THE HUMAN RESOURCE

Managing People and Work in the 1990s

The Human Resource

Managing People and Work in the 1990s

Roland Pearson
Visiting Lecturer in Human Resource Management
The Polytechnic of Central London
and
HRM Consultant
Educational and Personnel Services
Pinner

McGRAW-HILL BOOK COMPANY

London · New York · St Louis · San Franciso · Auckland
Bogotá · Caracas · Hamburg · Lisbon · Madrid · Mexico
Milan · Montreal · New Delhi · Panama · Paris · San Juan · São Paulo
Singapore · Sydney · Tokyo · Toronto

Published by
McGRAW-HILL Book Company (UK) Limited
Shoppenhangers Road, Maidenhead, Berkshire, SL6 2QL, England
Telephone 0628 23432
Fax 0628 770224

British Library Cataloguing in Publication Data
Pearson, Roland
　　The human resource.
　　1. Personnel management
　　I. Title
　　658.3

　　ISBN 0-07-707406-8

Library of Congress Cataloging-in-Publication Data
Pearson, Roland.
　　The human resource: managing people and work in the 1990s /
　　Roland Pearson.
　　　　p.　　cm.
　　Includes bibliographical references and index.
　　ISBN 0-07-707406-8
　　1. Personnel management.　　2. Labor market.　　3. Career development.
　　I. Title.
　　HF5548.P37　　1991
　　658.3—dc20　　　　　　　　　　　　　　　　　　　　　　　　　　90-19972

Typeset by Cambridge Composing (UK) Ltd, Cambridge
and printed and bound in Great Britain by Clays Ltd, St Ives plc

Contents

CHAPTER
1

Strategy and the human resource: how to manage 'personnel'?

Effective management of human resources in the 1990s will require more than competence in routine personnel administration. The purpose of this book is to define the role of human resource management in relation to organizational strategy and, in particular, to redefine the contribution of manpower planning.

The author's intention in this chapter is to raise some issues that will confront human resource managers in the coming years, and to ask whether previous experience in the personnel function has prepared them for an effective response. Competence in the routine of personnel administration is important, and can always be improved. Those who aspire to manage the human resources of an organization, however, must now turn their attention to strategic issues. To take the argument further, one might ask whether administrative competence is itself fully possible without the awareness of context that strategic thinking implies? Students of personnel management are required to consider organizational and social contexts when taking their professional qualifications, but the reality in personnel practice is rather different.

Teachers of personnel management will recognize the problem. The stark contrast between 'best practice' and documents produced by students from employers' files is often a lesson in itself. Job descriptions, which are crucial to both good administration and strategy, display neither competence nor strategic awareness. Tasks are listed haphazardly with little regard either to their relative importance, to their susceptibility to technology, to the skills required, or to the organizational context in which the work takes place. Personnel specifications emphasize experience at the expense of skills. Neither job descriptions nor personnel specifications show evidence of analytical ability, or even of curiosity about the direction of change. Competence, if such it be called, is limited to the requirements and traditions of the past. This narrow approach shows itself in more public ways: the Institute of Manpower Studies (Pearson and Pike, 1990) reported, for example, that many organizations were reviewing their policies for graduate recruitment and development, but without evaluating the success of previous practices. Whatever strategic thinking may be, that is not it.

One specialism, or competence, that might have given a strategic dimension to personnel management, is manpower planning. First promoted 20 years ago, it has since suffered both private and public failures. The private failures were those of communication within the personnel profession; reliance upon statistical analysis alienated many who could have learnt to apply simple but effective techniques to personnel management problems. The public failures were the manifest inability of governments and employers to avoid either heavy unemployment or skill-shortages. 'Manpower planning' was either ignored or ineffectual. The rationale of manpower planning, and its implications for human resource planning in the future, will be critically examined in this chapter.

Strategy and competence appear to occupy opposite ends of the managerial scale and they present the theorist with different problems. Competence can be understood generally as effectiveness in carrying out routine tasks, but is less easy to define in specific instances. Strategy is a much vaguer concept, which nevertheless becomes comprehensible as a sequence of definable activities. This chapter will consider the various meanings ascribed to strategic management, and to relate these to both *human resource management* and *human resource planning*. Attention is first directed to the challenges that will face human resource managers and planners in the 1990s.

Planning for scarcity

One feature above all others will characterize the human resource in the 1990s; its scarcity. In the UK, one third of the population will be above normal working age. By 1995, the number of young people leaving school will have dropped by 30 per cent compared with the mid-1980s. Similar trends are evident in almost all industrialized countries (Pearson and Andreutti, 1990). The impact of AIDS on mortality and procreation has yet to be fully assessed but, if the worst prophecies are realized, it can only compound existing demographic changes. Even if the Single European Market results in an overall loss of jobs in Europe, there will nevertheless be fierce international competition for those with professional skills (Pearson and Pike, 1990).

Liberalization of Eastern European countries will allow some skilled people, including manual workers and technicians, to fill vacancies in the West, but liberalization will only survive if it results in economic growth in their home countries. Growth, increasingly, depends on the pool of expertise available to an economy. The concept of '1992' could well be an irrelevance in the development of a world-wide labour market for skilled and qualified people. To what extent are those who manage human resources prepared for this challenge, and on what body of professional expertise can they rely?

In a rational world, scarcity of raw materials or energy sources should encourage better management, and they sometimes do. Scarcity of human resources should encourage the same attempts at parsimony and more intensive use. At national level, there would be heavy investment in education, training and re-training; within organizations, there would be evidence of a resolve to analyse jobs with care, to assess people effectively and to use them wherever their skills were appropriate. In the UK, on neither front are there grounds for optimism. The policy is to leave training to employers, who are assumed to know their own requirements. In other industrialized countries there is better state provision for both the training of school-leavers and of workers who become redundant. Massive redundancies in the early 1980s revealed the UK, by and large, as a nation unwilling to invest in counter-cyclical training, with consequent skill-shortages later in the decade. Inner cities deteriorated with their worsening employment prospects; some highly trained professionals went without work for a year or more. All this, of course, against a background of steadily increasing prosperity for those who obtained and retained employment.

On a narrow measure of productivity, output per employed worker rose substantially in the UK. The index for the whole economy rose by 20 per cent in the 10 years from 1979, and the index for manufacturing industries by 50 per cent (Economic Trends, 1990). The increasing reliance on the industrial production of other countries, however, combined with massive increases in consumer spending power, caused a worsening of the UK balance of payments as the 1980s came to an end. The star employment sector of the decade, financial services, was having difficulties both in disposing of people with the wrong skills and in recruiting people with the right ones. The Confederation of British Industry was forecasting business failures and redundances. Third World countries, inevitably, pursued human resource policies dictated by mountainous foreign debts. Complacency about management of the scarce human resource would be misplaced. More talk about *human resource strategy* has been accompanied by less effective action, particularly action motivated by a strategic analysis at national or organizational level.

One recent development in the effective use of the human resource is the flexible approach to employment now adopted by both employers and employees; a development that nevertheless needs strategic management. Flexibility in employment practices is well established; part-time and contract working is traditional in many parts of the steadily expanding service sector.

Flexibility in the use of employees' skills is less readily recognized or exploited. We will be discussing at a later stage the reasons for rigidity in the way workers are categorized, and what can be done about it.

At a macro-level, we have witnessed a dismembering of big corporate structures in private business, and the slow but steady adoption of ideas for privatizing government and the public services. This drift away from corporatism, together with an end to the trade union domination of work, offers opportunities for individuality in working methods that employees should not be slow to grasp. The Single European Market will favour the well-qualified 'knowledge worker' (the highly educated person who trades in information), whose services in the UK are already at a premium. Against a background of historically high percentages of unemployment, competition for the highly skilled will continue to be fierce. The latter will be able to make their own terms, and flexibility in their working lives will be one requirement. The issue of personal careers will be reviewed in Chapter 7.

The political, economic and social changes already evident in the 1990s offer many threats, but also many opportunities for business and employment. What is quite clear is that 'long-range planning' can no longer be seen as the linear extrapolation of a current trend; discontinuity is the norm. The late 1980s were characterized by political and economic surprises on a global scale. What often distinguishes a threat from an opportunity is the way in which a particular event is viewed, by individuals or by organizations. Progress will be made by those who regularly scan their environment, and assess their positions within it. This discipline is the first stage of the strategic process, which will be considered in more detail later in this chapter. The fact that books on strategic management, even those written in recent years, either leave the human resource out of account completely, or relegate it to a contingent role, is a major weakness in their own professed methodology.

So it is timely to look once again at the history of personnel management and manpower planning, and also to examine critically the concept of strategy. Since most controversy surrounds the last of these, we will examine 'strategy' first.

Corporate strategy: empty concept or merely confused?

No phrase dominated the management literature of the 1980s as successfully as 'corporate strategy', and perhaps none caused such evident confusion. Igor Ansoff (1987), one of the early writers on the subject, described strategy as an 'elusive and somewhat abstract concept'. More recently, Quinn (1980) has referred to major strategic issues as emerging first 'in vague or undefined terms'. Yet this ephemeral idea is included in the syllabus of many business courses otherwise devoted to highly practical subjects such as cost accounting and production control. The reasons for its attractiveness are not difficult to understand; they are both organizational and individual.

The economic stagnation of the late 1960s encouraged interest in the subject of 'long-range planning'; conferences and journals were devoted to it. There was a feeling that, somehow, large organizations should be able to predict the future. Getting the right experts to analyse and forecast long-term trends would reveal opportunities for revived profitability. The futility of this corporate crystal-gazing was exposed by the Oil Crisis of 1973, and the recession of the late 1970s and early 1980s. The effects were exacerbated in the UK by government policy, and the response of many large organizations was tactical rather than strategic; the 'knee-jerk' reaction of disposing summarily of substantial numbers of workers into an unfavourable labour market. This graphically demonstrated the absence of strategic thinking at both corporate and national levels. Some of the casualties never recovered their self-respect, and some have never returned to employment. Draconian shedding of labour costs affected the skilled and highly qualified as well as those whose abilities might sadly be correctly classified as redundant. We will return to this topic when we discuss the history of manpower planning.

Once profitability began to return, the feeling among many managements was 'never again'. The redundancy costs, and the accumulated ill will, would be avoided in future by thinking strategically. Japanese government and industrial long-term thinking were rumoured to be an example to follow; industry should be regarded as an arm of national policy. Not that the government in the UK during the 1980s offered much hope of close support for British industry, and their plans for the public services were to turn them, as far as possible, into commercial enterprises. Nevertheless, 'strategy' was in favour, and might have been encouraged by freedom from government control. Sir John Harvey-Jones (1988), lately chairman of the UK's giant chemical combine, ICI, has described how his particular brand of strategic thinking proved effective when the company became a loss-maker in the early 1980s. Bureaucratic corporatism was, of necessity, dropped in favour of global awareness, flexibility and creativity. Many of those using the word 'strategy' understood it less clearly than Sir John; they included both managers and management teachers.

Within institutions offering management education, the use of the word 'strategic' in course titles was motivated by an exposure to market forces. Strategy is associated most readily with the highest level of management; those investing in a business course would be likely to choose one that offered the hope of career progression to the 'strategic' level. The logic of this market thinking is clear, but delivering the product depends on understanding what 'strategic management' really is.

Strategy and policy

Using the word 'strategy' is, of course, much easier than defining it. Miller (1989), in discussing human resource strategy, stated that 'there is little consensus in the management literature or business practice about the meaning of the word strategy'. Chandler (1962) described strategy as 'the determination of long-term goals and objectives of the enterprise and the adoption of courses of action and allocation of resources necessary for carrying out these goals'. This seems to confuse strategy with both policies (long-term goals) and with plans (allocation of resources). Johnson and Scholes (1988), writers on corporate strategy, get around the confusion by sweeping all potential competitors into their net: 'readers will undoubtedly come across . . . terms such as: "business policy", "management policy", "corporate policy" and "strategic management", all of which deal with the same general area of study'. Perhaps they do, but the conflation does not help us to understand what is distinctive about strategy, strategic thinking or strategic management; and it is positively dangerous in at least one respect. Policy is not the same as strategy, especially when considering the management of human resources. Even in the development of business strategies, policy should be seen (Leontiades, 1980) as setting the limits within which these will operate. Policy is a distinctive concept, concerned with long-term goals and values.

Some commercial organizations may wish to treat customers, suppliers and employers in an ethical way; they may even find it profitable to do so. Some employees, in both public and private sectors of the economy, are bound by their professional affiliation to treat clients according to ethical codes of behaviour. Requirements of this sort are ongoing, whereas strategy relates to change. Policy may constrain both strategy formation and action, but it is itself an expression of values rather than of business needs. Irrespective of the vicissitudes of strategy, organizations may wish to provide guidance for management and other employees in the form of policy statements. Johnson and Scholes have coined the phrase 'recipe' to cover the 'beliefs and assumptions which form part of the culture of an organization'. Whether or not these are written down, they have the status of implicit policy; managers will violate them at their peril.

Organizations with sound policies should also follow the sound practice of presenting their beliefs and values as explicit statements, which can be taken into account in daily management and in the development of strategy. Where policies (or Johnson and Scholes' 'recipes', if you will) go unarticulated, strategic development will be impaired or prevented. Personal and organizational values are the ultimate arbiters of ethical action. In no aspect of managerial activity is this more appropriate than in the management of people.

Pigors and Myers (1981), whose viewpoint is that of personnel administration, described policy as 'a directive which invites participation and appropriate initiative from mature and responsible organizational members'; it can 'affirm a general principle or long-term aim'. On this basis, 'policy' rather than 'strategy' would be a better classification of the 'mission statements' often said to be the product of strategic thinking. As Pigors and Myers pointed out, the word policy had become debased with use, often by confusing it with procedure. Nevertheless, these two concepts are easily differentiated in managers' minds. Day-to-day operational sequences and standards are clearly distinct from overarching values and beliefs, however management books and teachers may confuse them.

To conflate policy with strategy, however, is to lose the analytical potential of two important words. For the purpose of this book especially, it is necessary to separate the concepts. Policy, like strategy, is subject to change; indeed, it will be maintained in this book that strategy is an expression of rapid change.

But policy, being the product of deeply held beliefs, changes only slowly. Research is integral to the development of strategy; its influence on policy is less direct or immediate.

Strategy and planning

Another confusion in this ill-defined area of management thought is the identification of strategy with planning. Since all managers plan, the phrase 'strategic planning' is used to describe the planning carried out by senior members of a management team. This fits the image required by some business courses but, once again, does little to clarify the essential nature of strategic management. And to categorize strategy as the sole concern of senior management supports the self-fulfilling prophecy that there are too few promotable managers who are able to think strategically. If the strategic process is made relevant to those in junior positions, their ability to adopt the same dsicipline when dealing with higher level decisions will be developed. And there is no reason, as we shall see, why this should not happen.

Leontiades (1980) provided a helpful distinction between policy, strategy and plans. In his view, policies establish broad purpose and direction for the total organization; strategies are alternatives that will be consistent with, and optimize on, the company policy; and plans specify tactical programmes and steps to fulfil strategies. Leontiades recognizes the interrelatedness of these aspects of management, but perhaps underestimates the importance of the strategic process in the derivation of all three.

Traditional planning techniques place a premium on rational development and sequencing, and have an important part to play once strategic development has reached the point of implementation. This is the arena of resource allocation, critical path analysis and rational organization. But strategy formation as a whole is a different matter. As long ago as 1960, Pfiffner described the strategic process as 'anything but linear'. It was 'a groping, cyclical process that often circled back on itself, with frequent interruptions and delays'. As Johnson and Scholes remind us, Pfiffner describes the process of strategy formation as being 'like fermentation in biochemistry, rather than an industrial assembly line'. All managers worthy of the name, plan and solve problems: all managers are capable of contributing to the strategic process, once the latter is made clear to them. Confusing planning and strategic thinking merely retards this aspect of personal development.

Johnson and Scholes (1988) describe strategic management as consisting of three sequential but interlocking activities:

- strategic analysis
- strategic choice
- strategy implementation

This formulation illustrates one general source of confusion about the concept of strategy: it is viewed, often by the same authors, as both process and product. Analysis and choice are the strategic processes by means of which the strategic product (the strategy) is derived. Once the strategic product is available, a further process, also referred to as a 'strategy', may be required to implement it. Tichy and others, writing in Ferris and Rowland (1988), define strategy as 'a process through which the basic mission statements and objectives of the organization are set and a process through which the organization uses its resources to achieve its objectives'. It will be more productive to differentiate strategic thinking from its outcome—the plans necessary to put the strategy into effect.

Once strategy is identified as a process, it becomes easier to compare it with problem-solving, which is one of the functions of management at all levels. A model of the problem-solving process is illustrated in Figure 1.1. The required activities are data-gathering, creative thinking, evaluation and implementation. These activities are universal, and their relation to Johnson and Scholes' formulation will be evident. They can be applied equally to solving departmental personnel problems or to the generation of a plan for the enterprise as a whole. This is not to say that these important principles are always observed. Managers are often encouraged to give attention to evaluation and implementation rather than research and creative thinking, and the quality of both operational decision-making and 'strategy' may suffer in consequence. Division of labour may require that the task of research be given to a staff specialist; in the development of 'human resource strategies', manpower research may have to be treated in this way. The danger is then that the human resource planner will be seen as someone who keeps the score, but does not play the game; a limited use of what should be a high-calibre member of staff. The trigger for the problem-solving process is described in Figure 1.1 as a 'perceived problem'. The perceived need does not itself suggest action. When a light bulb fails to respond to the switch, an investigation may reveal that a fuse has blown and that there are faults in the wiring; possible solutions include finding a fresh bulb, lighting a candle, or commissioning a full overhaul of the electrical system. Implementation will depend upon successful evaluation of the options, in addition to planning the delivery of the resources required.

Harvey-Jones discovered, as a chief executive of one of the UK's biggest enterprises, that waiting for events to force strategic change is not good enough; it is part of managers' jobs constantly to review the changes taking place around them. Quinn (1980) refers in his interpretation of the strategic process to 'environmental scanning', the active search for influences demanding a response from the organization. While this could be said to be a

Figure 1.1
The problem-solving process

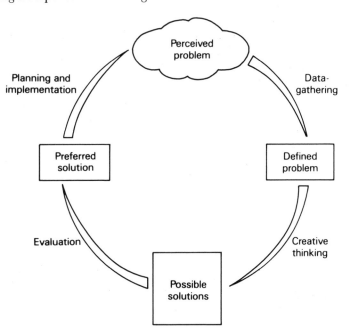

relevant, if not always obvious, duty of senior managers, it could and should be encouraged in managers at all levels, not least in the management of people.

An important area of junior managerial problem-solving is the control of staff. The persistent late arrival of an employee should prompt an investigation of circumstances, the legal and procedural implications, the impact on the rest of the staff and evaluation of alternatives before the disciplinary procedure is invoked. Managers who are aware of this problem-solving approach will not only act more skilfully in their work, but will be preparing themselves for the strategic tasks in more senior positions. We will return to the theme of management as a research activity; the growth of the 'knowledge industry' is giving the lie to Winston Churchill's wartime dictum that 'The scientists should be on tap but not on top'. Rapid change enforces strategic responses: management itself has become a research activity. Research training, so far from excluding those who receive it from the direction of enterprises, could now be an important if not essential preparation for it.

But are there distinctive features that set the concept of the strategic planning process apart from problem-solving in general? Johnson and Scholes' formulation suggests that the concepts substantially overlap. 'Strategic analysis' can be identified with the data-gathering in Figure 1.1, 'strategic choice' with the generation and evaluation of solutions. 'Strategy implementation' includes the formal planning phase of problem-solving. Figure 1.2 makes these identities clear. The close relationship of the strategic process with the model in Figure 1.2 is reinforced by the stance taken by writers on organizational problem-solving. Mayon-White's (1986) book of readings entitled *Planning and Managing Change* has much in common with treatise on corporate strategy. Several contributors refer directly to the strategic process, others to aspects of the four major activities in Figure 1.2.

'Strategic management' and 'strategic thinking' are processes rather than

Figure 1.2
The strategic process:
1 Johnson and Scholes
(1988); **2** Quinn (1980);
3 Ansoff (1987);
4 Ferris and Rowland
(1988); **5** Lupton (1971)

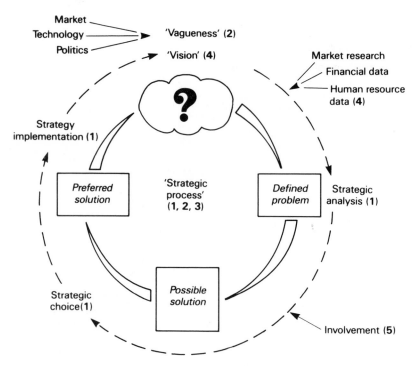

products; 'planning' is necessary to put the outcomes of strategic thinking into effect. The options to be considered during the strategic process, in planning and in the implementation of plans, will be constrained by the policies of the organization. Plans and policies are both vulnerable to changing circumstances; strategic management is the process which allows that adaptation to take place while maintaining the integrity of the organization and its members.

There are, however, two ways in which strategic management can be distinguished from the generality of problem-solving; the immediacy with which the 'problems' are perceived, and the complexity of the stages through which the options are arrived at. Strategic management is not crisis management, and strategic thinking is not 'executive action'. Impending disaster, however, can be averted only by swift and decisive management. The seriousness of the problem is evident, even if the contributory causes are not. Decisions must be taken on the best information available, which will always be inadequate: there is little time fully to engage the knowledge, skills and participation of the workforce. A direct leap to a less than optimal solution is unavoidable. Curiously, dramatic company 'turn-around' stories are often chosen to exemplify strategic management; what these actually demonstrate is the lack of strategic thinking by previous executives. 'Turn-arounds' are, at best, tactical cost-cutting exercises, as capable of killing a business stone dead as of saving it.

Identifying strategic management with crisis management has prestigious support, however. One respected writer on the topic, Igor Ansoff (1987), took the view that 'corporate strategy is unnecessary when things are going well'. But how often are things 'going well'? Twenty years ago managers might have been forgiven for believing that it was possible to control the long term; the 1970s and 1980s disproved that. Fat cat, complacent management comes before a fall. Never was this better illustrated than in the 1980s, when yesterday's fêted entrepreneurs became today's failed businesses, almost overnight. Often the personal obsession with the 'here and now' that had created the business, left no time or resources for environmental sensing, and courageous entrepreneurship was left dangerously exposed.

It is possible, however, for management to be pro-active, to scan the environment continuously, searching for opportunities and threats to organizational success. Managers of this type don't wait for crises to demonstrate their problem-solving skills; they actively seek reasons to change in the social and economic system, or within the enterprise itself. Management of this level of competence and awareness might justify a special description, and 'strategic' will do as well as any other. But it does indicate a quantum leap from other forms of managerial work. Managers at lower levels can choose to acquire this level of awareness, and organizations interested in the career development of their employees may choose to encourage it. Strategic thinkers, in this sense, are not a race apart. 'Organizational development', at its best, involves people at all levels in the strategic process.

A corollary of this, and a necessary element of the strategic process, is the way in which information is accumulated and decisions arrived at. The use of logical planning processes is eschewed; the way in which information is gathered is no less important than the decisions themselves. Ansoff claims that the formulation of corporate strategy is much more than an evaluation of strengths, weaknesses, opportunities and threats: the 'SWOT' of traditional business analysis. Quinn, Johnson and Scholes and others, describe the process of strategic management as 'logical incrementalism'. The traditional image of the manager as one who makes swift decisions and takes decisive action—the 'planning, initiating, commanding, monitoring and controlling' concept of the earlier management theorists—is turned on its head. The chief executive, though ultimately responsible for the strategic management of the organization, may eventually arrive at radically different plans from those that seemed appropriate when problems and opportunities were first sensed. The reason is the concentration on process rather than product; strategic management requires involvement of people with differing organizational viewpoints and differing levels of authority. The management of the inevitable politics, as Quinn points out, is an essential element in the strategic process. Debate, even conflict, increases the awareness among employees and employers of the factors that affect their joint future: the medium is the message.

But the use of consultative processes in strategic management does more than develop responsible organizational members; it improves the quality of the plans derived from the strategic process. In working through the stages in Figure 1.2, the early research phase will require the assessment not only of information collected in the routine of business, although there is often more to be gleaned from this than managers realize, but also additional investigations to fill gaps in knowledge. The creative thinking that is essential at the second stage may force a reconsideration of the data and generate the need for more research. Management of the strategic process is not swift and decisive, but slow and intuitive; 'fermentation, rather than the production line'. It is not inappropriate to describe strategic management as management by research.

Mintzberg (reported in Foster, 1989) seems to favour this interpretation. He has identified three main strands in the debate about strategic management; strategy as 'planning', strategy as 'vision' (usually ascribed to the chief executive), and strategy as 'corporate learning'. To describe strategy as planning is to make one of those words redundant. Like planning, vision has its place within the strategic process, but is only part of it. A personal vision of the business future must be tested against reality, and shared with others if it is to be implemented. Corporate learning incorporates the other interpretations, and is compatible with the model outlined in previous paragraphs.

The debate about the meaning and reality of 'strategy' in an organizational setting will continue. What is important is that writers and teachers of the subject should be prepared to make clear what they mean by it. For the purposes of this book, 'strategy' is a pro-active search for signals that the organization need to change, and the management of that change process. Much of the subsequent chapters will be taken up with the research and creative problem-solving aspects of management, with particular emphasis on the effective use of human resources.

Strategy, management and research

Within the author's lifetime the enthusiasm for the activity generally known as 'research' has waxed and waned. In the Second World War, reluctant respect was given to scientists who delivered code-breaking machines and radar. Post-war industry made profits from the products of the chemical research laboratory. Government continued to support research in universities and institutes on a large scale. Despite the current fear and disenchantment with atomic power, 'Britain's first atomic power station' was a matter of pride in the 1950s. The 1980s have seen a profound change of attitude towards government-supported research; the implication is that it no longer delivers the economic goods. Funding is far from freely available; those who believe they can profit from research should pay for it. Strategic management, on a national scale, is not evident.

Yet, if the government, and the public at large, have regarded scientific research as an uncertain ally, they have treated research into human and social problems with deep suspicion or outright antagonism. John Raven (1989) has recently written of both the paramount importance of social research in the modern managed economy, and of the indifference or antagonism that it encounters from those who would most benefit from it. Strategic management of the huge resources available to the state and its agencies should require that the 'research phase' of the strategic process be given its full weight and resources.

The attitudes of the general public, and especially of managers, towards research is as important as those of national policy makers. Vital wartime needs were met by scientific method and inventiveness, but neither leaders nor people were entirely at home with what looked like a Frankenstein's monster. Winston Churchill's remark that 'scientists should be on tap but not on top' has already been quoted. Those who had the task of putting the scientists' proposals into often dangerous practice coined for their persecutors the nickname of 'boffin'. The implication was, and unfortunately still is, that research is a separate activity, remote from the realities of management. Organizational structures have been deliberately devised to keep the researchers in their place. Career paths in research and in general management are often seen as incompatible. This attitude is as pernicious as race or gender prejudice, and has, in common with both, the nature of a self-fulfilling prophecy. If research staff are not admitted to the processes of management, they will not develop the additional skills and attitudes necessary to be effective. Strategic management provides both the opportunity and the need for these attitudes to change.

Another strategic issue that should bring both research and researchers closer to management are the changes affecting management itself. Technology has already enabled large organizations to dispose of significant numbers of middle managers, to empower those in direct contact with clients and customers to make decisions based on information directly available to them. Managers are needed for problem-solving, and will give more of their time to it, as against the routine operational aspects of earlier managerial work. They will be required to give more attention to the strategic process. The quality of their work, itself increasingly subject to performance monitoring, will depend on their ability to gather and interpret data. Research methodology is no longer the effete concern of scientists; it is the basis of management itself.

This identity of interest between research and management is, perhaps, easiest to accept in terms of technical information and market surveys. The use of social research to investigate the nature of the organization's labour market and its workforce is less likely to be seen as relevant. The paradox is that the need for strategic thinking about these issues has never been greater. Reasons for the lack of managerial interest in the social science of the workplace can be discovered in historical development of both personnel management and manpower planning.

Responsibility for people

The personnel profession in the UK had its origins in the Institute of Welfare Officers, which was founded during the First World War. This welfare function was a necessary one, given the rigours of industrial labour, as many a personal account has demonstrated. It continued to dominate personnel management until well after the Second World War. No one at this stage would have claimed that 'personnel officers', as practitioners were becoming known, should justify themselves beyond providing a service to employees. Seldom would the personnel officer have expected to have any particular impact upon business or operational decisions. The personnel department, however, gradually acquired a succession of administrative functions, to the extent that Peter Drucker, the management analyst, was moved in the 1960s to describe the personnel department as the 'dustbin'. Responsibility for canteens and suggestion schemes are much-quoted examples.

In the UK, the Industrial Training Act 1964 required employers to achieve certain training 'standards' if they were to satisfy the relevant training board and to secure 'levy exemption'. This exercise was often described by its intended beneficiaries in industry as 'grant farming'. Responsibility for administration of what was often a sterile, paper-shuffling exercise devolved upon the personnel department. Opportunities to prepare workers far-sightedly for coming industrial change were sadly missed.

The imaginative development of the human resource, in so far as this was consciously pursued, was the prerogative of operational managers. The John Lewis Partnership, whose philosophy and practice of management has been documented by Flanders, Pomeranz and Woodward (1968), conducted its experiment in industrial democracy at the instigation of the chief executive. Spedan Lewis had the perspicacity to see, as early as 1910, that the business of selling required employees with a stake in the enterprise. The sophisticated human relations research at the Glacier Metal Company was also encouraged by a chief executive, this time with a personal interest in industrial psychology.

The rare experiments at something more imaginative than paternalism were rapidly overtaken by the increasingly bitter and frequent shop-floor battles over pay that the Donovan Commission (1968) uncovered during the late 1960s. These battles were fought between employee representatives and first-line supervisors, with the personnel manager having, at most, an adjudicating role. The tight labour market should have been a spur to better understanding and use of the human resource; it was not. A factor in trade union strength during this period was an ability rigidly to control the categorization of work and workers, thus artificially maintaining labour shortages and, significantly, the number of unions with whom employers had to deal. In these circumstances, it is not surprising that those most concerned with the tactical, day-to-day effects of labour relations upon output—the operational managers—should have taken a leading role in managing them. Personnel managers consolidated their marginal, administrative, role by becoming 'keepers of the corporate conscience' with an interest in seeing that agreements were adhered to. In the public sector, white-collar unionism was in its infancy and the personnel function, in so far as it existed at all, was still concerned with welfare and administration.

The 1960s and early 1970s did witness some attempts at human resource management, of the type that will be discussed and recommended in later chapters. There were experiments in job redesign, of which the production-team approach at Volvo's Kalmar factory is the best remembered; there was an attempt to improve managerial competence by means of techniques such as management by objectives. These developments were enthusiastically embraced by the consultants who championed them; much less so by personnel managers, many of whom remained sceptical of their success. Then, as ever, disturbing the status quo was bad news.

The 1970s placed new stresses on those managing the human resource. Corporate mergers resulted for the first time in the loss of apparently 'safe' jobs by managers and professional specialists. The Oil Crisis of 1973 created a frightening level of inflation coupled with a world-wide trade recession. Governments had to manage inflation against a background of increasing trade union power and militancy. Employment legislation, intended to control the power of trade unions, was either dropped before it reached the statute-book, or repealed by a later administration. Laws prescribing the rights of individuals and trade unions at the workplace, originally intended as the sugar on the pill of trade union control, became the substance of employment legislation. In return for a measure of control over inflation through wage-freezes, workers were given property rights in their jobs through the Employment Protection Acts (1974 and 1978), and trade union power at the workplace was institutionalized. In personnel departments, welfare was displaced by a new imperative created by this legislation, the perceived need to treat employees as potential litigants. Personnel managers were expected to advise their operational colleagues on legal aspects of discipline and grievance-handling. Legislation intended to limit discrimination at the workplace had a similar, if less pronounced, effect. Much money was made by lawyers in providing training courses and advice as the frequency of applications to industrial tribunals increased.

The UK government's preoccupation with inflation had another consequence. The administrative activity in personnel departments was intensified by the bureaucracy required to maintain pay policies imposed by law. Those who had established pay structures, based on job evaluation, found themselves at an advantage, because the reasons for pay increases could be clearly demonstrated. Pay policies required the tacit, if not explicit, support of the trade unions, whose acceptance into government decision-making invited charges of corporatism.

At this stage the personnel function began to smell blood. Perhaps their kindly, marginal role was to be replaced by a seat at the table where business decisions were made. Operational managers were finding themselves out of their depth in the new world of pay policies and legally sanctioned trade union and employee rights. Personnel departments were strengthened by the appointment of industrial relations officers, often ex-union people themselves, whose task was to get the best short-term deals that difficult circumstances allowed: self-evidently tactical, rather than strategic, management was in order. Rising trade unionism among white-collar workers, together with reorganizations, encouraged the establishment of personnel departments in the public sector. The negotiation of job-evaluated salary structures was promoted by union pressures and by government pay policies, thus adding to the administrative importance of the personnel function.

That a similar role was being adopted by personnel managers in the USA is evident in the title of Pigors and Myers' (1981) long-running text *Personnel Administration*. Membership of the Institute of Personnel Management increased rapidly during this period, and passing examinations intended to test professional knowledge and competence became a necessary requirement. This was the era in which the Institute of Manpower Studies was established, with support from the larger employers whose preoccupation was the number of their employees. We will review the history of the specialism known as *manpower planning* later in this chapter. Strategy, let it be said, was low on most organizations' lists of priorities. Far-sighted decision-making, where attempted, was rapidly subordinated to tactical expediency.

In this state of increased visibility, but still uncertain corporate legitimacy, the personnel function entered the 1980s. It was ill-prepared for what was to follow. The Thatcher government was faced with high inflation coupled with a world-wide trade recession. Instead of bolstering what they perceived to be inefficient industries, they exposed them to the full effects of a high exchange rate. The result has been described as the 'Verdun effect' (Freeman, 1984) in British industry. Many firms went out of business, accelerating a long-term decline in manufacturing employment, and leaving some areas in the North, and even in parts of London, devastated. Unemployment had been growing on a long-term trend since the mid-1960s, but now accelerated sharply in spite of repeated attempts to redefine the contents of the index. In this environment trade unions lost both tactical effectiveness and the place that they had enjoyed in the corporatism of the 1970s. Industrial relations officers became an irrelevance; workers cooperated with the demands of managements who were themselves fighting for survival. For many businesses, closing down seemed as attractive as continuing the unequal struggle. Employment legislators turned their attention once again to the limitation of trade union rights. Personnel departments, often fearful for their own jobs, returned to a sad caricature of their administrative role as they prepared fellow workers for redundancy. Microcomputers were introduced to personnel departments not to provide sophisticated manpower planning but to calculate rapidly and repeatedly the amount of redundancy compensation owed to departing employees.

Once again the personnel function was marginalized; the managagement of the human resource was largely one way, and was firmly in the hands of chief executives chosen for their ruthless ability to get rid of 'dead wood'. Manpower planning decisions took the form of how many people should go, and how quickly. Any personnel managers who wished to do more than comply needed to be both very brave and to have a creative understanding of how manpower could be used. The previous history of the personnel function had prepared them for neither requirement.

As we move into the 1990s, there is evidence of a return to some of the experiments of the 1960s. 'Performance related pay', and the increasing interest in appraisal, can trace their origins back to 'management by objectives' and beyond. This time it is the customer, rather than the organization itself, that is being invited to assess the contribution of employees. *Total quality management* attempts to see the functions of a company or service from the customer's point of view. To what extent the personnel function, or profession, have been innovators in any of these activities is far from clear. They are undoubtedly the inheritors of a further administrative burden and the personal problems that these techniques bring about. Personnel management could be said to have come full circle. Welfare work and administration are back in vogue.

This attempt to describe the broad sweep of events, of course, does less than justice to the small number of far-sighted organizations for whom human resource management has been a central and creative activity; it also overplays the importance of personnel management in organizations that, even in 1990, would find the phrase 'job description' hard to comprehend. But what role do personnel professionals really want to play?

It is possible, of course, for personnel managers to rely on organizational inertia; they can stick to the administrative function in which many excel. Personnel records must be kept, documents prepared and filed, and recruitment procedures followed, even if they do not themselves have much influence on who is hired. For others this is not enough, as reference to the profession's own magazine *Personnel Management* will show. The adoption during the 1980s of a trans-Atlantic import called *human resource management*, or the even more grandly-titled *human resource strategy*, implies preparation for yet another assault by the personnel fraternity upon the citadels of power.

Once again we are faced with confusing phrases whose modish and ill-defined use does little to improve our understanding of difficult subjects. Guest (1989) has pointed out that the brand name *human resource management* has been applied with little discrimination to at least four types of product. The first is the least honourable, being simply an attempt to make old-style, discredited personnel management acceptable by retitling it. The magazine cover that accompanied Guest's article showed painters changing the name of the department on the personnel manager's door. That such a change should be necessary justifies the rather sad story told in previous paragraphs. Nor is the retitling merely a harmless attempt at self-marketing, because it gives the impression that new dedication and professional skills are necessarily available when the name is changed.

Retitling would be justified, perhaps, if it correctly implied that human resource management should encapsulate 'best practice' in personnel management. As Guest pointed out, however, what is best practice depends on circumstances. Best practice in a car manufacturing plant may require human resource managers to pay continual attention to keeping the production lines running; in a software company, the emphasis might be on assessment of skills and the maintenance of job satisfaction. Ten years before Guest's analysis, Legge (1977) had written of the essentially contingent nature of much personnel management, a tacit exceptance of its reactive role. Innovation, as Legge pointed out, depends very much on sensitive perceptions of the personnel manager's situation. Basing retitled personnel management on the shifting sands of contingency is not likely to promote the authority and influence that personnel managers believe is rightly theirs. More will be said about Legge's ideal of the innovative personnel manager.

Another justifiable use of the phrase *human resource management* would be to define it as personnel management with an emphasis on individuals; their needs for development, job satisfaction and a rewarding social environment. This would be an overt return to the welfare role, but at a higher level of professionalism. Such an approach could be satisfying and also appropriate to the 1990s, when the retreat of trade unions and the emphasis on skilled and qualified knowledge-workers allows and requires attention to individual needs. But this professional stance, almost that of the in-house psychologist, would again present personnel managers as providers of a valued service, which would require more specialized training than they currently receive, but not as participants in business decision-making.

In Guest's view, a tight definition of human resource management would include some of the professional understanding of people implied in the previous definition. It would also include a body of theory that would enable better use to be made of human capital, in the interests both of people and of organizations. Such theory would be firmly and unashamedly grounded in social science, not at the level of quick fixes for short-term problems, but in a way that encouraged and enabled integration of a flexible workforce with changing organizational tasks. The emphasis would be on measurement and improvement of performance, cost-effectiveness, retention of employees and, overall, a creative, problem-solving approach to the organization's needs.

Guest recognized the difficulties with such a radical approach; the ill-defined nature of organizational goals, and the apparent impossibility in many organizational cultures of aligning individual and trade union objectives with them. Strategic human resource management might be possible only where the fit between organizational and workforce objectives was sufficiently close. Miller (1989), writing in the same journal one month later, challenged both Guest's interpretation of 'strategic management' and his pessimistic conclusion. His interpretation was that strategic human resource management included confronting the differing interests of workers and management; industrial relations were to be one of the environmental factors to be reviewed in the strategic process.

Legge (1977) mounted an attack on the textbooks in personnel management for purveying what she described as 'normative' solutions to organizational problems. She implied by this criticism the tendency to prescribe best practice in terms of techniques that could be applied in all situations. In Legge's view, personnel professionalism requires innovation, but innovation that takes account of power and culture in organizations. The danger here, of course, is that the personnel practitioner may use Legge's contingent approach to personnel management as an excuse for going along with the status quo. Human resource strategies, as Guest conceptualizes them, are unlikely to be achieved that way. Legge's answer is that the personnel manager must always innovate, but the style of innovation must be suited to the circumstances. When power is limited, personnel managers should adopt the role of 'conformist innovator'; they should accept organizational goals for what they are, and use professional skills to support them. If staff-slimming is deemed to be necessary, for example, then the personnel manager will accomplish this desired objective with the least hurt to the people concerned. When the power of the personnel department is high, however, it may be possible to adopt the role of 'deviant innovator'. Perhaps people need not be sacked after all; a new organizational goal would be to hold on to skilled employees whose services would be hired to other employers while waiting for business to improve.

Is there any way in which the management of human resources can become the focus of an organization's activities, and in which personnel practioners can gain the influence that this focus demands? A comparison with a similar, but often more highly regarded, profession may point the way.

Finance directors do not confine themselves to collecting employees' subscriptions to the sports and social club, which might be seen as the equivalent of the welfare function in personnel; nor do they restrict their activities to the presentation of statutory accounts. The financial direction of a business requires much more than administration—it requires a knowledge of international economic trends, the ways in which financial resources can be acquired and, most important of all, the financial structure and internal resources of a business or public service. It might be objected that the two specialists are dealing with fundamentally different problems; that money is always money while people are individuals, and changeable at that. Yet the personnel manager categorizes people in some pretty crude ways for the purposes of the business, while good accountants are aware that money may take the form of revenue, debt, expenses, captial, loans, and so on. Nor will good accountants stand by while other members of the management team make errors that affect profitability; using their analytical skills they assist their colleagues to see where practical action will put things right. They may, for example, demonstrate how excessive overtime or working capital might be reduced. Given their range of knowledge, practical skills, and ability to conceptualize problems, it is not surprising that able accountants are more likely than their personnel colleagues to have a seat on the board, or to be promoted to chief executive. What is needed to give personnel management this degree of professionalism? Are there ways in which the personnel manager can analyse and conceptualize the workforce and labour markets with equivalent impact on business success?

The early 1970s saw a brief flirtation by the personnel profession with *human resource accounting* (e.g. Flamholz, 1974: revised 1986). The idea was to place a financial value on the human capital of the organization. The difficulty is that human capital usually appreciates in value with experience and accruing skills, as distinct from the depreciation that accountants routinely apply to the value of capital items. The appreciation is also very difficult to measure; training and work experience are worth more than the cost of courses and salaries. Useful though the financial measure may be in business, it is not appropriate in all circumstances. This is not to say that human resource managers should not be cost-effective in their daily work; Cannon (1979) has drawn attention to the many ways in which this can be achieved.

We will now proceed to a consideration of *manpower planning*, a discipline which might be seen to fulfil our requirements but which, like personnel management itself, has suffered a checkered history over the last 20 years. This review will indicate that the roles of 'conformist' and 'deviant' innovator are appropriate also for strategic human resource planners.

Human resource planning: the basis of a new professionalism

As implied above, readers are being invited to consider human resource planning not as a mere management technique, but as the means by which the personnel function can gain parity with the finance department in contributing to policy-making and planning.

Cynics will readily and rightly point out that the concept and practice of 'manpower planning' has been with us for over 20 years, and that its impact has not been spectacular. In 1990, only one out of a class of 20 personnel students admitted to the author that their employer used any formal manpower planning. To achieve the stated objective, 'manpower planning', like personnel management itself, must be redefined. The rest of the book is dedicated to this task. We need to consider not only what manpower planners currently do, but also what the human resource planners of the future might do. In addition we need to assess the impact of human resource planning on the personnel function, especially in its potentially strategic role.

But first we need to sketch the history of manpower planning to discover why this discipline, like personnel management, did not justify its early promise.

Early days: the dominance of statistics

Large career structures are a sitting target for the statistician. The behaviour of people, conceptualized as dots moving between boxes drawn on an organization chart, may be represented by formulae similar to those used by the physical chemist to represent chemical reactions. As career structures become more complicated so do the statistical calculations, but the computer comes to the rescue. Programs enable the manpower implications of possible procedures and policies to be modelled and analysed. Exponents of the statistical approach to manpower planning were Bartholomew (1967) at the

University of Kent, Morgan (1971) at Cambridge, and Smith (1970) working in the Civil Service. Much of Bartholomew's thinking was adopted by the Institute of Manpower Studies when it was established in the early 1970s. This at a time, it will be recalled, when companies were waking up to the idea that personnel management was as likely to be concerned with redundancy as with recruitment.

The application of quantitative methods to the management of human resources has much to commend it. 'Personnel management with figures' is greatly to be preferred to personnel management concerned merely with day-to-day administration within a legal framework, especially by those practitioners who yearn for a more creative role in the enterprise for which they work. But placing emphasis on one part of the social research process at the expense of all others had two adverse effects; it delayed the acceptance of manpower planning because potential users were frightened by its apparent complexity, and it encouraged the uncritical acceptance of existing categories of manpower and career structures, simply because they provided instant fodder for equations and computer databases. To be fair, even the early writers on manpower planning seem to have recognized the problem. Hughes, in a book edited by Bartholomew (1971), pointed out the danger that manpower planning wedded to the statistical description of large workforces would be seen as 'impersonal'. Morris, a co-author of Bartholomew's book, drew attention to the dangers of planning without taking account of organizational culture, and of regarding manpower as a cost rather than as a resource. In the same book of readings, Perlberg and Shaal described a manpower planning exercise for the Israeli Merchant Navy, and gave the opinion that 'an interdisciplinary approach is imperative'. The same claim appeared 12 years later in a book of readings edited by Edwards (1983). Half-way in time between the two, in a book devoted to manpower planning in the Civil Service, Smith (1976) pointed out in the introduction that 'hard maths must interact with the behaviour of people', and emphasized the potential for manpower planning as a benign influence on policy-making and day-to-day management. The rest of the book was given over to papers describing databases, simulation programs and statistical analyses.

Manpower planning has little value if it is not linked in some way to policy-making and strategic management, indeed this is its justification. Policy makers and those responsible for strategy are not necessarily highly numerate, and presenting manpower planning to them in the form of complicated equations does not guarantee their wholehearted understanding and support. The Institute of Manpower Studies recognized this problem in the mid-1970s, and began to encourage the presentation of manpower data in the form of easily understood histograms and pie charts. This change of emphasis was prompted also by the perception, in the wake of the 1973 Oil Crisis, that manpower planners should concentrate on auditing their existing staff rather than forecasting demand in an uncertain environment. Bennison and Casson's (1984) more recent book encapsulates this approach. Once again, the insight was not a new one; it had simply been brushed aside by enthusiasm for statistical analysis and computerized databases. Hughes, in Bartholomew and Morris (1971), had described forecasting as 'what would happen rather than what will'. Smith (1976) made much the same point, which was repeated in Bramham (1988), and in Edwards (1983).

But easily comprehended descriptions of data are not enough. The data must be properly conceptualized and correctly enumerated. It is all too easy to select inappropriate categories simply because they are sanctified by tradition.

Accepted grading structures may have more to do with job-evaluated payment systems than with making clear distinctions between types of work, or between the skills that workers need to be effective in each of them. The obfuscation necessary when payment systems are negotiated with employee representatives, for example, can lead to a distorted view of differences in skill between the various grades. The quality of manpower planning and of subsequent policy-making may both suffer. Bennison and Casson (1984) give an interesting account of the way in which the critical and detached eye of the manpower planning consultant can reveal home truths about manpower systems and the policies derived from them.

They quote the instance of manpower development in a large insurance company. The personnel staff supposed that all trainees had the opportunity to become senior managers. Diligent investigation of the personnel records revealed, however, that only those posted at some stage to a head office appointment actually made the senior ranks. The application of statistical forecasting techniques to the undifferentiated career structure would have resulted in a totally misleading picture of promotion prospects. Statistics would have legitimized a wrong conceptualization, and policy makers would have been led into error.

Categorization, the central problem in social research, can lead the manpower planner into other types of error. Mangan, writing in Edwards (1983), interprets manpower planning as econometrics and points out that the heterogeneity of the workforce is not recognized in economic theory, presumably any more often than it is recognized by manpower planners generally. Smith (1976) takes a sanguine view of the stratified categories of workers in the Civil Service, which he sees as presenting a favourable structure for the ministrations of the manpower planner; yet officers from the same nominal grade may perform very different work requiring very different skills depending on department and location.

While statistical analyses can be in error through too facile an acceptance of traditional and undifferentiated manpower categories, the opposite can also lead to unworkable prescriptions. A Hungarian economic policy adviser, interviewed on television, referred to the impracticality of expecting redundant miners, with their fierce adherence to their work and its social structure, to accept alternative employment—a world-wide phenomenon. Loveridge, in Edwards (1983), whose predeliction is to interpret manpower planning as an aspect of sociology and industrial relations, points correctly to the dangers of ignoring workforce traditions in the formulation of manpower plans.

So a methodology of manpower planning too closely linked with the statistical analysis of obsolescent or unvalidated manpower systems has a number of dangers. The obscurity of the analytical methods may alienate the very people, policy makers and employee representatives, whom they are intended to influence. Even on their own terms, such analyses may be erroneous because they take too little account of ingrained tradition, of technological change and how it may be received, and even the skill and knowledge content of existing jobs. Economic history and occupational psychology must become part of the multi-disciplinary study required of the human resource planner. As the 'new realism' of the 1980s shades into the microchip industrialization of the 1990s, we ignore these factors at our peril. But there are other strands in the history of manpower planning as a specialism that should be brought to the reader's attention.

The corporate view: shadow of the 1970s

What might be christened the corporate view of manpower planning was advocated by Bell (1974) in his book entitled, appropriately, *Planning Corporate Manpower*. In it, he made the following statement:

> The demand forecast must derive from the obligations of the company, which are set out in the business plan. The analysis of resources provides the means of translating the objectives into manpower terms.

McBeath (1978) took a similar line when he stated that 'Manpower planning follows from and is complementary to organizational policy'.

There is no indication here that the workforce available to an organization, and the variety of skills that they possess, might be its most valuable assets. Nor is there room for the thought that available skills might influence business objectives. Bell's approach requires that top management should not only possess a clear set of objectives, but should also be prepared to pass these on to the manpower planner. Are these realistic expectations? Not in the managerial experience of the author, nor of his postgraduate students who practise manpower planning and who are frequently faced with the need to do so in the absence of clear statements of corporate policy. Rajan and Fryatt (1988) noted during a study of manpower needs in the City of London, that corporate objectives were conspicuous by their absence in the firms they interviewed.

Strangest of all, however, is the assumption in the second half of the quotation from Bell. The analysis of resources may in fact reveal that corporate objectives cannot be translated into 'manpower terms'. The manpower planner who believes that workers with relevant skills are always to hand, is planning with pre-industrial concepts. In the early eighteenth century, labour was differentiated merely by titles such as 'domestic servant' or 'shepherd'. When, additionally, much of the potential workforce was incipiently unemployed, it was easy to conceive of the labour supply as something to be drawn upon at will. The early, labour-intensive, phases of the Industrial Revolution revealed that the unemployed might not always be there when they were needed. This included the remote areas where water power was to be obtained, but trained adult workers were not. Employers resorted to the extreme procedure of recruiting child labour. This commodity could be obtained from workhouses and domiciled within the factory—an option not available to employers today.

In our own times, a company might declare that its corporate aim was to supply artificial intelligence systems for business use. Yet the current output of appropriate university departments, and the limited opportunities for training, might seriously hamper the achievement of corporate plans for an entry into high technology. Manpower planning is not subordinate to corporate planning; the two are interdependent.

Loveridge (Edwards, 1983) stated that entrepreneurs always seek flexibility in the face of commercial uncertainty, and for this reason may distrust both corporate and manpower planning. In commercial enterprises—and in the 1990s these may well come to include much of the current public sector—manpower planners will do well to anticipate the market and technological changes affecting their businesses, and to prepare plans realistically based on an audit of available skills. Sometimes they must be prepared to make clear that desired short-run corporate objectives cannot be translated into manpower terms, much as an accountant may have to draw attention to cash flow problems. Perhaps for this reason, Edwards (1983) was more cautious than Bell in accepting the dominance of corporate over manpower plans: 'The manpower plan influences corporate strategy and is in turn influenced by it'. He rightly pointed out that neither recruitment nor demanning are necessarily automatic or immediate options.

The corporate view, however, has another serious disadvantage. It shares with the statistical approach a tendency to ignore the appropriateness of manpower categories. A corporation is a financial and statutory entity, not a human one. When speaking of corporations, we usually imply large public and private bureaucracies. In the Civil Service, for example, a member of staff classified as an executive officer might work in a local social security benefit office. Someone with the same job title might assist policy makers in Whitehall. The types of work are very different and require totally different skills: planning at the corporate level would ignore these important differences. Sales staff in private sector corporations carry out a wide range of duties, from the purely administrative to delicate negotiations with a quasi-legal character. Nevertheless, a corporate decision to amalgamate the sales departments of two divisions, and make 'surplus' staff redundant, might totally ignore the varied skills of the people concerned, and the varied ways in which they could be used. Planning with skills, rather than 'head counts', in mind may enable the manpower planner to suggest not only alternatives to redundancies, but also new directions for business development. Manpower analysis may become the source of corporate plans rather than being complementary or merely subservient to them. The analogy is again with accountants, but this time in their role as activator of hidden assets.

Corporate managers in the 1980s, however, might have been forgiven for assuming that the management of redundancy is what manpower planning is all about, so briskly was 'slimming' pursued. Redundancy demonstrates the failure rather than the successful outcome of the manpower planning process. It is a sad fact of life in contemporary Britain that large corporations, which once appeared to offer job security in return for loyal service and an acceptance of a stereotyped role, have so frequently reneged on the deal. In axeing 'dead wood', corporations were often ridding themselves of a problem of their own making; the failure was of the organization's human resource policies and procedures, not of the people sacked. The ineffectiveness, so perceived, of staff was created earlier by a lack of enlightened career development. The corporate view can ignore social responsibility in addition to the varied skills of the workforce.

Pearson and Heyno (1988) have investigated the re-employment of a wide range of managers and professionals following redundancy. Sixty per cent had changed their occupational classification, regardless of age or gender. Had the flexibility of the skills that they had acquired during their working lives been recognized by their previous employers, it is doubtful whether redundancy would have been justified or necessary.

Tactical manpower planning: a proposal ignored

Corporate manpower planning, and the statistical approach, both depend on the existence of large, stable organizations. Is there an alternative view, that takes account of the existence of small organizations, often in the service sector, for which average numbers of employees, and average wastage rates, have little meaning? Is there a way of conceptualizing manpower planning as a day-to-day tactical exercise?

Bowey (1974), in a book, significantly, out of print, made proposals along these lines. Although she contributed an original formula for the calculation of wastage rates, that compensates for distortion caused by less committed short-term staff, her book is not dominated by mathematical formulae. She concentrated not on manpower planning for the big battalions, but on the situational needs of managers faced with changes such as sudden staff shortages, or the need to move the location of their businesses. Her concern was with the availability of potential employees when required by the entrepreneurial business.

On the subject of categorization of employees, or on the multiple uses to which their skills can be put, she has little to say. She was prepared to advance explanatory theories, however, for the phenomena that analysis revealed; 'push' and 'pull' explanations for employee wastage, for example. She suffered, perhaps, from being ahead of her time. Her conception of manpower planning as a situational requirement is better suited to the free market 1980s and 1990s than to the corporate 1970s. It does not, however, support the strategic view of human resource management.

Practical manpower planning

The approach adopted by Bennison, and the Institute of Manpower Studies, in the middle of the 1970s was to make manpower planning comprehensible to the average manager. This objective was also adopted by Bramham (1988). Both concentrated on the use of simple, non-mathematical techniques to solve short-term problems at an organizational level. McBeath (1978) took a similar line, this time with the emphasis firmly on the 'control' of manning levels. The late 1970s was the period when demanning became the prime concern of many personnel managers. Like Bramham and Bennison, Pettman and Taverner (1984) adopted the approach of supplying the manpower manager with a practical workbook, concentrating on data collection and information systems. In none of these books, however, do we find an explanatory or unifying theory to bind the various strands of manpower planning together, and to assist the translation of research into policy.

How should we define manpower planning?

If manpower planning, as the discipline has been known for 20 years, is to become the much-needed backbone of personnel professionalism, then it must itself be capable of clear definition. At this point the reader will be more aware of the variety than the unity of the activities subsumed under the title of manpower planning. These include processes of statistical analysis, often applied to large, supposedly stable, organizations with the object of creating long-term plans. Simple techniques may, however, also be used to analyse the day-to-day needs of small enterprises. Manpower planning is also assumed to encompass issues of the supply of trained manpower by the educational system, and the demand for it throughout the UK. Definitions applied to manpower planning by various authors seem generally inadequate.

The Department of Employment defined manpower planning in 1976:

> A strategy for the acquisition, utilization, improvement, and retention of an enterprise's human resources.

The word 'retention' can presumably be excused on the grounds that knowledge of the massive redundancies to come was not available at that time. Bramham (1988), was perhaps, being more realistic when he defined manpower planning as 'essentially concerned with the effective use of human resources', as was McBeath (1978):

> The task of manpower planning is to determine and specify the optimum manning requirement now and in the foreseeable future.

Already, in these seemingly similar definitions, we can sense differences of emphasis; between strategy and tactics, and between the manpower plan as an end product and the processes required to derive it. The effective deployment of existing human resources, for example, could require the use of work study, motivational theory, and job design, rather than statistical analysis of payroll trends. While the word 'strategy' in the Department of Employment definition might imply the use of statistical forecasting, 'acquisition' suggests that a knowledge of personnel assessment methods might also be desirable.

Bennison and Casson (1984) emphasized the importance of the process of planning, as distinct from the product. The latter, which they refer to as the 'manpower map', takes account of various scenarios apparent to planners and their fellow managers. The 'manpower map' is to be revised continually as circumstances change. McBeath (1978) places stress on the function of manpower planning as the basis of manpower control; the planner as policeman.

A number of writers on manpower planning, and no doubt many personnel managers, have expressed concern about the frontier between planning and personnel management. The Department of Employment definition, for example, would seem to contain a great deal of the personnel manager's job. Smith (1976) draws a fine distinction by describing manpower planning as 'quantitative personnel management'. Nevertheless, Leek's contribution to Edwards' (1983) book on manpower planning is a straightforward description of personnel selection and training procedures, as might be taught to people studying for membership of the Institute of Personnel Management. It might be possible, but self-defeating for our purpose, to define personnel management in terms of day-to-day administration, and manpower planning as the separate development of personnel policy and strategy. Alternatively, manpower planning could be incorporated unequivocally within the training and activity of personnel managers, a development that would make the clarification of its content even more necessary.

Perhaps the biggest stumbling block to a comprehensive definition is the word 'planning'. In a political context it can imply direction and the loss of liberty; 'planning agreements' intended to involve government in the direction of manufacturing industry were not welcomed by the private sector in mid-1970s Britain. Lester (1965) was wise to title his book *Manpower Planning in a Free Society*, knowing the likely reaction of US citizens and businesses to intervention by the government, particularly federal agencies. At least one elderly civil servant of the author's acquaintance, when speaking of a colleague, used the word 'planner' as a term of abuse.

But 'planning' is seen not only in opposition to 'freedom', but also to 'doing', as Loveridge points out; planning constrains the achievement of the self-motivated entrepreneur. It is but a short step from there to suggesting that business or manpower planning are a waste of effort that could be better expended in getting 'real work' done. Smith (1976), in an analysis taken up by Bennison and Casson (1984), disposed of this objection in a satisfying way. Management, he wrote, consisted essentially in making decisions about the use of resources to achieve objectives; the entrepreneur could hardly object. Planning, he added, was intended to provide the best possible framework of information within which decisions could be made. Significantly, in view of what the author is about to suggest, Halsey (1972) described the purpose of social research (particularly sociology) as being 'to inform the political debate'. In the same publication, he drew a relevant distincion between planning as 'futurology' and as 'sought ends'. It may well be part of the manpower planner's art to keep a realistic balance between the two.

So it appears desirable to concentrate on the process of manpower planning, rather than its outcome, which should be subject to constant revision. Manpower audits and forecasts should be revised at least as often as financial forecasts already are. The purpose is to provide information relevant to decision-making within an enterprise or public service, the research arm of policy creation, and an integral part of the strategic process. Edwards (1983) referred to manpower planning as 'the art of designing a manpower strategy'. Returning to the potential meanings of the word 'strategy' discussed earlier in this chapter, we can see that at least one interpretation of Edwards' definition would suit the interpretations of personnel management and manpower planning that we are beginning to carve out. Practitioners will need to be multi-skilled craftsmen, oriented towards the solution of problems rather than the pursuit of a cosily delineated academic discipline. Herein lies yet another danger.

It is possible to approach the problem of illuminating manpower and business decisions from another angle. We can regard work and workers as a legitimate subject for social research, as on many occasions not directly connected with manpower planning they have been. We now start not with statistics, which is but one way of describing our data, but with conceptualization of the work and workers whom we wish to study. The analogy, in a more directly recognizable social research setting, would be with the process of taking a census of population. The first step is to decide the categories within which we wish to collect data; age, gender, standard of education, domicile, and so on. The next stage is to enumerate the data by means of questionnaires. The enumerated data must then be described in ways that enable it to be readily comprehended and analysed: graphs, histograms, charts and tables all suggest themselves, in addition to the statistical models sometimes used in traditional manpower planning. Finally, we need an explanatory theory that will suggest policies and action needed to change the status quo, should we be required to do so. Sociology, psychology, geography, or economic history, might all contribute to our understanding of the processes revealed by our data, and indicate possible lines of policy formulation. There is no reason, apart from the early espousal of the subject by the statisticians, why manpower planning should not be accorded the same methodology and rigour. The objective is unity in method, and diversity in interpretation. Manpower planners, in studying the behaviour of workers and problems of labour supply and demand, are engaged in social research. Conceptualization of appropriate manpower categories is at least as important as statistical description, especially given the onward march of industrialization, which affects at different stages every country in the world.

The proposed definition of manpower planning now becomes: 'A process of social research whose primary objective is improving the quality of work'.

This definition is in no way intended to restrict the current range of manpower planners' activities; indeed it should extend it. Labour markets will be studied with a view both to increasing the availability of skills and for the benefit of those without work. Within organizations, studies of wastage rates and absenteeism will be augmented by research aimed at discovering how work is perceived by those who leave and by those who stay. In all investigations using surveys (the majority of current manpower planning), equal weight will be given to each stage in the methodology; categorization, enumeration, description and explanation. Statistics will have an honoured but not overriding status. Ethnography and experimental research can be introduced where their methodologies are appropriate. Most important of all, critiques of manpower research can be grounded in the accepted standards for social research in general.

Human resource planning for the future

The argument so far may be summarized as follows. Personnel management as a function has failed to break out of its administrative strait-jacket. As demands grow for line managers to take more responsibility for the people who work for them, and computers reduce the number of staff required for record-keeping, personnel could easily lose even its administrative role. Yet the impact of larger markets, technology, and the greater need to meet the needs of consumers, all require that more attention be paid to human resources. To mark the change in emphasis, we will refer to the future developments in this subject as 'human resource planning'; 'manpower planning' will be used when describing past history.

Human resource planning, defined as social research at the workplace, can provide human resource managers with a practical means to justify and express their professionalism in ways that will directly affect profitability and effectiveness. But human resource planning demands that its practitioners take on board what may be unfamiliar concepts. These were identified above as four stages in the research process: categorization, enumeration, description, and explanation. Both categorizaion and explanation interact closely with policy-making and with the strategic process

CASE STUDY 1
How many graduates should we recruit?

A statistical technique

The technique used in this case was the *stationary population model* described by Rowntree in Smith (1970). It relates regular annual intake and wastage rates (the percentage leaving per year) to the number of employees available within an organization (the stationary population). Rowntree pointed out that such models were artificial, in the sense that they assumed the purposive continuation of a recruitment procedure over many years, but that they nevertheless allowed the long-term implications of policies and procedures to be explored.

To understand the construction of a stationary population model, consider the following simple example. Assume that the annual intake of recruits is 100, subject to wastage of 10 per cent per annum. At the beginning of the first year, 100 trainees are recruited, of whom 90 are left at the beginning of the second year. These are joined by 100 new recruits, yielding a total population of 190. At the end of the second year, 10 per cent of each of the intakes have left, reducing the population to 171 (81 + 90). To these are added a third intake of 100 to make up a population of 271. Repeating the calculation for the number of years judged to constitute a 'career' in the organization yields an estimate of the static population for the particular type of employee. The result can be expressed graphically as in Figure 1.3.

The static population indicates the probability of being able to promote experienced ex-trainees to senior positions. For instance, if the static population of qualified engineers within an organization were 300, and there were 200 senior engineers' posts to fill, the organization would have little choice between candidates, unless some were promoted soon after recruitment. With a static population of 1000, promotion could be more selective.

An historical context

The history of graduate recruitment reflects many of the social attitudes and prejudices discussed by Wiener (1981) and others, and whose origins can be traced to the nineteenth century. The attitudes of industry to graduates, and of graduates to industry, have always been wary, and the role of graduates in industry has been difficult to define. Like the professions, industry was forced into accepting this source of recruits by the deflection of the brighter school-leavers into higher education by the expansion of the universities and polytechnics in the 1960s and 1970s.

Whether graduates would accept industry was another matter. For many years, many graduate occupations provided parallel means of advancement to those on offer in industry and commerce, which were entered directly by school-leavers. Graduate careers were defined in terms of steady progress in the apparently more 'gentlemanly' atmosphere of the learned professions, the public service and education. Not only did industry appear to involve more risk and rough and tumble, but it was situated in undesirable locations and lacked social status. As Wiener pointed out, 'fees', or a salary from the public purse, have a respectability that industrial profits and salaries do not. Some enlightened industries were offering management training schemes to graduates before the Second World War, and their reputation was enhanced as the trainees developed into successful managers. Most industrial and commercial companies, especially small- and medium-sized ones, looked at that time to school-leavers for their future management talent. Technical skills were developed at night school and in provincial colleges, some of which were destined to become universities.

After the Second World War, it became fashionable for prominent companies to pay visits to the better-known campuses in search of a small intake of graduates. Issues of prestige, and 'me-too-ism', were probably as important as purposive attempts to acquire high-quality trainees for the future. The 'milk round', as this exercise rather slightingly became known, had begun.

Many are the tales of misuse of graduate talent; of unimaginative training schemes, based on the idea that graduates should get to know industrial life from the bottom, and in the lowly roles accorded in the past to school-leavers. Such training exposed the new recruits where they were most vulnerable (knowledge of the company and commerce in general) and prevented the use of their strength (an analytical mind). The sheer boredom and deflation of this initial experience, heightened by the contrast with the glossy literature used to attract recruits in the first place, was responsible for high turnover. This, in turn, reinforced the perception of many industrial managers that 'graduates are not suited to industry'. Scientists and engineers were offered interesting, if limited, careers because technical advance was in vogue, and because these graduates' contribution to profitability could be demonstrated. Management, in the form of unchanging administrative practices, was carried out mainly by people without higher education. Even in 1990, only 25 per cent of British managers have a university or polytechnic education (Pearson and Pike, 1990), but industry, much reduced in terms of total employment, has become the largest single sector (18 per cent) for the recruitment of graduates.

Poor practices in the recruitment and employment of graduates still persist. These will be discussed further in Chapters 4 and 7.

An organizational context

This case study concerns the recruitment of graduates by a British industrial company with subsidiaries throughout the UK and overseas. In common with similar organizations, the company began to take graduate recruitment seriously when it perceived that the expansion of universities, and the formation of the polytechnics, would decrease the number of bright school-leavers. The number of recruitment visits to the university careers offices increased and, through familiarity, some of the long-standing prejudices began to break down. Graduates were taken sufficiently seriously as a source of future talent for the numbers joining the company each year to be reported to the main board. Training schemes were available for engineers and accountants.

The year in question was a bad one for graduate recruitment, because confidence was reduced by a trade recession. Many campus visits were cancelled, but token attempts were made to keep faith with the more popular university careers services. As is sometimes the way with senior management, the economic reasons were later forgotten when they criticized the reduced entry of graduates (less than one third of the previous year's total). Questions were asked about the effectiveness of those coordinating graduate recruitment at head office. The newly appointed director of personnel was moved to enquire: 'How many graduates should we recruit each year, and why?'

Central personnel staff, faced with the need for a quick answer, and in an effort to initiate manpower planning, decided to rephrase the personnel director's query in the following way:

- What are graduates for?
- How do we calculate the appropriate number?

Both these questions are capable of simple or complicated answers. The first can be answered simply by saying that the purpose of the 'graduate intake' is to provide for the future senior management of the company. This simple answer avoids equally important questions about the balance between technical and managerial skills, and the motivation of qualified people to undertake these different types of work. It raises other questions about the career objectives and career development needs of the graduates, and the extent to which a decentralized company can meet them. It raises yet further questions about the need for new ideas, and about the acceptablity of the creative graduate to a traditional and bureaucratic management.

Deciding how many graduates to recruit is a matter of forecasting demand. This in turn requires assumptions about the rate of company growth. On this important and delicate matter, the staff were to receive no guidance from senior management beyond a statement that 'you had better assume that things will stay pretty much the same'. Bennison and Casson (1984) have pointed out the sensitivity of manpower forecasts to assumptions about rates of growth or contraction.

The paradox is that the quality of staff within a company can be influenced only in the long term; graduates must not only be recruited, but also absorbed effectively into the manpower structure and the social environment of the company. Yet long-term forecasts of economic climate and growth, and therefore graduate demand, are highly vulnerable to fallible economic forecasts.

These difficulties were sidestepped, rather than overcome, by some rough and ready assumptions without which manpower planning could not proceed. The central recruiting team decided to concentrate on graduates as the source of future management talent; it would be assumed that most graduates would be capable of developing the appropriate skills and career orientation, whether these were apparent at recruitment or not. Some would opt for specialist careers, or leave the company. This wastage would have to be allowed for, but no assumptions would be made about separate streams for specialists, professionals and managers. In the absence of any strategic guidance from senior management, the team decided to assume that the company would neither contract nor expand. Within a few years this was proved dramatically incorrect, as was the cognate assumption that careers lasting 40 years could be offered to graduates joining the organization in their early twenties. The plans for closures and redundancies were either unarticulated or not communicated.

Planning graduate intake

For statistical analysis the planning team chose the static population model (Smith, 1970) that was described at the beginning of this case study. This was used iteratively, trying out different assumptions about intake until the results made reasonable sense. Figure 1.3 illustrates the application of Smith's approach to two possible scenarios. One of these was that recruitment should continue at the lower rate apparent during the recession, and the other that an intake of 100, possible during times of business confidence, should be maintained whatever the economic climate. Direct intake to operating divisions was to be supplemented with trainees sponsored by head office when necessary.

The team also decided to ignore the topping up of graduate numbers by recruitment of managers and specialists in mid-career; this would be essential in the early years of the proposed policy, because recruits direct from university would, by design, not fill all the vacancies for qualified employees. Later, the calculated level of recruitment direct from the universities would take up the slack, and mid-career recruitment would diminish.

In addition to assumptions about intake and length of career, the static population model required data about the likely wastage rate of graduate staff. Experience throughout the company at that time suggested that it would be advisable to assume loss rates of 15 per cent per annum during the first five years of service, and five per cent thereafter. These assumptions, like the others, were highly sensitive to economic and market conditions.

Figure 1.3(a) shows the long-term effects of recruiting 50 graduates per year, allowing for the anticipated losses. A static population of 559 graduates would be available for selection for senior management posts. The next stage of the analysis demanded an assumption about the number of senior management jobs that need to be filled, in the long term, by graduates.

The company had just instituted a policy of identifying and giving special treatment to those managers whose contribution was felt to be essential to the proper functioning of the company. The intention was to retain these people by various fringe benefits in a time of national incomes policy. To that extent the company was identifying in a rather graphic and purposeful way its essential internal labour market. This group numbered 300 throughout the UK divisions.

The next stage of the analysis was to see, by trial and error, how readily this group of 300 key staff could be obtained, long term, by promoting graduates. Figure 1.3(b) shows that very few options are available at this level of intake. One would be to promote all available graduates to the key group within eight years of joining, plainly unrealistic in view of their varied talents and aspirations, or to promote some very much earlier, before they had acquired sufficient general experience. Whatever might otherwise be practical or desirable about this level of intake, it would not achieve the stated long-term objective.

An intake of 100 graduates per annum was plainly within the capability of the company, since 140 had on occasions been recruited in one year. Figure

Figure 1.3
Application of Smith's model to graduate recruitment
(a) Intake of 50 graduates per year
(b) To maintain senior grade of 300, all remaining graduates promoted after 7 years' service
(c) Intake of 100 graduates per year
(d) To maintain senior grade of 300, about one fifth of remaining graduates would be promoted after 10 years' service.

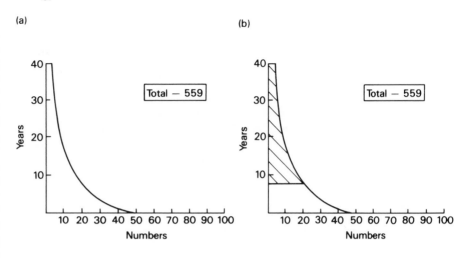

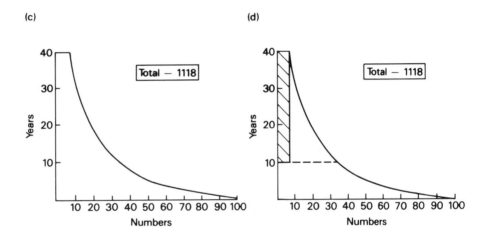

1.3(c) shows the implications of translating this figure into the annual long-term procedure. The static graduate population would become 1118. From this, to quote but one option, it would be possible to select about one fifth after eight years' service to fill key positions in the company (see Figure 1.3(d)). This expectation would motivate the more ambitious graduates if it were made explicit, and it would allow the company to choose people who had proved themselves at a lower level as good general management material. Other options were available, and it is an important outcome of getting the intake sufficiently large that the organization then has freedom to manouevre in planning for senior management succession.

In the event, the planning team decided that 100 graduates per year was the right target for the company. Resources were provided in terms of publicity material, the long-term commitment of general managers, and funds for centrally-sponsored training schemes. But 'the best laid schemes of mice and men', as Burns might have remarked, did not always work out in the commercial realities of the 1980s. The planned recruitment of graduates brought many talented people into the company, but it could not compensate for fundamental problems of unsuitable product mix, for directorial myopia, nor for a highly unfavourable market. Ten years after this study was carried out, the company, one of Britain's most prominent multinationals, had been taken over twice, first by its bankers, and then by a better-managed conglomerate. The corporate entity that the graduate recruitment procedure was intended to support, no longer existed.

So had the manpower planning exercise been a waste of time? Some would say that commercial success, or lack of it, would have had little to do with the number of graduates available. Yet commercial success was beyond the remit of the central personnel staff who planned graduate intake, and it is possible to surmise that without the regular intake of talent, failure would have been one step nearer.

Planning and strategy

This case study provides some general lessons that relate to the arguments presented in Chapter 1. These can be itemized as follows:

1 Planning the recruitment of people with important skills is a strategic issue. It requires collaboration and information from those planning the commercial development of the organization, because of its long-term and company-wide implications.

2 Human resource planners can, however, initiate the strategic process, even in the absence of information from senior management, by means of research based on existing personnel records.

3 Planning decisions are improved by taking full account of historical and organizational contexts. Assumptions about growth rate are crucial, and must be regularly reviewed as part of strategic human resource planning. Realistic categorization of the functions that employees are intended to fill, both now and in the future, is necessary for effective forecasting.

4 Strategic analysis does not necessarily require the use of complex statistical techniques; scenario assumptions are at least as important as mathematical analysis. In this case, more elaborate calculation would have stretched the underlying assumptions too far. The manpower system, in Bennison's terms, is more important than the statistical method used to analyse it. Most important of all, statistical exercises of this type must be regularly reviewed in the light of growth expectations and changing patterns of employment.

References

Ansoff, I. (1987) *Corporate Strategy* (revised ed.), Penguin, Harmondsworth, London.

Bartholomew, D. (1967) *Stochastic Models for Social Processes*, John Wiley & Sons, Chichester.

Bartholomew, D., and Morris, B. (1971) *Aspects of Manpower Planning*, English University Press, London.

Bell, D. (1974) *Planning Corporate Manpower*, Pitman Publications, London.

Bennison, M., and Casson, J. (1984) *The Manpower Planning Handbook*, McGraw-Hill (UK) Ltd., Maidenhead.

Bowey, A. (1974) *A Guide to Manpower Planning*, Macmillan, London.

Bramham, J. (1988) *Practical Manpower Planning* (4th ed.), Institute of Personnel Management, London.

Cannon, J. (1979) *Cost Effective Personnel Decisions*, Institute of Personnel Management, London.

Chandler, A. (1962) *Strategy and Structure: chapters in the history of American industrial enterprise*, MIT Press, Cambridge, Mass., USA.

Donovan, The Lord (1968) *Royal Commission on Trade Unions and Employers' Associations 1965–68*, HMSO, London.

Economic Trends (1990), HMSO, London.

Edwards, J. (1983) *Manpower Planning: strategy and techniques in an organizational context*, John Wiley & Sons, Chichester.

Ferris, G., and Rowland, K. (1988) *Human Resources Management: Perspectives and Issues*, Allyn & Bacon Inc., Boston.

Flamholtz, E. G. (1986) *Human Resources Accounting* (revised and expanded ed.), Jossey-Bass, San Francisco.

Flanders, A., Pomeranz, R., and Woodward, J. (1968) *Experiment in Industrial Democracy: a study of the John Lewis partnership*, Faber & Faber, London.

Foster, G. (1989) 'Mintzberg's Strategic Force', *Management Today*, April, 74.

Freeman, C. (1984) 'Keynes or Kondratiev? How can we get back to full employment?' in Marstrand, P. (ed.) *New Technology and the Future of Work and Skills*, Frances Pinter, London.

Guest, D. (1989) 'Personnel Management and HRM—can you tell the difference?' *Personnel Management*, January, 48.

Halsey, A. (ed.) (1972) *Educational Priority Vol 1: EPA problems and policies*, HMSO, London.

Harvey-Jones, J. (1988) *Making it Happen: reflections on leadership*, Fontana/Collins, Glasgow.

Johnson, G., and Scholes, K. (1988) *Exploring Corporate Strategy* (2nd ed.), Prentice-Hall International (UK) Ltd, Hemel Hempstead.

Legge, K. (1977) *Power, Problem Solving and Innovation in Personnel Management*, McGraw-Hill (UK) Ltd, Maidenhead.

Leontiades, M. (1980) *Strategies for Diversification and Change*, Little, Brown, Boston.

Lester, R. (1965) *Manpower Planning in a Free Society*, Princeton University Press, Princeton.

Lupton, T. (1971) 'Organizational Change "Top–Down" or "Bottom–Up" Management', *Personnel Review*, Autumn, 22.

Mayon-White, W. (ed.) (1986) *Planning and Managing Change*, Harper & Row, London.

McBeath, G. (1978) *Manpower Planning and Control*, Business Books, London.

Miller, P. (1989) 'Strategic HRM: what it is and what it isn't', *Personnel Management*, February, 42.

Morgan, R. (1971) 'Manpower planning in the Air Force: an exercise in linear programming' in Smith, A. *Models of Manpower Systems*, English University Press, London.

Pearson, R., and Heyno, A. (1988) *Helping the Unemployed Professional*, John Wiley & Sons, Chichester.

Pearson, R. and Pike, G. (1990) *The IMS Graduate Review 1990*, Institute of Manpower Studies, Brighton.

Pearson, R., and Andreutti, F. (1990) 'The European labour market review—the key data', IMS report No. 165, Institute of Manpower Studies, Brighton.

Pettman, B., and Tavernier, G. (1984) *Manpower Planning Workbook*, (2nd ed.), Gower Press, Epping, Essex.

Pfiffner, J. (1960) 'Administrative Rationality', *Public Administration Review*, Summer, 125–32.

Pigors, P., and Myers, C. (1981) *Personnel Administration: a point of view and a method* (9th ed.), McGraw-Hill, Tokyo.

Quinn, J. (1980) *Managing Strategic Change*. Quoted in Mayon-White, W. (ed.) (1986) *Planning and Managing Change*, Harper & Row, London.

Rajan, A., and Fryatt, J. (1988) *Create or Abdicate?: The City's human resource choice for the 90s*, Institute of Manpower Studies/Witherby, London.

Raven, J. (1989) 'Democracy, bureaucracy and the psychologist', *The Psychologist* 2 No. 11, 458.

Smith, A. (ed.) (1970) 'Some statistical techniques in manpower planning', CAS Occasional Papers No. 15, HMSO, London.

Smith, A. (ed.) (1976) *Manpower Planning in the Civil Service*, HMSO, London.

Wiener, M. (1981) *English Culture and the Decline of the Industrial Spirit 1850–1980*, Penguin Books, Harmondsworth, London.

CHAPTER 2

New markets for people and jobs: categorization and efficiency

Labour markets: where people and categorization meet

Labour markets are a prime strategic concern for anyone seeking to supply goods or services and, of course, needing employees to do it. It is also true that labour markets are as restricted or open as you wish them to be. The case study at the end of Chapter 1 touched on the topic of categorization, and the effect that the chosen categories had on subsequent manpower planning. Categorizing employees as 'graduates' and 'senior managers' was necessary for planning to proceed within the time-scale allowed, but was a palpably incomplete picture of the company's internal labour market. The human resource planning of the 1990s should regard all manpower categories as provisional, and emphasize the flexible use of people.

Categorization becomes doubly important, and more than doubly difficult, when attempting to understand and manage the external labour market. Neither governments nor employers can avoid studying labour markets if they are to achieve their economic objectives. They represent the most obviously 'social' topic within manpower research: the categories used, in all their superficiality, may determine not only social policies but the life-opportunities of millions.

Human resource planning in the 1990s must reconsider how its raw material is used. What is the basis of the categories used by managers and by policy makers in describing the labour market? Why does the industrial past dominate the way we think about people, and how should categories change in the face of continuing industrialization and the development of human skills? This chapter addresses these issues, and links the answers to the problems of unemployment and equal opportunity. Each of these topics is important in their own right, and together they provide a basis for the wider consideration of human resource planning as social research in Chapter 3.

But first we need to assess whether the labour market is a 'market' in any recognizable sense: to what extent is the human resource simply a factor of production?

Market forces and people

In the UK, the word 'market' acquired political meanings during the 1980s. The ruling political party emphasized the disciplinary virtues of the 'market economy', while those with different values spoke of the 'social market' or 'market socialism', implying the uses to which market-generated wealth should be put. This latter perspective gained support from the European concept of the Social Charter. Its proponents, notably France's Jaques Delors, support the Charter as a means of distributing the economic benefits of the Single European Market. In fast-changing Eastern Europe, it was the economic benefits of a change from communist to free market systems that most attracted the man in the street. Capitalist, socialist or communist, the 'market' had new significance for all.

In the UK, the prevailing ethos in the 1980s was that all organizations, particularly those in public hands, would work more efficiently if exposed to the full rigour of market forces. Under the Conservative administration, retail distribution was held up as the example of market efficiency, and executives from major retail chains were invited to investigate the workings of the social security system and the management of the National Health Service. Certainly, British retail management could teach others, including even the Japanese, how to go about distributing goods to potential customers. Yet doubts remain, and not only among adherents to left-wing politics, as to whether retail marketing is the correct model for major social and economic phenomena. If I am prepared to pay £20 for a pullover, a selection is available in a multiple store to meet my need. If £200 is a price that I would contemplate, a 'niche player' will supply this narrower market with specialized goods to my taste. The phrase 'labour market' can suggest that supply and demand for people is similarly controlled.

In a crude and unspecific way, the retail analogy is correct. During the early 1980s, the UK government used the unemployment created by stringent monetary restriction to bring down inflation. Whether this was a deliberate act of policy, or passive acceptance of a situation created by an overvalued currency and world-wide recession, will probably never be known. The objective was achieved—for a while. 'Market forces', in the guise of reduced demand, had lowered the real cost of supply, at least in the short term. The question, of course, is not whether the exercise of political power to achieve macro-economic objectives can be effective, but whether is has long-term success in generating wealth. Even highly developed economies still require economic growth if the quality of life of its citizens is to be improved. Those advocating the adoption of a Social Charter to accompany the Single European Market in 1992 would not deny that the efficient generation of wealth is a necessary condition for its success. For less-developed countries, the process of wealth creation is, literally, a matter of life and death.

The following examples illustrate that serious, yet largely ignored, labour market ineffiencies can exist in economies that are generating wealth as never before. They are each taken from reports published towards the end of the 1980s, when Britain again seemed in the grip of inflation, but when most citizens were enjoying unprecedented prosperity.

The first concerns the efficient use of the female portion of the labour force, an emotive issue and one that affects all countries. This book is not concerned with the wider issues of feminism, however, but rather with the full use of available human resources. Chapman (1989) published the results of a longitudinal study of the careers of British graduates in the first three years after graduation. The researchers produced evidence to show that women graduates suffered disadvantages in three ways: they were more likely to be found in lower status, sub-professional employment; they were, on average, lower paid; and they had lower career aspirations that worsened when they married. The career aspirations of male graduates after marriage were higher than before.

Chapman explained these findings on the assumption that those who control the gateways to career success still think in terms of male and female occupations. School teachers, those who recruit for vocational higher education, employers and, most important, women themselves, consider that 'careers' are for men, and transfer this perception to students, clients and employees.

We will examine the concept of 'career' in a later chapter. Since there is no evidence to show that women do not possess the skills to succeed in traditional male occupations like science and engineering, Chapman's report supports the contention that wealth-creating capacity is going to waste. This is true of the UK, and probably of every other economy in the world. Women, by and large, are confined to the secondary labour market of temporary and part-time work, even if they possess graduate qualifications. If they do not, their plight is even worse. In the UK, the Equal Opportunities Commission (1988) pointed out that while women made up on average 42 per cent of the workforce, most were 'still working in lower paid, low-status jobs which offer restricted training and promotion opportunities. This is especially true of minority ethnic women and all those who carry extra responsibility for family care'.

The male professional is assumed by Chapman to be secure in his career, which is supported rather than inhibited by marriage and children. The second example paints a rather different picture of some men's careers. Hogarth and Daniel (1988) have studied the phenomenon of long-distance commuting that was brought about by the lack of jobs in the northern counties of England compared with the relatively prosperous South. About 100 000 people, mostly married males from professional and managerial occupations, were found to leave their families to work in London or the surrounding counties during the week. Travel was arduous and unpleasant, especially if undertaken by the cheapest routes; loneliness increased the strain, associated often with overwork. While many professionals would accept separation from their families for brief periods as a natural hazard in building a career, most long-distance commuters saw no end to their deprivation. The explanation was simple: there were jobs to suit their skills in the South, but no comparable housing at a price they could afford. In one way this can be seen as a labour market working efficiently. Skills were available where needed, and at a price that employers were prepared to pay. Employers did not, of course, pay the full cost of the availability of skills and, except on a myopic view of labour economics, the long-distance commuter would not be seen as an efficient form of labour. In effect, social costs had been externalized, and transport revenues artificially increased.

The third example concerns a massively inefficient labour market in the City of London—one of the attractions for 'industrial gypsies' from other parts of the country. Gross employment had increased by at least 30 per cent since deregulation of the financial markets was first announced in 1984. Employment fell back slightly following the 'crash' of 1988, but looked set to increase steadily into the 1990s. The shortages of staff had been brought about, according to Rajan and Fryatt (1988), not only by growth in business, but by changes in technology and by specialization of the products offered to customers. Most serious of all, each of the competing institutions had been prepared to pay ever-increasing salaries to poach employees from others, rather than to train people in the skills needed in the changed environment. The lack of strategic thinking, as defined in Chapter 1, and even of traditional manpower planning, was manifest.

Whether we look at the effects of public policy, or at managerial decisions about hiring and firing, the labour market does not work efficiently. Its imperfections can act as a significant brake on economic progress. Many more instances could be cited of the failure of the free market to provide the necessary skills, where and when they are needed.

Part of the problem lies in the way in which workers and potential workers are categorized, by both policy makers and managers. The more specialized we perceive work to be, the smaller the apparent labour market, and the more arduous and expensive is the recruitment process.

We will consider first why the simple supply and demand model of the labour market does not work, even on its own terms, and then why inappropriate categories are applied to the workforce. The latter enterprise will require a historical view of the continuing process of industrialization, and an awareness of the directions in which technology is influencing the workplace: in short, the approach will be strategic.

Two meanings for 'labour market'

It should be evident from the foregoing discussion that the phrase 'labour market' has two distinct meanings, one economic and the other descriptive. In classical economic theory the market is the meeting place of supply and demand, where the willing seller exchanges goods with the willing buyer. It is in this sense that workers may be said to 'price themselves out of the market' by making exorbitant wage claims. The other, descriptive, meaning should be apparent from the accounts of the three labour market failures by Chapman (1989), by Hogarth and Daniel (1988), and by Rajan and Fryatt (1988). Their approach was to describe workers and jobs available without attempting to link the two in the mathematical model implied in Figure 2.1. Where labour markets are referred to in this book, it will usually be in this descriptive sense.

Problems with supply and demand

The simple theory of wage determination, which is assumed to predict the availability of labour at differing levels of reward, and the relation between supply and demand, are illustrated in Figure 2.1. If this model works, up to a

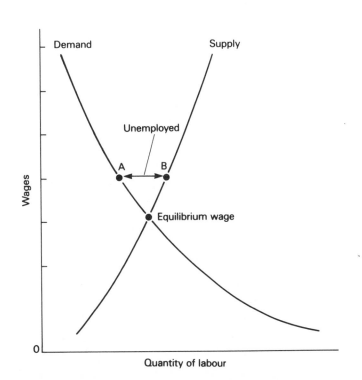

Figure 2.1
Classical supply and demand model for labour

point, for the sale of goods in a competitive retail market, why does it fail for the supply and demand for labour?

Briefly, the problems are threefold. The simple theory ignores the self-awareness of workers, the diversity of their skills, and the presence of monopolies in the market. People are not an inanimate commodity like coffee or potatoes; they at least partially understand their own position. They are able to make choices about whether to work or not, and to balance monetary gain against quality of life.

The requirements of jobs and the skills of workers vary widely, so we are dealing with many labour markets rather than one. Sometimes the inability of workers to move between these markets is overstressed. Pearson and Heyno (1988) have demonstrated the ease with which many unemployed professional people are able to change occupations in the process of getting back to work. Skills acquired in one job may be readily transferred to another. Workers themselves are often unaware of the flexibility of their skills, and both employers and trade unions, through ignorance or self-interest, may foster unrealistic and over-restrictive categories of work. In so doing, employers reduce the range of recruits available to them, and trade unions become locked into defensive, rather than creative, roles.

There are, however, some classes of work that require high intelligence and extensive training; there are others where the chief demand is for a high level of manual dexterity; and there are jobs that require exceptional skills in dealing with people. Temperament or ability may make it difficult for people to move easily between all these classes of work; in the economists' phrase, these markets are not 'cross elastic'. Training can improve the 'elasticity' of the workforce, but British employers, at least, have shown a reluctance to train the people who work for them. From the poor performance that brought the industrial training boards into being in the 1960s, to the decision to devolve training to local agencies in the late 1980s, the achievement has been, at best, patchy.

But there is a third factor that contributes to inelasticity in labour markets: monopoly power in the hands of either buyer or seller of the commodity. A town with one factory, or government department, as its major employer is subject to monopoly (strictly, 'monopsony') power of the buyer. A trade union that represents key workers in a public service (such as the electricity power workers in the UK, at least before privatization) enjoys monopoly power as a seller of labour. Simple supply and demand relationships do not operate in these conditions.

So the simple notion that the labour market consists of a unitary commodity, whose cost varies directly with one set of supply and demand forces, must be abandoned in favour of a pluralistic view. We are dealing, in any economy, with a multiplicity of labour markets, and with the fact that individuals have only limited ability to move from one market to another. This opportunity is highest among the best educated and trained, but since one unskilled job is very like another, the opportunity also exists at the lower end of the scale. For human resource planners working within organizations, crude labour market analyses at national level will have only background significance. The figures are over-aggregated for detailed use, and any statements about supply and demand are likely to be too remote. National labour market information is being computerized in the UK to make up for this deficiency.

The International Labour Office (ILO) is interested in comparisons between developing and less-developed countries. It published (Bourgignon,

1988) a comparative study of the wage–employment relationship in the two environments. Bourgignon concluded that in developed economies the relationships between wages and employment ('elasticity') varied so widely that they could not be considered in isolation from macro-economic policy, and the variation in the other constraints experienced by the employer. These were liable to change with time, and with the development of the informal ('black') economy. In developing countries an additional confounding factor was the side-by-side existence of modern and subsistence economies. The subsistence sector can, up to point, act as a 'sink' from which labour is always available. The 'gastarbeiter' system in Germany operates in a similar way as 'guest workers' can be returned to their country of origin when demand falls.

Research into these complicated relationships must continue, as it should into any social or economic system, but, in the short term, the findings are unlikely to be of direct use to organizational strategists or human resource planners.

'Labour market' as a descriptive concept

This brings us to the descriptive meaning of 'labour market'; the way in which the phrase is normally used. The 'labour market' for an individual is the perceived range of jobs available to him or her. From the employers' point of view, the 'labour market' for, say, computer programmers, is the number of people with the range of skills and aptitudes that the organization will accept for this type of work, and who are also available within travelling distance. Increasing wages, by and large, does not automatically increase the number of school-leavers with 'A' levels, nor does it make computer programming any more attractive to those whose chief desire is to work with people. As human resource planners, we do better to categorize and enumerate our 'labour markets' correctly than to engage in economic theorizing on the basis of doubtful and over-simplified assumptions.

If there is one outstanding example of the fallibility of manpower planning at the macro-economic level, it is the failure of all forecasting bodies to predict accurately the rising unemployment in the UK during the 1970s and 1980s. Figure 2.2 shows how far their estimates went astray. Bennison and Casson

Figure 2.2
Inaccuracy of employment forecasts
Source: Adapted from Evans, A. (1979) *What Next at Work?: a new challenge for managers*, Institute of Personnel Management, London

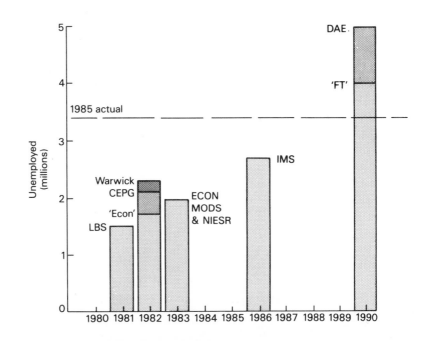

(1984) wisely emphasized the virtues of auditing rather than forecasting future demand in an uncertain market. This approach places a premium on appropriate categorization of people and jobs, and then their accurate enumeration. Strategic thinking demands that plans can readily be changed when the unexpected occurs. The organization that understands its current workforce and recognizes its sources of new recruits is best able to make an effective response to unexpected problems. So the social research skills of categorization and enumeration, together with scenario planning (the preparation of written descriptions of likely economic, social and business developments) are preferred to elegant but inaccurate forecasts based on past numerical trends.

General levels of employment are a product of macro-economic cycles and structural changes in the economy. They are also subject to frictional effects such as the lack of information about job opportunities, immobility of labour and over-restrictive hiring practices. Precise calculation of the combined effects of these factors is impossible. Economic models use historical figures collected by government departments and attempt to extrapolate from them. Their complexity apart, forecasting techniques of this type cannot take account of sudden catastrophic events, like the 1973 Oil Crisis or, indeed, the consequences of the 1987 world stock market crash. So what is true for the organizational level is also true for national manpower planners; concentrate on the analysis of the current situation, and leave the crystal ball to the fortune-tellers. Strategic thinking will not enhance its reputation by making definitive predictions and then being consistently and catastrophically wrong. Realistic auditing of current resources, together with a qualitative awareness of future trends, offers the best hope for effective management of organizations and nations.

Rajan (1986, 1987) has published two useful books on the changing occupational structure of the UK. His approach is essentially descriptive: which sectors of the labour market are expanding, and which contracting? In tentatively predicting the future for employment, he relies on surveys of employers' current intentions in preference to historical government statistics. In research of this type, whatever the country, the first question must be how to categorize jobs and workers.

Which categories should we use?

The problem here is one of avoiding the obvious. Appropriate categories will change as a country, region or organization becomes more highly industrialized, and as sophisticated technology is introduced. Appropriate categories will also change with general levels of education. What the strategic manpower planner should most firmly bear in mind is that the use of inappropriate categories will either reduce the efficiency of an organization or an economy, or unreasonably restrict employment opportunities. These issues have social implications at all times, but when skilled vacancies are difficult to fill, they also directly affect economic performance. This is true whether we are engaged in strategic planning for a company in the North of England, for a German bank or for the Republic of Uganda.

Effective categorization is not a once and for all exercise; industrial and social change ensure that constant revision is necessary. The continuing process of industrialization and technological change, which is discussed later in this chapter, will ensure that. For the purposes of strategic planning, however, we need to be aware of some common but useful categories applied to labour markets.

'Industrial' versus 'subsistence'

Developing countries are often said to have dualistic economies. This is the existence side by side of industrial and subsistence sectors. Mountjoy (1982) described this phenomenon in relation to the progress of industrialization in the less-developed countries. He pointed out that the distinction is not between industry and agriculture as a mechanized and scientifically-controlled agriculture is part of the industrialized sector. Within this it will be possible to identify agricultural specialists, mechanics and trained animal husbandry workers, as meaningful categories of labour. In the subsistence sector, however, work may be very difficult to categorize. Skills, in the industrial sense of the word, may be undifferentiated, and yet roles may be complex. Agriculture and the production of goods is likely to be for personal consumption, or for barter transaction. Yet the subsistence sector is nevertheless an important reservoir of manpower and aptitudes, and cannot be ignored in any satisfactory manpower audit. The appropriate categories will depend on the rate at which the efficiency of subsistence agriculture can be improved. The objective, in the early years of the European Common Market, was to enable workers to leave uneconomic farming and to move into industrial work; much of the vexed Common Agricultural Policy was to allow this necessary process to occur without undue hardship. The important topic of dualistic labour markets in developing countries has been subjected to comparative study by Potter and Unwin (1989).

British readers may find all this rather remote, but I would urge them to think again. No more than 10 miles from the prosperous financial centres of Britain and major cities throughout the world, we can find examples of a growing subsistence economy. In the UK, the long-term unemployed, whose plight has been investigated by Warr (1987) and others, often learn to accept their reduced circumstances, and to survive on a low nominal income. Such people are isolated socially, as well as economically, from the industrialized mainstream. National manpower strategists should not ignore them. Tax authorities, of course, often wish they could get to know more about the more successful members of this 'hidden' economy! The late 1980s saw massive movements of populations bent on achieving not only greater political freedom, but also greater freedom to use their skills to create wealth for themselves and their families. People with industrial skills may be trapped inside a subsistence economy.

The 'working population'?

When we have decided which citizens are currently part of the industrialized economy, or could later be drawn into it, we have to decide how many of those currently constitute the 'working population'. This will be decided by the product of two other factors: the percentage who are of 'working age', and the 'activity rate'. The activity rate is the percentage of potential workers who wish to participate in the visible economy. In the UK, the most significant development in the labour market since the Second World War has been the entry of married women into the paid workforce, thus increasing the activity rate.

Assessing the population of working age requires both demographic statistics and a knowledge of local customs: activity rates may be projected from past trends, mediated by an appreciation of social, economic and technological change. As so often in the human resource planning process, we need both an accurate description of the way things are, preferably in numbers, together with a feel for the way they might develop,

**'Primary',
'secondary' and
'tertiary'**

These are the traditional categories of economic activity in an advanced, industrialized country. The primary sector includes the direct exploitation of the environment by agriculture or mining. The numbers employed in these activities have declined in industrialized countries. The secondary sector includes all types of manufacturing and this sector, too has declined as a source of employment in all Western countries since the Second World War.

It is the tertiary, or service, sector that is the biggest headache for the human resource planner. At the moment, it is taken to include such diverse activities as teaching, banking and office cleaning. One possible sub-categorization is to segregate the publicly-financed services provided by local or central government from those provided by private enterprise or parastatal organizations. This way out of an over-subscribed category may have more meaning, however, when talking about demand rather than supply, because the work done in the two sectors is likely to be similar. Jones (1982), whose major concern is the impact of the microchip on employment world-wide, and who may be counted a member of the 'alarmist' school, has suggested two potentially useful sub-categories of the service sector; the 'quaternary' and the 'quinary'. The quaternary sector would include domestic work of all types, whether paid or not. This would have the additional benefit of giving recognition and dignity to the economic contribution of 'housewives' and 'househusbands', as well those more obviously engaged in paid 'domestic work'. The quinary sector would include all activities and workers concerned with processing information—those, in fact, most likely to be affected by the introduction of information technology. Financial services have been one of the fastest growing elements in the tertiary sector: banks, insurance companies and building societies would all be included in the quinary category. After deregulation of financial markets, it would make good sense to recognize that technology has also broken down barriers between traditional occupations in the financial sector.

**Industrial
sectors?**

Rajan and Pearson (1986) commented that industrial sectors (shipbuilding, car manufacture, etc.) are singularly unhelpful categories, and government forecasters would probably concur. The reason is simple: employers use directly the skills of many different workers, and hire (from the 'service sector') the services of many more. This is one of the ways in which the multiplicity of skills in an industrialized economy fails to fit the categories perceived by the statistician. Organizations within one sector may draw upon workers from another (or even upon workers from another country) for the skills they need, and workers can change 'industrial sector' without changing the work they do, or change the nature of their work while remaining within the same sector. Add to this the problems of getting accurate figures from employers, and then aggregating them into meaningful totals, and the problems of human resource planning at the regional and national level can be understood.

In the UK, there are several standard classifications, each of which must be used with care. There is a Standard Industrial Classification (Central Statistical Office, 1979) that categorizes organizations by the product or service they provide. For the categorization of workers, an occupationally-based system called CODOT is available. For local manpower planning, national figures are disaggregated and held in a computer system called NOMIS, available to subscribers.

**Workers
themselves**

We encountered some of the problems of assigning individual workers to appropriate categories in Chapter 1, and in Case Study 1. The fundamental problem of the strategic human resource planner is to conceptualize 'skills', and 'significant experience', and then to assign workers provisionally to the currently appropriate category. The potential of job evaluation schemes as the source of workable categories will be explained in the next chapter.

In Phyllis Deane's (1979) phrase, industrialization requires the availability of an 'expanding, mobile, and adaptable labour force'. This is as true of advanced industrial nations as it is of countries taking their first steps towards an industrialized economy. The paradox is that industrialization itself is a cause of over-specialization, unless categories are viewed critically and strategically.

Work and non-work

Work has been defined as 'activity directed to goals beyond the enjoyment of the activity itself' (Warr, 1983). This definition makes no stipulation that work should either be enjoyable for its own sake or that it should earn a cash reward, but neither does it exclude these possibilities.

In the UK, work is generally associated with pay; voluntary work is not considered to be 'real work'. Job satisfaction is seen as a perk for the fortunate few. In this social climate, status depends crucially on the possession of paid employment.

Writers in the 1950s were already predicting that 'automation' would bring about mass unemployment, and that policy makers would have to engineer the 'post-industrial society'. If machines could take over routine work, then let them do so; the consequent wealth must be shared in such a way that workers could be liberated from drudgery. A flowering of artistic interest and communal endeavour would ensue.

After the massive economic upheavals of the 1980s, we still await the post-industrial society. Workers were released, right enough, but into unemployment or insecure and often equally routine service jobs. More important, the Protestant work ethic has, if anything, intensified, making it even more difficult for people to accept a society in which work could include unpaid service to the community, and in which there might be such a thing as a social wage, giving dignity where present social security payments and bureaucracy take it away.

Human resource planners should be realists; it is far from safe to assume, in advanced industrialized countries or probably anywhere else, that the post-industrial society is in prospect. We are trapped in a world of work that still depends on Marx's 'cash nexus', both for the operation of labour markets and for upholding human independence. This does not mean, however, that countries currently struggling to industrialize should not learn from those that preceded them, nor that advanced countries should not do their best to improve the quality of work which is offered in exchange for pay. If we have a market economy, then let it be a market; employers should compete for workers' skills, not merely by offering pay, but also by offering the conditions in which those skills can be most effectively and pleasurably deployed. Something of the kind is encapsulated in the proposed Social Charter, which some European politicians hope will complement the Single European Market. Nor need it be considered 'left wing' to point to the lack of industrial training in the UK, or to suggest that the market would be a good deal healthier if the government took the problem seriously instead of assuming, against all the evidence, that individual companies and industries will do it for themselves.

Employment and unemployment

Some readers of this book will be personally aware of countries and cultures in which this categorization is well nigh irrelevant. In industrialized societies, however, unemployment has a real and very personal meaning. Employment is the provider of important aspects of human experience: time structure, social interaction outside the intense relationships of the family, collective purpose and regular activity, status and identity. In pre-industrial societies, the question may never arise, because work is performed within the family unit and is related to an agricultural economy. Work can always be found, and the rewards of work, be they meagre, can nevertheless be shared. Industrialization, whatever its benefits, breaks this bond between producing, consuming, and the status that goes with each. Even in a welfare state, the unemployed person is subject to the rigours of reduced income, and to the restriction on his or her freedom that the system of welfare payments demands.

We must be careful, however, not to regard work in an industrialized economy as the sole provider of the human needs listed above; nor must we assume that employment always fulfils its potential in these respects. To see unemployment as removing the benefits of working life is to concentrate on worklessness as 'deprival' (in academic terms, we are using 'deprivation theory'). Another academic viewpoint that concentrates on the removal of autonomy from the unemployed by making them subject to a network of state regulation, while also removing a major part of their income, is referred to as 'agency theory'. Unemployment not only deprives people of the positive aspects of work, it also limits their capacity to act on their own behalf. The psychological effects of unemployment are discussed in more detail below (Pearson, 1988), and in Chapters 6 and 7.

It is no accident that the heading for this section is also the title of a book by Marie Jahoda (1982). She is a prominent 'deprivation' theorist. In this book, she looked again at the major study that she conducted into the effects of mass unemployment in an Austrian company-town in the 1930s, and compared her findings with the facts of unemployment 50 years later. She began one of her chapters with the following quotation:

> We entered Marienthal as scientists; we leave it with only one desire: that the tragic opportunity for such an inquiry may not recur in our time.

What shocked not only social scientists, but also social workers, journalists and politicians, in Britain as well as in other countries, was the poverty that the unemployed and their families endured: ragged, starved children; undernourished, aimless adults. While the rise to power of totalitarian regimes in the 1930s had many causes, unemployment was undoubtedly one of them. These conditions did not improve during the economic revival of the late 1930s, and came to public attention once again during the evacuation of city children to the countryside at the outbreak of war. The 'corrosive evil' of unemployment was the erosion of physiological and psychological well-being by poverty, as much as by lack of work. This, let it be said, was a state that much of the population of Britain and other countries had to endure over many centuries, both before and after the Industrial Revolution, with only the most basic and degrading social provision to mitigate it. To this extent, the full employment, welfare state period after the Second World War could be seen as an atypical interlude, perhaps a brief respite between a bleak past and an even bleaker future. It is all too easy to concentrate on unemployment and overlook the other aspects of poverty.

But 1980s unemployment has taken place against a background of relative prosperity, and its effects have been softened by this coincidence. While unemployment restricts income, no one is currently allowed to starve because of it. Relative poverty is as likely to be the result of lack of skills and bargaining power in the economic hierarchy as it is of unemployment. A television documentary, 'London isn't working', revealed that many out of work would prefer to stay that way, even though taking a job would result in a real increase in income. Although 10 per cent of the working population of Greater London were unemployed, it appeared that they still wished to be choosy. Unemployed office workers do not see vacancies in hamburger restaurants as the answer to their problems. As Marie Jahoda put it, the 'absolute deprival' of the 1930s has been replaced with the 'relative deprival' of the 1980s.

Jahoda entitles another of her chapters, 'Can we humanize work?', which both accepts and regrets the fact that while unemployment has adverse effects, paid employment does not necessarily provide a satisfying life. Work at one end of the scale can be mindless and yield little recognition beyond the pay packet; at the other end of the scale, demanding work can become so stressful that health is seriously impaired. If unemployed people seem reluctant to get on with job-seeking, experiences like this may lie behind their hesitation. To quote Jahoda again:

> . . . there exists a stratum of society—its size is hard to determine—of degraded, frustrated, unhappy, psychologically unhealthy people in employment whose personal morale is as low as their productivity, who are unable to provide a productive environment for their families, whose lack of commitment in employment colours their total life experience and, depending on the size of the group, the level of civilization in which they live.

Perhaps not all the members of this group are unskilled and unqualified. High status does not necessarily mean high job satisfaction, and it appears that lack of 'agency' is not confined to those out of work. We will return to this topic later in the book, when we discuss the psychology of job satisfaction.

The subject of unemployment is a sensitive one in all industrialized countries. It is sensitive from the point of view of those without work, as I have explained above, and it is sensitive from the point of view of politicians whose economic policies are measured, partially, by the level of employment. In the UK, the world-wide economic upturn brought in its wake a reduction in the historically high unemployment figures, but there are reasons for thinking that the reduction would have been a good deal less if consistent methods of categorization and enumeration had been used. Between 1980 and 1989, 29 changes had been made to the method of calculating the number of the unemployed. In 1989, members of the Royal Statistical Society began to complain that the integrity of statisticians was being compromised by political pressures on the Civil Service.

Briefly, the method used to exclude those without jobs was to restrict the 'count' to those claiming unemployment benefit, and then to make this social provision as difficult as possible to claim. Every society has its 'scroungers', and public sympathy is generally against them, but to maintain that figures derived in this way give a true picture of those seeking work is to mislead not only the general public, but those whose task it is to construct effective employment policies.

Expressing unemployment as a percentage is misleading in another way: people do not experience it as a partial state. For the individual who is out of work, the unemployment rate is 100 per cent. While the general level of unemployment, however accurately reported, provides an optimistic or pessimistic background to the search for a new job, it is personal experience of available vacancies in a particular area, and of the response of employers to applications that determines the individual's view of the situation. Policies should be for people, and not solely a response to percentages.

Even on their own terms, however, there are reasons for believing that simple percentages are a misleading method of measuring unemployment. The size of the workforce is arrived at by multiplying the number of people of working age by the 'activity rate', the proportion of each gender and age group wishing to take up paid employment. The first term in this product can be objectively arrived at from census data; the second requires the measurement of a social attitude, a far more subjective matter. It would be naïve to suppose that all those officially counted as unemployed really want a job, or that that all those currently holding jobs would necessarily do so if there were some dignified alternative. In the UK, workers over 60 no longer have to sign on in order to obtain unemployment benefit, and are thus excluded from the 'claimant count' on which the official unemployment figures are based. Those aged 16 and 17 were removed from the British unemployment statistics in 1989. In 1987, the UK began the procedure known as *restart* interviews; these were undertaken among the long-term unemployed, and revealed some who had found unofficial but rewarding means of livelihood, and who would no longer claim benefit if it meant discussing their life-style with a government-appointed interviewer. The scale of the 'hidden economy' has never been effectively measured, but it must be considerable.

In other sectors of the market, unemployment is seriously underestimated. The 'claimant count' excludes two important groups: those currently engaged in Training Agency-sponsored programmes, who may return to the register at a later date, and the vast majority of married women wishing to work and who are unable to claim benefit in their own right. The impact of these two groups on the severity of unemployment is very different. While one would not wish to deny the long-term consequences of youth unemployment (some youngsters in mid-1980s Britain were well into their twenties without having had a job of any consequence), demography is working to the advantage of the legislators. The teenage bulge is now well past its peak (see Figure 2.3). Human resource planners are now worrying about a shortage of young workers, especially graduates. The Department of Employment is using this 'demographic time bomb', as it is called, to get employers to consider alternative sources of

Figure 2.3
Fall in number of young workers entering the labour market
Source: Hutt, R. (1984) 'Supply side consideration', *Manpower Studies 7*, Winter 83/84, 22–26

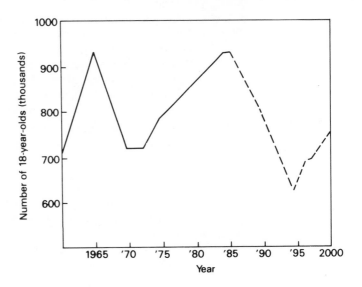

workers, particularly ethnic minorities and older people, and to provide appropriate training.

National labour market statistics, once again, obscure data of importance to human resource planners. The Institute of Manpower Studies (Pearson and Pike, 1990) has pointed out that the 'demographic time bomb' does not affect all social classes equally; the size of the middle-class families, from which most students in higher education still come, was maintained through the 1980s. The 18-year-olds from social classes I and II, will however, decline in number by about 15 per cent by the middle of the 1990s. The number from the remaining social classes continues its steep fall well into the 1990s. Even here, the local labour markets are affected differently, both in terms of the severity of the decline, and in the rate of recovery from it (Waite and Pike, 1989). Strategic human resource management requires us to look beyond the obvious.

The participation of married women in the labour market has been growing steadily since the war, encouraged by the increase in white-collar jobs at the expense of manual labour, rising expectations of material prosperity and convenient birth control. Recently, an expanding part-time labour market has given a further impetus to the employment of women. The 'growth in the number of people at work' claimed by the Conservative government is largely concentrated in this area. Re-employment programmes intended primarily for redundant workers often attract married women wishing to return to work after bringing up a family. Tax allowances for child care were conceded in the 1990 budget, though the Prime Minister had expressed fears about the effect of working mothers on family stability.

One increasing, and potentially cohesive, group subsumed within the official figures are the long-term unemployed; those who have been without work for over one year. In the mid-1980s, one million, roughly 50 per cent, of the recorded unemployed fell into this category. Many of these had experienced repeated rejection to the point at which they were resigned to living on social security. For them, the 'farming' of benefits, plus, perhaps, a little judicious participation in the hidden economy, was becoming a way of life. They seemed to have lost motivation, particularly the motivation to make job applications. A Manpower Report (Manpower Services Commission, 1986) demonstrated that, over the age of 20, the probability of being long-term unemployed increased with age. Surprisingly, long-term unemployment was not concentrated within the ethnic minorities.

People from professional or managerial backgrounds may be found among the long-term unemployed. Research by Pearson and Heyno (1988) into this category has provided pointers to ways in which this group may be helped. Although the 'Bridge' programmes set up in the 1980s by the British Manpower Services Commission were intended as much for short-term as for long-term unemployed, about one quarter of those attending had been out of work over one year. Those in the long-term category were found to return to work less easily than others, but the job-getting process could be accelerated by personal assessment and help with job-getting skills. The emphasis was upon getting a job for yourself, rather than on allocation to a 'training place'. The former enhances self-reliance and dignity, in a job with reasonable security; the latter offers training at the whim of the employer without a guarantee of continuing employment. Pearson and Heyno's research suggests that it is the recognition of existing skills, rather than training in new ones, that is the crucial factor. Although these authors' experience is confined to unemployed but qualified people, the approach pioneered in the UK 'Bridge' programmes may well have applications elsewhere. Career development from redundancy is discussed in Chapter 7.

Levels of labour market analysis

We have already discussed labour markets at national level. In the UK, a Labour Market Quarterly Report is published by the Department of Employment. The problem with documents of this sort is that they tend to be selective in the topics chosen for analysis, which is perhaps inevitable, and also tend to reflect government policy, which is not. Read critically, however, they provide a background for strategic manpower planning. The World Bank produces an annual World Development Report, which reviews population, industrialization and labour force trends in all countries, with particular reference to the Third World. Many countries produce annual reports covering changes in population and employment, and indicating training needs. A supplementary reading list on the industrialization of developing countries is provided at the end of this chapter.

While national and international labour market trends are necessary reading for strategic human resource planners, they are not sufficient for planning the effective use of human resources within organizations. Trends in local and regional labour markets provide the basis for assessing recruitment problems and opportunities. These are available in the UK from regional Manpower Offices, and are contained in the NOMIS database referred to previously.

For human resource planners, however, the most important labour market is not the external one, be it international, national, regional or local; it is the internal labour market, the human resources within the organization for whom they work. The reasons are twofold. The internal labour market is the most accessible, provided that its full potential is known. It also determines the categories to be used when investigating all other labour markets. In Chapter 3, we will look at the analysis of what Bennison and Casson (1984) call the manpower system within organizations, and at ways in which this is used to assess the external labour market in relevant ways.

The complexity of labour markets

The foregoing discussion will have revealed that study of labour markets is far from an exact science. Precision in analysis, let alone in forecasting, is unattainable. Most important, however, is the realization that labour markets are not immutable or totally objective entities. They are categorized according to the viewpoint of particular manpower specialists, and are always subject to reformulation. They are also subject to the rules and weaknesses of all social research, a point to which we will return later in Chapter 3.

At this point, it is necessary to consider the powerful strategic forces that affect work and the way we structure it; the industrial past and the technological future.

The concept of industrialization

The British Industrial Revolution exemplifies the way in which economic and social systems can alter dramatically when a number of favourable factors concur. Strategic human resource planners in 1780, had they existed, would have had the greatest difficulty in forecasting manpower needs for the cotton industry, not because they lacked the techniques or computer hardware, but because of the rate of change.

The Industrial Revolution was more than an isolated historical curiosity. It owed its origins to economic and social forces operating before the eighteenth century (Hill, 1969), and it initiated a process of change that is yet far from complete. Kemp (1978) described industrialization as 'a fundamental revolution . . . which was to lead to the development of the world as we know it today'. Industrialization both requires and creates social and economic adjustment in every country it affects. The developments that we observe around us in manufacturing industry, commerce, banking, and in the public service are all products of a restless industrial society whose explicit goal is economic growth. For readers born in the UK and in other Western countries, this goal is the routine material of politicians' speeches; for many others it is a matter for deep current concern. As a student from Uganda once put it, 'How do we get enough economic growth to pay enough teachers so that our population can be skilled enough to support more economic growth?' Debt crises will cease to occur only when Third World economies are sufficiently in balance, and this means supplying goods the rest of the world wants to buy. It is not too fanciful to suggest that the world manufacturing base, which in living memory has moved away from its birthplace in Europe and America to Japan, and thence to other Pacific countries, may in turn become the staple of African economies.

Since industrialization is pervasive, and a continuing influence for change in peoples' working lives, its nature and its contradictions should be appreciated by those who aspire to plan strategically, particularly when planning the use of human resources.

Discussing industrialization is a lot easier then defining it. Kemp (1978) attempts a neat definition when he describes industrialization as 'the embodiment of human knowledge in production'. This might be criticized for focusing too narrowly on industrial production, and ignoring the wider changes that industrialization has brought about. The reader is challenged at this point to jot down some ideas about the characteristics of an industrialized society. He or she may be surprised at the variety of ideas, and ways of categorizing work that their analysis suggests. It is important not to be fooled by what Kemp calls the 'popular imagery' of films like Charlie Chaplin's *Modern Times* or the 'dark satanic mills' of Blake's poem.

A group of people challenged to carry out this exercise might well have come up with different lists; some would see different factors as more important or evident, and some lists would be longer than others. This is consistent with industrialization being a process, rather than a single definable concept, a matter of interest to strategic planners who wish to know what stage of industrialization an organization or country has reached.

Here are some features that might enable us to answer the question.

Mechanization and technology

With the current emphasis on new technology, it is difficult not to see the application of mechanical and, nowadays, electronic devices as a central aspect of industrialization. Kemp (1978) draws an interesting distinction between the use of craft techniques in the earlier British Industrial Revolution, and the later liaison between science and industry that Germany so successfully developed. In modern phraseology, the 'knowledge base' of German industrialization was much greater. The recent arguments about the role of the universities in assisting British industry shows that in this country the relationship has yet to be resolved.

Division of labour

Long before the Industrial Revolution, work had been organized on a craft basis. Many English surnames derive from occupations dating back to Medieval times and before. Categorization was then at the level of occupation, so that each craftsman would complete a whole product, or at least a major process in its manufacture. When mass markets demanded that the inefficiencies that can exist in the craft system be removed, tasks became more specialized. It was to root out the idiosyncracies remaining in that system that Taylor proposed 'scientific management'. Long before Taylor, Adam Smith (republished 1970) drew attention to the economic advantages of getting workers together in a factory, and dividing the work between them in a logical way. He was writing before the extensive introduction of machinery to the factory system; 'organization' predates 'mechanization' as a key aspect of industrialization.

Deskilling It is often assumed that the combined effect of the division of labour and mechanization is to devalue or make obsolete workers' skills (Jones, 1982). While this process would be expected to lower the self-esteem of the worker, it often also has the dire consequence of redundancy. Yet deskilling and redundancy are not inevitable results of industrialization. It may be here that state intervention is needed to supplement and support a free economy.

The problem arises from the over-identification of skills with people. On this assumption, when the need for certain skills diminishes, then so do jobs; the previously skilled person has to choose between unskilled work or no work at all. But people can develop new skills to meet new needs, much as the industrialized cotton industry required that the mechanization initially in the hands of clock-makers should develop into a full-scale engineering trade. In addition, changes occur at different rates in different parts of the economy Handloom weavers were still operating in the smaller textile factories in 1850, and in highly specialized work do so today. The 'choice' is between a mass labour market and a specialized one; making the choice, however, may require more information and sophistication than most workers can muster. This is as true in the 1990s as it was in the nineteenth century. A free market is only truly free when labour market information and training are freely available and comprehensible. Without this sophistication, however, workers shed from one industry are taken up by another, as when males displaced from the textile mills by women were able to obtain work in the mines and in the steel industry.

The extent to which service industries will similarly absorb the unemployed resulting from structural changes in the current British economy is problematic (Rajan, 1987). The early stages of industrialization provide a livelihood for an expanding population, which need not be highly skilled, but what happens to displaced industrial workers in an advanced economy is not quite so clear. Their first resort is the expanding service sector but, as commercial competition increases, mechanization may remove this option.

Urbanization Although industrialization is only in its early stages in many developing countries, and is proceeding far too slowly in Africa (Mountjoy and Hilling, 1988), there are often problems of urban squalor, sprawl and unemployment. People migrate from villages into the towns, hoping for a better living than subsistence agriculture can provide. Industry has not expanded fast enough to be able to offer the jobs that they seek. In the UK, a growing mercantile economy had supported a flourishing network of towns long before the Industrial Revolution began to dictate how work should be done. Displaced agricultural workers were moving into the towns throughout the eighteenth century, building up the workforce that industrialization would tap. For a while, the use of water power detained textile factories in remote upland areas, but steam power allowed them to be sited where it would suit the entrepreneur best—near the supply routes and plentiful labour of the towns. Living in close proximity with others became the norm for a large proportion of the population, and a whole new set of problems was created.

Capital

The Marxian associations of this word can hide from us the fact that industrialization requires the accumulation and deployment of large amounts of capital under any political system. In the early stages of British industrialization, capital was needed more to finance the organization of the productive process than for mechanization. Capital could be obtained from the profits of expanding trade and efficient agriculture—a full-scale banking system emerged later. In other countries, and in more recent times, the existence of an elaborate capital market involving banks and joint-stock companies has been the precursor of industrialization rather than its outcome. In some instances, the use of state capital has made an essential contribution. For studies of industrialization, the reader is referred to the books by Kemp in the list at the end of this chapter.

Public control—or the lack of it

One reason why the cotton industry achieved such dominance in Britain's industrialization was that the longer-established woollen trade was shackled by taxation and state control, and by long-standing monopolies for merchants and workers alike. The cotton industry was new enough to create its own rules. Of course, the environmental problems caused by the rapidly expanding industry, and demands for improved transport systems, eventually brought about government intervention, both at national and local level. In other countries, partnership between entrepreneurs, financial institutions and the state has been the preferred route to industrialization, particularly in Japan. In the 'Russian model', favoured by some countries outside the USSR, large-scale industrialization has been driven by a process of state planning and control. As Eastern Europe begins itself to abandon this model, it is apparent that there is a sad legacy of industrial pollution and health hazards; neither state control nor capitalism avoid this cost of an industrialized economy.

Emphasis on consumption and productivity

An important precursor of economic growth is the separation of production from consumption. Self-sufficiency is achieved by supplying limited personal needs by personal effort; it presupposes the ownership of both tools and sufficient land. The depopulation of UK agriculture in the eighteenth century created a situation in which workers could buy food with money earned in factories, where they made goods required by others. Once this separation has been achieved in an industrializing economy, consumption of an expanding range of goods is possible in increasing amounts, and the 'take-off' of economic growth is under way. Expanding sales are obtained by reducing costs, increasing the productivity of workers, in terms both of hours worked and methods used, and encouraging the substitution of machines for manual labour.

Trade unionism

Phyllis Deane, a historian who has specialized in the Industrial Revolution, has already been quoted in this chapter. She pointed out that 'An inescapable condition of successful economic growth is the existence of an expanding, mobile, and adaptable labour supply'. Neither the old craft guilds, nor trade unions, have been noted for their cooperation in regard to mobility and adaptability. Yet the process of industrialization was not unduly affected. In spite of the Chartists, who were largely based in the textile industry, trade unionism made little headway among the unskilled and semi-skilled workers until the New Unionism of the late nineteenth century. Trade union strength was concentrated in the craft-based trades in engineering. In the face of the entrepreneur's desire for greater productivity, the combination of workers to protect their interests may be seen as an outcome of industrialization.

Flexibility of labour is, of course, related to another fundamental requirement of an industrial economy—wage payment. Feudal and mercantile economies had previously operated with a system of land tenancy and home manufacture, a crude prototype of the small business culture. Factory production requires a footloose labour force, paid at 'market rates', leaving a surplus for investment in plant, machinery and raw materials. We return to the subject of payment systems in Chapter 5.

Professionalism

The existence of the 'shop-floor', with its organized processes and subtle class distinction between unskilled, semi-skilled and skilled workers, is the self-evident result of industrialized production. What is not so readily seen, perhaps because its results are almost too familiar, is the extent to which present-day white-collar work is also an outcome of industrialization. In the factory itself, the functions of owner–managers were divided and subdivided; the factory clerk was replaced by the sophisticated accountancy and administrative departments that we see today. Outside the factory, urbanization and subsequent municipalization created demand for local government services, with a consequent growth in professional work. Central government felt compelled to take on many monitoring functions, increasing the size of the Civil Service and its specialist departments. Expanding and interdependent commercial activity and capital investment required increasing numbers of financial and legal experts. Health and education made increasing demands on the public purse, partly because of requirements of industry itself, and partly because growing prosperity raised public expectations of a better life. People in white-collar jobs yearn for professional status, which confers self-esteem, and controls entry and job demarcation. Whether these elaborate systems of job control are appropriate in modern organizations is a matter worthy of the human resource planner's attention. Unemployment is becoming more common among these groups, so the promise of a lifetime career in return for working for qualifications is not always fulfilled.

Counter-culture

An interesting facet of British industrialization is the rapidity with which it produced its own counter-culture. A reaction from the land-owning classes against the town-based industrialists was to be expected, and there are echoes of this in British culture and politics to the present day. Commentaries on the squalor of industrial cities, and the regimented nature of factory work, were common even in the first half of the nineteenth century, though they probably did not take sufficient account of the conditions under which the alternatives of agricultural work and domestic service were performed. But criticism went deeper than that: Ruskin, Carlyle and Marx pointed out the ways in which workers were being separated from the products of their labour. This unhealthy trend, as it was seen, was the target of the 'Arts and Crafts' movement of William Morris, whose hand-blocked wallpaper designs based on 'natural forms' can be seen in West End stores to this day. And, of course, there was the desire of the rising and prosperous middle classes that their sons should enter professions rather than 'trade'. Martin Wiener (1985), among others, has linked the decline of Britain as an industrial power to this flight of educated people from manufacturing to more respectable ways of earning a livelihood.

In recent times, industry has come under pressure from environmental lobbies, who fear both pollution and the depletion of natural resources. 'Green issues', as they are called throughout Europe and the United States, are set fair to dominate the politics of the 1990s. Third World countries, which have yet to taste the advantages of a fully industrialized society, are less perturbed by its possible disadvantages.

Novel economic structures

Industrialization of distribution through chain and department stores was added to industrialization of production in the UK and elsewhere. Engineering and chemical industries were developed to serve the needs of leading producers, and railways were both essential to full-scale industrialization and financed by its growing and elaborating capital structure.

Into the future: industrialization as process

In talking about the process of industrialization, we are referring to a sequence of events; particularly what precedes industrialization, and what follows it. In a number of ways, the Industrial Revolution in the UK was atypical, and there are notable differences between, say, the industrialization in present-day developing countries and the path followed by European nations in the nineteenth century. Attention will be drawn to some of these in the following discussion. Despite the differences, there is a discernible pattern, which may help readers to understand the changes in work and manpower demand that are taking place in their own countries right now. Which factors, first of all, favour the onset of industrialization?

Population growth

Growth in population is a dominant factor, in the sense that it affects both the desirability of industrialization and its feasibility. Deane (1979) discussed the complex interrelation between falling death rate and rising birth rate that caused a steady rise in the population of the UK before 1780. Mountjoy (1982) described similar changes in the population of developing countries. As the population increases, so it becomes more difficult to support it by subsistence farming using methods that rely on large acreages of land per person. Intensive agriculture requires the removal of some workers from the land, usually into towns, thus improving profitability and creating a market for surplus agricultural production. Those freed from agricultural work are available to form an industrial labour force. So both growth in population and the intensification of agriculture are likely to precede full-scale industrialization. In the economies of developing countries, as described above, the existence side by side of industrialized and subsistence sectors is referred to as 'dualism', a concept that we have already noted in relation to labour markets.

Markets

Another important precursor of industrialization is the availability of markets for cheap, mass-produced goods. A home market is created by a growing population that is learning to specialize, making some goods for itself and buying others. The demand for cheap cotton clothing from an expanding urban population, together with increasing trade in Britain's traditional mercantile export markets, were the twin stimuli for a textile-led Industrial Revolution.

Technology It is common, nowadays, to talk about industrialization in terms of hardware; we hear constant reference to the 'microchip revolution'. In developing countries, for example, the debate is about whether investment should be in state-of-the-art capital equipment, or in what is referred to as 'intermediate technology'. Schumacher (1974) favoured the latter. Mountjoy (1982) sounded a note of caution, however, pointing out that products will have to be sold in world markets, to acceptable standards of price and quality, if a return on capital is to be obtained. But the British Industrial Revolution was achieved without recourse to high technology, even by the standards of the time. Innovations occurred only as market pressures made them inevitable. The industrialization of the UK was a matter primarily of organization rather than of technology.

Capital Capital is the retained surplus from productive activity. In the UK, profitable development of agriculture, and mercantile ventures overseas, together with some pre-industrial developments by landowners, all assisted the accumulation of capital to finance industrialization, once its potential profitability had been demonstrated. Developing countries today find that the pace of desperately needed industrialization is slowed by lack of capital, and by the lack of income to service debts. This capital is needed both to purchase factories and plant and to finance stocks and distribution. High-technology plant may be required if products are to compete in world markets. Kemp (1978) ascribes the difference in the rates of industrialization for sparsely populated Canada and teeming India partly to the greater readiness of the City of London to invest in the North American Dominion.

Transportation Industrialization makes increasing demands upon the infrastructure, especially systems of transport. Raw materials must be delivered, often from thousands of miles away, and products distributed. The improving road system in the eighteenth century favoured the onset of the British Industrial Revolution, as did the sea-going mercantile economy that had preceded it. Railways rapidly replaced the canals as the industrialized factories both demanded them and provided the wealth for their building. Cheap and easy transport was to revolutionize society as industrial organization and technology revolutionized production. Similar patterns may be discerned in other developed economies.

Education Britain's industrialization was achieved with the labour of a largely illiterate workforce, and with the ideas of untutored inventors. Later in the nineteenth century, education became more important; it is argued that Britain's decline as an industrial power was in part due to a failure to recognize the importance of education in science and engineering. The use of high technology, expensive in itself, carries with it the additional burden of training workers in its effective use; a further problem for developing countries.

Culture The phrase 'enterprise culture' has taken on particular political overtones in the UK in recent years. For this reason, some may be reluctant to accept that entrepreneurship is a necessary precursor of industrialization. But it is difficult to deny that Britain's industrialization was achieved by profit-oriented entrepreneurs, who operated largely outside government control, but with the help of the economic and environmental factors described above. Earlier historical periods, the Renaissance and Reformation, had an influence in promoting the 'Protestant work ethic', which culminated in the 200 years of mercantile activity preceding the Industrial Revolution. A similar spirit is evident in the industrialization of the USA and Canada. In continental Europe, however, a vast peasant population delayed improvements in agriculture and subsequent industrialization. Vested interests delay the introduction of technology and economic growth quite as much as the fear of deskilling.

Outcomes of industrialization

If certain factors are necessary before industrialization takes place, what are the consequences of industrialization, and how universal are they? In some instances, of course, the outcomes are an intensification of the precursors; industrialization accelerates urbanization as agriculture becomes more efficient, and workers turn away in increasing numbers from the countryside to the towns and cities for employment. Capital investment in industry produces increasing profits, and the accumulation of capital encourages the establishment of sophisticated banking systems and joint-stock companies. This in turn allows financial resources to be mobilized for large-scale projects in transportation.

While industrialization may begin as a largely entrepreneurial activity, it does not remain so; factory conditions and urban concentration generate public health problems, which demand responses from both local and central government. Municipalization is as much a product of an industrialized society as are manufactured goods. Gathering the population together in large units facilitates observation of their living conditions. Reformers wish to see these improved, and the population itself begins to expect a higher standard of living. Better hospitals and schools are eventually provided, not only for reasons of social conscience, but because a healthy and well-educated workforce is good business. The British public school system owes something to the need for colonial administrators, and its traditions have been emulated, among other places, in Hastings Banda's Malawi. The burden of educating the mass of the population, however, falls on the shoulders of the state system. The specialization associated with industrial society encourages the emergence of professionalism. Specialization in manufacture, too, encourages the development of new industries and new forms of manual employment. Overall, the level of public consumption is raised dramatically, and workers submit to the discipline of mass production in order to purchase an ever-widening range of consumer goods. They also make attempts to control the terms of their bargain with employers through membership of trade unions. Since industrialization is an international phenomenon, highly geared economies can 'overheat' and experience balance of payments problems.

When is industrialization complete? Some people have discerned a trend towards a 'post-industrial' society in certain Western countries; it is assumed that the need for disciplined work will wither away in the face of technology, and in face of the need to limit production to conserve dwindling natural resources. The recent high unemployment in these countries, however, has revealed that most citizens would prefer to work than to be idle, and not only because they get more money for so doing. Unemployment has been created by massive sectoral swings in the economy away from manufacturing industry towards services. In the UK, a very small proportion of workers is engaged in primary production, agriculture and mining. Heavy industry has contracted sharply over the last 20 years, and many consumers prefer to buy goods manufactured abroad. The computer has enabled the industrialization of the service sector, with results that can now only be guessed at. Once under way, the process of industrialization ensures that the patterns of work, and the skills required, will undergo continual change. It is against this background that strategic human resource planning has to take place.

Is it possible to see any pattern in the way economies develop once industrialization has taken place? Jones (1982) identified three phases, starting in 1780: the steam revolution, the electric revolution and the atomic revolution. Another attempt to make sense of the sequence of economic events since the Industrial Revolution is the 'long-wave' theory of Kondratiev, which was adopted enthusiastically by the American economist Schumpeter. This theory is outlined by Jones, and described in more detail by Marstrand (1984) and by Freeman, Clark and Soete (1982). Those interested in the recent history of Britain's declining manufacturing industries, will find a readable account in Pagnamenta and Overy (1984).

At this point, the reader is invited to take part in yet another thought experiment. Think about each aspect of your own job: how far would you agree that it is conducted in an industrialized setting, and what pressures, if any, are likely to cause changes in your working methods? Becoming sensitive to these issues is necessary for developing a strategic approach to the constant changes that characterize the world of work. Figure 2.4 illustrates the process of industrialization in a developing country (based on the description in Mountjoy, 1982).

Those interested in reading more about the concept and process of industrialization are directed to the references already given, and to the bibliography at the end of this chapter.

Figure 2.4
Process of industrialization in a developing country
Source: Adapted from Mountjoy, A. (1982)

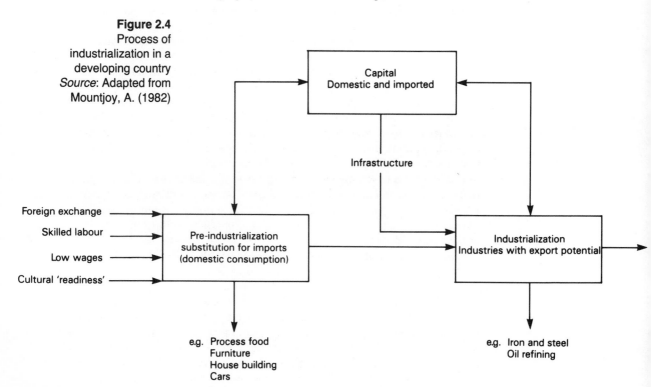

Automated production and automated thinking?

The Industrial Revolution stands as a monument to the outcomes, both good and bad, of organized work and the use of technology. New machines, and the control of labour, allowed mass markets to be supplied, and employment and wealth to be created. But technology changed the patterns of work and employment: women replaced men in the fast-growing textile industry, at cheaper wage rates; fewer workers were needed per unit of output. Products appeared that could not have been manufactured at all without the use of specialized machinery. Market expansion did not go on for ever, and when it faltered, unemployment grew apace. The folk memory of those times, and of the Great Depression of the 1930s, remains strong. Small wonder that the microchip is looked at askance by many workers, who perceive yet another opportunity for their labour to be replaced by machines. There is also the fear that if work is augmented yet again by technology, then the quality of working life must suffer.

The Industrial Revolution turned many workers into machine-minders. Perhaps the 'microchip revolution' will now turn them into computer-minders. Most sinister of all, will the computer become a people-minder, replacing the human supervisor?

But what is it that computers are capable of taking over? What human skills can they replace, now or in the future? In later chapters we will be looking at the skills and attitudes of individual workers. We digress into that area now so as to be able to make sense of the remaining two subjects in this chapter: technology, and the transfer of technology. We also need to be able to understand the ways in which computers can take over both manual labour and brain work.

Human skills

Skill, like industrialization, is difficult to define. People readily recognize the skill in playing sports; mostly activities which all are capable of to some degree, but which are raised to high level of efficiency and elegance in the hands of experts. Craft skills fall into the same category; most of us can use a chisel, albeit at risk to life and limb, but in the hands an expert woodcarver the same tool becomes the begetter of graceful and moving images. Least commonly understood are mental skills, perhaps for the obvious reason that their display is less public. The skill of the violinist in performing a work is more evident than the skill of the composer who wrote it. Somehow, we have to allow for skills that require the manipulation of symbols, as well as for those which involve bodily coordination. Researchers prefer the latter, because outcomes are more easily measured, and processes more easily observed. For the purposes of subsequent discussion, we will classify skills in the following way:

1 Psychomotor or 'action skills', which require bodily coordination. This type usually appear not to require conscious mental processing, and may even deteriorate if such processing is forced upon a skilled person.
2 Symbolic skills, which include language, calculation and visualization. These require both conscious and unconscious mental processing.

The American cognitive psychologist, Ulric Neisser (1983), has provided a useful analysis of skilled performance. He describes the characteristics of action skills as follows:

- they allow tasks to be carried out in a variety of ways
- they require accurate perception, anticipation and precise movement
- they allow actions to be adapted to a changing physical environment

As an example, think of a woodcarver adapting his movements to the grain of the wood and working with precision, yet achieving an individual style.

Symbolic skills, however, depend on the order in which operations are carried out, rather than on precise timing. But the sequence has also to be pursued to a logical conclusion if the skilled output is to be achieved. So two features of symbolic skills are logical sequence and purposiveness.

But if wood is the medium to which the woodcarver applies his psychomotor skills, then what is the corresponding medium for symbolic skills? Neisser makes the interesting suggestion that this medium is the relationship between the symbols that are being manipulated; think of a mathematician achieving an 'elegant' solution to a theoretical problem.

Those concerned with education, training and personal selection know that individuals vary considerably in both psychomotor and symbolic skills. They will also know that skills respond to practise. Perhaps not so well known is the extent to which action skills benefit from mental practise; Neisser gives a good example of this in his review. This observation must cast doubt on too sharp a division between psychomotor and symbolic skills.

Most important of all, from the point of view of the human resource planner, is that when we talk of a 'skilled worker', or the possibility that computers may 'deskill' work, we need to be clear exactly what skills are assumed. An agreement between management and unions to regard certain worked as 'skilled' may have more to do with maintaining industrial harmony than with skilled performance in Neisser's terms. The human resource planner's objective should be to assess the realities of such situations, so the cost of using people in a less than optimum way is clearly identified.

Are computers skilled?

The human resource planner also needs to come to terms with the extent to which computers, and computer-controlled devices, can replace human beings. Is it true that they can simulate the human skills that we have just discussed, psychomotor and symbolic?

Robots demonstrate the computer's ability to replace human psychomotor skills. They are being used in increasing numbers in manufacturing industry, with car factories leading the way. Robots offer considerable advantages over human workers, especially when work is disagreeable, dangerous or difficult for a human being to reach. They can be programmed to transfer, machine and assemble parts. They can be programmed, in a process called 'lead-through', which looks very like the training given to a human operator, to carry out paint-spraying. But are robots really displaying psychomotor skills, as defined by Neisser? This could be one of the central 'human resource' questions of the 1990s.

And what about symbolic skills? Computers and human beings can both be conceived as having memory and processing capacity, and both store and manipulate symbolic information. In fact, more is known about how computers do this than about human mental processing. Psychologists use computers as analogues for the human brain, and it is thought that biological materials will be used in future to replace silicon chips and other semi-conductors used to carry computer circuitry. The performance of computers differs from that of human beings, however, in some important ways.

Mental processing is impossible without memory, which requires both retention of symbolic information, and its recall at the appropriate moment. To understand the difference between retention and recall, consider the embarrassment of the tutor who suddenly forgets a student's name in class, and then remembers it as soon as she gets back to the office. The retentive potential of computers is increasing daily, but is still less than that of the human brain. In normal functioning the computer's recall, however, is wellnigh perfect.

For routine and repetitive calculations, the computer is clearly superior: it is fast, logical, reliable and maintains the purposive element in Neisser's description of symbolic skills without boredom. The speed with which computers were adopted by the accountants emphasizes this point. The computer also deploys the same qualities in problem-solving, provided that the solution may be found by an exhaustive search of a finite number of options. Where the number of possible options is very large, however, because each immediate course of action leads in turn to many more, then the human capacity to make heuristic guesses is superior. The attempt to build heurisitc reasoning into computer programs is an important aspect of artificial intelligence, which is discussed later in this chapter.

Language is a uniquely human achievement. Computers simulate language in a stilted way in order to respond to a human operator, and this can sometimes appear to have the qualities of a conversation. But words entered via a keyboard are used merely as 'triggers' for a computer program that produces an appropriate 'word-string' in response. The computer cannot be said to understand the meaning of statements made either by itself or the operator. The word processor may correct spelling, but not grammar.

But neither computers nor human beings can carry out a task, whether symbolic or psychomotor, without receiving information from the outside world, or without communicating their conclusions. Human sensory devices, sight, touch, hearing, taste and smell, are sophisticated and highly effective. Robots can be equipped with touch-sensors, and with vision systems using digitalized TV pictures; voice recognition is under development. Recognition of written characters is possible, but does not match human reading skills. Communication with computers is usually maintained by the cumbersome method of keyboards; and output is obtained from printers or display screens. In perception and communication, the human being is clearly superior.

For the immediate future, therefore, it appears that people are going to be most useful when deploying their skills in perception and communication, especially when dealing with other people. They also have the edge in creative problem-solving. But routine and repetitive work should be relegated to the computer whenever possible. The sensible response from those who plan and develop the human resource is not to use computers less, but to educate people more.

Whether computers are to be assigned only to routine work, however, depends on the development of artificial intelligence.

Thinking computers?

A report by d'Agapeyeff and Hawkins (1987) stated that over 1000 'expert systems' were then under development in the UK, and that most large organizations employed staff working on the application of artificial intelligence to their business.

The question as to whether machines can think goes beyond computer technology to some very basic and hotly debated issues in philosophy and psychology. The reader might like to stop reading at this point and consider the following question: what do we mean by 'thought', and why should it be a uniquely human activity?

For the seventeenth-century philospher Descartes, the one certain basis of human knowledge was *cogito ergo sum*, 'I think, therefore I am'. Thinking was taken to include feelings and dreams as well as logical reasoning. But even if I am sure that I am thinking, how can I also be sure that other people are doing so? If I have to rely on observation to infer thought in other people, then the same goes for machines. Alan Turing, whose 1936 paper on 'Computable Numbers' laid out the conditions for a programmable computer, asserted that a machine displaying intelligent behaviour should be referred to as 'intelligent'. One reason for research in artificial intelligence, in fact, is to shed light on human reasoning processes. Readers are referred to Boden (1987 and 1988) for a detailed discussion of this issue.

John Searle (1984) dismissed the idea that the computer, or any other machine, can think, on the grounds that mechanical or electrical devices cannot possess conscious awareness or intentionality. So far as we know, computers, unlike Descartes, are not aware that they are reasoning, nor can they 'will' to take action. While they can manipulate symbols, they do not comprehend the meaning that the symbols convey. As Searle puts it, they are capable of syntax, but not of semantics.

Turing, however, was in no doubt about the future for intelligent computers; in a play by Hugh Whitemore (1987) about Turing's life, he is quoted as saying, 'I am sure that by the year 2000 it will be perfectly correct to speak of an intelligent machine, or to say that a computer is thinking'.

How far have we progressed towards Turing's goal? Current work on artificial intelligence, to be frank, is rather like manpower planning—a collection of techniques with little conceptual basis. This 'broad church' includes work on the simulation of psychological processes using computer programs, and the development of computer vision and natural language interfaces. But most important of all for the human resource planner is the design of what are known as *expert systems*.

An expert system has been defined by Oakley (1987) as 'the embodiment within the computer of a knowledge-based component derived from an expert skill, in such a form that the system can take intelligent decisions about a processing function'. He went on to say that 'An additional characteristic, which many would consider fundamental, is the capacity of the system, on demand, to explain its own reasoning'.

Expert systems are sophisticated databases, that require special types of programming language to develop, and special search devices, called 'inference engines', to allow the knowledge stored in the database to be made available to users. The knowledge consists of facts, assertions and, most significantly, 'if-then' rules. The purpose is to encapsulate the knowledge and decision-making capacity of human experts, so that less skilled people can have access to it. The threat to the exclusiveness of specialist, professional work is obvious, but the threat is currently more apparent than real.

The expert system has to converse with the human user, preferably in natural language, so that the expert advice can be elicited and new rules added, and so that the system can justify its own reasoning. Providing these requirements has proved more difficult than expected. The debate continues, and it is hopeless to expect a book to be up to date on this important and developing topic. Strategic human resource planners, however, should ensure that they attend to the latest developments as these are published in newspapers and periodicals.

We now return to the subject of human skills. It is easy to see, as educated professionals, how robots and standard computer systems can take over the work of unskilled and semi-skilled people; we can perhaps accept it with a certain equanimity as the price of change. But expert systems are a different matter; here we are dealing with a computerized threat to professional work. The as yet imperfect expert systems can nevertheless diagnose diseases, analyse geological data for oil search, unravel complicated legal problems, and work out configurations of computer hardware to suit particular customers' needs. The process of industrialization, which created, as never before, the need for specialists, is now providing the means of replacing their work.

Technology transfer and employment

Neither countries nor organizations are compelled to adopt new technology; rejection or delay may be the result of ignorance, indolence or deliberate policy.

The author worked for a multinational company for 25 years. At its peak, the Dunlop Group employed 100 000 people world-wide. The company owed its existence to the invention of the pneumatic tyre by John Boyd Dunlop. This took place at the turn of the century, and the product had been under development ever since. So the ethos of the company might have been assumed to favour technology, and to an extent this expectation was fulfilled; innovation did take place, but the technology was craft-based, and 'science' was looked at askance. The company established after the War a world-wide network of research centres, whose purpose was purely defensive. Other people's technology was to be monitored, rather than the company breaking new ground for itself. Any discoveries we might make were to be patented and locked away, but were not to be developed.

There was a determined attempt to reverse this strategy in the 1960s and 1970s to develop new products, but this effort seemed to be inspired more by a desire to impress City of London investors than genuinely to create new markets. Dunlop was repeatedly out-smarted by the technically more adventurous Michelin company. From 1970 onwards, employment declined steadily in the UK, dropping to a few thousand employees in the early 1980s. In 1985 the company was taken over by a more successful British conglomerate, BTR. This was as near a confession of strategic failure as makes no difference.

It has become folklore to blame technology for the loss of jobs, but it is easy to forget that there are other causes of a decline in employment: managerial incompetence, restrictive labour practices, and a general failure to realize that at the end of the day it is the customer who pays the wages. There are influential people, as well as the fearful and ignorant, who suggest that the introduction of new technologies should be delayed or rejected entirely in the interest of labour-intensive production that, they claim, would improve employment prospects. Schumacher (1974) has urged 'alternative technologies' on developing countries; Shirley Williams (1981) suggested the same solution for unemployment in the UK. We will now consider some research that suggests that this advice is not entirely sound in the British context, and then review some of the problems that world technological advance presents for developing countries. But before we go much further we shall need some concepts to help us understand the arguments.

Technology as concept

The word technology has become too easily associated in the public mind with micro-electronics. It was used in that way in the previous section. When we talk of 'new technology' we mean computers; 'information technology' is used to refer to telecommunications and data processing. Yet there is a range of 'new technologies', including micro-electronics, but also biotechnology and atomics. 'Information technology' goes back beyond Caxton and his printing press to the discovery that it was possible to convey meaningful messages by drawing on the walls of caves. The computer is doing nothing really new in terms of information processing; it is just doing it faster.

Technology may usefully be defined as 'a means of altering materials or information'. This definition has the virtue of allowing us to see technology in a historical context rather than being mesmerized by late twentieth-century microchip science. Any tool, even a simple agricultural implement, that increases human effectiveness, is an example of technology. But it is undeniable that there is a great deal of difference between the woodcarver's chisel, which is essential to the purpose and allows a display of human skill, and a robot that displaces human labour entirely. Perhaps we should learn to distinguish between 'necessary' and 'contingent' technology.

Product versus process

Technology affects production in two ways: it can be introduced into a product to enhance its value to the customer (in so doing it may increase both demand and employment) or into the production process, sometimes to improve the quality of output, but more often to increase output per worker. Process technology is more likely to be associated with reduction in employment.

Invention, innovation and diffusion

Britain is said to be good at discovering things and developing new theories; the USA to be good at turning new scientific ideas into marketable and profitable products and processes. This illustrates the difference between 'invention' and 'innovation'. Innovation requires the spread of existing technology between companies and between countries, a process known as 'technological diffusion'.

Armed with these concepts, we can look critically at technological transfer in two environments: late 1970s Britain, and the more general situation of developing countries.

Technological innovation and diffusion in the UK: the North-South divide

This example is based on research by Goddard and Thwaites, entitled 'Unemployment in the North: jobs in the South', and published in Marstrand (1984). It describes the difference between the rate of technological diffusion in the two regions. A strong causal link between technology and employment is implied.

The North of England was the cradle of the Industrial Revolution, not only for the UK, but for the world. Over the last 100 years its once thriving heavy industries have declined, and since the 1930s there has been a growing disparity between North and South in both employment and prosperity. Readers unfamiliar with the UK will no doubt be able to think of parallel situations in their own countries. Successive governments have tried to redress the imbalance in the UK by regional aid and incentive schemes, but 'regional policy' has now fallen into disrepute. Goddard and Thwaites argue that the lower level of investment in technology in the North has contributed to its industrial decline.

The researchers conducted two comparative surveys of technological developments, one concerned with innovation, and the other with diffusion. In the first study, they asked manufacturing companies whether technology 'new to the plant' had been introduced between 1973 and 1977. In the second, they assessed the spread of specific technologies through particular industries. The first survey revealed that manufacturers in the South of England showed a greater propensity to innovate than those in the North, a commitment that was additionally expressed in the greater numbers of research staff employed by southern companies. Even in the South, innovation consisted of introducing technology developed elsewhere; there was little evidence in either region of original research or invention, and this was true of both process and product technology. The North had fallen particularly far behind in product innovation, although it was 'average for the UK as a whole' in the introduction of new processes. The diffusion study revealed that the introduction of microprocessors into products had occurred faster in the South.

Human resource planners, of course, will be interested chiefly in the effect on jobs. Taking the sample as a whole, Goddard and Thwaites observed that introduction of new technology into products had very little effect on numbers employed in the innovating companies; in many instances, additional workers had been taken on. If it were not for the biasing effect of one very large organization, whose shedding of labour may have had other causes, the increase in employment by product-innovating firms would have been quite marked. Process innovations, which are more likely to be aimed at productivity gains through manpower reductions, were indeed often followed by job losses, but even in these instances employment sometimes increased. The diffusion study showed that innovating firms experienced above average employment growth, a growth that was not confined to technical experts. However, growth was biased towards managers and technical experts and away from shop-floor workers. Nevertheless, Goddard and Thwaites concluded that failure to innovate had rendered northern companies more liable to job losses.

Technology and developing countries

Industrialization is a mixed blessing; together with its economic benefits it brings pollution, overcrowding into urban areas and a mechanist outlook that appears to spread from the productive process to the fabric of life itself. Yet the industrialized nations are those with the highest per capita income, and the best education, health and welfare services. There is little doubt that most developing countries would prefer the problems of industrialization to those they currently face. What are the limiting factors that prevent rapid industrialization, and how might they affect manpower policies?

The first Industrial Revolution took place in the absence of any serious competition in world markets. A mercantile tradition, a growing colonial empire and rising prosperity and population at home, all helped to ensure a ready market for everything that the enterprising manufacturer could produce; markets led, technology followed. Industrialization now has to take place within a sophisticated and interdependent world economy. Manufactured products can be sold only at competitive prices and at acceptable quality; the Japanese and other Pacific countries have based their spectacular industrial advance since the War on this principle. What holds the others back?

One very important factor must be the need to invest in new technology; quality and competitive prices are achieved only by appropriate process and product innovations, as the Goddard and Thwaites study in the UK indicates. Yet technology appears to threaten one important objective of industrialization in developing countries—the spread of prosperity through increased employment.

To discuss fully the problems of developing countries in adopting and exploiting new technology is beyond the scope of this book. The reader's attention is drawn to the following authorities on the subject (the author has used them to illustrate the issues, without being proscriptive about their solution): Jones (1982), Mountjoy (1982), Schumacher (1974) and Stewart and James (1982). The reader is also referred to the list of papers at the end of this chapter for information about the technical development of individual countries. The central question is whether we need to introduce technology at all.

Jones, who was concerned like other writers in the 1970s and early 1980s about its effect world-wide on employment, does not believe that technology is deterministic. As Armstrong (in Marstrand, 1984) puts it: 'there is nothing acting with the force of necessity' to make us adopt industrialized production. Up to a point this is true. But no government can ignore forever the yearning of its people for better health, food and education. At some point, technology enters into the delivery of all these advantages, the 'necessary' technology of any state providing its population with a minimum standard of living. Once 'necessary' technology is accepted, the 'contingent' technology of industrial production, finance and entertainment cannot be far behind.

But we recognized earlier that industrialization is much more than the introduction of technology. Organization is at least as important as mechanization, and precedes it in the industrialization process. So a developing country can start its industrialization by acquiring some managerial and engineering skills, and putting a plentiful labour force to work on labour-intensive projects. Reservoirs are being built in this way in Ethiopia. It is the introduction of technology that presents a developing country with its most difficult choices. The essential questions are as follows:

1 How to strike a balance between the needs of primary production (mining and agriculture), manufacturing industry and, eventually, the service sector? A growing population must be fed, and primary products must be sold abroad to raise foreign exchange. The productivity of agriculture must be raised to release resources for further industrialization.
2 How to raise sufficient capital? Incurring large foreign debts returns a country to colonial status. Relying on multinational companies for industrial and technical development leaves the latter in control of the economy.
3 How to compete in world markets with products that are manufactured by 'intermediate' technology? Is it possible to acquire the necessary expertise to adapt the technology of other countries, or even create it from scratch? Could the adapted technology be sold to others?
4 How to strike a balance between wealth creation for the nation as a whole, and prosperity for specific regions? In opting for the first, how is the wealth created by siting high-technology plant in the most favourable areas to be shared with the rest of the population?
5 How to prevent the capital created by expensive technical developments from falling into the hands of those who will spend it on imported luxuries rather than creating an expanding market for home-produced goods?
6 Technology can be used effectively only by a workforce with a good general standard of education, followed up by training in specific techniques. In addition to the cost of capital investment, how is this educational investment to be funded?
7 If the successful introduction of technology depends on entrepreneurial skills, how are entrepreneurs to be identified and encouraged?

8 If the successful introduction of technology also depends on the readiness of the population at large to accept change, how are social institutions to be adapted to make this more likely?

9 Which industries should be selected to lead the process of change?

10 Above all, what is the role of the state in the introduction and development of technology? Rigid control, on the now-discredited Russian model, active partnership as in Japan, or to leave it entirely to entrepreneurs?

These questions are no mere academic niceties; successive groups of overseas students on manpower studies courses try to find satisfactory answers for their own countries.

So shaking off the industrial past requires an understanding of the ways in which the process of industrialization has created the apparently stable forms of work that we experience in daily life. Then we need to accept that stability is largely illusory, and that technology is already available that could alter almost every form of work which the Industrial Revolution created. Finally we need to accept that 'industrial revolutions' could take place several times in a working lifetime. This should create the appropriate frame of mind in which to plan strategically the use of human resources during the 1990s.

Consumer demands in the 1990s: markets in Europe and elsewhere

The previous discussion has made the point that labour markets are simply a way of categorizing workers, and that the categories will change with what is technically feasible in production and administration. Important as this awareness is to strategic human resource planning, it is not enough.

Technology will be applied if there is an economic advantage in doing so, and only then if management are aware of its potential. 'The object of production', wrote Adam Smith, 'is consumption'. The first stage in the Industrial Revolution was the organization of production, not its mechanization. The machinery was available, but was not used until the entrepreneur was compelled to look for ways of increasing output. What compelled him was the rapid expansion of markets. Human resource planning and strategy in the 1990s will be as sensitive to market forces as it was 200 years ago.

It would be a commonplace to state that markets for goods and services are now world-wide. At the time of writing, awareness campaigns have been conducted by the British government, and businesses in the UK are cautiously preparing, with varying degrees of enthusiasm, for the Single European Market. Trade links and mergers with companies in continental Europe, and an expansion of language training, indicate that the opportunities are not going unnoticed. For some years, however, the Japanese have been preparing springboard sites in the UK to take advantage of the expected trade expansion in Europe. Add to this the unexpected opening up of the East European states, and the walls of the new trade citadel appear fragile indeed. The hunger for consumer goods is as strong in Eastern Europe as the hunger for democracy, and vast markets for these have suddenly opened up. Germany, by *de facto* reunification, has the potential to become a manufacturing giant: Western 'industrialized' countries in general, including the USA, have been rapidly losing manufacturing capacity. The British textile industry, the engine of former industrialization and prosperity, is now confined to manufacturing for niche markets with high-technology plant from abroad. There are now more British workers in the financial sector of the economy than in manufacturing. It is difficult to see how this trend can be reversed. Manufacturing, by and large, will be the prerogative of the Pacific Basin, moving later, perhaps, to Africa. The older industrial nations are moving on to the knowledge-based industries of finance, personal services and consultancy.

Employment and work categories are determined not only by the items consumers want, but also by standards of service and by personal preferences. The poorer countries, including the newly-opened markets in the former communist bloc, will for some time to come be satisfied with mass-produced but serviceable products of the capitalist economies. In Western countries themselves, individuality is the key to sales. The customer is buying not merely a service or hardware, but delight with the purchase. Marketing departments and sales staff explore customer requirements as never before, computerized manufacturing and 'just in time' delivery of parts allow products to be tailored to individual needs, and 'total quality management' aims to meet customer-determined standards of performance at every stage. True, this Utopian vision is not everywhere observed in practice, but it is the standard towards which manufacturers and service providers now have to move if they are to keep their customers.

Rajan and Fryatt's (1988) description of the twin effects of technology and market deregulation on the services provided by the City of London was referred to at the beginning of this chapter. Financial products moved from the standard and bureaucratic to individually devised and supplied packages; technology supported this by faster data processing and decision-making programs. The net effect on employment was significant, not only for the financial services industry, but in its implications for employment in sophisticated economies in general. The demand is for 'knowledge-workers', trained in conceptual thinking and able to assemble and analyse complex situations. Clerical workers, who formed the backbone of an earlier, more standardized and leisurely age, are less in demand.

Strategic human resource planners would be well advised to inspect their own organizations for similar trends. Outside the financial sector, better design may be expressed in physical rather than conceptual ways. And better design now includes the desire of many consumers not to harm their environment. The UK has been running down its higher education in science and engineering, just when it appears that specialists in these activities will be in demand. The strategic issue, however, is that providing goods and services will depend more than ever on good education in all disciplines. More than that, it may at last become a generally accepted good in its own right—the ultimate individualized product.

The mobile worker

At the beginning of this chapter, we discussed briefly the phenomenon of 'Britain's industrial gypsies', the largely white-collar workforce that commutes weekly between northern cities and London. Adopting an historical perspective, we can see that, in one sense, this is nothing new. Before the Industrial Revolution, the servants' home would be where their masters lived, and would change with employment. Skilled workers (the name 'journeymen' is suggestive) would go where their crafts were in demand. Soldiers and sailors were, in the nature of their employment, mobile workers. Nevertheless, the vast majority of the population did not move far from the place where they were born. Industrialization accelerated the steady movement of people from the country to the towns that had commenced with the improvements in agricultural productivity in the eighteenth century. This, however, was a once and for all change for most of those who made it. The need for social stability and the inability to pay for long journeys by public transport, placed a premium on living near to work. Towards the end of the 1980s part of the argument between the architectural profession and its critics concerned the desirability of integrating work and home so that daily commuting could be avoided.

Both manual workers and professionals, of course, expect to move to their work if this is an explicit condition of employment; site engineers may be employed on North Sea oil rigs, or on construction sites in the Middle East. As Hogarth and Daniel (1988) point out, however, the 'industrial gypsies' contain many for whom such wanderings were neither an accepted nor an acceptable aspect of their careers. However socially and psychologically undesirable this feature of late twentieth-century Britain may be, strategic human resource planners should be aware that long-distance commuting will be undertaken by some of the professional workforce, at least when faced with local unemployment.

In labour markets, however, mobility has meanings beyond the geographical. Rajan and Fryatt (1988) reported, with disapproval, that the reaction of the City of London to deregulated financial markets was to poach each others' professional and qualified staff at ever-increasing salaries. Cash incentives joined unemployment as the carrot and stick of the late twentieth century labour economy. But carrots and sticks do not always work with human beings.

It was emphasized earlier that labour markets are as much a matter of psychology as of economics. We need to know how individuals themselves think and behave in these markets. The facts and figures need to be balanced by interviews and survey questionnaires that tell us about personal experience and reaction to perceived economic conditions. More emphasis should be given to fieldwork research to help human resource planners understand this neglected area. Studies of job satisfaction refer to conditions of stability; it is the transitions that give working lives their variety and meaning, and which suggest opportunities for strategic management and creative use of the workforce.

Enforced mobility and financially induced mobility then appear only as part of the picture; other forces are at work. In the description that follows, the focus is upon the professional and managerial workers as a category, since their behaviour is of special importance in the knowledge-based economy of the 1990s. Information about the job and career movements of this group are not easy to come by, although plenty of data exists. Every application form submitted to a potential employer contains a career history, but there is a reluctance to collect and analyse it. In the UK, the Data Protection Act is an excuse, if not a reason, for neglecting this ready-made data source. Strategic human resource planners would do well not to waste this valuable source of labour market information. The value of analysing career data is illustrated by the following examples.

Nicholson and West (1988) sent questionnaires in the mid-1980s to members of the British Institute of Management. Those who replied received a follow-up one year later. Their sample included both managerial and professional categories. The subsequent analysis gave many interesting insights into the career development of managers, especially women. We return to this research in full in Chapter 7. For the moment we are concerned particularly with mobility.

Nicholson and West discovered that a high proportion of managers make regular 'spiralling' moves in their working lives. These involve increased responsibility, changes of occupation and frequently also changes of employers. This process achieves not only higher rewards, but also greater job satisfaction. Interestingly, the individual career moves are often unexpected. Many moves that took place in the year between the two questionnaires were not predicted when the first was filled in.

Nicholson and West's findings are summarized in Table 2.1. For professionals and managers, career mobility has become the order of the day. This conclusion is supported by independent information from courses aimed at helping unemployed and other job-seeking professionals. A picture of the white-collar labour market emerges that is at once more complex and more complete than the traditional image of middle-class career development. Three categories of job-changer can be discerned; these will be referred to as the *opportunists*, the *seekers*, and the *unemployed*.

Table 2.1
Historical change in mobility

Date of survey	Number of employer changes:				
	0	1	2	3	4 or more
1958 (N = 646)	34%	24%	21%	11%	13%
1966 (N = 815)	33%	23%	19%	12%	13%
1971 (N = 964)	17%	16%	19%	14%	33%
1976 (N = 1304)	13%	16%	17%	17%	37%
1983 (N = 1364)	9%	13%	16%	18%	43%

Source: Nicholson, N. and West, M. (1988) *Managerial Job Change: men and women in transition*, Cambridge University Press, Cambridge

The *opportunists* are the employed managers and professionals whose career and occupational changing behaviours were reported by Nicholson and West. These deserve the title 'opportunists' because, according to these authors, their career changes are often unexpected. They frequently require moves between employers, between functional specialisms, or both. Opportunists, almost as a matter of course, enlarge their repertoire of skills at every move. This group contains many successful people whose careers, surprisingly, are largely unplanned.

Opportunists are marked by their confidence and adaptability. They like challenge, recognition, opportunities for learning and creativity. Most significantly, in the light of perceived skill shortages, the opportunists often make 'spiralling' moves that entail both a change of function and an increase in responsibility. Skills are nothing if not transferable.

The *seekers* are another employed category. They are dissatisfied in some ways with their current job, and would like to make a constructive move. They may perceive themselves as lacking useful skills, or lacking outlets for those they are aware of. Unlike the opportunists, they see their working lives as constrained by lack of personal development. A sample of seekers attended courses offered by the Polytechnic of Central London to employed managers and professionals who were considering a change of employment.

The *unemployed*, self-evidently, are managers and professionals currently

Figure 2.5
Distinctions between
opportunists, seekers
and the unemployed

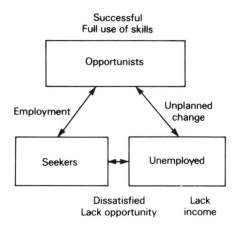

without work. Usually, the workless state was induced by some sudden action on the part of employers. Like the seekers they are searching for new employment, but with greater financial incentive and less social support. Like the seekers they often feel that their narrow range of skills limits their labour market. Like the opportunists, their chances of advancement may appear in a random, unplanned way, but with confidence damaged by redundancy, however, their ability to perceive and grasp them may be a good deal less. The relationship between the three categories of job-changer is shown in Figure 2.5.

The MSC-sponsored 'Bridge' programme at London Management Centre (Polytechnic of Central London) helped 1400 people between 1983 and 1988. One third of these were women and one fifth from the ethnic minorities. Their ages ranged from the early twenties to 62. Follow-up questionnaires revealed that, six months after each programme, 90 per cent of respondents had returned to work, and that age, gender or ethnic origin had very little effect on re-employment. The major ingredients of the programme were self-assessment, conducted in a group setting, and advice and practical work to improve applications and performance at interview. Full details of the development and content of the programme may be found in Pearson and Heyno (1988).

This experience provided a perspective on career development unavailable to the personnel managers and others who make managers and professionals redundant. The high re-employment rate gave the lie, if such were necessary, to the assumption that 'redundant' equals 'useless'. Over 50 per cent of those re-employed made some significant change in occupation, often without formal re-training, indicating a repertoire of transferable skills frequently unrecognized in previous employment, and this does not apply only to the young.

People returning to work often claim better remuneration and improved job satisfaction in their new posts. We return to the psychological and human resource implications of changing occupation in Chapter 7. For now it is sufficient to make the point that, while categories of work are constantly changing, there is no reason to suppose that workers cannot respond to shifting requirements; whether they will do so depends on those with a responsibilty for the effective use of people, and their effective knowledge of labour market changes.

Nor is this flexibility to be seen as a mere convenience for people who, no longer expecting security in employment, adopt a more hedonistic and reactive stance to work. High pay for valued 'knowledge work' may well support frequent holidays and changes of employer for personal reasons. The emerging equality of careers for women will trigger 'career breaks' for members of both sexes. But the evidence is that employers, too, want an end to 'lifetime' employment.

Atkinson (1984) has noted the phenomenon of the 'flexible firm'. Readers working in the public services in the UK, and perhaps elsewhere, will be well aware of the arguments over privatization. But private employers have also come to rely more on contract services, regrading many workers from the industrial to the service sector. The flexible firm goes further than privatization, however. It seeks to leave itself with as few long-term obligations to the workforce as possible. Short-term contracts are the order of the day, not only for cleaners, but also for systems analysts. Part-timers will be used to meet peak demands, and Training Agency-sponsored trainees will be farmed to fill low-level jobs. Only 'core' workers, whose long-term support is deemed to be essential to the maintenance of the business or service will be offered any semblance of an external career, and this will be subject to achieving measured results. In such an environment, individuals manifestly become personally responsible for rationalizing and developing their careers. The interest-free, but not cost-free, career development grants offered by the UK Training Agency are a portent of what is to come.

Flexible firms may, however, fail to meet their varying needs from their traditional external labour markets. They may also, on occasion, wish to promote the development and flexibility of existing members of their staff. The message of the research described in the preceding paragraphs is that both employees and their skills can be used flexibly, provided that the personnel function has the expertise and strategic capability to make it happen. People need not be hired and fired simply to meet changing requirements for skills; nor need employers put up with poor performance of those unhappily locked into dead-end jobs. Work categories all too easily become stereotypes.

Categorization by age

What was not by any means clear, as the 1980s drew to a close, was whether employers were poised to take advantage of the opportunity presented by this new flexibility in the labour market. That they desire the end is evident from Atkinson's research; whether they desire the means is more problematic.

Figure 2.6 shows the change in the distribution of the workforce by age between 1988 and 2000. Employers in key service industries like retail distribution have responded by increasing the pay of their young recruits, and also started to use older people, particularly pensioners, to replace younger workers. This achieves twofold flexibility: the labour market is enlarged, and the employer is able to use people who, because they are already in receipt of a basic income and value more leisure, will settle for part-time work at hours when peak demands have to be met. What it does not reveal is any great flexibility in the use of skills, because the work demands no more than average intelligence. Categorization by age, no less than categorization by gender, should cease to be a factor in strategic human resource planning.

Figure 2.6
Estimates and
projections of the
population of working
age, Great Britain, 1988
and 2000
Source: Government
Actuaries Department,
1987-based projections.
Reproduced from *The
Labour Market
Quarterly Report*, Nov.
1989 by kind
permission of The
Training Agency

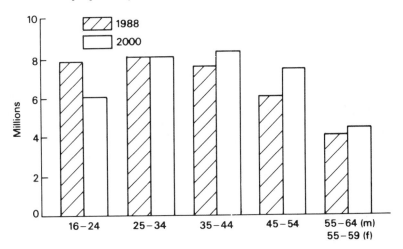

Categorization by race: the ethnic minorities

After gender, ethnicity is probably the most powerful source of human categorization. The subtlety of the categories used will vary with the sophistication of the categorizer: 'black-white', 'black-coloured-white' or, perhaps, 'this person is a member of the Ibo nation'. The Western stereotype of ethnic minority unemployment is black youth in the inner cities; unskilled, unmotivated and a prey to racial discrimination. This is a social and ethical problem that employers alone cannot solve. Yet it is possible for employers to set an example by the attitudes they adopt, and there are many instances of this around the world. We will return to this topic when we consider the interaction between human resource planning and policy.

For the present, the point can be made that the size of the labour market is diminished unnecessarily by each irrelevantly excluded category. As with the inappropriate use of age and gender, so racial discrimination will reduce the pool of much needed skills. There is hopeful evidence that employers in London are prepared to look beyond any prejudices that they may have and not to discriminate against unemployed professionals. Pearson and Heyno (1988) have observed that the re-employment rates among these groups, at least those given training in making and following through applications, was little different from unemployed professionals as a whole. The non-European immigrants who formed nearly 20 per cent of the participants in Pearson and Heyno's programme were at least as well qualified as the others, were slightly younger, and contained a higher proportion of males. They also contained a higher proportion of engineers and accountants, but a lower proportion of managers and administrators. Almost without exception, their first language was not English. This group will be discussed in greater detail when we come to consider the use of objective tests in selection.

Testing is only one aspect of selection, however. Rejection can occur solely because the candidate is personally disliked by the selector, and this frequently happens. It can also be the result of competition from better-qualified candidates, from failing a valid selection procedure or from unfairness arising from an invalid one. It is important to distinguish between prejudice and discrimination; the first may arise from irrational feelings aroused by ethnic categories, but may nevertheless be controlled by the prejudiced person. What is important is whether prejudice then results in unfair discriminatory behaviour.

Objective testing can serve to increase or diminish unfair discrimination, depending on the expertise and values of the selectors. Where education is lacking, well-designed and valid tests have an important part to play in ensuring that the employer is not unknowingly sacrificing standards of performance in order not to discriminate.

Describing the external labour market: some examples

The time lag in the production of books and indeed, many journals, means that labour market information presented in them is usually out of date. Some trends, of course, continue long enough to be relevant for strategic planning, even when the figures themselves are not. The data provided as a conclusion to this chapter, in Panels 1, 2 and 3, are examples that readers will be able to update or make relevant to the country where they work.

Conclusion

Case Study 1, at the end of the previous chapter, concerned the recruitment of graduates to an industrial company. Human resource planning for this group depended not only on statistical analysis, but also on an understanding of the categorization of work and the history that lie behind the concept of graduate recruitment. The interaction between change in industrialized society and the categories that we assign to both work and workers has been developed in this chapter.

The labour market, expressed in the form of simple supply and demand economics, is seen to have little value in strategic human resource management. Many of the traditional categories used in describing workers and jobs must also be regarded with some scepticism. The reason for both these caveats is the pervasiveness of the process of industrialization; once a nation or an economy has embarked on this road, it can neither halt the process nor assume that jobs, or the way they are carried out, will remain static for long. Once intitiated, industrialization draws increasingly upon technology and promotes its development. Market forces, increasingly world-wide, will ensure that the technology is adopted, either in products or in the process of manufacture.

The response to this situation must be for both employers and employees to maintain a flexible view of work and of the people required to do it. Stereotyping by gender, age or ethnicity, quite apart from their social and moral implications, show little awareness of the strategic needs of human resource management. Stereotyping by category of work has the same effects. In the next chapter we will consider how an understanding of their methodology can help planners to make more, rather than less, use of the human resource.

Once a labour market has moved from the imperceptible change of an agrarian society to the rapid development of an industrial one, the categories applied to people as workers, and to the work they do, must be kept under constant review. Most important of all, basic education must provide core skills, and the perception that they can be transferred between different types of work. From that point onwards, training should be seen as integral part of work, each assignment being seen as personal development in addition to its role in achieving corporate objectives.

The analysis of labour markets is at its least reliable and informative, for strategic purposes, when it relies solely on the concepts of the economist. As a descriptive process, however, labour market analysis is essential background to strategic planning. The source of effective categories lies in the organization itself, its current manpower system and its future needs. as Chapter 3 will explain.

References d'Agapeyeff, A. and Hawkins, C. (1987) *Report to the Alvey Directorate on the second short survey of expert systems in UK Business*, Published by the Institute of Electrical Engineers on behalf of the Alvey Directorate.

Atkinson, J. (1984) 'Manpower strategies for flexible organisations', *Personnel Management*, August, **28**.

Atkinson, J. (1989) *Corporate Employment Policies for the Single European Market*, Institute of Manpower Studies, Brighton.

Bennison, M. and Casson J. (1984) *The Manpower Planning Handbook*, McGraw-Hill (UK) Ltd, Maidenhead.

Boden, M. (1977) *Artificial Intelligence and Natural Man*, Harvester Press, Brighton.

Boden, M. (1987) *Artificial Intelligence and Natural Man*, MIT Press, London.

Boden, M. (1988) *Computer Models of Mind: Computational Approaches in Theoretical Psychology*, Cambridge University Press, Cambridge.

Bourgignon, F. (1988) *The Measurement of the Wage–Employment Relationship in Developing and Developed Countries: a short survey*, International Labour Office, Geneva.

Central Statistical Office (1980) *Standard Industrial Classification*, HMSO, London.

Chapman, A. (1989) *Just the Ticket? Graduate men and women in the labour market three years after leaving college*, HELM working paper No. 8, Polytechnic of North Staffordshire.

Deane, P. (1979) *The First Industrial Revolution* (2nd ed.), Cambridge University Press, Cambridge.

Equal Opportunities Commission (1988) *The EOC Strategy for the 1990s*, EOC, Manchester.

Evans, A. (1989) *What Next at Work?: School Leaver Decline and Effective Local Solutions*, Institute of Manpower Studies, Brighton.

Freeman, C., Clark, J. and Soete, L. (1982) *Unemployment and Technical Innovation*, Frances Pinter, London.

Hill, C. (1969) *Reformation to Industrial Revolution*, The Pelican Economic History of Great Britain, Pelican Books, Harmondsworth, London.

Hogarth, T. and Daniel, W. (1988) *Britain's New Industrial Gypsies: long-distance weekly commuters*, Policy Studies Institute, London.

Jahoda, M. (1982) *Employment and Unemployment: a social psychological analysis*, Cambridge University Press, Cambridge.

Jones, B. (1982) *Sleepers, Wake!*, Wheatsheaf Books, Brighton.

Kemp, T. (1978) *Historical Patterns of Industrialization*, Longman, London.

Manpower Report (1986) *Labour Market Quarterly Report*, Spring/Summer, MSC, Sheffield.

Marstrand, P. (ed.) (1984) *New Technology and the Future of Work and Skills*, Frances Pinter, London.

Mountjoy, A. (1982) *Industrialization and Developing Countries*, Hutchinson University Library, London.

Mountjoy, A. and Hilling, D. (1988) *Africa: Geography and Development*, Hutchinson Unwin Hyman, London.

Neisser, U. (1983) in Sloboda, J. and Rogers, D. (eds.) *The Acquisition of Symbolic Skills*, Plenum Press, London.

Nicholson, N. and West, M. (1988) *Managerial Job Change: men and women in transition*, Cambridge University Press, Cambridge.

Oakley, B. (1987) 'Expert systems: artificial intelligence research comes of age', A lecture for the public given on 19 May at the Royal Society, London.

Pagnamenta, P. and Overy R. (1984) *All Our Working Lives*, BBC Books, London.

Pearson, R. and Heyno, A. (1988) *Helping the Unemployed Professional*, John Wiley & Sons, Ltd, Chichester. (Passage on pages 42–43 reprinted by permission of John Wiley & Sons, Ltd.)

Pearson R. and Pike, G. (1990) *The IMS Graduate Review 1990*, IMS, Brighton.

Potter, R. and Unwin, T. (1989) *The Geography of Urban–Rural Interaction in Developing Countries*, Routledge, London.

Rajan, A. and Pearson, R. (1986) *UK Occupation and Employment Trends to 1990: an employer-based study of the trends and their underlying causes*, IMS, Brighton.

Rajan, A. (1987) *Services—the second industrial revolution: business and jobs outlook for UK growth industries*, IMS, Brighton.

Rajan, A. and Fryatt, J. (1988) *Create or Abdicate? The City's human resource choice for the 90s*, Witherby/IMS, Brighton.

Schumacher, E. (1974) *Small is Beautiful*, Abacus, Sphere Books Ltd, London.

Searle, J. (1984) *Minds, Brains, and Science: The 1984 Reith Lectures*, BBC Books, London.

Smith, Adam (1970 republished) *The Wealth of Nations*, Pelican Books, London.

Stewart, F. and James, J. (1982) *The Economics of New Technology in Developng Countries*, Frances Pinter, London.

Waite, R. and Pike, G. (1989) *School Leaver Decline and Effective Local Solutions*, Institute of Manpower Studies, Brighton.

Warr, P. (1983) 'Work, jobs and unemployment', *Bulletin of the British Psychological Society* **36**, 305.

Warr, P. (1987) *Work, Unemployment and Mental Health*, Clarendon Press, Oxford.

Whitemore, H. (1987) *Breaking the Code*, based on the book *Alan Turing, the enigma* by Andrew Hodges, Amber Lane Press, Oxford.

Wiener, M. (1985) *English Culture and the Decline of the Industrial Spirit*, Pelican Books, London.

Williams, S. (1981) *Politics is for People*, Penguin Books, Harmondsworth, London.

Bibliography on industrialization

Ashton, T. (1973) *The Industrial Revolution (1760–1830)*, Open University, Milton Keynes.

Berger, M. (1975) *Industrial Policies in Nigeria*, Munchen, Weltforum.

Davies, R. (1979) *Industrialization of Soviet Russia*, Macmillan, London.

Gwynne, R. (1985) *Industrialization and Urbanization in Latin America*, Croom Helm, London.

Henderson, W. (1972) *Britain and Industrial Europe*, Leicester University Press, Leicester.

Henderson, W. (1975) *The Rise of German Industrial Power*, Temple Smith, London.

Hobsbawm, P. (1977) *The Age of Revolution*, Abacus, Sphere Publishing Ltd, London.

Kemp, T. (1983) *Industrialization in Nineteenth Century Europe*, Longman, London.

Kemp, T. (1983) *Industrialization in the Non-Western World*, Longman, London.

Kilby, P. (1969) *Industrialization in an Open Economy: Nigeria 1945–66*, Cambridge Univeristy Press, Cambridge.

Martin, S. and De Souza, J. (1977) *Agriculture and Industry in Brazil*, Cambridge Centre for Latin American Studies, Cambridge.

Martin, R. and Hawthorn, B. (1986) *The Geography of De-industrialization*, Macmillan, London.

Mathias, P. (1983) *The First Industrial Nation—an economic history of Britain 1700–1914* (2nd ed.), Methuen, London.

Onyemelukwe, J. (1984) *Industrialization in West Africa*, Croom Helm, London.

Preobrazhenskii, E. (1980) *The Crisis of Soviet Industrialization*, Macmillan, London.

Rweyemamu, J. (1973) *Underdevelopment and Industrialization in Tanzania*, Oxford University Press, Nairobi.

Trebilcock, C. (1981) *The Industrialization of the Continental Powers 1780–1914*, Longman, London.

Tranter, N. (1985) *Population and Society 1750–1940*, Longman, London.

The UK labour market 1990

Officially recorded employment in the UK is at an all-time high—26 million. Part-time work is responsible for much of the recent increase, which now accounts for a quarter of all employment. Women take most of the part-time jobs, thus being the main reason that employment as a whole has risen. A major feature in the UK labour market is thus its part-time, female workforce. The number of men who accept part-time work is also increasing, including some people who do multiple jobs rather than work for one employer.

The official working age is from 16 to 65 for men, and 16 to 60 for women; women now want equal access to work, and men equal access to pensions.

Unemployment is the second most notable feature of the UK labour market. It has recently fallen from its all-time high of 3.2 million to 1.6 million, which is still an historically high figure.* This reduction is based on official figures, the subject of some scepticism, being based on the 'claimant' count—people who are eligible and claiming unemployment benefit. This leaves out of account those technically ineligible, including many of the new labour force, married women. Household surveys reveal higher numbers of people who are seeking work. These broad generalizations hide significant regional variations in employment and unemployment; until recently the most pronounced falls in the official figures were taking place outside the more traditionally prosperous areas of London and the South-East. The fall in unemployment overall has now ceased, and it is once again on the increase.

Ethnic minorities feature disproportionately among the unemployed, although more are taking up self-employment, a sector that is finding increasing favour among all races.

Despite unemployment and the increasing female labour force, employers have been reporting shortages of workers, particularly younger workers and skilled craftspeople. The number of school-leavers is due to drop by 25 per cent by the middle of the 1990s, and abandonment of training during the 1980s recession reduced the opportunity to acquire skills. Britain has the second lowest percentage in Europe of pupils remaining in education after the official leaving age.

The effects of the Single European Market look like having more impact on the way business is organized than on employment. Free movement of labour will be technically possible, but will favour those with special skills. Transfer of professional qualifications is, paradoxically, a likely barrier (Atkinson, 1989).

In common with other industrialized countries, Britain's economy has been moving steadily away from its manufacturing base towards service-based employment. Whether this trend could, or should, be arrested is a matter of political debate.

(Figures from the Labour Market Quarterly Report, May 1990)

* 2.0 million 1991

The Malaysian labour market 1984

The management of the Malaysian economy is dedicated to the alleviation of poverty by industrialization. The population of working age in Malaysia (1984) is estimated to be about 7.8 million, of which 5 million are considered to be in the labour force. This excludes housewives, students, retired or disabled persons and those not seeking work. One third of the labour force are female, although females make up over half of the population of working age. Women outside the labour force are biased towards those of childbearing age, but participation is high in the 20 to 24 age group. Both men and women are more likely to be employed if they live in a rural area, the opposite of what might be supposed, but this effect is moderated by age. Participation is higher for older females in the rural sector, but higher for middle-aged men in the urban areas. Although the quality of the rural areas vary, the urban–rural split does not correspond directly to dualism as defined in Chapter 2.

An important feature of the Malaysian labour market is migration. This takes place both within Malaysia and between Malaysia and other countries. The government regards migration as a necessary process in achieving its economic and social objectives. The propensity to migration within the Malaysian Federation had increased from 96 per thousand of the population in 1970, to 143 per thousand in 1980. Migration took place from the rural to the more urbanized states, with their higher level of development and earning potential. However, there was a strong inter-rural migration, with migrants seeking better land and social conditions. The Ministry of Labour admits to a categorization problem here, because those who settle on the outskirts of towns may be classified as rural rather than urban, even though engaged in the urban economy. Migration tends to take place among the young, and the non-Chinese races. Migrants are better educated than non-migrants. These changes are in accord with the New Economic Policy enunciated by the Malaysian government in 1970, and dedicated to raising the educational and economic opportunities for the Malay population. Alleviation of poverty is seen in terms of reducing the population (largely Malay) in the subsistence sector. In 1980, the proportion of Malays in the manufacturing and service sectors of the economy was increasing, as they departed from their earlier, mainly agricultural role, but not sufficiently rapidly. While urban unemployment was recorded at 5 per cent, this was expected to increase if the erstwhile rapid growth of the manufacturing sector were to falter.

Malaysia is part of a complex Pacific labour economy, and both inward and outward migration of workers takes place. Malaysia loses skilled workers to Singapore, and gains them from Indonesia. Many of the latter (130 000) are classified as illegal immigrants. Overall there is a shortage of skilled workers.

(Adapted from Labour and Manpower Report 1983/84, The Research and Planning Division, Kuala Lumpur, Malaysia)

The labour market in Malawi

At least superficially, Malawi remains one of the most stable countries in the subcontinent and has attained a high degree of self-sufficiency in food, together with a significant expansion, improved infrastructure and regional development. This has been achieved despite the lack of significant mineral deposits or other exploitable resources, a feature that partly accounts for Malawi's severe underdevelopment during the colonial era. Historically, this situation underpinned the country's role in the southern African political economy as a small, peripheral labour reservoir. With a population estimated at more than 6.8 million in 1984 (just over 5.5 million were recorded in 1977), at an average density of 57.7 per square kilometre, creation of additional earning opportunities has clearly been crucial . . .

Malawi's development programme during the late 1960s and 1970s centred on capitalist agriculture, particularly the estate form of production. The chief commodities were cash crops, particularly tobacco, sugar and more recently also tea. World market prices for all three were buoyant over that period. Tobacco and tea production are inherently labour intensive and, because of the low cost of labour, capital intensive sugar cultivation was eschewed in favour of labour absorption . . . The labour requirements of estate agriculture were met from two sources, namely expropriation from peasant production, and returning international migrants.

Over the 1966–77 censal period, about a third of a million migrants are estimated to have returned to Malawi without precipitating a significant increase in *measured* unemployment . . . The majority of each year's returnees, varying from 55 to 73 per cent, were absorbed by the peasant sector. It is not clear to what extent this was their preference or the result of a lack of wage earning opportunities, although the percentage returning to the peasant sector does appear to have risen as the absolute number of returnees increased during the early 1970s. Under the circumstances, *disguised* rural unemployment and underemployment are sure to have increased significantly.

There is evidence that many returnees to Malawi engage in seasonal wage employment, thus necessitating periodic male (and sometimes female) absenteeism. This is almost certainly a consequence of the depressed subsistence conditions and increased land pressure in the peasant sector . . . Wages and working conditions on the estates are poor . . . some 27 000–30 000 predominatly rural Malawians still find employment in South African mines each year.

Less clear, however, is how sustainable the chosen development path will be, given the degree of ongoing surplus extraction from the peasant sector, which has experienced growing population pressure and land scarcity.

(*Source*: Potter, R. and Unwin, T. (1989) *The Geography of Urban–Rural Interaction in Developing Countries*, Routledge, London)

CHAPTER
3

Auditing human resources: methodology

Management and social research

In Chapter 1 we traced the development of personnel management and manpower planning, and explored the relationship between them. Failure to respond to the realities of working life was perceived as a threat to the validity of both. In Chapter 2, the discussion of labour markets demonstrated the necessity of categorizing work and workers if human resource planning were to take place. The same discussion also demonstrated the necessity of keeping these categories under constant review. Changing consumer needs and the steadily increasing power of technology will ensure that work and working methods place changing demands on people throughout their lives. As the research into professional careers has demonstrated, people have the skills and adaptability to respond, provided that managers and strategists will let them. Jobs are regularly redundant, people are not.

Meeting the challenge of changing demands and changing categories of work, is the purpose of human resource strategy. In Chapter 1 it was suggested that the methods of the manpower planner were implicitly those of social research, and that those of the human resource strategist should be explicitly so. We will now look more closely at the process of social research that was briefly outlined at the end of Chapter 1. Before doing so, it is necessary to counter an objection to this interpretation of manpower planning that is as understandable as it is unjustified.

Managers, especially commercial managers, are often sceptical about social research, and fearful of 'sociology', with its overtones of student revolt and union militancy. Old suspicions die hard. In 1989, one of the author's students was explaining the process of manpower research, along the lines suggested in this book, to a group of general managers from one of Britain's largest enterprises. His ideas were gaining approving nods until he inadvertently let slip the phrase 'social research'; the atmosphere cooled immediately. Subsequent presentations included the principles, but omitted the label.

The academic world has some responsibility for this state of affairs. Tendentious presentation of social studies and social science to students has fuelled the scepticism and fear of business managers, and perhaps reduced the effectiveness of the very students whom the academics hoped would 'change society'. Society does change, as recent events in Eastern Europe have demonstrated; what is needed is a constructive response to the changes as they occur. Strategic human research planning is concerned with constructive responses in the world of work, improving both its effectiveness and its satisfactions.

Halsey's (1972) statement, that 'the purpose of social research is to inform the political debate', was quoted in Chapter 1. He made it while discussing the problems of objectivity in social research, in this instance an attempt to discover the causes of under-achievement in primary schools, and possible methods of correcting it. Halsey develops this theme as follows:

The problem of the entanglement of analysis with value assumptions is intrinsic to sociological study. To get it straight, we must first distinguish the 'scientific' problem from the 'value' problem: to ask separately what is possible and thereby, with the issue and alternatives sharply defined, to decide on preferences and priorities. In this way the challenge to social science becomes clear and the task for the sociologist is, literally, to inform the political debate.

Halsey, let it be said, went on to point out that this separation was by no means easy. But it is difficult to imagine a clearer exposition of what researching the human resource, let alone other social topics, might be about. It is apparent that there is a premium not only upon objectivity, but also on clarity of presentation. Halsey, long before strategic management became a vogue phrase, was stating its principles.

Significantly, social research theory and methodology are accepted without question in a different but related area of management; market research. Here the same methodologies that the human research strategist applies to the study of people in their roles as workers are applied to the study of their wants and needs as consumers. To accept market research as a legitimate tool of the free market economy, and to reject human resource research as Utopian, or worse, is partial and perverse. An organization that aspires to 'strategic management' should surely embrace both.

Human resource planning, revealed as strategic research, will seem a less specific, and perhaps more worrying, discipline than the earlier treatises on manpower planning might have led readers and practitioners to expect. They are urged to have patience as they are about to discover that the skills and insights of the manpower planner have many more uses than earlier definitions of their craft would suggest. Human resource planning need not be confined to speculation about future demand for rigid and out-of-date categories of workers. Once the implicit social research content of human resource planning is made clear, the way is open for human resource strategists to apply their techniques to a wider range of problems.

Gathering social data on a national and international scale is, of course, nothing new. A bureaucratic revolution followed industrialization in Western countries in the last century and has since spread to all parts of the world. Gathering data about population and working patterns became part of the administrative stock in trade, as the descriptions of labour markets at the end of Chapter 2 will have demonstrated. Those who categorize and enumerate the national labour market have a part to play in the development of strategies for people. Governments may choose to ignore the data that they produce, or to use their findings in a perverse way. But effective action to improve the prospects of workers and the use of their skills must include a consideration of the national statistics; in future, data covering the EC and other multinational trade blocs will also be important.

Planning at national level is largely reactive, however. Responsibility for human resource strategies that enlarge the wealth-creating capacity of society and improve the job satisfaction of individual workers rests at local level, and chiefly within employing organizations themselves. National statistics are usually out of date, and fail to reflect the rapid technological, economic and social changes that characterize late twentieth-century labour markets throughout the world. Compilers of national statistics can keep the score, but cannot play the game.

Employers, of course, may be reluctant to accept the challenge. Strategic use of human skills requires both an expertise and a dedication of management time that some may see as an unnecessary expense. Even when the expertise is afforded and available, it may not be heeded. After more than 20 years of formal training for personnel managers in the UK, the quality of job descriptions and personnel specifications leaves much to be desired; selection procedures are seldom validated; job and induction training are regularly the subject of unflattering comparison with practice in other countries.

The research role of the human resource planner was explained in Chapter 1; no organization can claim to be thinking strategically unless it fully understands the potential of its own workforce, and no organization can claim to be thinking strategically unless it takes account of the continuing and accelerating process of industrialization to which it is being subjected. This process has little to do with national boundaries, since dualistic economies may contain both subsistence agriculture and an industrial urbanized sector that has more in common with the developed nations than with its own hinterland. Those working in the subsistence sector have the luxury of using all members of a family or tribal group in undifferentiated and inefficient work; the price paid for this particular luxury excludes all others. Industrialization, on the other hand, brings material benefits but encourages the categorization of work and workers in ways that inhibit further technical advance. Strategic human resource planners will be aware of this danger, and will wish to give equal attention to changes in the environment and to auditing the resources already available within the organization.

The 1990s offer both encouragement and justification for this approach. In the UK, the changed perceptions of trade unions, and the skill-shortages with which employers enter the decade, provide both freedom and stimulus to look at manpower systems afresh. The intrusion of micro-electronics into the world of work, which we considered from the point of view of national labour markets in Chapter 2, should prompt regular fundamental reassessments of human resources in both service and manufacturing organizations.

Human resource planners need a pro-active approach and particular skills of their own, if they are to rise to the challenge. These are crucially dependent upon a conscious recognition of the methodology that they use, its potential applications and its dangers.

Manpower planning: implicit methodology

Organizations and the labour markets that surround them are open social systems. Within organizations, the differing types of work, and the status accorded to each, constitute what Bennison and Casson (1984) have referred to as 'the manpower system'. Correct perception of these systems is doubly important: it affects the ways in which the potential of workers is seen within the organization, and it structures management's perceptions of its external labour market. As Walshe, McGill and Pearson (1982) pointed out, defining the organization's manpower system is a necessary first step in local labour market analysis.

The investigations that both Bennison and Walshe describe, in common with many others, seldom make their methodological assumptions explicit. In the past, as Chapter 1 has shown, manpower planning has been uneasily suspended between theoretical statistical approaches, and down-to-earth surveys that do not challenge readers, students or practitioners to consider their wider development within a methodological framework. If they did, manpower planning might creatively include other methods of research beside

Figure 3.1
An outline of the social
research process

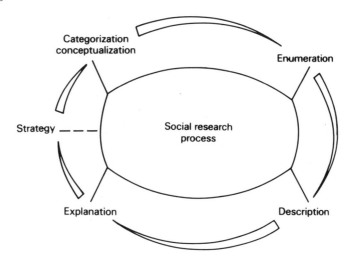

the ubiquitous survey. Is it possible to present a more inclusive yet unified
model, that provides a structure for what in the past has been known as
'manpower planning', and which also acts as a stimulus for assessing the
human resource in new and effective ways?

Figure 3.1 illustrates the processes inherent in manpower research. The
diagram makes no assumptions about the starting point, which would differ
according to the purposes of the investigation, and with the personal values
and paradigms of the researcher, but it does imply that there is a necessary
link between the research process and the development of strategy and with
the evolution of policy. Policies and strategies developed without research are
rhetoric, while research without organizational implications is difficult to
justify except in academic terms.

Adopting this model allows us to see the history of manpower planning in
perspective. The early statistical phase was dominated by description;
categories were taken as given, and enumeration depended on existing
manpower records. Description itself took the form of presenting manpower
systems as mathematical, often computerized, models. To summarize the
arguments in Chapter 1, this approach gave us techniques, but no insight into
the better use of individual workers. The apparent complexity of the models
discouraged rather than encouraged their use by personnel practitioners.

The 'corporate' phase of manpower planning, identified with the 1970s,
made the questionable assumption that corporate policies and strategies
would spring to life, *sui generis*, without reference to the skills and desires of
those who worked for the corporation. In terms of Figure 3.1, research would
not be seen as integral with, or even relevant to, the development of corporate
strategies and policies. The role of the human resource planner, in this unreal
situation, would have been to take the business strategy for granted and to go
to the market for its human resource needs. We need look no further than the
skill-shortages in the financial services and high technology industries to see
the fallacy in such an approach. Organizations would not embark on policies
of expansion without researching their ability to raise adequate finance in an
acceptable form, yet human resources are assumed to be there for the picking.

The assumption that strategic development (or even planning) is a 'top-
down' process is, in any case, highly debatable. Quinn (1980) refers to
strategic development as 'logical incrementalism', meaning that strategy is the
product of data-gathering and negotiation, involving many interested parties

within the organization. Well-informed human resource specialists are as likely to influence strategy as to be influenced by it.

The small-scale manpower planning, which I attributed to Bowey, was a useful but neglected contribution to the development of sound human resources research. Bowey emphasized the situational nature of planning, as against forecasting; in so doing she focused on the relationship between the workers immediately available to an organization and its immediate needs. This approach is more likely to encourage questioning of manpower categories than those dominated by statistics or assumed corporate needs. More important, it also emphasized the process of manpower planning, and its relationship to plans for a department or organization, rather than refining techniques of description.

The research conducted by the Institute of Manpower Studies was initially based on the statistical approach of Bartholomew and others, but graduated during the 1970s towards a more complete use of the model in Figure 3.1. Bennison and Casson (1984), particularly, emphasized the essential stage of conceptualizing the manpower system, not as management assume it to be, but as it really is. Their emphasis in the research process was on categorization. They also favoured scenario planning as against forecasting, promoting the use of a manpower map, based on best and worst cases evaluated by scenario planning, rather than upon the extrapolation of trends. Description, in the reports published by the IMS, tends to be in the form of histograms and percentages; readers do not require extensive mathematical training to understand their implication. The Institute promoted the use of computerized models with the objective of encouraging managers to explore the implications of different manpower strategies. The Institute's work, however, reflects its relationship with sponsors by leaving the latter to provide their own explanations. Human resource planners within organizations cannot, of course, afford this luxury, since the product of their research must be strategies likely to be effective within their own environment. This requires that explanations, however tentative, must be provided in psychologically and economically relevant terms.

Since, to some readers at least, the processes in this methodology will be unfamiliar, it is necessary to explain them in some detail, and to give examples. We begin with a closer examination of categorization, and why this is sometimes wittingly or unwittingly, too superficial for our strategic purpose.

Categorization

Philosophers will argue, perhaps interminably, about the nature of reality, and the extent to which it exists beyond sensory experience. Human life would be impossible, however, without the ability to conceive categories among the thousands of stimuli that bombard our senses each and every day. In the inanimate world, we need to be aware of the categories of solid, liquid and gas, yet many gases are invisible. Ideas such as 'hot' and 'cold' objects, 'wild' and 'tame' animals, 'edible' and 'poisonous' plants, are necessary to our very survival. In some cases the discriminations will be crude but effective, in others finely drawn and necessary only if we are making a special study of an academic subject. The more elaborate the system of categories that a person uses when discussing or contemplating a topic, the more of an expert he or she is likely to be. In an effort to appear 'practical', it is easy to use over-simplified categories to describe research to an unsophisticated audience. This lack of sophistication should not extend to the research itself.

The dangers of categorization are at their most acute when the subject of research is people. To make sense of our daily lives we need, for example, to categorize people as shop assistants, nurses, bus conductors, policemen and so on. Working clothes or uniforms, emphasizing the uniformity of categorization, are used to reinforce our perceptions. As part of our social education, we learn the behaviour to be expected from these categories, and the response required from ourselves. Powerful though working roles are in determining social categorization and response, they tell us very little about individuals, the full range of their skills, attitudes or their domestic lives. Of course, many more subtle discriminations are needed in daily interactions with others; to confuse a Lord Mayor with a popular comedian, or a maiden aunt with a nightclub hostess, would be to court social disaster. Social education requires the development of ever-finer distinctions between people. This type of discrimination is seldom allowed for in traditional manpower planning.

In the world of work, poor categorization has financial as well as social consequences. Good candidates may be rejected because insufficient information is obtained during an interview or because an interviewer persists against the evidence in assigning them to inappropriate categories. Use of category systems like 'blue-collar' and 'white-collar', more appropriate to an earlier phase of industrialization, may blind management to the talents of a modern workforce. Distinctions between 'scientists' and 'technicians' need to be justified, not merely by a graded salary scale, but also by demonstrable differences in the level and content of work.

Pay scales are a common and highly misleading method of categorizing human resources. Grades may be arrived at by some method of job evaluation, agreed with trade unions, and then become the basis for recruitment, promotion and human resource planning. 'A shortage of people in grade 6' may or may not be a cause for concern, depending on the validity of that particular category as a measure of the skill and responsibilility necessary to effective job performance.

Job-evaluated pay scales are intended to reward people according to the responsibility and other demands of their work; no assumptions are made about the occupational categories to which they belong. The consequent grades have little relevance to human resource planning. All we know is that two or more people obtained the same number of points in the grading process. The total points awarded each worker may derive from very different scores on each factor. There is no implication that each could perform the others' job. It is only by looking at the common, highly rated factors (see Table 3.1) that common skills become evident. As with other aspects of life, rough and ready categorization may be necessary to get safely through the working day, but categories that are appropriate for one activity in management may not be appropriate for another. Nowhere is this caveat more important than in human resource planning.

Categorization, of course, is merely the arrangement of people or objects in groups; similarity in one particular respect is all that is required. Children arranging toy bricks in the nursery do as much. To say why the groups are different we need concepts. These may be simple, like the concept of shape that is available to the child; they may be more complicated abstract concepts like 'intelligence' or 'education'.

Categories and concepts   The words 'concept' and 'category' have both entered this discussion and it is necessary to make clear the relationship between the two. Categories are the

Job factor	Points awarded			
	Maximum	Production controller	Commerical manager	Personnel Manager
Education	50	20	20	40
Relationships	50	30	40	50
Analysis	50	40	40	50
Accuracy	50	35	35	30
Decision-making	50	30	30	30
Mental effort	25	20	20	10

Source: job evaluation table for a small manufacturing firm

simplest level of concepts, and are necessarily limited. For academic study, professional analysis, and for strategic management, we need more abstract tools of thought; we need to be able to think conceptually.

Cognitive psychologists, whose job it is to try to understand and explain the workings of the human mind, identify two types of concept (Sokal, 1974). The first, and most easily understood, is the least used in daily life. It is referred to as the monothetic concept, because all members of such categories have at least one feature in common. Monothetic concepts are the simple reductions made by physical scientists in order to understand the world. All acids, for example, have at least one feature in common. Such knowledge was not available, of course, until the end of the eighteenth century, and its concepts are still being developed. Before this, many scientific ideas were as confused as ideas about people still are, some 200 years later. In physics, categories such as electron, proton and neutron are also precisely defined and understood, although the 'fundamental' particles of physics have an almost human capacity to change their nature with more detailed research. At any one time, however, a group of physicists might be reasonably clear what they jointly understood by the idea of an electron. Such precise knowledge is necessary for the laboratory experiments that are the physical scientist's stock in trade.

Monothetic concepts are met in ordinary life, as well as in the laboratory, however. Children sorting bricks would use not only colour but would also be able to identify those that are square, those that are circular. They quickly learn to identify the invariant feature, and could place the bricks in different boxes according to a required category system. Such simplified systems are plainly inappropriate for plants or animals, let alone for human beings. Categories such as 'sales clerk' may have validity at a particular time, in a particular organizational setting, but they do not assist us to understand the uniquely human characteristics of a member of the group.

People, and many other things in everyday life, are categorized in more elaborate ways. To take the range of occupations mentioned above, some shop assistants, bus conductors or policemen may be graduates, but many are not. Some might have high general intelligence, and many not. We are in the world of averages rather than sharply defined categorization. A range of characteristics is surveyed, and individuals are assigned to the most appropriate category. It is no longer necessary for all members of the group to share one invariant feature; membership is statistical rather than absolute. Such categories are referred to as 'polythetic'. Abstract as they may sound, polythetic categories are much more common in everyday life than monothetic ones. Dogs with very different appearances are categorized together for the purposes of a dog show; dogs remain dogs even when they lose one leg in an accident. Classifying an object as a table is a matter of use rather than appearance. Wittgenstein's (1958) famous example of the category of 'games' requires abstruse relationships to be perceived between one member of this group and another.

Uncomfortable though it may be for human resource planners themselves, and awkward though these ideas may be to explain to colleagues, polythetic categories are part of their stock in trade. In practice, this means regarding all simple category systems as provisional, liable to change or become useless with time, and treating them as averages rather than sharp dividing lines between one employee and another. A 'sales clerk' may be a 'sales clerk' for purposes of job location and pay. Inspection of his or her job content may reveal considerable similarity with other occupations, offering the opportunity of transfer if computerization or reduced sales volume makes the original occupation redundant. A particular sales clerk may gain a degree through part-time study and thus become one of the graduates available to the organization as a whole. Such considerations might appear to be self-evident, and so they should be, but they were not taken into account during many a 'redundancy exercise' during the 1980s. A procedure of 'last in, first out' would be applied, regardless of the skills to be lost and the flexibility that human beings can bring to their work.

An organization that categorizes and enumerates its human resources at regular intervals is beginning to think strategically. To be fully strategic in its use of people, however, it is necessary to use the categories and conceptual systems that are appropriate to the investigation, and to be prepared to change these with changing circumstances.

Some examples relevant to human resource planning will help us to understand the use of concepts in social research. We may, for instance, wish to categorize the reasons that people give for being away from work; sickness, sanctioned absence, holidays and so on. Having established these categories, recorded absence could be grouped under these headings. But the subject of our study would not be the individual categories so much as the overall phenomenon of 'absence behaviour'. This 'concept' is an abstraction from the real world of employees not being available for work. We may also need a higher level concept that would incorporate both absence, of all types, and the loss of workers from the organization; 'withdrawal from work' might suggest itself. We would have to decide whether withdrawal from work was to be regarded as voluntary, or whether to include forced redundancy and dismissal. We would need to be sure that all possible aspects of withdrawal, including stress-related illness, were considered. These relationships are illustrated in Figure 3.2.

Concepts form an ascending ladder, from simple categories to the most abstract. Figure 3.2 shows that 'withdrawl from work' could be incorporated under the general heading of 'employee behaviour', and so on up the ascending hierarchy of concepts. Conversely, the concept of 'employee behaviour' is defined in terms of lower-level concepts, and is ultimately measurable in terms of categories at the lowest level.

Concepts may be defined in one of two ways; in terms of other concepts, or in terms of some objective measure. When we were discussing the concept of 'industrialization' in Chapter 2, you may have noticed that it was defined in terms of other concepts; 'organization', 'mechanization', 'urbanization' and so on. Such concepts may be judged in terms of their usefulness in helping us to make sense, not only of academic study, but of the world in general. For the

Figure 3.2
A conceptual map of
'withdrawal from work'

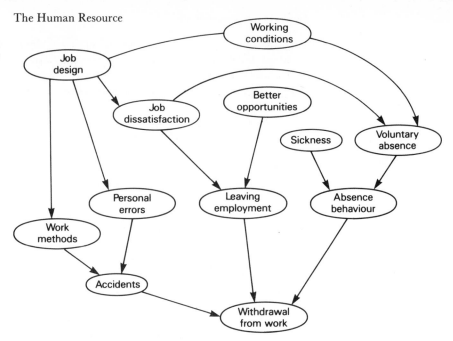

human resource strategist 'industrialization' is just such a concept. But neither human resource planning, nor any other form of social research, has a claim to being scientific unless some of its concepts can be measured objectively. For this we need not only a concept but also an indicator. Although 'industrialization' itself would be difficult to measure, the introduction, within a specified time-span, of 'process and production innovations new to the plant' (Goddard and Thwaites, 1984) provides a measure of propensity to innovate, one manifestation of industrialization.

Take the concept of 'unemployment' as an example. As we discovered during our discussion of labour markets, this concept is not as clear-cut as might at first appear. We could choose to define a category of labour called 'the unemployed', which might be those seeking work but unable to find it. We could, perhaps, enumerate this category by reference to the numbers of people both claiming unemployment benefit in one week and also being able to convince officials that they were available for work. Both concept and indicator might be vulnerable to criticism, but we would be in some position to commence research on the subject of unemployment.

In personnel selection, a subject to be discussed in the next chapter, concepts, categories and indicators are important, but seldom properly thought out. We may claim, for example, that it is necessary for suitable candidates for managerial vacancies to be 'assertive'. How is the concept of 'assertiveness' to be defined and how is it to be measured? In the terminology of social science, how do we operationalize our concept by providing an objective measure that two or more people can agree on? Operationalization is the basis of all scientific activity. Within the objectives of this book, it is also the basis of human resource planning. The strategic planner is required to conceptualize human resource systems, to operationalize the concepts and to apply the appropriate measures to the chosen systems.

Assertiveness would, in fact, be difficult to operationalize; measurement would depend on observation of specific behaviours under controlled conditions. Group discussions are used in selection with this sort of purpose in mind, and their success depends crucially upon the careful briefing of observers.

Operationalization can also be illustrated by reference to other aspects of work behaviour. We may, for instance, wish to advance the theory that withdrawal from work is related to 'job satisfaction'. Such a conjunction could be important in developing strategies for effective management of the workforce. The danger is that the argument could become circular, in that both 'withdrawal from work' and 'job satisfaction' would be measured by observing absence. The problem is resolved by defining the conceptual content of 'job satisfaction' (no easy task, see Chapter 6) and establishing independent measures for each component: the result would be a questionnaire to be administered to employees to assess their subjective views of work content. We would need to be reasonably sure that 'job satisfaction' was a valid concept, that it represented something distinct in thinking about work. We would also like to know that it was related in consistent ways to other concepts in human resource planning, such as labour turnover and organizational size.

In studying attitudes to work it is desirable that the concepts should be relevant to the people concerned, rather than being imposed by the researcher. Pilot interviews, in which representatives of the target population are allowed to speak freely about their feelings, can provide the investigator with suitable ideas. A suitable technique is known as *repertory grid* (Fransella and Bannister, 1977). This has been used by Hutt (1983) in pilot interviews to assist the design of a survey of nurses' attitudes towards the prospect of returning to work after a career break. Nurses were asked to distinguish between different types of work they had done during their careers, thus revealing the concepts that they used. The questionnaire could then be constructed to investigate these relevant concepts.

Enumeration

Establishing valid concepts and categories is the first stage in social research, certainly in conducting the surveys that are its most common manifestation. The second is to discover reliable and valid indicators for valid concepts. These two stages were undervalued in much early manpower planning, and this neglect contributed to its unreality and lack of acceptance.

Unreliability may, of course, present itself in quite tangible ways. We may find, for instance, that a supervisor's records of absence behaviour differ from those maintained by the salaries department; further investigation is required before either can be accepted as reliable. Establishing the reliability of a test used for personnel selection would require statistical correlation of results obtained on two separate occasions.

The methods of enumeration employed in manpower research fall into three broad and interrelated categories. We may deliberately manipulate one of the variables affecting the situation under study, and observe the effect on another, while attempting to keep all other variables constant; the experimental method. This is seldom practical, and sometimes unethical when research concerns human beings. Direct observation, however, without manipulation of those observed, can be both practical and ethical, depending on the use to which the observations are then put. An example would be measurement of relative interest in college courses by means of library records, which, for the duration of each course, results in the more frequent borrowing of books to be found in the reading lists? This approach to observation is known as the use of non-obtrusive measures. Use of deliberately different teaching methods in each course would give this methodology an experimental character.

Survey methods allow us to enumerate systems as they are. Categories are chosen, and data gathered within those categories. Sometimes sufficient resources are available to put questions about aspects of categories nominally to the entire population; the census method. The best known example of this procedure is the national census. Casley and Lurey (1981) believe that conducting a census is the most valuable first step in improving the economic performance of a developing country. The same argument could be used to support an audit of manpower in a low-performing industrial company.

Censuses suffer from a number of drawbacks. Large-scale data collection is expensive, time-consuming and draws heavily on supplies of trained enumerators. The time taken both to collect data and evaluate it causes the census to be out of date when published. Expense precludes frequent revision. Some enumerators are less able than others and may allow bias to affect the results. Even good enumerators have difficulty in contacting all respondents in their area, some of whom may be reluctant to answer questions. The word 'enumeration' is strictly reserved for census data where, ideally, every member of the population is counted within categories. Its meaning is stretched slightly here to include counting within samples. Sample surveys, as distinct from censuses, can be conducted with less resources and therefore more frequently. Since fewer enumerators are required they can be better-trained and more thorough. Success depends on the validity of the initial assumption, that the sample is representative of the whole.

Representativeness is assured in two ways: the sample must be large enough, and it must be related in a rational way to the population being investigated. Statistical formulae exist to calculate the sample size required to achieve a given level of accuracy. Random samples are often used to ensure that each member of the population has an equal chance of being included. Randomness can, paradoxically, be assured by systematic sampling. We could contact, for example, every fifth member in an alphabetical list of the population under study. There should, of course, be no reason to suppose that the first letter of a surname is associated with the sample in a biased way.

Sometimes random sampling could result in a significant minority being completely excluded from the survey, so arrangements are made to include members of the minority group according to their importance. This is known as stratified sampling. When the survey is being used to test a particular hypothesis, enumerators may be instructed to find members of the population whose characteristics correspond with the groups to be compared, a technique known as quota sampling. In all cases, the survey design is aimed to achieve statistical significance and representativeness, at less cost and effort than a census would entail.

Questionnaires are used to collect data for surveys. They are completed during interviews, which may be face to face, or conducted by telephone or post. These procedures are subject to a type of bias called reactivity; the respondent reacts in a particular way to the interviewer or the questionnaire, and either fails to cooperate or biases answers in a particular way. This may take the form of not answering or making a biased statement, either through lack of understanding or lack of trust.

Response bias, a related source of error, can seriously affect the randomness in the sample, since certain members of the population may be more likely to cooperate than others. A well-known but useful example is the restriction of telephone surveys to those listed in the phone book. The random sample must be both willing and able to respond.

One of the important tasks of questionnaire designers is to test the reactions of a pilot sample to their questions. The approach to the selected members of the population should be such as to encourage cooperation. Tact and reassurance may be needed if the respondent fears that the information may be identified with individuals and used against them. The reader may like to consider the reaction of a workforce to the unheralded arrival of an interviewer who begins to ask them questions about absence behaviour.

Sample surveys, and censuses for that matter, can be conducted on data that already exists, and without questionnaires or interviews. This opportunity is afforded by the existence of records that the investigator is able to sample in a random or systematic way. Personnel record files should readily suggest themselves to human resource planners as a valuable source of data about the nature and behaviour of the workforce. As the case study at the end of this chapter indicates, however, their value in this respect could often be improved.

Computerized personnel records appear to be an even more tempting source for manpower research. Alas, computerized records are often compiled more for ease of administration than for ease of analysis, like the manual files before them. Payroll records are often just that; a means of ensuring that workers are regularly and accurately paid. Opportunities to gather and classify useful information about employees at the same time are just not taken. There is also a lamentable tendency, moderated in recent years by the need to keep minimal data against the possibility of an industrial tribunal hearing, to dispose of information about leavers. Needless to say, these are a prime source of data about employee behaviour. Long hours spent on the categorization of existing data, and putting up with maddening omissions, may give enthusiastic planners a sense of realism; most records are not compiled with their needs in mind. Specially designed surveys may be necessary from time to time to supplement the planner's database. Strategic human resource planning cannot be achieved without cost.

So far, we have discussed the gathering of what are referred to as 'primary data', that is, data which results from the investigator's own research. When working within one organization, the planner will usually gather and analyse data of this type. If information is required about, for instance, the local labour market, then 'secondary' sources will probably be used; the investigator will rely upon reports published by the Department of Employment or the National Census. Human resource specialists who work within government departments or agencies may rely heavily upon research reports produced by other civil servants or academics. Use of secondary sources does not relieve the researcher of the obligation to give attention to categorization and enumeration. Far from it! Many official reports concentrate on recording figures in tabular form and these will need to be carefully examined and re-tabulated to suit the needs of the research project. In developing countries, for example, reports produced for the World Bank are likely to concentrate on the financial aspects of a problem, rather than on the social effects of changing work patterns.

Description
Research into human resources should be conducted by carefully selecting valid concepts and categories, and then by using valid indicators to measure their occurrence in a representative sample of the population under study. That has been the message of this chapter so far, although the argument will be modified later in this section. So far we have concentrated on means rather than ends. The objectives of social research, of which human resource planning is an example, are to influence operational strategies and

organizational policies. In Halsey's (1972) already twice-quoted phrase, the purpose of social research is 'to inform the political debate'.

An advertisement for a 'Human Resource Planner' for London Underground, the corporation that runs the capital's rail-transit system, in the late 1980s was subtitled 'Making Data Talk'. Research findings can be influential only if they are clearly understood, first by the researcher who is required to provide an explanation, and then by those who need to take policy-making or strategic decisions. There is an element of journalism in the presentation of all research findings, as is evident in the catchy titles now used for papers in professional publications. Nor need this indicate a lowering of standards; the presentation of data in many newspapers and on television is often exemplary. Human resource planners need not be ashamed of learning from the media.

The commonly used methods of data presentation, and therefore of describing research, are tabulation, graphs and diagrams. Diagrams include histograms and pie charts. It is also possible to present research findings as mathematical equations, although this is more common in physical than social science. Since the human resource planner will be concerned to influence managements and government policy makers, trends and research findings should be communicated as simply and directly as possible. Equations are more suited to an academic audience. They can, of course, be used in another way; incorporated into computer models of the system under review, a career structure perhaps, they allow policy makers to test the effects of possible changes. Since the obvious course of action may also be the least suitable, the ability to explore alternatives is a powerful incentive to strategic thinking.

The use of diagrams is essential in all aspects of strategic management, whether these are directly concerned with human resource issues or not. Organizational systems are notoriously difficult to describe in words; a simple input–output diagram will focus discussion of a problem on essential issues, while organizational relationships can be expressed in a systems diagram, of which a career structure is only one example. Diagrams showing cause–effect relationships between various aspects of organizational functioning, reveal multiple causes and discourage oversimplistic reactions to problems. Human resource planners should be prepared to use their analytical skills in the service of all aspects of policy- and strategy-making, thus ensuring that the issues relating to people are given full attention. Figure 3.2 demonstrates the use of a multi-causal diagram in the analysis of a problem of absence behaviour in a factory. The research had revealed that working conditions were related to voluntary absence; factors contributing to perceived working conditions could be discussed to see whether improvements could be made. Alternative explanations could be investigated.

The problems of data presentation are the problems of data itself, indeed of research as a whole. The choice is between richness and comprehensibility. The more detailed the presentation, the harder it is to understand and to generalize. In research we may choose to spend a long time interviewing a few members of staff in order to get a full understanding of their attitudes to a proposed change in working methods—this has the virtue of richness—but generalizing the findings to a large number of similar works could be hazardous. A questionnaire administered to the workforce as a whole would reveal general attitudes, but their use for the management of individuals would be slight.

In data description, this dilemma gives rise to problems in both tabulation and the presentation of diagrams. The age distribution of a workforce is one of the oldest and also one of the most important tools of manpower and human resource management. The reason is that the shape of the histogram suggests immediately to management that strategic problems of recruitment, retention or redundancy are likely. Designing a histogram, however, requires the choice of class intervals. If these are too narrow, the histogram will 'break up' because there are too few instances in some or all of the categories, so five-year class intervals may have to be 'collapsed', to use the technical term, to 10 years. The danger in this unavoidable simplification is that 10 years is a long time in a working career. People at the age of 29 may be very different from others of 39, and between those ages may themselves change in many ways. With the swiftly altering attitudes to careers that are reported elsewhere in this book, only the most tentative assumptions can be made about the group of workers 'in their twenties', let alone any other decade. Yet this data may be all we have; it must be properly presented, and then used with circumspection. Strategic thinking requires that statistics are balanced by common sense, and by an awareness of social and economic change.

This point can be made again in relation to tabulation. Table 3.2 illustrates the association between different aspects of a manpower situation. It has a meaning, however, only if the numbers in each cell of the table are large enough, and if the number of cells is small enough to allow the reader to take in the relationships between them. This is one reason why summary tables should be used in the main text of a report, the detailed tables reporting individual items being confined to the appendix. Summary tables are also the starting point for statistical analysis, to reveal the strength of association between variables, or the significance of an apparent difference between two distributions (see, for example, Table 6.7). If we look for interesting associations where the numbers in cells of the table are too small, their significance may not be supported by the size of the data. Strategic recommendations derived from this analysis are vulnerable to attack. If we collapse the data to obtain significant associations, however, the subtlety of differences within the workforce may be lost, again with consequent weakening of policy and strategic recommendations. Statistical significance is itself no final arbiter. The stated level of significance represents the acceptable risk in making an inference from the data. Whether this is pitched at one in 20, one in 100, or one in 1000, is finally down to personal judgement. The same argument applies to the regression lines plotted to reveal correlations between the two variables, the basis of forecasting by trend lines, among other uses. Apart from ignoring the fact that catastrophic change could nullify the assumption of a trend, the correlation itself is assumed to be statistically significant. Given the likelihood of secular change in the environment, time spent in raising the significance level of such data may well be wasted. Though computer models may be able in some sense to compensate for this problem, their output is derived from regression equations, and they share their faults. Policy makers and strategists should use

Table 3.2
Readiness for promotion to product manager (30 managers interviewed)

Experience	
21 have potential but lack experience	3 already doing similar work satisfactorily
5 of doubtful potential	1 doing similar work unsatisfactorily

system models to explore alternatives, but not as the sole basis for final judgements or recommendations.

Explanation

The psychologist Hans Eysenck said that there is nothing so practical as a good theory. It is unfortunate that 'theory' should have come to mean the opposite of 'practical' in the minds of non-scientists, and particularly managers. Theory is the mainspring of research, and research is essential if enterprises, whether public or private, are to become strategic by learning from past experience. In no area of an organization's activities is this more important than the use of people. The human resource planner needs theory, derived from experience of manpower systems, in order to categorize a workforce appropriately for the task in hand, to explain his findings to others and to suggest which line of inquiry should next be followed.

Theories, of course, are provisional. The purpose of further investigation is to refine or falsify earlier theory. The replacement of theory does not make it 'impractical', any more than the replacement of worn parts in a motor is an impractical procedure. The replaced components have given service, and the discarded theory has done the same.

There is no denying that theorizing in a social environment brings with it problems not usually found in the closed world of the scientific laboratory. Social systems are open systems, subject to irregularities in the social, economic and political environment. In a laboratory, the physical scientist controls temperature, pressure and other extraneous variables so as to concentrate on the sole effect of the factors to be purposively changed and measured. Theories in physical science are also provisional, but they can usually be stated more explicitly than theories about human beings. They are thus easier to falsify.

Theories about labour markets and manpower systems may derive from any of the human sciences: psychology, sociology, economics, geography and economic history. As reported in Chapter 1, a plea for manpower planning to be an interdisciplinary study was made as early as 1971, shortly after the subject was appropriated by the mathematicians. It is important, however, to distinguish between interdisciplinary and multi-disciplinary approaches. Edwards (1983) put together, under the heading of manpower planning, a series of essays relating to their specialist subjects by economists, psychologists and industrial relations experts. This provides a multi-disciplinary approach without a unifying methodology. This book is dedicated to the premise that it is the research methodology that binds the strategic study of human resources together, leaving room for interdisciplinary contributions at the explanatory stage. The important difference is that the disciplines do not re-interpret human resource planning each for its own purpose, but contribute each perspective to a unified concept of what planning in this area should be.

It is significant that many published reports in the general area of human resource planning stop short at description, leaving the explanation to the sponsor or to the general reader. The reason is not far away, and illustrates the important relationship between explanation in research and subsequent strategy- and policy-making. The organization that sponsors research is, so the shrewd research team might think, best left to draw their own conclusions without the implication of criticism. If the researchers have an underlying theory, they keep it to themselves. This is a pity, because other research teams' work has to start theoretically from scratch.

Where possible, however, the human resource planner should be prepared not only to explain the data from manpower research to other workers in terms of known theory, but should also be prepared to make that explanation available to management or sponsors. Discussion of theory is, once again, part of the strategic process.

Theory makes its entrance, of course, rather earlier in the process of manpower research, in fact at the point of categorization. The researcher will use at least an implicit theory in deciding under what headings to collect data, and the categories might owe a great deal to earlier workers' research and explanations. Research is often conducted to establish the extent to which an existing explanation can be generalized to a different setting.

If the research is particularly original, or takes an unexpected turn, new theory should be generated. While this should be a matter for rejoicing in academic circles, the implications will need to be handled sensitively in relation to policy-making and organizational strategy. The human resource planner may need a Janus face, looking in one direction towards the policy makers, and in the other towards the theorists. This stance is not only possible, it is also both practical and creative. For nearly 20 years, the University of Aston (in Birmingham, England) ran a research degree programme known as the Interdisciplinary Higher Degree (IHD) Scheme. Students from a wide range of first degree disciplines were sponsored by employers to undertake research projects that were aimed at the improvement of some aspect of organizational functioning—technical, systems or related to the management of people. The scheme achieved both the immediate objective of problem-solving, and developed good research students who also became good managers. It could quite reasonably be said that research, so far from being a remote alternative to a career in management, actually enhanced the student's managerial ability. They were, in addition to other skills, able to think strategically. We will return to this topic in a later discussion of career development.

Cause: the crucial issue

In developing theory, policy and strategy from research data on human resources, we cannot avoid the issue of cause. Managers will want to change working conditions and discourage behaviour when either are perceived to have an adverse effect on business effectiveness; they will want to promote conditions and behaviour that improve output and quality. Assumptions are made about these matters in everyday management; human resource strategists should be able to assess the extent to which variables are causal.

In physical science, experimental design allows the control of extraneous variables, so that the experimenter can concentrate on the effect of one variable on another. Philosophers of science doubt whether even this allows valid ascription of cause. Karl Popper (1959) maintained that the physical scientist's rigid control does not permit the assumption that, because B varies with A, this necessarily 'proves' the theory that A causes B, even when other potential variables are held constant. In his view, proof is never possible, only disproof by means of an experiment that falsifies the statement that B varies with A. Science is not a matter of proof, but of falsification.

In our pursuit of human resource strategies, however, this philosophical point need not disturb us too greatly because practical problems are even more pressing. One of these is the difficulty of achieving the physical scientist's control over variables; some of those taking an intelligence test may be jet lagged, for example. Another is knowing whether the conclusions obtained in research, say within a small government office, could also be applied in a much larger one many miles away. This is the problem of generalizability. Common sense, and a readiness to be open to new data, must be a practical weapon in the armoury of the human resource strategist.

Common sense is also needed in considering the general problem of cause in human resource research, even without the issue of falsification discussed above. The nearest we are likely to get towards establishing cause in our work is to discover that two phenomena occur simultaneously, or that one variable co-varies with another. Examples would be research showing either that those with post-school education also scored above average in an intelligence test, or that intelligence scores varied with the level of educational qualification obtained. In the first case, we could claim an 'association' between education and measured intelligence: in the second, a 'co-variation' between intelligence and educational attainment. In neither case would assumptions of cause be justified, although common sense might dictate that, in the absence of other evidence, we accept that the first causes the second. We could, however, explore the possibility that a third variable, social class, was related by heredity and educational opportunity to both the others. This explanation is referred to in research parlance as the 'intervening variable'.

As with categorization, there is no guarantee that we have got it right; merely a provisional conclusion for further investigation as opportunity arises. This has important implications for the use of research in policy-making and this issue will be the subject of further discussion in Chapter 8.

Theory generation and theory use, especially in the case of human systems, will often require more than explaining the effect of one variable upon another; 'this varies with that because . . .' Variables may interact in multi-causal systems like the one illustrated in Figure 3.2. Systems like these are difficult to research but, once mastered, provide a more realistic basis for strategic management than simple cause and effect systems, or decisions with no theoretical underpinning at all. There is nothing so practical as a good theory because, like a carpenter's saw, it is a tool of the trade. From time to time, however, the tool may need resetting and sharpening.

Quality and utility in social research

The strategic process requires that human resource planners, technologists, financial experts, and indeed anyone else who can contribute, be brought together to work on common problems and to understand each others' points of view. There are blocks, however, that strategic teams will have to overcome if they are to work effectively. One of these concerns the professional's desire to be right. Readers of learned journals will have been irritated by the statement that 'further work is needed before the conclusions stated here can be fully accepted.' This is to place the theoretical purity of research above the strategic and policy aims.

Data is never sufficient, and taking decisions on the basis of some hard information is much better than working solely by personal hunch. Colleagues should not, however, be surprised or distressed by the need to review conclusions as new data come to light. If this holds for carefully controlled experiments in the laboratory, how much more should it be the case for the uncontrolled or partially controlled observations and surveys that the human resource specialist will carry out.

Why social research is so vulnerable to criticism is a topic to be explored in its own right. The concept of validity has already been introduced, once in relation to the conclusions derived from research, and once in relation to the effectiveness of selection procedures, particularly psychological tests. Two types of validity apply when discussing a research project: *internal* and *external validity*.

Internal validity refers to the consistency and appropriateness of the methodology used, chiefly the extent to which it was possible to exclude random and unassessable variables. This is an aspect in which research in physical science is strong; researchers will go to great lengths to control temperature, humidity, light and so on, if these might be thought to affect the outcome. People are poor raw material for those who wish to conduct experiments in the social sphere; they have two major drawbacks. The first of these is that people differ markedly, in background, in attitudes, in skills. While the researcher may try to match samples selected for different treatment, this matching is always far from perfect. The second is that people are self-aware, and legitimately contaminate the researcher's motives with their own. Most often, in normal conversation, we wish to say things that are socially acceptable; it is difficult to break this habit when the conversation is yielding data for an experiment or survey.

Because of this lack of control, and uncertainty about data, there will always be doubt about the cause of a particular effect, in more than the Popperian sense mentioned above. Often, this is a matter of multi-causality. Which of several reasons for an effect should we accept as the basis of our strategic decisions? It might be difficult, for example, to separate the effects of parental influence, educational background and general intelligence on the acquisition of a particular skill, since these variables could be closely related.

External validity concerns the extent to which the findings of a research project, however internally valid, can be generalized to groups or persons excluded from the research. This may be because the research itself affected results, perhaps because a test used to select subjects also affected their later responses, or because the experiment itself was too unlike real life. The most important aspect of external validity for the human resources strategist is the transferability of conclusions from one place to another or from one time to another. A test used validly to select engineering apprentices in the South of England may not also be valid in Scotland, perhaps because of differences in the educational system. Still less may it be valid in the Caribbean, for reasons that are explored in Case Study 4. The results of a questionnaire survey to establish job satisfaction among workers in 1975 may not hold good in 1990. Values and social perceptions change. Prediction of future behaviour by extrapolation of trend lines is particularly vulnerable to invalidity caused by changes in the environment. If some administrative change is made on the basis of the trend line, the expected change in trend may occur by accident, thus falsely justifying the original action. The world of economic management is particularly susceptible to this problem.

So there are good reasons for the human resource strategist, or any other purveyor of social data, to be cautious about conclusions. But there is a difference between proper caution and waiting forever for perfect data before suggesting action. Managers grow understandably impatient with exaggerated caution. Provided it is clear to all that the file is always open for amendment, strategic management can continue.

Raven (1989) began an article on the necessity of research to the proper formulation of public policy (or strategy) by referring to Rothschild's (1982) analysis that too much social research was overly academic and individualistic. Policy-relevant studies (strategy is also implied here) tend to be messy, and require research to be pushed to the uncomfortable stage of making recommendations. Raven reinforced these arguments by saying that research was a necessity rather than a luxury in a modern managed social and economic environment. He also pointed out that the necessity for research to establish what their 'customers' really wanted would conveniently be ignored by administrators who wanted to do their own thing regardless—an observation no less true of the senior managers of some private organizations. Raven generalizes this problem into a discussion of the unresponsiveness of all large organizations to the needs of their supposed customers. He sees the answer in a form of appraisal for administrators and managers in these organizations that would take account of their track record of innovation. Towards improved, customer-responsive innovation, Raven suggests that the primary need is comprehensive research into matters of social concern, and organizational structures in which managers are constrained to listen to the findings.

Raven's article was written for psychologists, but he mentioned a wide range of social research. Human resource strategists may wish to focus rather closer to the people who are their special area of expertise; the workforces of public and private enterprises. Meyer (1982) called for the balancing of economic research and theory with an investigation of motives: 'Economics tells you what people do, but not why'. Raven himself subtitled his article 'Why psychology should replace economics as the key discipline in policy development'. While it would be inappropriate to suggest that human resource strategists should replace market research specialists in the decision-making processes of enterprises, they undoubtedly deserve a place alongside them. Among other common concerns, they share the methodology of social research.

In the next chapter we consider the central human resource issue of personnel selection; in so doing we will see how social research methodology underlies administrative practice. In the case study that concludes this chapter, we will concentrate on the two first stages of the social research model: categorization and enumeration.

CASE STUDY 2
Assessing the internal labour market: researching human resources

To conclude this chapter we will look at a routine but necessary aspect of human resource planning—auditing existing staff to assess strengths for strategic development. The purpose is to illustrate the use of simple research techniques, and to reinforce the points made earlier about methodology.

This case concerns a medium-sized company in the fire-protection business. Until the time of this study, it had enjoyed continuing commercial success. It had been acquired by a large conglomerate, but operated independently in marketing and manufacture. There were about 1100 on the payroll, of whom 400 were staff. The clouds on the horizon were the ending of patent protection for one of its major manufacturing processes and, unbeknown to most of the directors, an intention by the parent group to dispose of the company to raise much-needed cash. At this point, the manpower planning manager was asked to conduct an audit of qualified employees and managers, and to make a presentation on the subject to the company directors and a member of the parent board. Two months were available for the research. This left little time for gathering and analysing data.

First hopes were pinned on the personnel records but these, as so often is the case, were woefully inadequate for the task. They contained many letters on administrative matters, but even basic demographic information was missing. The planning manager realized that interviewing staff at the three widely scattered sites would be the only satisfactory way to get the data he needed.

The next task was to decide which information to collect in order to present a balanced picture of managerial strengths in his report. This fell into the following groups:

- Demographic information
  - gender
  - age
  - length of service
- Quality information
  - academic qualifications
  - current function
  - occupational experience
  - managerial experience
- Attitudinal information
  - readiness to move home
- Judgemental information
  - suitability for promotion within existing function
  - suitability for a more generalist role

The last of these categories of data was required because the then managing director had plans to convert the existing functional structure into a product-oriented one.

Data was collected in 20-minute interviews with the 130 staff above clerical or routine technical level who were in the UK at the time of the survey. Readers will recognize the census method. A standardized form was used to guide each interview, and for provisional recording of subsequent data. Enumeration was conducted by tabulating answers in columns, for later aggregation and conversion into descriptive diagrams.

Age and length of service were recorded directly from the interviewee's answers, and data presentation was by histogram with an appropriate class interval. The results are shown in Figure 3.3. Gender presented no problems of categorization, neither in theory nor practice; all those interviewed (1978) were male. To his shame, the manpower planning manager does not remember finding this remarkable; nor did the members of the board when the information was presented to them!

Categorizing qualifications presented a more difficult problem. Employees possessed a range of different degrees and professional qualifications; their relative intellectual value would probably take an informed committee some weeks to decide. The planner decided to take a short cut by assuming that the significant dividing line would be between graduate qualifications and the others. Full membership of major professional bodies would be categorized within the graduate group. Higher national qualifications presented a further problem, but these were categorized with graduates as those with HNDs and HNCs appeared often to be doing the same jobs as graduates. Categorization problems of this kind are often best solved by reference to the realities of the workplace.

The significant finding was that over half the key employees interviewed had graduate-level qualifications as defined in the previous paragraph. This was substantially higher than the percentage of graduates among similar employees in the company's parent group.

How people use their qualifications and abilities is at least as important as the attributes themselves. Enumerating experience, both functional and

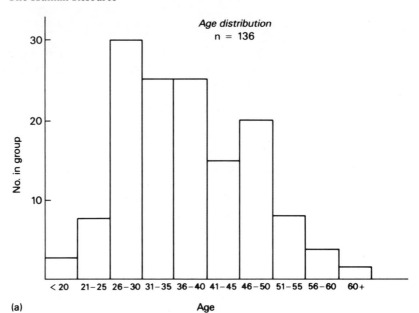

Figure 3.3
Age and length of
service distributions for
non-clerical staff (fire
protection company)

(a)

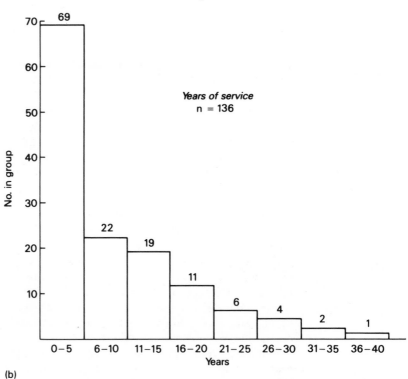

(b)

managerial, requires a category system for both. Here we encounter one of the
most difficult problems in manpower categorization. These difficulties may be
summarized as follows.

Occupation?   Within a medium-sized company, like the one under investigation here,
categorization by occupation is deceptively simple. Occupational boundaries
are apparently reinforced by departmental ones; acccountants are to be found
in the 'accounts department', and production managers in the 'works'. But the

manpower planning manager's concern was not so much with the current use of people as with their potential. The managing director, it seemed, would be more interested in where the company could go than in being told what he already knew from his daily interaction with staff. Potential is measured by the totality of work experience, rather than by current function. Many unsuitable decisions about promotion, and especially also about redundancy, have been made on the basis of the current function of an employee. The production manager, for example, who might also be a qualified accountant, has skills that could be used not only in finance but in other areas of company activity. It was necessary to audit not only current function, but also past occupations in order to give a rounded picture of the human resource.

In the event, the manpower planning manager chose a set of occupational categories that were closely related to the organizational structure. Neither the time available for the study, nor the sophistication of the intended audience, allowed more subtle category systems to be used. During the interviews that provided the data for the audit, staff were asked to describe their duties and responsibilities in present and previous jobs, and to give an indication of the level of their responsibility on each. On the basis of this information, the manpower planning manager assigned each job to the appropriate category. In so doing he had to assess whether the experience claimed would have contributed significantly to the development of knowledge and skills.

Significant experience? Experience is a product of environment, the demands made on skills and time. For experience to be significant, it is necessary that an employee should do more than observe what is going on in a particular department, or perform some temporary function within it. If that were sufficient, the unimaginative 'graduate training scheme' that encourages trainees to spend short periods 'getting to know all aspects of the company' would, within their first year, produce many highly experienced managers. Significant functional experience requires that the employee should have responsibility to management and colleagues for measurable tasks within a department, and a sense of identification with it. How much time this requires is debatable, but the manpower planning manager chose to regard one year's work within a function as the minimum to claim experience of it. Modules of experience reported on Figure 3.4, which also illustrates the category system used, were assigned on this basis.

Managerial responsibility? If the human resource planner has problems with categorizing occupations, they are as nothing compared with categorizing managerial responsibility. In the late 1980s, there was a heated debate in the British Institute of Management, business schools, the Training Agency, and among training managers, about the feasibility of defining management as a range of 'competencies'. There was general agreement that managers were not receiving sufficient training. One school of thought maintained that the identification of competences would assist in the targeting of training effort and in accreditation. The counter-argument was that management was a holistic activity, requiring both knowledge and skills, and that it was a process rather than the application of a repertoire of distinct and measurable activities. 'Competencies', as distinct from 'competence', were a side issue.

These sophisticated arguments were unavailable to the manpower power planning manager some years before the 'competencies' debate, and they might not have helped if they had been. Decisions had to be taken quickly.

Figure 3.4
Experience of staff by
occupational category

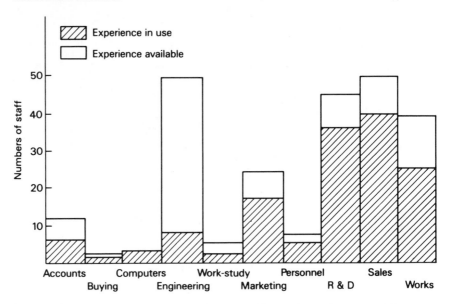

Figure 3.4
Experience of staff by
occupational category

The manager's solution was to consider two dimensions of managerial activity: allocation of resources and staff supervision. The allocation of significant resources, particularly money, would be considered managerial activity: whether or not staff supervision was also part of the job. Those whose jobs required them to oversee staff, but not to plan and allocate resources, were to be categorized as supervisors rather than managers. The application of this rough and ready system is illustrated in Figure 3.5.

Mobility?   Prediction of staff mobility is important from two points of view: likelihood of loss to the organization and willingness to move within it. Wastage of staff, especially in the early days of manpower planning, was the best-researched area of worker behaviour, and the various indices of labour turnover were the major contribution of the statistical school.

In this instance, wastage rates for the level of staff being evaluated were not available because nobody had thought to collect them. Among professional

Figure 3.5
Distribution of staff by
managerial and
supervisory experience

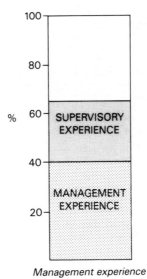

Management experience

Figure 3.6
Categorization of
employee attitudes
towards moving home

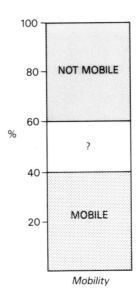

and managerial staff, of course, the decision to leave is highly personal, and is not satisfactorily represented by the indices calculated for large groups of people doing the same type of work. The former tend to make highly purposive choices made on career advantage rather than immediate gain and the circumstances affecting that gain, and the opportunities to pursue it, change rapidly. But some indication can be obtained by observing past patterns of job choice, and by listening, even in a short interview, carefully to the feelings expressed about perceived quality of work, and of life in general.

People are unlikely to give a direct or particularly accurate assessment of their own feelings in answer to a direct question about whether they might wish to leave the company; and asking 'Would you be prepared to move to further your career?' would elicit only a guarded reply. The manpower planning manager was forced to rely on inferences drawn from the tone and content of the interview, and the data about previous job moves, especially how changes of domicile were justified to family and friends. Current family circumstances could also be assessed. As Figure 3.6 shows, a straightforward decision about the likelihood that employees would be prepared to move was not always possible. Although attitudinal data is difficult to obtain and interpret, however, attempting to do so should be part of the human resource planner's professionalism.

**Management
potential?** Judgement of potential is notoriously difficult, even when a well-designed appraisal system is in place; both people and jobs change, and success at one level does not guarantee success at another. Assessment by one superior may not match assessment by another, for a variety of reasons. In this instance, assessment of potential was easy for some of the staff interviewed, those who already had product manager roles. Even in a short interview it was possible to gauge their competence and enthusiasm for demanding work of this type. Others, however, had experience across a range of functions, but were untried in general management. Others, yet again, had the motivation required but lacked experience outside one functional role. It was necessary to assess the evidence from both past job history and the tone of the interview that general management potential was there. A good interviewer who can adopt a neutral stance, and who is not directly concerned in the interviewee's work, can often

see qualities that go unnoticed in the everyday commerce of manager–subordinate relations. Given the time available for the whole audit, however, it must be admitted that assessment of potential was its least satisfactory feature. It may well be the human resource strategist's most difficult task.

The results of this part of the study are shown in Table 3.2. This rather ad hoc categorization suggested that some members of staff were ready for greater responsibility, that others had potential but needed wider experience. Management development programmes could be devised to meet this need.

The accumulated data was duly presented to the company directors in the presence of a representative from the group main board. All seemed gratified by the picture that had been created of a well-qualified team. Whether they had also grasped the strategic implications is less certain. The data could be summarized as follows:

1 The study had covered all available members of the staff in important posts within the company.
2 A high proportion of this group were young and had been employed by this company for a comparatively short time.
3 Their potential was revealed by good academic or professional qualifications, and by experience in a variety of functions, often already at managerial level.
4 Such people might reasonably be expected to seek other jobs unless good career opportunities were offered to them. The management style of the company was highly paternalistic, and it seemed to the manpower planning manager that trusting younger people with greater responsibilities would not come easily to the existing board.
5 There was potential to expand the engineering activities of the company without recruiting additional staff. In view of the problems with some of the existing products, such a move might have been good corporate strategy.

This study illustrates two major issues related to human resource planning. The first is that it is possible to do useful manpower research in a short time, even when existing records are poor. This requires the purposive choice of manpower categories, and both a knowledge and an acceptance of their shortcomings. Explicitly addressing the issues of categorization, enumeration, description and explanation contributes to the validity of the work.

The second issue is that a thorough research job of this type does not guaranteee a good outcome for the staff interviewed or for the researcher. The group main board representative showed the greatest interest in the conclusions, and asked for a personal copy of the report. Within two years the parent board had sold the company to raise much-needed cash; in the ensuing staff changes, the manpower planning manager found himself free to pursue his research in an academic environment!

In other circumstances, it would make sense to audit the key staff of an organization at least once per year. Computerized staff records, unavailable at the time of this study, would help, but both judgement and direct contact with the people being audited, would still be advisable. Computer records are no better than the categories used and the data enumerated within them. Career decisions, as we shall see, are often made opportunistically, rather than as planned changes in life-style. As such their likelihood is difficult to assess and record within computerized databases. Analysis of well-structured and representative data, however, can help management to understand the organizational influences upon individual career decisions.

References   Bennison, M. and Casson, J. (1984) *The Manpower Planning Handbook*, McGraw-Hill (UK) Ltd, Maidenhead.

Casley, D. and Lurey, D. (1981) *Data Collection in Developing Countries*, Clarendon Press, Oxford.

Edwards, J. (1983) *Manpower Planning: strategy and techniques in an organizational context*, John Wiley & Sons, Chichester.

Fransella, F. and Bannister, D. (1977) *A Manual for Repertory Grid Technique*, Academic Press, London.

Goddard, J. and Thwaites, A. (1984) 'Unemployment in the North: Jobs in the South', from *New Technology and the Future of Work and Skills*, Marstrand, P. (ed), Frances Pinter, London.

Halsey, A. (1972) *Educational Priority Vol 1: EPA problems and policies*, HMSO, London. Passage on page 77 reproduced with the permission of the Controller of HMSO.

Hutt, R. (1983) *Sick Children's Nurses*, Institute of Manpower Studies in association with the DHSS, IMS, Brighton.

Meyer, B. (1982) 'The research programme of economics and the relevance of psychology', *The British Journal of Social Psychology*, **21**, 81.

Popper, K. (1985) *The Logic of Scientific Discovery*, Hutchinson, London.

Quinn, J. (1980) 'Managing strategic change' *Sloan Management Review*, **21**, 4, 3.

Raven, J. (1989) 'Democracy, bureaucracy and the psychologist', *The Psychologist*, November, 458.

Rothschild, Lord (1982) *An Enquiry into the Social Science Research Council*, HMSO, London.

Sokal, R. (1974) 'Classification: purposes, principles, progress, prospects', *Science*, **185**, 115.

Walshe, K. McGill, D. and Pearson, R. (1982) *The Methodology of Labour Market Analysis*, DHSS/Institute of Manpower Studies, Brighton.

Wittgenstein, L. (1958) *Philosophical Investigations* (2nd ed.), trans. Anscombe, G., Blackwell, Oxford.

The science of selection

Selection in a free market

Personnel selection, is self-evidently, a pivotal issue in human resource strategy. This is no less true because long-term commitments to employees are giving way to short-term contracts. There is less time for adaptation and training when recruits are expected to become quickly effective, to make their contribution and move on. For that reason alone, the topic would rate a chapter at this point in the book.

Yet selection is also an excellent illustration of the potential for 'management by research'; the move away from the administrative to the strategic in human research management that has been advocated in earlier chapters, and which will be developed in succeeding ones. In essence, an effective selection procedure is an exercise in social research. Jobs are described and analysed to establish the factors that make for successful performance. The selection procedure assesses personal characteristics related to those factors. The research hypothesis is that what is tested during selection will predict job performance at a later date. The administrative approach to personnel management places stress on procedures rather than outcomes; the hypothesis frequently goes untested. Human resource strategy assumes that we will learn from our mistakes.

Selection also relates in an important way to the discussion of labour markets in Chapter 2. When good candidates are at a premium, it is important to be clear what the characteristics of a 'good candidate' really amount to. How much of the current personnel specification is traditional, related to out-of-date expectations of the educational system or perceptions of the social requirements of the job? The human resource strategist should regularly review both national and local labour markets, not to bewail their inadequacies but to devise ways in which organizational needs can be matched to the people available. This flexible approach must also be applied to the organization's internal labour market—indeed, it may be said to start there.

In its early days, manpower planning concentrated on the formulation and analysis of what Bennison and Casson (1984) referred to as 'manpower systems'. These were diagrammatic models of organizations, taking the form of a hierarchy of grades, that were assumed to correspond to different types of work and to different levels of pay and status. 'Manpower systems' also indicated by means of arrows the flow of people between grades, and between the organization and its labour market.

The inclination of manpower planners at this time was to concentrate on career management, assessing the implications for the workforce if grades were kept constant in size, or for the organization if promotion prospects were maintained regardless of the need for people in particular grades. These approaches corresponded to 'pull' or 'push' views of promotion in large organizations. The appropriate statistical models were known as 'replacement' and 'Markow', and both required assumptions about wastage rates from each grade. They are capable of summarizing and describing accumulated data, but not of providing theoretical explanation. Categorization is crude, often related more closely to the status of employees than to their effectiveness. How the flows are regulated, within the organization, or between the organization and its external labour market, goes unquestioned.

This way of looking at organizations nevertheless had its value. It encouraged a critical assessment of long-term policies for career development, at least in the management of large concerns with low turnover rates. As our earlier discussion of labour markets has revealed, however, the 1990s will see less opportunity for this approach. The fluid nature of employment, which became evident during the 1980s, and which Atkinson (1984) incorporated into his concept of the flexible firm, implies that much greater importance should be given to the selection process. People may stay with a particular employer for a comparatively short time, but that stay should be as productive as possible. The responsiblity for management of careers is passing to employees, and management of personal contracts looks like replacing career structures as the concern of employers. Human resource planners will become 'casting directors' rather than 'actors' agents'. The career management task, where it still exists, will itself depend more on assessment of individuals than on the description and adjustment of rigid structures. Skill-shortages will place a premium on the human resource planner's ability to allocate people to the work that they can do best. Appreciation of selection theory and practice will overtake the more traditional emphasis on career management within organizations.

It was implied in the opening to this chapter that recruitment takes place all too often without careful thought about the nature of the job, the factors that will make for success, and the measures which could be applied to discover whether candidates possess the desired skills or personal characteristics. Where these issues do receive attention, the selectors may be said to be using the psychometric method of selection, because of the psychological devices that are used to assess candidates. The phrase 'psychological devices' calls to mind tests, but the psychometric method can be conducted effectively using only interviews, provided that these are structured to gather job-related information.

Neither does the use of tests and questionnaires, however enthusiastically they may be sold, ensure that more successful candidates will be appointed. The tests must be related in some logical way to the requirements of the job. Even then, error-free selection cannot be assured; psychometric selection is an experiment in social science. Every recruitment programme is an exercise in predictive validity. The previous chapter introduced the process of operationalization, relating a measurable quantity to a concept. To validate our selection methods we need to operationalize both performance in the job and performance in the selection procedure. Validity is measured by the strength of the relationship between these two variables. This is unlikely to be particularly high unless the chosen measures are also reliable.

There is more to effective selection procedures than psychometrics, however. Identifying satisfactory candidates is only half the battle; they must also be motivated to accept the offer of a job. Neither manpower planning, in its earlier manifestations, nor psychometric selection, gave sufficient attention to the social relations between candidates and selectors. This point has been well made by Herriot (1984), who warned that the psychological contract between candidate and employer may be broken off, by either side, both before and after recruitment. When talented people are in short supply, the balance of power shifts towards them, and the risk to the employer is increased.

Herriot pointed out that psychometric methods can be criticized from two points of view. The first concerns the lack of concern for the social aspects of selection. The selection procedure may be applied in such a way that candidates are alienated and quit the procedure, or recruits may leave shortly after starting work because its nature was not fully explained. The second criticism relates to the psychometric method itself. Those who profess to use it may fail to do so in a professional way. Among other things, professionalism requires the validation of the selection methods. To quote Herriot (1988) on graduate recruitment, 'If we consider the pre-selection stage, few organizations even have stated criteria, let alone explicit weightings of certain areas'. Pre-selection is the stage at which many graduates are weeded out before meeting the employer for an interview. To understand this criticism, we need to know rather more about selection theory.

Psychometric methods: some essential concepts

Selection procedures can look like meaningless ritual, and frequently that is how they seem to the candidates subjected to them. Yet the fact remains that the selection methods used daily by thousands of different employers are, consciously or unconsciously, a prediction of a given candidate's likely success in the job. This is true whether the selection procedure is organized or informal, well-considered or slapdash. As the late Professor Alec Rodger used to tell his students at Birkbeck College, 'selection is concerned with satisfactoriness for the employer and satisfaction for the employee'. The employer anticipates that the person chosen will both perform the job effectively, and remain with the organization at least long enough to repay the cost of any training given.

The grounds for these predictions may be scientific or impressionistic, and are frequently a mixture of the two. Managers who state categorically that they 'can tell a good candidate the minute he walks through a door' are sometimes maddeningly right. Intuition has its uses; what is much less satisfactory is that impressive-looking and expensive selection instruments sometimes show little advantage over intuition. The fault often lies with those who profess to use psychometric methods without fully understanding them. What are the conceptual bases of the selection process? Is it possible to regard personnel selection as a science?

Even at their most sophisticated, selection procedures do not produce infallible results; everyday experience suggests that they are not totally predictive. But the psychometric method can be defended as systematic, if not scientific. This approach requires accurate job analyses, detailed job descriptions, personnel specifications and task analyses. Tests and structured interviews are devised to provide information about an individual's suitability in terms of skills, aptitudes, and disposition. Sometimes, these psychometric techniques are combined into a 'battery', and administered at an assessment centre, along with practical tasks and group exercises.

The claim to scientific prediction rests on some ideas that we have already encountered in Chapter 3, chiefly those of concept, indicator and operationalization. A scientific prediction is one that links the perceived suitability of a candidate to later effective performance in the job. The concept of 'good performance' must be operationalized as a measurable quantity. Examples would include production output, sales obtained or patients successfully treated. Whatever the measure, it is referred to in psychometric theory as the 'criterion'. The concept of 'candidate suitability' must also be operationalized, as performance in test or interviews, or perhaps by reference to success in a previous job. This variable is known as the 'predictor'.

Having established two measurable quantities, scientific prediction requires that we establish the relation between the two. It is this stage that is so often lacking in the daily use of tests and interviews by personnel managers. In social research, including scientific selection, we must be aware of the need for reliable and valid measures. Readers may like to return to Chapter 3 to remind themselves of the meaning of these terms.

A predictor, be it a test, an interview or an assessment centre, cannot be predictive unless it is reliable. That is to say, it must give reasonably repeatable results with the same candidates. Reputable test designers will provide customers with the reliability coefficient for the tests that they offer for sale. These are derived by one of two methods: *test–retest* or *split–half*. The test–retest method is the obvious way of seeing whether a test gives repeatable results. It has its dangers, because the test is applied to human beings and not to inanimate machinery. Humans have the capacity of learning, and some improvement may be anticipated from one presentation to the next.

The split–half method consists of dividing the test into alternate questions, and administering the halves on different occasions to the same subjects. Learning can still affect the result, in terms of understanding the test situation, and familiarity with the content. The subjects, however, are presented with different items on each occasion. The correlation coefficient between the results for each subject on the two tests becomes the 'reliability coefficient'.

Once the reliability of a test has been established, it is logical next to inquire to what extent the reliable test can predict job performance; in the language of both psychometry and social science, we need to establish the validity of the test. For most purposes, it is the predictive validity of the selection procedure that determines its usefulness. Yet there are many barriers to establishing this elusive property.

The most important of these barriers is the difficulty of knowing whether the criterion, no less than the predictor, is a reliable quantity. For decades, the 'criterion problem' has dogged the efforts of occupational psychologists to measure and correlate work performance. Readers need do no more than think about the criteria of success in their own jobs to see how convoluted the problem is. Performance is, of course, measured daily. Managers need to assess the value of their staff, and often use highly subjective criteria to arrive at an answer. Appraisal interviews are conducted on the assumption that subjectivity can be avoided, though not always convincingly. Performance-related pay is predicated on the idea that job performance can be both objectively measured and related directly to rewards. This link has been made in the past, with varying degrees of success, in the use of payment by results systems on the factory-floor. The Hawthorne studies (Roethlisberger and Dickson 1939), and many others since, have shown how these are regularly subverted by those they are intended to motivate, so that the ability of an employee to carry out a repetitive task would be inaccurately measured by payment or output.

But the importance of repetitive production-line tasks is diminishing as automated and robotized production takes over. Many manual jobs now require a much higher degree of personal responsibility and a much wider range of skills than hitherto. The success of a particular worker may depend as much on an ability to coordinate a number of actions as on the possession of task-specific skills. The argument that 'the whole is greater than the sum of its parts' applies with even more force to managerial work. In high-level manual work, such as the maintenance of complex systems, knowledge and general skills in problem-solving are replacing the craft skills of old. Middle managers with mere 'competence' are being replaced with computerized information systems. Management at all levels now requires the strategic approach outlined in Chapter 1.

The definition of a criterion, then, depends first on establishing what constitutes success in a particular job. The second stage is to find a measure of that success, and then to decide how far the worker has control over it. We may say for example, that the success of a general manager is primarily financial, and that this can be measured by profits earned, or by market share obtained. But how far are either profitability or market share entirely within the manager's control? Three years of steady success may be blighted by one year of failure, strongly affected by macro-economic conditions outside his or her control. The criterion, if it is to be representative at all, may have to take account of average performance over a period of years. Criteria, to be valid, must be chosen on the basis of careful consideration of the purposes and nature of the job.

Criteria must also take account of the range of objectives that a worker is expected to achieve. Is the manager, for example, expected to obtain short-term profitability at the expense of the future reputation of the company? Are there cognate objectives related to the human resources of the company? Plainly the criterion must take account of the differing aspects of successful management; in psychometrists' terms, it must have content validity.

Theory into practice

The reader would be right to suppose that establishing a satisfactory criterion is no easy task, and even those conducting scientific investigations into the effectiveness of selection procedures often have to make do with second best. Monahan and Muchinsky (1983), in a study of selection research over three decades, stated that the criterion used in most cases was a 'supervisor's rating'. Anyone familiar with the ways of supervisors would be wary of such a subjective measure. An improvement can be obtained by getting ratings on the major components of the job, and then combining the individual scores into an overall criterion. It may be necessary to weight the scores to reflect the relative importance of the components in job performance. Job evaluation can reveal those factors that are important in job performance, and also indicates their perceived value. Rating performance on these important factors offers one method of getting reasonably accurate and relevant criterion measures.

Having established a workable, if far from perfect, criterion of performance, and discovered a reliable predictor, the next stage is to establish the relationship between the two. Ideally, this would be accomplished by assessing a range of candidates for a job, recruiting across the range of scores and then observing performance when they had all settled into their work. This is both time-consuming and, in many cases, impractical. But it is the surest way of establishing the predictive validity of the test or selection procedure. Testing current employees to establish 'concurrent validity' may have to suffice.

The relationship between the score at selection and later performance is illustrated in Figure 4.1(a). Ideally, the graph of criterion performance against predictor score would be a straight line, allowing direct and accurate prediction of performance level. Since neither predictor nor criterion, however,

Figure 4.1
a) The idealized relationship between the score at selection and later performance
b) The effect of cut-off score in the selection of candidates
c) Differential validity of a test for two groups of subjects

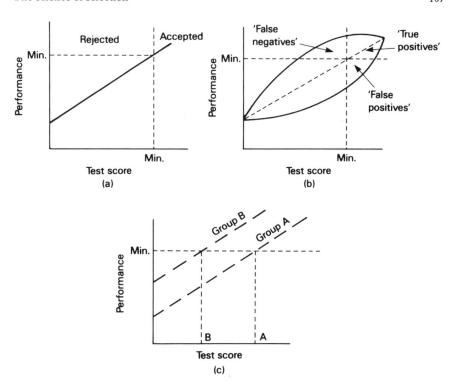

are 100 per cent reliable, the graph will exhibit considerable scatter. The correlation of one quantity against the other (see Chapter 3) is referred to as the coefficient of predictive validity. Some very important consequences arise from the fact that this coefficient is always less than unity; 0.6 might be considered good.

Figure 4.1(b) shows the effect of using a particular cut-off score in the selection of candidates. Here, the use of this score results in about 25 per cent of those tested joining the organization. The cut-off score corresponds to the lower limit of criterion performance. Candidates scoring above the cut-off will be accepted, those scoring less will be rejected. This process, which is the necessary consequence of the psychometric method, does not result in the desired selection only of successful performers, nor does it result in the rejection only of those who would be unsuccessful. Some of those selected will not reach an acceptable criterion performance, in spite of scoring above the cut-off at selection. Some of those who would have been successful in their work are rejected. Those who are both selected and successful are referred to as 'true positives'; those who are rejected and who would have been unsuccessful are the 'true negatives'. The extent to which a selection procedure identifies each of these groups is a measure of its satisfactoriness. All selection includes the risk of selecting 'false positives' and 'false negatives'. To those who seek assurance in the validity (perhaps infallibility) of psychometric selection procedures, this comes as a sad surprise. To those who are disappointed by the predictive power of the average employment interview, the fact that even the best-researched selection procedures can fail may be some comfort.

Selection, however, is not necessarily about predicting the success or otherwise of the individual candidate. Human resource planners should be the first to agree that an organization would also welcome an improvement in the average performance of the workforce, whether this takes place within a department or on a wider scale. The decision to use a particular selection procedure should depend ultimately upon this consideration.

Figure 4.2 demonstrates the improvement in work performance that may be achieved by using a test of moderate predictive validity (0.6). The oval shape in Figure 4.2 illustrates the scatter of test results that would be obtained at this level of validity. Two other concepts are necessary in evaluating the utility of a test: the selection ratio, which is the percentage of tested candidates who are appointed, and the percentage of current employees whose performance is considered satisfactory.

We will first assume that the current average level of work performance is represented by C2 on the criterion axis; 50 per cent of the currently recruited employees perform satisfactorily. By applying the moderately valid test and appointing only those who achieve at least an average score (a selection ratio of 0.5, represented by T on the test axis), average work performance is improved. Consider the ratio of true positives to false positives indicated by Figure 4.2 to assess the improvement. Using what are known as Taylor-Russell tables (McCormick and Tiffin, 1975), we could demonstrate that use of the test will increase the percentage of satisfactory employees in the selected group by 34 per cent.

The test yields less benefit if the existing procedures result in the appointment of a higher fraction of satisfactory employees (C1 corresponds to 75 per cent currently satisfactory). If existing procedures result in lower average performance than C2 (C3 indicates only 25 per cent of existing employees currently performing satisfactorily), then the benefits of the test are correspondingly greater.

The selection ratio itself has a marked effect on the value of the test. If the latter has only moderate validity, a high proportion of success can still be obtained by appointing only very high scorers. The penalty is that the proportion of false negatives is increased so potentially good candidates are discarded. When the selection ratio is high, the test will have little selective effect. When the selection ratio is low, however, and the average performance of the existing staff is low, significant improvements in job performance are possible even with a moderately predictive test. When measured against the extra cost of the selection procedure, the performance gain could still look very attractive.

Figure 4.2
The effect of selection ratio on the effectiveness of a selection test
Source: McCormick, E. J. and Tiffin, J. (1975) 6th ed, *Industrial Psychology*, Prentice-Hall, New Jersey

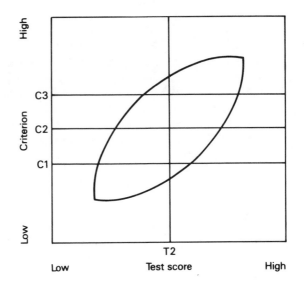

What makes a good test?

So far, we have considered three types of validity in selection: there is the validity of the performance measure, and the concurrent and predictive validity of the predictor. Predictive validity depends not only on the validity of the criterion, but also on the test's ability to sample effectively all relevant aspects of performance. This last is known as content validity.

Testing for personality characteristics provides a good example of the problems of content validity. In Chapter 3 we used 'assertiveness' as an example of a quality that selectors might desire in satisfactory candidates. Questionnaires or group exercises might be used as indicators, but users would need to be assured not only that they had defined 'assertiveness' operationally, but also that the selection methods were fully sampling 'assertive' behaviour. As implied earlier in this chapter, the careful thought given to the definition of criterion measures should improve the human resource planner's understanding of manpower requirements.

A selection procedure can be assessed, as in the foregoing discussion, in operational terms; does the test or selection procedure correlate with job performance, either among those currently employed or those recruited? For this purpose, the test need have no obvious relationship with the work done, either in appearance or via some related concept. Face validity indicates the relevance of test appearance to stated ability. For example, a test of skill in filing documents that requires the subject to list words in alphabetical order has high face validity. This may be important in gaining acceptance by those to be tested, but has little to do with the test's predictive validity. Personality questionnaires, or personality tests as they are sometimes called, usually depend on low face validity; the candidate is often unaware of the aspect of personality related to a particular test item. Some items, apparently like the rest, are included to discover whether the candidate is giving answers on the basis of social acceptability, the 'MD' (motivational distortion) items in the Cattell 16PF personality questionnaire being an example.

The essential feature of an effective test is that it should be predictive of job performance in a particular situation. The user does not necessarily have to understand its conceptual basis. An understanding of their conceptual bases, however, will make the choice of appropriate tests quicker and less haphazard. If we can think conceptually about work, a necessity for strategic human resource planners, then tests can be chosen for validation on the basis of their underlying concepts, and the relation of the latter to job content.

It will help here to consider intelligence tests and academic performance as related but separate predictors of job performance. Academic success is used extensively as an indicator of suitability, and every application form contains a space for listing exams passed. Intelligence tests are frequently used in personnel selection; they have high reliability and reasonable face validity which helps their acceptance by candidates. What they measure has been a matter of heated and continuing debate by psychologists for over a century. Graduate candidates, usually when the job market is working in their favour, have been known to resist being tested on the grounds that their academic achievement says all there is to say about their mental abilities. For some subjects, such as classics or mathematics, where logical ability is needed more than factual knowledge, this assertion could be true. But the dispute raises the question whether tests and examinations are measuring the same thing and, if not, what are they measuring? We are concerned with the conceptual basis of each method of selection.

Let us suppose, for want of a better definition, that human beings vary in the speed with which their mental processes operate, the cause being largely biological. The man in the street has little difficulty with such an idea, being quite ready to classify acquaintances as 'quick on the uptake' or 'slow-witted'. Although this ability will be needed in varying degrees during academic study, in vocational training and at work, it may not correlate very well with any of these. Psychometrists would claim that intelligence tests are tapping into an ability that is fundamental to, but separate from, attainment. The educationally subnormal are very unlikely ever to achieve a university degree, however hard they might work, while gifted children find most academic study so easy that it requires wilful negligence on their part not to do well. In between, performance on academic or work-related tasks requires a combination of intelligence and motivation to succeed. Selectors may legitimately be interested in each of these factors, so that both intelligence test scores and examination results have a separate but related part to play in selection.

Academic achievement and intelligence are different concepts, and the tests used to measure them must each have concept validity. One way of establishing the concept validity of intelligence is to note that it is correlated with academic performance, as logic suggests that it should, but that the correlation is only partial, as required by its separate nature. The validity of the two concepts, as useful but separate ideas, is established by this relationship. Selectors should not confuse them.

Intelligence tests may be used to illustrate the remaining interpretations of validity in relation to selection procedures. If the items in a test consisted only of questions related to knowledge acquired at school or college, it would not be achieving the objective suggested above. A test, supposedly of basic reasoning power, would actually be measuring academic attainment, and not discriminating sufficiently in favour of the former. Ability to exclude unwanted concepts while measuring the desired concept is known as discriminant validity.

An intelligence test based solely on spotting relationships between words might be doing at least part of its job, provided that the items were loaded on reasoning speed rather than academic achievement. But we might discover that some people did better on similar reasoning tests based on numbers or on pictorial problems. We would suppose that intelligence consisted of ability in all of these related but not identical skills. The American view of intelligence is that it depends not so much upon a general factor, as European theory has taught, as upon many separate skills. The American assumption is more egalitarian ('everybody is good at something'), but requires a more extensive range of tests to establish separate skills. In the UK, psychometrists might look for, and be interested in, different components of a test, but would nevertheless feel that the total test score was measuring some overall factor. The important aspect of this argument is that if we wish to measure a general factor, we also measure sufficient contributing abilities to make the final score meaningful; the test, in short, should have content validity. We last met this idea when considering the criterion of performance.

This section of the chapter has introduced some complex ideas about the basis of selection, and they are useful whether formal selection tests are used or not. Selection tests have the virtues that they can be standardized, and that their predictive validity can be established by correlation of an objective score against job performance. The selection interview is much more difficult to standardize. Indeed, it is the author's view that selection tests and selection interviews have different roles to play in the selection process. This point will be taken up later in the chapter. To assist those new to the concepts of validity in relation to personnel selection, definitions will be found in Table 4.1.

Table 4.1
Definitions of validity

—*Construct*: tested construct relates rationally to others
—*Concurrent*: test predicts current behaviour
—*Predictive*: test predicts future behaviour
—*Content*: test samples adequately the aspects of the construct
—*Discriminant*: test excludes aspects of unrelated constructs
—*Face*: test looks as if it measures the construct

One more concept related particularly to tests is required for the subsequent discussion—the idea of test norms. For any reasonably large group, intelligence test scores are distributed as shown in Figure 4.3. This is the familiar bell-shaped or Gaussian curve of normal distribution. The same shape would be found if the distribution of heights or weights were plotted as a graph. Dividing the x-axis into segments, deciles or quartiles, allows the selector to indicate how the candidate has performed in relation to the group. This relative performance, of course, depends on the chosen reference group. Test suppliers should be prepared to provide norms for a range of reference groups, but human resource specialists will probably wish to develop norms of their own as their data banks increase. Graduates can be measured against graduates, and technical assistants against people of similar background.

Figure 4.3
Distribution of scores in
an intelligence test

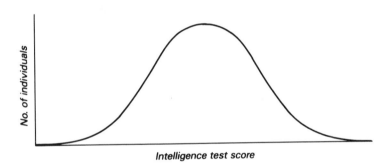

Intelligence test score

Are tests fair?

The role of the human resource planner is to provide objective information upon which strategic decisions can be made. It is assumed that all decisions at a strategic level must involve people, their capabilities and inclinations. It is a sad fact that organizations have a very limited understanding of the capabilities of their employees. Those who could make a contribution in different areas of specialist work are made redundant because their potential is assumed to be limited to one. Often the employees themselves are unaware of the fleixibility of their skills.

Tests are the basis of objective assessment, whether of applicants or of existing employees. The flexible use of people is likely to require more testing rather than less; tight labour markets require that candidates be allocated to appropriate work, rather than being selected or rejected for one job. The utility of reliable and valid tests in human resource planning is considerable.

The difficult labour markets of the 1990s may reflect the situation of 50 years before, when the wartime need for every able person to contribute in some way to the war effort was paramount. Psychological testing was pressed into service then, as it was in the American forces in the First World War. The psychometric selection of employees for peacetime jobs was brought to an abrupt halt in the USA during the 1960s by the Civil Rights movement. If it could not be proved that tests were fair to blacks as well as whites, litigation against the test user might follow. Whatever the practical utility of the test, the potential costs were too great.

Fairness is a difficult philosophical concept, and also a psychometric variable. The British Institute of Personnel Management, some 30 years ago, defined their specialism as concerned with 'achieving both efficiency and justice'. By implication, personnel selection, whether of new recruits or of internal candidates for promotion, should be concerned with both ideals. Unfortunately, they conflict. The efficiency of an organization may depend upon accepting only able people; justice for less able people in society may require that organizational considerations be overruled in the interests of giving them a chance of training and development. Organizations can do this only at the expense of efficiency or of greatly increased training costs. Employers may well feel that it is the task of the state, to whom they pay taxes, to educate disadvantaged groups to the point at which they could compete effectively for jobs with the rest of the population. In the interest of good public relations, or through a sense of social responsibility, employers may decide that they will give a disadvantaged group 'a chance'. This is a matter of policy, based on social values, which will in turn contribute to and constrain human resource strategy. The relationship between policy and strategy was discussed in Chapter 1. The human resource planner's role is to ensure that the extent of the likely performance deficits is known and allowed for in budgets for both formal and informal training. Tests can play an important part in this, aiding rather than denying the achievement of social fairness. To some, of course, tests will always be seen as 'racist instruments', designed to keep a minority in its place, rather as the '11-plus' examination in Britain was assumed to favour middle-class as against working-class children in selection for grammar school education. To others, tests reveal real differences between racial groups, which have biological origins. The responsiblity for choice finally rests upon the shoulders of the human resource specialist; fairness, in the sense of social justice, is determined by the intentions of those who apply selection procedures, whether these include psychometric testing or not.

But justice and fairness have other meanings here that are closely related to efficiency, the other essential item in the IPM definition of personnel management. Fairness can mean that a particular selection procedure gives equal opportunity to both the majority and to minority groups, even if less of the latter are actually selected; that is to say, that the test has equal validity for both groups. The human resource planner whose concern is with the efficiency of the workforce will use the test to select those most likely to be successful in the job, regardless of membership of any social group.

Some difficulties in the way of this approach are simple and others are complex. One of the more easily identified problems is uncertainty about the validity of the criterion, because this is common to all selection procedures, whether they require decisions to be made about different social groups or not. If the criterion of later job successes can be attacked for lacking content or discriminant validity, then users of a particular selection procedure are vulnerable to accusations of unfair discrimination. This is so whether psychometric testing is used or not. The defence against such accusations, and an expression of realistic social values, is simply to observe good practice; validation of selection procedures is essential to the strategic use of people, whether or not different social groups are involved.

If the predictive validity of a test is different for two different social groups (see Figure 4.1(c)), then different cut-off scores should be used. If the test is equally predictive for the two groups, then the same cut-off may be used, and the action defended by reference to supporting data.

More subtle issues, however, affect the use of tests. One of these is social, and the other concerns the detail of the particular tests chosen. The first has been referred to as 'situational bias', which is the effect of test administration on applicants from particular groups. Members of the group may be unused to taking written tests and find the procedure particularly threatening. If the administrator of the test belongs to the majority population, particularly one that is considered to be an elite, then those taking the test may feel inadequate. While good tests provide practise questions, and good test administrators do their best to put the applicants at ease, it may be difficult to gauge how far those anxious to do well may view the entire procedure as alienating.

More subtle still, and even more complex, is the issue of bias within the test itself. Written tests consist of two main elements: general instructions and the test items. In order to answer each item, the applicant has to understand the spoken instructions of the administrator, and the written instructions within associated with each item. The able administrator can encourage questions to clarify the spoken instructions, although anxious applicants may not wish to reveal their lack of understanding. Once the test has begun it is not possible to help them to understand what mental response the written instructions are asking for. So unfamiliarity with language will inhibit performance, whatever the stated content of the test. If the test is also intended to reveal verbal ability, and itself is based on the relationships between words, then the bias is taken one stage further.

But differences between groups are not confined to language—social and cultural background may also affect the outcome of the test. So items in the test may be biased for reasons of language and for reasons of culture. The process of answering a particular test item is illustrated in Figure 4.10. Case Study 3 at the end of chapter demonstrates how the differential effects of language and item bias may be investigated. Human resource planners should request help from the test supplier if they suspect that either issue is affecting the validity of the tests they use. Confirming item bias requires statistical analysis, for which reputable test suppliers will have computer programs.

During this discussion the author has used 'selection procedure' and 'test' almost interchangeably. This is to emphasize the fact that the discriminatory aspects of psychometric testing is only one source of discrimination in selection. Omitting psychometric tests from a selection procedure does not guarantee that it is free of unfair discrimination, quite the opposite. Tests are more open to checks on validity and item bias than interviews, since the data is more objective. If anything, the selection procedure that does not depend on objective testing needs even more careful attention from the human resource planner than those which do. Defending such procedures from accusations of discrimination requires very careful record keeping.

Describing jobs

Both efficiency and justice in selection depend crucially on the ability of human resource planners to describe fully and accurately the nature and quality of work done in the organizations for which they are responsible. A professionally-prepared job description is the essential basis for specifying the human qualities required, and the criteria for successful performance. Outside the scope of this chapter, job descriptions are required for job evaluation and equitable payment, and for appraisal and training.

The unsatisfactory description of jobs limits the range of candidates who apply, and causes many of those who do to withdraw at a later stage. To the vast majority of job-seekers a vacancy is identified with a job advertisement. However, the situations vacant columns give a distorted picture of job opportunities.

In the widest sense, a vacancy exists when someone realizes that it would be profitable to share out the work in an organization, together with the rewards for doing it; for example when a sole trader takes on a partner. Vacancies can also be created by the arrival of a well-written 'curriculum vitae', suggesting to an employer that the sender could contribute to the development of the business. In these cases, issues of scientific selection, or of fairness, hardly arise. The 'vacancy' in the first instance is a matter of adjustment between one partner and another; in the second, the candidate has created it in his or her image.

In the larger organizations, however, vacancies are part of a bureaucratic process. There are agreed manning levels, expansions may be planned, or staff may leave. At this point, vacancies exist and how successfully advertisements communicate 'what the employer is looking for' to candidates depends very much on the professionalism of personnel departments. In most large organizations, written job descriptions should be available; whether they are well-written or kept up to date is another matter. There are many possible ways of presenting formal job descriptions, one of which is illustrated in Figure 4.4.

Figure 4.4
Format of a job
description

JOB DESCRIPTION

JOB TITLE:

REPORTING TO:

DEPARTMENT/SITE:

OVERALL SCOPE AND PURPOSE:
(*in 30 words or less, why the job?*)

DUTIES:
(*a list of specific activities, in the form 'to ensure. . . .', 'to maintain. . . .', 'to control. . . .', etc.*)

RESPONSIBILITIES:
(*a general accountability for people, equipment, money and materials*)

SPECIFIC TARGETS:
(*quantified targets that the job-holder is required to achieve*)

LIAISON:
(*amount of contact with people inside and outside the organization*)

Considerable thought is required to complete such descriptions accurately, and the process is often skimped. Even when diligently researched, however, job descriptions may be criticized for giving too rigid a prescription of the nature of the work; it is clear, say critics, that jobs are negotiated on a day-to-day basis with others, both inside and outside the organization, and that individuals often achieve very similar work objectives by totally different strategies, according to temperament. While these arguments have some basis in experience, and no one would suggest that descriptions should become tablets of stone, it is fair to say that an organization that cannot provide written job descriptions does not know what sort of candidates it will be seeking, and will probably waste its own and the applicants' time.

What are the essential elements in a job description? The first is that it should indicate the job context: where the job is situated in relation to the organization, which department and to whom the job-holder will report. It would be useful to record under this heading any special conditions, good or bad, under which the work is performed. Jobs may be noisy and frequently interrupted, isolated from other people, or present particular hazards.

The next consideration is job content, and in particular the separation of routine duties from the responsibilities of the job. Responsibilities can usually be classified under the headings of people, materials, money and buildings. Delineating these will give some guide to the managerial content of the work. They will be a better guide to personnel selection if they are quantified: how many people, of different levels of competence, is the job-holder responsible for? What levels of spending without higher authority are allowed? Tasks should be analysed for their skill content, so that selectors need not be mesmerized by candidates with similar job titles. The transferability of skills will be discussed in greater depth in Chapter 7.

All jobs have their routine aspects, and these should be spelled out. They will be distinguished from the responsibilities because the action required will be precisely specified. Responsibilities require accountability without indicating what the job-holder is required to do; in fact, initiative and discretion may be encouraged. Jobs near the top of an organization will be stated mostly in terms of responsibilities; jobs near the bottom mostly in terms of duties.

Another aspect of job content may be specified targets. It was suggested that responsibilitites should, where possible, be quantified. If so, the job-holder can check the level of performance required. The same is true of particular objectives that the job-holder is required to achieve. This feature will be more evident in executive jobs than in those concerned with administration. Most jobs, however, contain some quantifiable tasks. Jobs associated with projects, such as civil engineering or advertising, are likely to be rich in quantifiable objectives.

The final stage in assessing job content is to consider job relationships. To what extent is the successful performance of the job likely to depend on good relationships and communication both within the organization and with people outside? Answers to this question will be required when considering the personality of a successful job-holder.

Where are we to get the information needed to answer the questions raised by the job description? The starting point, but only the starting point, might be the previous job description, if one already exists. As Chapter 2 has already made plain, jobs have been changing their character ever since the Industrial Revolution; under the influence of high technology they are doing so ever more rapidly. It is wise not only to update a previous job description, but to indicate in the course of re-writing it where further developments can be foreseen. This may cause the subsequent personnel specification to be broadened, and also allow the recruiter legitimately to offer prospects of career development to candidates.

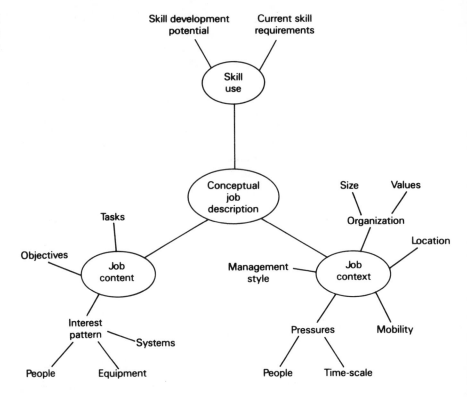

Figure 4.5
Concepts related to job
description

Good sources of information are people doing similar work, the job-holder's manager and other people who depend on the job-holder in various ways. A form of job description, called role analysis, is sometimes used in bureaucracies—this makes extensive use of the expectations of others. Too great an emphasis on this source, however, can reduce the scope for initiative in the job, as it becomes the lowest common denominator of performance. Job-holders become more effective by applying gentle pressure to those with whom they work, rather than by minimally meeting their requirements.

Figure 4.5 illustrates the concepts surrounding a job description, and provides a framework that ensures that all the essential questions are asked. It is capable of expansion by the human resource specialist to meet the requirements of particular organizations.

Specifying people

A well-completed job description will go some way towards suggesting what sort of personality, in the broadest sense of the word, might carry out the duties and responsibilities well: standard of education, previous experience and temperament should all be considered. These features can be formally listed in the personnel specification, which in turn forms the basis of an advertisement. A professional human resource specialist will distinguish between those features that are essential to the satisfactory performance of the job, and those which are desirable. To maintain a wide choice of candidates it is important not to overstate any requirement, especially education. The *seven point plan*, devised by Rodger (1952) is still a frequently used format for a personnel specification. It is illustrated in Figure 4.6. The seven point plan is no mere random list; it is based on a carefully thought out structure covering both the ability and the willingness to work in particular way in a particular place. It can be used both to specify people and as the basis of an interview plan.

The elements of the plan that concern ability are *physical characteristics*, *general ability* and *special abilities*, and *circumstances*. The last of these, unlike the others, is a feature of the social and physical environment of the applicant. Willingness to apply abilitites to desired objectives is demonstrated by *attainments*, *disposition* and *interests*

In considering physical characteristics we are taking account of social impact as well as physical strength. Both are sources of prejudice and discrimination unless the requirements are objectively spelled out. Jobs stated to need great physical strength will often exclude women; racial discrimination can enter covertly into a specification of 'acceptable appearance'. Where good grooming is an essential aspect of the work, however, this should not be omitted solely because it might be thought to be discriminatory. Justifiable stipulations are just that.

Attainments cover educational achievement, work experience and achievement in spare-time activities. Care must be taken not to over-specify the length of experience that is essential to job performance; there is a tendency for those who now do the job to overestimate the time taken to become proficient. Similarly, it is easy to overestimate the educational qualifications required to perform a job satisfactorily. As we shall see in Chapter 7, it is counter-productive to identify skills and relevant experience with a particular job title. Like overspecification of educational attainments, this unduly and unnecessarily restricts the effective job market.

General ability, the heading used in the seven point plan to cover intelligence, takes us back to the discussion of psychometric tests earlier in this chapter. Specification under this heading should be either fairly general or very specific. If testing is either impractical or inadvisable, it is better to state the requirement in terms of observable behaviour at interview: 'satisfactory candidates will exhibit the ability to discuss their previous jobs in a logical and objective fashion'. Stating this requirement as 'satisfactory candidates will

Figure 4.6
The seven point plan

PERSONNEL SPECIFICATION

PHYSICAL CHARACTERISTICS:
(*Appearance, manner, speech, and health*)

ATTAINMENTS:
(*Education, work, and spare-time activity*)

GENERAL ABILITY:
(*Intelligence*)

INTERESTS:
(*Mechanical, outdoor, social, artistic, etc*)

DISPOSITION:
(*Reliability, acceptability, self-reliance, influence*)

SPECIAL ABILITIES:
(*Mechanical, computational, musical, etc*)

CIRCUMSTANCES:
(*Location, salary, redundancy, family commitments, etc*)

be of above average general intelligence' assumes that interviewers are able to gauge intelligence and also have some mental picture of norms for the general population. Since verbal fluency is often mistaken for intelligence in ordinary conversation, and since very few people will have conversed with a sufficiently large sample of the general population, specifications in these terms are unlikely to result in accurate assessment.

If tests of intelligence are used, the human resource specialist has the option of using norms provided by the test supplier, or of developing norms by testing sufficient candidates and plotting the distribution curve for the scores. In the long run, development of norms related to recruitment needs has much to commend it. When an organization sets out to test candidates for the first time, of course, there is no choice but to use norms developed by the test suppliers or by other users. In specifying general abiilty, therefore, the human resource specialist must consider how intelligence is related to the particular job, and whether the requirement is to be specified in terms of the general population or the organization itself.

The word personality is much abused in general use, not least in phrases such as 'television personality', which confuse personality with charisma, or even with 'person'. It almost becomes possible to imagine that some people have personalitites and that others do not. At the other end of the scale, and equally misleadingly, the word is associated with instability, almost as psychology is confused with psychiatry; phrases such as 'personality problems' (which, by the way, are often organizational problems) tend to this distortion. In developing his seven point plan, Rodger preferred to keep the word personality to represent all aspects of a person; personality as holistic.

Yet it is essential to identify important personality characteristics if personnel specifications are to be effective. While not all managerial or sales jobs require greater than average assertion, many will, just as many jobs in the public sector require sensitivity to others. Once the necessity to specify personality characteristics is accepted, there is no lack of words to do so. There are a great many words describing personality traits, not all having generally-accepted meanings. Rodger avoided this difficulty by selecting just four traits that had particular relevance to the world of work: reliability, self-reliance, acceptability and influence. It is not intended, of course, that all acceptable candidates should be strong on all of these traits—that is neither likely nor particularly desirable. The human resource specialist should, however, be prepared to consider whether the job requires particular strengths in any of these aspects of personality, and whether weakness on any might rule a candidate out. As with physical characteristics, it is important not to let prejudice influence selection, any more than when considering gender or race.

The previous discussion is based on an assumption that behaviour is at least in part determined by enduring aspects of the personality, and not entirely by circumstances. Ascribing personality traits to others is one of the ways in which human beings give order and structure to their lives. We feel better able to cope when our family, friends and working colleagues are acting 'true to form'. Selection, as observed earlier in this chapter, is a matter of prediction. There do appear to be some aspects of personality that are relatively enduring, but even these change to some extent over time, and behaviour is manifestly influenced by social and physical surroundings.

If there are deeper and relatively enduring aspects of human personality, then there are also more superficial and less enduring aspects. Rodger identified *interests* as one such aspect that might affect job choice and personnel selection at a particular time in a person's life. Interests are nearer to attitudes than they are to traits. They affect the relative attractiveness of such aspects of work as whether it is conducted out of doors, whether it is scientific, mechanical or artistic, and whether it is concerned mainly with manipulating people or helping them. It is easier to specify the lack of interest that will indicate the unsuitability of a candidate rather than strong interests that are necessary. Interests, unlike intelligence, are not normative, and are best viewed as highs and lows within each individual, rather than in comparison with others. Prudent human resource specialists will be careful not to overspecify the pattern of interests essential for a particular job.

Earlier in this chapter we discussed the relationship of specific skills to general intelligence. Even in the British tradition, which relies on the concept of intelligence as a general factor, there is acknowledgement of two major sub-factors: spatial-mechanical and verbal-educational. The idea of two sub-types of intelligence underpinned the proposal, now abandoned, to select 11-year-old children for different categories of education. Published intelligence tests usually contain components that are intended to assess each of these separately. The two major sub-factors are assumed, in turn, to be made up of others concerned with skills in mechanics, drawing, literary tasks, languages and so on. Rodger's original advice was that where a candidate showed evidence, preferably by test score, of a high general intelligence, then the sub-factors were of less importance; where the general factor is not high, however, specific abilities should be given more attention. To an extent these can be gauged by the quality of job experience, and by work-related tests.

Six of Rodger's seven points concern the individual. The seventh point acknowledges that environment also has a place in determining whether a candidate wil be suitable. The job must have a salary limit and, if the candidate is prepared to accept less than current earnings, this needs careful investigation. Family ties might make it likely that the candidate would not remain long in the job if accepted. Until recently, closed shops would ensure that the membership of a trade union, or the willingness to join, could be an important factor in job success. However well-qualified an applicant may be on the other six points, circumstances must be right if the joint goals of selection, satisfactoriness and satisfaction, are to be achieved.

The seven point plan has been available for 50 years; it has stood the test of time, but it has not escaped criticism. Some of the criticisms have already been implied, and others will now be discussed. Most of all, critics object to the way in which plans like this appear to atomize human personality. It is felt that there should be a more holistic way of viewing human beings. There is also the feeling, quite close to Herriot's social view of the selection process, that the seven point plan is too individualistic, separating the individual's skills and disposition from the social environment: 'it takes two to tango' and, perhaps, to suffer a personality clash. Creativity may be more a function of a working group than of individual brilliance.

Yet the *reductio ad absurdum* of the social view of work is that we need not select at all, anybody would do for any job. If this is manifestly untrue—and it is—then specification has the virtue that it is possible to review selection decisions, and adjust selection procedures in the light of experience. Reluctance to specify appropriate candidates implies a reluctance to take responsibility for the outcome. That is not the road to strategic human resource management.

Rodger is also criticized for taking the organization too much for granted. He used the phrase, 'fitting the man to the job', in days when this was less likely than now to invite accusations of sexism. The analogy was with an engineer fitting a bolt into a hole in a sheet of steel. The selection decision was seemingly dependent on the unwavering characteristics of a bureaucratic hierarchy. Some jobs, perhaps, are still like that, but not many; in the 1990s there will be fewer still. Yet few managers, let alone human resource specialists, would deny that satisfactory performance immediately after recruitment depends upon specifying what that job requires. Indeed, success at this point may well be essential if a particular recruit is to get the opportunity to develop new skills and to change as the organization changes. The mechanical analogy may be both more realistic and more acceptable if the successful applicant is seen as an expansion bolt, able to gain entry to the organization, and then to press gently but firmly for changes. But it would be wrong to assume that Rodger felt that there was only one side of the bargain. His methodology was described briefly as 'FMJ–FJM': 'fitting the man to the job; fitting the job to the man'. Rodger can retrospectively be accused of sexism, but not of failing to realize that organizations, whether they are aware of it or not, adjust the nature of work in both obvious and in subtle ways to the idiosyncracies of human nature.

If the seven point plant has both longevity and robustness to its credit, it has also not lacked competitors. Munro-Fraser's *fivefold framework* (Figure 4.7) also has its adherents. This has the advantage of being two points shorter, and places rather more focused emphasis on physical characterisics, motivation and adjustment. Physical characteristics are re-cast as *first impressions*, emphasizing the powerful effect of appearance, speech and apparent health on interviewers. Motivation is viewed, not as an aspect of interests, but as a trait in itself. People are assumed to have a reserve of energy that they pour into any activity which is related to desirable goals. This energy is revealed, according to the rationale of the plan, by setting attainable goals and then pursuing them steadily and purposefully to completion. McClelland's (1961) theory of achievement motivation, a trait assumed to be dependent upon social conditioning in childhood, seems to support this particular notion. It is further assumed that motivation, in this sense, can be generalized from one activity to another. Adjustment, stability in relations with others, is seen as a key factor in job success. The remaining two factors, *brains* and *abilities*, and *achievements*, are closely kin to general ability and attainments in Rodger's plan.

This discussion of ways in which it is possible to specify good candidates for jobs has two objectives. First, human resource specialists should be able to take an analytical view of work, and the many-faceted people who perform it. Analysis is a prerequisite of the strategic approach. Secondly, well-tried formats for personnel specification have been introduced, not primarily as models to be slavishly followed, but as the basis from which practitioners can develop their own plans for particular jobs in particular situations. Analysis

Figure 4.7
The fivefold framework
Source: Munro-Fraser
(1971)

F—Face to face impact

A—Acquired knowledge and qualifications

B—Brains and innate abilities

M—Motivation

A—Adjustment

requires only that jobs and people be looked at from several different aspects; this adds to the holistic view of both, rather than detracting from it.

Criteria by objectives

Validation of selection procedures depends on the establishment of criteria for job success; only then can tests and other selection methods be tested for predictive validity. Job success, however, is the product of the application of the appropriate and necessary skills. So it is important to distinguish between product and process in the performance of a job, much as we did when considering, in Chapter 2, the application of technology to manufacturing. Criterion validity of a test presupposes that the skill detected by the test is effectively deployed so that desired objectives are achieved. It is this distinction that justifies the attitude of those who would base selection on evidence that the applicant has, in previous situations, achieved the set objectives. How this was done is less important than the fact of achievement.

Some 20 years ago, the technique known as *management by objectives* enjoyed a vogue in Britain and in other parts of the world. There were three purposes that its supporters wished to achieve: getting managers to regard their jobs in an entrepreneurial way; taking responsiblity for setting and achieving objectives that supported those of the organization; and placing emphasis on output at the expense of method. Up to a point, what managers did was their own affair; what they achieved was the concern of their employers. Rewards were assumed to favour the successful achiever.

The procedure of management by objectives was as follows. The organization's plans were analysed to discover *key result areas*. The manager's job was then analysed to discover which key result areas his operations supported. *Key tasks* for the manager within these key result areas were then identified, and he or she was then asked to consider what would be reasonable *performance standards* for each task. These were to be numerically defined wherever possible. Regular performance reviews allowed the achievement of standards to be measured. Where the practically achievable standards were too low, the manager was encouraged to devise an *action plan*, making changes that would ensure higher performance in future.

Two major difficulties stood in the way of the successful adoption and exploitation of the management by objectives system, which apparently offered better results for employers and better career development for employees. It was said that individualistic objectives militated against teamwork, by setting members of a team against each other. Whether there was any truth in this criticism is hard to gauge, since teamwork can be built into the objectives if needed. Rising staff unionism, and the undermining of cosy, but unproductive, relationships seems more likely. Secondly, there was the problem that, in a decade of pay held back by counter-inflationary policies, it was difficult to reward managers and key staff for achievement, whether management by objectives was used as the measure or not.

The early 1980s were, in several countries, a period of recession and redundancy—an inauspicious time to introduce this particular approach to self-management. It may be significant that, in Britain, it is a more entrepreneurially-minded public sector that is introducing performance-related pay, based on the management by objectives concept. Whatever the difficulties of this reward-led system, it will have the virtue of focusing management's attention on criteria, and perhaps also on their explicit description. Human resource planners and other specialists should take heart;

they can begin to test the criterion validity of selection and promotion procedures.

But they should remember that test and personality questionnaires measure skills and attitudes. Criteria measure the achievement of objectives. Tests are necessary to establish likelihood of success in new recruits; as careers develop, the criteria themselves become the predictors of further success, relegating tests to diagnoses of strengths and weaknesses that the achiever will learn either to surmount or bypass in order to reach organizational and personal goals.

Selection is social?

Herriot's (1984) advocacy of the social interactive approach to recruitment was mentioned at the beginning of this chapter. He pointed out a useful contrast between the organization selecting graduates by what they understand to be a psychometric approach, and the person-centred attitude of most career advisers, who see themselves as helping their graduate 'clients' to surmount developmental hurdles in their lives.

Herriot states that neither approach is satisfactory, because both are too narrow. What is lacking is an understanding of the continuous social interaction between organization and employee, and the fact that successful performance is determined by the effectiveness of this socializing process. There is no once-and-for-all developmental change from education to employment, and no once-and-for-all fitting of the satisfactory candidate to the organization. Readers may like to consider how far this view fits their own experience of selecting people for jobs, and of being selected. The logic of Herriot's analysis dictates that employers should spend more time telling candidates about the requirements of the jobs they are offering than in devising and administering psychometric procedures. That way there would be less opportunity for false expectations on either side. In another publication (Herriot, 1989), the same author underlines the number of occasions during the selection process on which the candidate is able to withdraw. The further the selection procedure has progressed, the more costly is the withdrawal of the candidate to the recruiter. Frankness in the early stages about the nature of the organization, and its selection procedure, makes for cost-effective selection, may well improve the recruiter's image and may save the candidates' time. As with issues of prejudice and discrimination, the demonstration of criterion-related validity also helps candidates to appreciate that participating in tests and exercises is not a ritualistic charade. Herriot has gone so far as to suggest that graduate candidates should take tests at a centre, rather than repeating them at a number of employers' premises. In addition to saving time at a crucial time in their education, candidates would then own the test results, and it would be up to them whether they chose to reveal them. Although some way short of this ideal, it is good practice for those administering tests to agree to explain the outcome to candidates, and to offer counselling.

It is hard to deny that recruitment is a social, and not merely a psychometric process, but the two do not have to be seen as alternatives. Giving candidates accurate and relevant information about jobs and employers enhances rather than replaces valid psychometric procedures.

Selection methods

So far we have concentrated on intelligence tests as an example of selection techniques. By now the reader will be in no doubt that the choice of selection methods should be based on a careful analysis of the job. This starts with the preparation of a job description and personnnel specification, and may continue with an analysis of tasks carried out, and of skills required.

But what selection methods are available? The following discussion is based on the list in Table 4.2. Managers who do a lot of selection interviewing may sometimes feel that they have slipped out of their intended role into those of the career counsellor or psychiatric consultant. Candidates who present themselves as having these needs, of course, are not usually helping their chances of selection. Selectors prefer to appoint those with a clear view of their career objectives and no apparent signs of mental distress. There are certain, particularly stressful, jobs for which qualified psychiatric assessment would be apropriate, however. A discussion of reactions to previous employment that, in a skilled selection interviewer's hands, gives indications of a candidate's disposition, might well not predict likely reaction to, say, the stresses of work as a bomb disposal expert. Selectors would be wise to hand over the assessment on this score to those with relevant training; in fact most would be keen to do so.

Table 4.2
Selection methods

1 Clinical
2 Personality questionnaires
3 Repertory grid
4 Group discussion
5 Ability tests (tests of general or specific abilities)
6 Attainment tests (e.g. the exam at the end of this course)
7 Work-sampling
8 Assessment centres (a combination of the techniques listed above)

A desire to leave the extremes of personality assessment to interviewers with clinical training, however, does not deter selectors from freely categorizing candidates by personality traits: 'I thought the second person we interviewed this afternoon was rather withdrawn'. The seven point plan suggests assessment of personality on four traits (see above): reliability, self-reliance, acceptability and influence. Evidence to support judgements on each is gathered by getting the cadidates to talk about their experience. The Cattell 16 PF questionnaire, as its name implies, offers ratings on 16 possible traits; the Kostik and OPQ questionnaires, 20 and 30 traits each.

On the face of it, getting a candidate to complete a questionnaire is more objective than making judgements based on statements during an interview. The questions are standardized, and so is the scoring. The problem, of course, is the candidate; can we be sure that the questions mean the same to everyone, and how far does mood affect answers to what, in essence, are attitude questionnaires? The skilled interviewer can detect the effect of mood in the candidate's responses, and make allowances. The interviewer can rephrase questions that the candidate has apparently misunderstood. We are faced, in using these questionnaires, with doubts about reliability and validity. In clinical use, reliability may be unimportant, even undesirable; what is important is how the patient feels at the time. The Goldberg *general health questionnaire* is used in this way. In personnel selection, the objective is to discover the existence of stable traits, and reliability is important. Reliability coefficients of around 0.5 are quoted by suppliers of personality questionnaires. Human resource specialists considering the use of these should inquire into the reliability of any new questionnaire that they may be offered.

Figure 4.8
The difference between
the 16PF personality
factor profiles for the
same person measured
three months apart

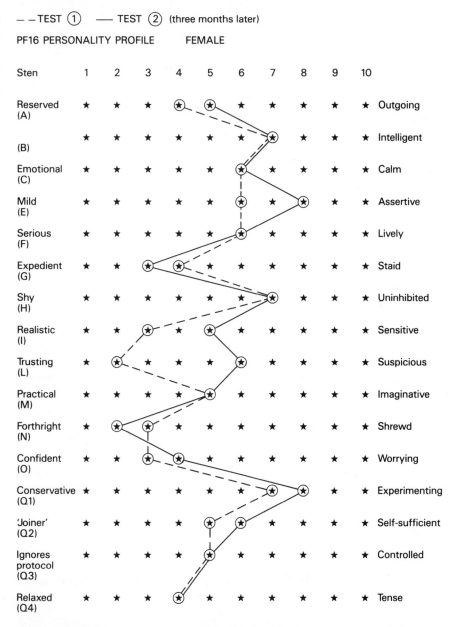

Figure 4.8 shows the difference between the 16PF personality profiles for the same person measured three months apart. While some traits do seem to endure, their expression is less extreme at some times than at others.

Questionnaires of this type can, of course, be criticized on grounds of both concept and predictive validity; will there be 'congruence' between what the test measures and the trait concept, and will the indicated trait have any meaning in terms of work behaviour? In asking these questions, we are challenging not only the concept validity of the questionnaire, but also the ability of the selector to analyse the criterion requirements of the job, and the predictive validity of the questionnaire. Answering such challenges is not easy. The traits recorded on the profile chart are revealed during test development by factor analysing the responses of large samples of respondents. They are statistically separate from each other, but this does not assure psychological validity. The statistical traits may, of course, be validated against observed behaviour and clinical practice. That this causes some difficulty is illustrated by the multiple names attached to traits on profile charts (Figure 4.8).

The predictive validity of questionnaires also depends upon the ability of the human resource specialist to define the job, and to specify the person who is likely to be successful doing it. This is true whatever the selection method. At best, only a few personality traits are likely to seem particularly relevant, either as requirements or contra-indications. Questionnaires that offer a wide range of personality information probably cloud what is already an ill-defined issue. The more recent personality questionnaires for use in selection tend to select traits that relate to behaviour at work, and this is welcome.

The attraction of personality questionnaires for human resource specialists is understandable. Many selection decisions later appear to have been ill-advised for reasons that can be ascribed to the job-holder's personality. Whether that ascription should be made is another matter. If a substantial number of unsuccessful trainees for sales appointments can be shown to have scored low on factor A ('reserved—assertive') on the 16PF, then there may be the basis for using this factor in future selection decisions. If only one or two show this correlation, then reasons should be sought elsewhere. 'Personality clashes', the stuff of boardroom battles, are as likely to be the result of faulty organizational structure, or badly defined objectives, as they are to relate to the traits of either party as revealed in a personality profile. The combative nature of candidates should, in any case, be evident from their occupational histories.

Personality questionnaires are more at home in counselling rather than selection: here the cooperation of the persons tested is more likely, and the outcome can be discussed openly with them and kept confidential from others. If used for selection, questionnaires should be regarded as providing tentative data, which will be validated through evidence obtained during a subsequent interview.

In a book comparing the virtues of personality questionnaires with those of intelligence tests, Heim (1975) made the point that the former impose categories upon the candidate. She pointed out that a more realistic picture of personality could be obtained by giving opportunity for free response; the *Brook reaction test* was cited as an example. The problem is that the interpretation of responses is lengthy, and would not be considered cost-effective in selection. An alternative would be to use the technique known as *repertory grid*

Repertory grid is based on Kelly's (1955) theory of *personal constructs*. In brief, this asserts that people act in ways that are consistent with the way in which they make sense of the world. Making sense amounts to drawing distinctions between groups of things, people or ideas. The distinctions are 'constructs', some of which are shared with other people, and others that are personal. The repertory grid is the method used to elicit the constructs that are important to a person at a particular time, and to arrange them in a structure that is a model of the person's world view. The important difference between repertory grid and personality questionnaires is that the former do not assume an unchanging pattern of personality; constructs are liable to change and elaboration as new information becomes available, and behaviour changes accordingly.

The elaboration of a construct series is an indication of expertise. A layman, if asked to say why one of the following—potato, tomato—differed from apple, might make an obvious but correct distinction and reveal the possession

of a 'fruit–vegetable' construct; a botanist might go on to demonstrate much
finer distinctions. The ways in which candidates make distinctions between
people indicates the ways in which they are disposed to act in given situations;
their depth of knowledge about people, ideas or things is demonstrated by the
elaboration of their constructs. Both can be investigated in a structured
interview, or by computerized questionnaire. The latter, however, might suffer
from a lack of face validity; candidates might prefer the apparently more overt
personality questionnaire while in fact getting a worse deal from it.

Clinical interviews, questionnaires and repertory grid are ways of drawing
inferences about candidates' personalities. From what they say, or the
response that they make on paper, the selector attempts to predict future
behaviour. A more direct way of attempting to assess people's personalities is
to do what we do every day—observe their behaviour in real situations, make
guesses about personality traits and use these to predict what might happen
on other occasions. This is formalized in selection procedures as group
exercises: selection for training as an army officer includes an exercise in
which candidates in turn assume the leadership of a group charged with some
complex task; would-be management trainees may be asked to take part in or
chair group discussions. The selectors observe the behaviour of all candidates,
whether they are leading the discussion or not.

The face validity of group discussions and other team exercises is high,
because much of the activity is plainly related to work. But there are problems
of validity within the exercises in the categorization of behaviour, and the
reality (ecological validity) of the situation. The difference between 'made
many constructive suggestions' and 'constantly challenged the authority of the
chair' may be a fine one. Whether people behave 'on parade' as they would
when participating in a group out of sight of the selectors is debatable.
Nevertheless, they do break the barrier between inferred and observed
behaviour. If the exercise itself requires the completion of a task, such as
getting a delicate case of instruments across a 'ravine' or making a committee
decision on the allocation of funds, then success or failure can be objectively
demonstrated. Reasons for success or failure may be rather more problematic.

Intelligence tests have the advantage over personality questionnaires in
reliability and predictive validity (Heim, Watts and Simmonds, 1974). The
narrow range of skills and behaviour tested by the former may, however, be a
reason for omitting them from selection procedures. The use of aptitude
testing in general is based on the assumption that, if basic skills are present,
they can be developed during training. In conjunction with acquired job
knowledge, the trained skills are the basis of effective performance. An
example would be the use of manual dexterity tests to predict success in
mechanical assembly tasks, or alphabetical sorting skills to predict success in
filing correspondence. As work of these types is done away with in the onward
march of industrialization, however, the usefulness of such tests begins to
wane. We are more likely to be selecting the multi-skilled than the single-
skilled. As one of the case studies at the end of this chapter reveals, tests of
programming aptitude as a specific skill are not particularly valid.

The objective demonstration of specific skills and knowledge is the purpose
behind attainment tests. A typing or shorthand test indicates not only the level
of skill a person possesses, but objectively demonstrates the level of actual
output that should result from well-motivated performance. Written or oral
examinations investigate not only knowledge but mental and presentational
skills. They are little used in the selection of employees, apart from Civil
Service trainees and indirectly in the assessment of candidates for the

membership of professional bodies. They could be used more, since they give comparatively objective data, and have face validity for particular types of work.

The argument against the use of examinations in selection is one already voiced in Chapter 2, that skills can be transferred between jobs, and that job knowledge is acquired in a new post as it is needed. This might be seen as favouring the concept of a general factor in intelligence; people with a high general intelligence can do most things quite well. In fact, evidence for the ready transferability of skills from one occupation to another is accumulating, and will be presented in Chapter 7.

Many selected candidates lack specific knowledge of a job before being engaged, yet acquire it quickly enough to be considered effective. We might hypothesize that professional examinations, which appear to be testing job knowledge, are actually assessing intelligence, determination to complete demanding tasks and transferable skills like analysis and written presentation. They are none the worse for that, although for some purposes the direct assessment of skills and intelligence may be more appropriate. As the mobile jobs of the future move away from adherence to one trade or profession, general testing will become more important.

Selection tests with the highest face validity are known as work-sampling tests; as their name suggests, a segment of daily work is administered to candidates, who are allowed to show how they would complete the task in real life. An example is the 'in-tray' test often used in assessment centre routines. A set of memoranda and other documents are presented to the candidate in the form of a file or in-tray. He or she is asked to assume that they are new to the job, and to take the most appropriate action; items overlap and interact, and the session may be interrupted by telephone calls. Scoring is far from straightforward, since the test is open-ended, and different forms of behaviours may be equally effective. The final appraisal may be more of style than of effectiveness. Nevertheless, the candidate will have had a good opportunity to experience this work at first hand, and this may lead to self-selection. Material from the exercise can be used at interview to explore reasons for actions, and thus indicate work-related personality traits. Work-sampling can, of course, also be applied to the selection of candidates for manual work. Robertson and Kandola (1982) have demonstrated the validity and acceptability of this method of selection.

So far we have reviewed the use of selection methods as if they were mutually exclusive; in fact, given a sufficiently large budget, they can be used in combination. The greater the range of activities in which candidates engage, up to the point of exhaustion, the greater the amount of information about them, and the more they will feel they have been given a chance to succeed. When the penalties of failure are high, or the commitment to the candidates' future is strong, then assessment centres may be used in order to take advantage of a wide range of assessments for selection and career development purposes. An idea of the complexity of assessment centres may be obtained from Table 4.3, which is reproduced from a paper by Dulewicz and Fletcher (1982). The authors state, somewhat wistfully, that the intelligence test was highly predictive of success in the centre as a whole. It was presumably one of the lowest cost items used at the centre. The cost of administering a large battery of tests and group exercises should not be underestimated, nor the opportunity cost of the senior management time required in the training and use of observers.

Table 4.3
Tests and exercises
used at an assessment
centre

In-tray exercise (items of managerial work)
Committee presentation
Committee discussion
Letter writing (situation requiring tact)
Business decisions (group exercise)
Business presentation

Source: Dulewicz, V. and Fletcher, C. (1982) 'The relationship between previous experience, intelligence, and background characteristics of participants and their performance in an assessment centre', *Journal of Occupational Psychology*, 55, 197

The human resource specialist must be prepared to assess the cost of selection against its potential value. This, like so much that is neglected in the strategic use of human resoures, depends on the capacity and willingness to get a clear picture of work and jobs, and what makes for their successful execution at a particular time in technological and economic history. There must also be a willingness to keep and analyse data, particularly about failures. That way the specialist can establish criteria of successful performance and choose tests, or batteries of tests and exercises, with predictive validity.

The social aspects of selection

Selection can be seen as picking the best person for the job. The previous discussion has emphasized the importance of assessing skills as a means to this end. But jobs are more than tasks, they are part of a social network. Here we pick up once again the examination of selection and early employment as social interaction.

Herriot (1984) has emphasized this aspect of selection, particularly in relation to the recruitment of graduates for large organizations. Small organizations can react and adapt to the arrival of a new recruit; large organizations are those to which Alec Rodger's phrase 'fitting the man to the job' most readily applies. Neither formal working procedures nor informal social norms can be flouted without cost to the individual employee.

Successful recruitment, in the sense of obtaining good candidates who also stay sufficiently long to recover the costs of initial training, depends on fully informing applicants of both the content and the context of work that they will be asked to perform. This requires both awareness and frankness on behalf of those charged with responsiblity for selection. Unfortunately, the odds are often against this. Selectors are cast in the role not only of judges, but also of salespeople. In attracting talent they emphasize the benefits to future employees and omit the rest. Selling goods in this way leads to complaints and lost future business, but gains today's commission. Selling jobs in this way also mortgages the future, but also solves the immediate problem. Neither selling nor recruiting with only short-term results in mind may be called strategic.

As implied above, a strategic approach to recruitment starts long before the candidates appear on the scene, with the thorough investigation of the work to be offered. The objective is to produce full and accurate job descriptions and personnel specifications. Professional and strategic human relations specialists will use well-tried formats for both, or develop their own. The purpose is to ensure that jobs and suitable candidates are considered from a variety of viewpoints. The danger as in all aspects of human resource planning, is inappropriate categorization. Jobs with the same job title may have been developed successfully by previous encumbents in different ways, and the diversity may be important to the way the organization functions. Disguising variety in a generalized job description can be a recipe for built-in failure. An organization which can show to candidates that it appreciates and accommodates individuality has the best chance of attracting them.

If jobs may have individuality, then people certainly do. Personnel specifications should clarify both the essential aspects of a good candidate, and those where variety is acceptable. Unfair discrimination in selection for jobs takes many forms, racial and gender discrimination being the most prominent. Discrimination and prejudice are often confused in the minds of campaigners and politicians; the strategic human resource planner cannot afford this confusion. Prejudice, based on stereotypes of gender, race, class and other labels, is not evil but necessary. It is part of coping with the everyday problems of life, which would be impossible without some psychological short-hand. The ethical and strategic issue is the danger of failing to acknowledge prejudice, and carrying it unacknowledged into the selection process. For certain, strictly limited, purposes the law in the UK allows distinctions to be drawn between sexes and between races. Beyond those, personnel specifications should state explicitly that selection criteria do not include race, sex or religion. Only by overt statement can prejudice be prevented from turning into discrimination; once this is articulated, selectors are free to search for appropriate skills.

The next stage in this process is to advertise, and it is at this point that the carefully evolved descriptions of the job and job-holder face their first major hazard. With the exception of hole-in-the-corner advertising by box numbers, and anonymous advertising through consultants, the copy usually carries the organization's name. All recruitment advertising is, by default, also corporate advertising. Human resource specialists find themselves referred to the corporate agency, 'to get the image right'. Corporate advertising affects not only relations with customers, but relations with the financial community, governmental agencies and the workforce in general, so caution in the presentation of copy is understandable. It is not caution from which the human resource specialist has most to fear, however. The agency may distort the straightforward and informative statement of the vacancy as presented in the job description and personnel specification. In an attempt also to remind potential investors of the wisdom of buying shares, hyperbole about the organization's prospects may creep into the copy. This can give the impression that rather special people are required when the opposite is the case. Public service organizations may wish to present an image of 'worthiness', that the good potential candidate may, incorrectly, interpet as dullness. Not only do these embellishments distort the picture of the work to be done, but they also take up space that could better have been devoted to giving a more detailed description of the real demands of the job.

It has been emphasized elsewhere in this book that a distinguishing feature of the strategic human resource planner will be the ability to support arguments for better strategies, policies and procedures with objective data. In the battle against corporate distortion of job advertising this data seems hard to come by. We do not know the characteristics of able candidates who might have applied, had the advertising been more objectively presented. Yet it would not be impossible to find out, certainly where organizationally important professional work is concerned. Sampling frames for suitable candidates exist within the professional associations. Members could be invited to give their reactions to a range of the organization's advertisements, with the explicit aim of improving communication with potential employees. Both understanding of the job and attitudes to its image could be explored. The very act of conducting research in this area could improve the acceptability of the organization to professionals; there are 'action' as well as 'policy' implications.

Product advertising is designed to attract a large response. Advertising vacancies, however, is a matter of concentrating on getting the widest field of suitable candidates, rather than the largest number of replies. Improving communication through recruitment advertising is as much to discourage unsuitable candidates as to attract people who could perform the work well. Yet another advantage of careful job analysis is that advertising can become the cost-effective rapier rather than the expensive blunderbuss.

What applies to employment advertising also applies to the application form. Strategic human resource planners would be well-advised to research the effect that standard application forms have on response. 'Difficult' forms have, in the past, been used to check the motivation of graduate candidates to join some of the more prestigious management training schemes, but procedures designed for the 1960s may no longer have the desired effect. To go to the other extreme and rely solely upon career histories provided by candidates is equally ill-advised; some will have been instructed in the art of presenting their skills and experience in a comprehensible way, others will fill an over-lengthy document with extraneous information that will result in rejection for lack of any positive features. The ideal is a carefully designed application form for each vacancy; as the next best thing, organizations should present candidates with a general document that requests face-valid information in concise form. The purpose is clear, if the means of achieving it often is not: the ability to select people for further consideration on the basis of evidence of necessary skills. Unless biodata, as general family and career background are called, is to be used as a valid selection device, most information about family and other circumstances can wait until later in the selection process. Mere listing of job titles and employers is less important than encouraging candidates to describe the content of relevant jobs. Selection of candidates from application forms is a chancy business, as research by Herriot, Glendinning and Wingrove (1984) revealed. They asked selectors from a transport company to explain their reasons for selecting particular graduate candidates for interview. Survival of candidates through this process was a haphazard affair. The lack of coherence between the selection criteria used by different selectors was a major factor in this. Selection criteria appeared to be based upon stereotyped images of the acceptable candidate. Candidates who filled the white space on the form were more likely to be selected, perhaps because diligence in form filling was equated with motivation to work. This stage of selection, no less than the final decision on whom to appoint, depends on the use of explicit and relevant measures.

An important social aspect of selection is the way in which candidates are turned down at this point in the procedure. They will have invested effort and time in their applications, and should be accorded equal courtesy in turn. Informing them that there were many excellent candidates but they have not quite made the grade, is not good enough. An organization that really understands its own selection procedure should be able to be more explicit. If possible, all suitable candidates should be seen at interview, the most social of the social aspects of selection, even if the selection decision is strongly supported by test data.

The role of the interview?

Readers may have been surprised that the list of selection techniques earlier in this chapter made no mention of the interview. This is still widely used in selection, in spite of having dubious reliability and validity, and being vulnerable to racial and other forms of prejudice, and to bias caused by the timing of information. A review by Arvey and Campion (1982) substantiated these criticisms, but pointed out that interviews which may predict certain important characteristics such as social and verbal fluency, are an acceptable substitute for more complicated and expensive forms of selection that managers might not understand, and are necessary in order to inform the candidate about the employer.

All forms of selection are improved by careful analysis of the work to be carried out. Interviewers should be armed with both a job description and a personnel specification, and should have prepared questions that are likely to reveal information on the essential characteristics needed in the job. They should use 'open' questions wherever possible, encouraging the interviewee to talk, and 'probing' questions to follow up interesting leads that are relevant to job performance. 'Closed' questions should be used sparingly to check facts; excessive use of this type of question will bring the interview to halt.

Should the interview be regarded as a selection technique, in the same category as an intelligence test? A case can be made that it should not. In the hands of skilled interviewers, for selection or social research purposes, the interview is a highly effective information-gathering device. It yields data that is far richer than that obtained by most other devices, because it does not limit the responses of the candidate. That richness, however, makes the information more difficult to classify. A well-drafted personnel specification provides headings under which relevant information can be gathered, but the interviewer should use the interview plan in a flexible way that reflects the uniqueness of each candidate.

Candidates should not feel that they have 'failed' an interview in the same way that they might 'fail' an objective test of some specific ability. The interview is an information-gathering device; subsequent discussion of that information by the selectors determines the candidate's success or failure.

The interview is reliable if two skilled interviewers would have obtained the same information; it is valid if this information is relevant to job performance. It is the subsequent discussion of candidates that needs to be checked for predictive validity. Reliability and validity at all stages are improved by careful analysis, and explicit statement, of job requirements.

Even if the interview is eventually abandoned as a selection device, and this does not seem likely, it will be retained as the major social event between first contact with a candidate and the final selection decision. It is the principal, if not the only, opportunity for the candidate to obtain detailed information about the content and context of the work. Candidates' questions should, of course, be answered, but they should also be encouraged. Self-selection is at least as important as selection by the organization; the more candidates know, the more clearly they can measure their own ability and motivation in relation to the work offered.

Ipsative and normative assessment

The individuality of human beings, particularly in their roles as candidates for jobs and as workers, is emphasized throughout this book. The stereotyping of people that was necessary in statistical manpower planning for large organizations and groups actually made it more difficult to use employees flexibly. There may seem to be an inconsistency, however, in advocating careful description of jobs and specification of job-holders, and then pleading for the treatment of candidates and employees as individuals. Yet the paradox is easily resolvable. Care in description and specification means putting into those documents only what is essential, and being prepared to change the content as changing markets, technology and individual working methods make this advisable. The strategic approach to the use of people requires only that the change should be from one carefully thought out analysis of requirements to another. When making selection decisions, it is good practice to compare candidates with the personnel specification rather than against each other.

For certain, limited aspects of selection, candidates are assessed against other people—the most obvious instance is the weight to be given to scores on an intelligence test. The scoring methods for personality questionnaires, such as the 16PF, also have a normative element, since each score is converted to a normalized rating for given populations. Selectors should take careful note of these, since the reactions of people in Middle America, for example, to the questions may be very different from those of youngsters in urban Britain. Once again, developing local norms should be a legitimate and important task for strategic human resource specialists.

Interest questionnaires should not be regarded as normative data. It is the pattern of a person's interests, rather than the relation of individual scores to those of other people, that is significant: A cannot be said to be more interested in music than B, but A can be said to be more interested in music than, for example, outdoor activities. We are here confronted not with normative assessment, but with the relationship of various factors within one personality. This is ipsative assessment. It is more familiar, perhaps in career guidance than selection, but it has its place in both. Careers advisers make an attempt to sum up the separate information they have obtained from tests, questionnaires and interviews in order to suggest what lines of work would suit the client; selectors should do the same, with a different purpose in mind. It is this composite picture of each candidate that is compared with the personnel specification to discover suitability. Direct comparison of candidates with each other, though difficult to resist, moves attention away from the original analysis of the job towards stereotyping and prejudice. At this point it is possible to undo what can be achieved by following the procedure described above. The effective comparison is between candidate and specification, not between candidates. Selection in this way is an ipsative rather than a normative process.

Ipsative assessment, the full understanding of each candidate, has other advantages. If the organization is expanding in a difficult labour market, selectors may wish to allocate a range of candidates to the most suitable work, rather than selecting or rejecting them for one particular vacancy. In this case, a full understanding of each is essential to cost-effective allocation.

Categorization: how candidates see it

Market researchers use a technique called 'market segmentation', which can also be applied in the strategic management of human resources. In market research the categories differentiate between groups of customers; in recruitment they differentiate between groups of candidates. The following example will illustrate how this can be used in the recruitment of graduates; in essence it is an attempt to meet Herriot's proposal for more fruitful social exchange with applicants.

Readers of Case Studies 1 and 7, especially if they are directly concerned with graduate recruitment, will appreciate the complexity of the process. This illustration of market segmentation follows naturally from changing assumptions about the motivation of graduate recruits. In Case Study 1, it was assumed that at least some graduates would stay with the company throughout their careers. In Case Study 7 (Chapter 7), the assumption is that early and effective use of recruits, whether they remained with the company or not, is more important than long-term prediction of career development.

The company had taken the trouble to assess the motivation of candidates who applied for the various types of training that it offered to graduate entrants. There were basically four groups. The first were the 'direct entry' graduates—those who had obtained degrees in vocational subjects, mainly in applied technology and engineering. This group had usually received practical training in industry during their studies. They were uninterested in general training with their new employer and, above all else, wished to demonstrate their skills directly in technical work. They were appointed to fill vacancies, rather than joining training schemes.

The second category were those who wished to enter a graduate training scheme leading to a recognized professional qualification, perhaps in accountancy or engineering. Here the quality of training offered was more important than the general reputation of the employer; graduates would take a view about the desirability of staying once the professional exams or guided training period was complete. The title 'professionals' seemed appropriate for this group.

In some ways similar to the second category, but less attracted by the idea of professional qualifications, were the 'specialists'. These came from a variety of degree disciplines, but now wished to develop a specialist skill in industry; personnel or marketing expertise are examples. Like the 'professionals' they were attracted to a particular company by the apparent quality of the training offered. In this case the training was project-based, similar to that offered to the final category, but less demanding.

The fourth group were attracted by the idea of a higher degree project to start their careers. Their existence came to light when projects were offered under the Aston University IHD Scheme, as-described in Case Study 7. They were highly qualified graduates who might not otherwise have considered employment in industry. They brought to this an individual and objective approach, developing skills and attitudes of later use in general management; they were categorized as the 'generalists'.

'Direct entry', 'professionals', 'specialists' and 'generalists' were labels appropriate to a particular company at a particular time. Identification of these four groups, however, helped the human resourcing team to develop advertising that targeted the needs of each, making clear how the company could respond.

Nevertheless, the basic principle of market segmentation could be applied with advantage in any organization. What work satisfactions are being offered, and to whom? Advertising can then make these points clear, with increased likelihood that suitable candidates will apply. Throwing money at the problem, by offering higher and higher salaries in increasingly expensive advertising, smacks of the despairing rather than the strategic. The opportunities for skill use and skill development (see Chapter 6) offered by a job are also where the advantages lie for the employer; people like to do a good job and develop themselves in the process. Money is only a temporary palliative if skills are under used. Every decision to recruit should now be based not only upon a job description, but also on appropriate job design.

The long-term goal: improving the human resource audit

This has been a long and densely written chapter. The ideas in it will be familiar to some readers, and are important to all concerned with effective use of human resources. Many years after occupational psychologists first proposed the concepts of predictor and criterion in selection theory, many organizations still disregard the bases of good selection practice with a negligence that would be considered criminal if adopted in financial management. Too much emphasis has been placed on the difficulty of defining criteria, but just to try would raise the effectiveness of many organizations. Perfection is not necessary to improvement. Strategic decisions encourage learning, even if wrong.

The advent of microcomputers has encouraged personnel departments to use customized software to store personnel data in an accessible way. At least as much attention must be given, however, to the nature of the data as to computerization. One way to learn what is important is to pay more considered attention to the selection process, both for internal and external candidates.

Which predictors are being used, either to select people for promotion, or for entry to the organization? How satisfactory have selection decisions been over recent years? What criteria are used to decide that question? How valid, then, are the predictors? A thorough examination of the data required to answer these questions will suggest, better than the handbook for standard software, the data that should be stored on the personnel database. No other aspect of this process is more important than the recording of the emerging and developing skills of the current workforce.

Readers who would like to extend their knowledge of current selection issues, and the associated theory, are referred to Smith and Robertson (1989).

Conclusions

This chapter has shown that social science concepts, mostly psychological in this case, are important to the development of human resource strategy. Selection theory affects the way the labour market is viewed and used, whether we are considering psychometric method or social interaction. At the centre of good selection practice is the concept of operationalization—making both jobs and candidates measurable. Though the interview is the dominant selection technique, and is likely to remain so throughout the 1980s, the human resource strategist should be aware of the wide range of alternative or supplementary techniques.

Important concepts introduced in this chapter were: predictor and criterion, reliability and validity, norms, ipsative and normative selection, and tests and questionnaires. Two case studies will be used to illustrate these ideas. The first describes a study of the recruitment of computer staff. It indicates, among other issues, the off-hand way in which selection can be approached, even in a modern industry. Superficial categorization, the lack of job descriptions and personnel specifications, and the unprofessional use of tests, all appear as villains in this piece. Technological change is a factor in deciding appropriate criteria of job performance; this case study also shows how technological change may be evaluated.

The second case study raises issues about the use of intelligence tests with candidates from different cultural backgrounds. It also illustrates the use of tests in general, and the normative use of the resulting data.

In the next chapter we consider which factors make for effective job performance, and consider the subject of job descriptions in greater detail. The related topics of job satisfaction and careers are the subject of Chapters 6 and 7.

CASE STUDY 3
Selection of computer specialists

In the early 1980s, the Manpower Services Commission were concerned about the training needs of computer programmers and systems analysts, with particular regard to training the young unemployed. In collaboration with the University of Aston, they set up a research project to investigate the methods used for selecting computer staff, the likely technological changes in this occupation, and the training methods currently in use. This case study considers the first two of these issues.

The researchers (Spurgeon, Patrick and Michael, 1984) evaluated the aptitude tests used to select applicants for entry to computer programming and systems analysis. They did this by consulting the rather sparse literature on the subject. Some coefficients of predictive validity were available, but there were the usual problems with criteria of subsequent performance.

A test used widely in the industry since the 1950s had been validated against supervisors' rating of performance in 1964, and found to have a moderate predictive validity of around 0.3. Another test had been validated only against subsequent success in a computer studies course, for which the coefficient of predictive validity was zero. A multiple aptitude test used in America, and subsequently adapted for British use, contained one sub-test that was negatively correlated with success in analogue computing. A standard intelligence test (AH2) was found to give satisfactory prediction of success on a computer training course.

Spurgeon's literature search thus revealed two faults with selection tests: there was little published validation and, where validation had been carried out, predictive validity was not impressive. The number of passes at 'O' level (the lower school leaving examination at that time in the UK) were predictive of subsequent course assessment, and of success in getting a job.

The next stage of the research was to investigate the views of employers and the procedures that they used, by means of a postal survey of a sample of computer users and suppliers. There were problems here in selecting the sampling frame, because of the wide variety of organizations employing computer staff, and their geographical dispersal. Response rates could also bias this type of research. Spurgeon and his co-workers decided that the response they received was representative of the industry as a whole.

The survey of employers revealed that 'A' levels (the higher school leaving qualification in the UK) was the most-used predictor of success in computer training, to the exclusion of graduate qualifications and, even more surprisingly, experience in the industry. Employers regarded 'personal qualities' as important, but were not able to articulate what they meant by the phrase. They regretted the shortage of candidates with these undefined qualities. No employer had carried out a validation study of the tests they used, and only 50 per cent of employers used them. They were loath to offer training to entrants to computing work, preferring to poach trained staff from other employers. The research team were struck by the lack of systematic selection, based on formal and complete job descriptions. Notional grades in the career structure seemed to relate only loosely to the selection criteria applied to entrants (see Figure 4.9). This was all the more surprising because the survey of future trends indicated that the pattern of employment, and the probable demands on candidates, were changing.

Another questionnaire was employed to elicit opinions from experts about the likely changes in computer technology. The purpose was to ensure that recommendations made in the report would be relevant to the future of the

Figure 4.9
Notional career
structure for computer
staff

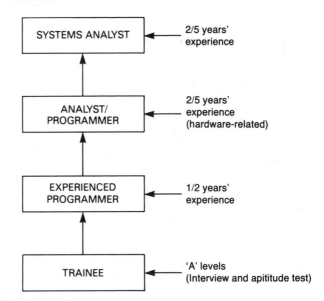

computer industry rather than its past. Predictive validity should be based on the appropriate criteria.

Technological forecasting is notoriously difficult, partly because the rate of technological innovation (see Chapter 2) is dictated by both market demands and the availability of new techniques. Another difficulty is that the opinions of 'heavyweight' experts dominate the thinking of other well-informed people. Human resource planners are often in the same position as the research team—they need opinions about the future direction of the organization they work for, but such views as are available are coloured by corporate politics. Spurgeon used a forecasting technique known as Delphi.

Delphi operates in the following way. Experts are nominated by organizations operating in the relevant technical area, and are consulted by post so that opinions remain anonymous. Feedback is statistical, so that each expert can see how close his or her own views are to the group norm. Individual responses remain confidential. Consensus is not required, but experts are asked to justify differences from the general opinion. Reference to Chapter 3 will show that this method of canvassing expert opinion has aspects in common with the ethnographic style of research, in that respondents were given considerable freedom in choosing responses.

Spurgeon's research team engaged 70 experts who were asked first of all what major events they foresaw in the computer industry over the following five years, and then within 10 years. The experts, rather than the research team, provided the concepts and categories. By analysing the replies, the researchers were able to identify 73 possible events that figured prominently in the individual replies. They returned to the experts to ask for estimates of the probability of occurrence of each within the 0–5 and 5–10 year timescales. These probabilities were assigned a mean value by the research team who then asked the experts to reconsider their individual estimates and to justify divergencies. Mean probabilities were then recalculated and submitted once again to the panel of experts. This time there was substantial agreement.

The potential for Delphi in the formation of corporate strategy should now be evident to the reader. While organizational politics might continue to colour the acceptance of the outcome, planners could nevertheless gain access to reasonably unbiased data to assist decision-making.

The conclusion from the Delphi research was that work in the computer specialisms was moving up-market. Operating jobs would be deskilled or disappear; those providing services to computer users would need to be multi-skilled, and to be trained in the broader aspects of business as well as in systems design. The development of new programming languages was considered unlikely. Artificial intelligence developments would demand very high-grade skills, but from comparatively few people. Overall, the demand for computer specialists was expected to increase slowly.

The implications of this research study are salutory, and extend well beyond the computer specialisms. Those responsible for recruiting and training staff were using methods developed in the 1960s that were invalid even in their own terms and no attempt had been made to revise selection to meet the future needs of a changing industry. The experts who had made the predictions in the Delphi study worked within or alongside an industry that was using out-of-date methods of selection. Their opinions apparently had no effect on human resource planning. The lack of strategic thinking is clear.

For our purpose, this investigation demonstrates how three modes of research can jointly contribute to the understanding of an important human resource problem. Literature surveys are useful in indicating both the quantity and quality of the research already conducted. Postal surveys, properly designed, can elicit structured but representative data from a wide range of sources. Expert opinion can be tapped systematically by means of the Delphi technique, and in such a way that prestigious members do not bias the views of the group as a whole.

CASE STUDY 4
Testing ethnic minorities

Background

The previous case study highlighted the importance of defining jobs in realistic ways and of validating the selection procedures, including tests, used to predict the future performance of candidates. This case study concentrates on the tests themselves, particularly the problems that arise when using intelligence tests with members of minority populations. It is based on research by Pearson and Smith (1990).

Standardized tests, used singly, in batteries, or in combination with other selection methods in assessment centres, offer the selector the opportunity to make decisions based on objective data. The predictive validity of tests can be established by correlating numerical test results against a measure of subsequent job performance. On the face of it, the objective use of test data should favour the employment of minority groups by substituting objective measures of performance for those based on educational qualifications that are subject to educational and cultural disadvantage. They are also free of the effects of prejudice and discrimination that can influence selection by interview.

Unfortunately, tests themselves have been attacked as discriminatory, particularly in the USA, resulting in the rejection of testing for fear of litigation. The argument (Angoff, 1986) hinges on the differential predictive validity of the test for different ethnic groups. Ethnic minorities perform worse on average than the indigenous population on ability tests. Does this mean that job performance will subsequently be found to be inferior? If so, wherein lies the unfairness? More important, does inferior performance indicate some immutable difference, or can remedial action improve the performance and employability of the minority group?

The opportunity to investigate differential test performance arose from the attendance of professionally trained people from a variety of ethnic backgrounds at a programme designed to help them find new jobs, usually following redundancy. The programme was called 'Bridge', and was sponsored by the Manpower Services Commission between 1983 and 1987. The objectives and structure of the programme are described in the discussion of unemployment in Chapter 2, and the techniques used are described, and related to career development, in Chapter 7.

As part of the career guidance aspect of the programme, participants were offered the opportunity to take a test of general intelligence, and about 80 per cent did so. The utility of the test was twofold. Unexpectedly high scores indicated those whose educational or occupational achievements did not match their ability, and who might be helped to obtain more challenging employement. In contrast, surprisingly poor scores indicated those whose test performance, and job prospects, might be impaired by lack of facility in English. Those who scored low on the test and whose first language was not English, were advised to attend classes to check their spoken and written skills. None ever rejected the advice as unfounded or impertinent.

The test used was the AH3, devised by Heim and co-workers, and details are given below. The test instructions are spoken in English by the administrator and must be fully understood by the test-taker if performance is not to be impaired. The practise items at the start of each of the three sections of the test allow takers to question the test procedure, if they are confident enough to do so. The written instructions, which the taker is not allowed to question while the test is in progress, are also in English. The verbal sub-test makes explicit demands on the understanding of English words and phrases. When low scores are obtained by people for whom English is not the first language, it can be difficult to know how far this indicates genuinely poor cognitive ability rather than inadequate language skills. The latter is remediable, while the former is unlikely to be. In the perceptual ability section of the test, the same doubts can be raised about the cultural significance of the pictures used in test items.

Test results are determined by the speed with which test-takers can solve the problems that are presented to them. The contribution of each of the factors mentioned above to overall processing speed is illustrated in Figure 4.10. The hypothesis that the research set out to test was that differences in performance between ethnic groups may be more easily ascribed to linguistic and cultural causes than to basic cognitive abilities.

'Ethnic minorities'   The stereotype of ethnic minority employment is black youth in the inner cities; unskilled, unmotivated and a prey to racial discrimination. The social and ethical problems presented by this larger group are not the subject of this case study, although the findings may be relevant; the non-European immigrants who formed nearly 20 per cent of the participants in the programme were at least as well qualified as the others, were slightly younger and contained a higher proportion of males (Table 4.4). They contained a higher proportion of engineers and accountants, but a lower proportion of managers and administrators. Almost without exception, their first language was not English. Since the dearth of potential 'knowledge' workers in the British labour market during the 1990s may well be compensated by recruitment from Europe, and from as far afield as the Pacific Rim, test findings from both Eurpean and non-Europeant subjects are directly relevant to the concerns of human resource specialists. Additionally, the Single Market of 1992 may in any case lead to a significant increase in Europeans seeking

	Non-Europeans	All participants
Average age	40	41
Women (%)	20	28
Post 'A' level qualitifications (%)	86	70
Unemployed under 6 months (%)	52	60
Managers (%)	11	17
Engineers (%)	19	12
Commercial (%)	7	11
Financial (%)	13	7
Teaching (%)	7	8
Clerical (%)	6	7

Table 4.4
A comparison between the qualifications, personal characteristics and occupations of the minority group with those of all participants

employment in the UK. The implications for career guidance of clients from the ethnic minorities is even more evident.

For the purposes of analysis, three separate groups were identified: native English speakers educated in the UK, Europeans whose first language was not English, and non-Europeans whose first language also was not English. The third group would generally be classified as 'ethnic minority' members on grounds of appearance, but they included various Middle Eastern, Asian, Chinese and African races and nationalities.

The test

The purposes and structure of this test are described in a paper by Heim and co-authors (1974). The AH3 test was originally intended for use with teens and young adults. It is a timed test with a steep gradient of difficulty. Groups of more highly intelligent subjects are given shorter times to complete each of the three sections, which cover verbal, numerical and perceptual abilities. The authors claim that the test is free of sex bias, and its use in 'Bridge' programmes has demonstrated little susceptibility to the age of subject. Scores were found to vary over the whole range; none of those attending the Central London 'Bridge' programme completed the test correctly, though a few came close. The test was administered to mixed groups attending each presentation of the programme in accordance with the published instructions and using the short time limits. Attendance at the test session was voluntary.

Analysis

Test performance was analysed in two ways. The first compared the mean performance of the three ethnic and linguistic groups by calculating means and standard deviations for total and constituent scores. The significance of apparent differences was established statistically by means of t-tests. Differences in relative performance between the verbal, numerical and perceptual sub-tests could indicate the contribution of linguistic and cultural factors to overall test performance. Test results analysed in this way were those obtained by people attending the last seven programmes and taking the test, a sample of 433 in all.

The purpose of the second analysis was to establish whether items in the test itself were disproportionately difficult for one or the other group, once their overall test performance had been taken into account; the *Mantel Haenszel* procedure (Holland and Thayer, 1986). The analysis was carried out using the programme operated by the National Foundation for Educational Research in England and Wales (NFER). In order to obtain adequate sample sizes for the non-UK groups, data were used from earlier 'Bridge' programmes, in addition to those used in the first analysis.

Table 4.5(a) shows the mean total scores, mean sub-test scores, standard deviations and sample sizes for each of the three groups. Tables 4.5(b) and 4.5(c) present a comparison of each possible pairing of the three groups, giving the difference in mean scores together with an indication of their levels of statistical significance. The purpose is to demonstrate where differences in performance occur, and how important they are.

Table 4.5(a)
Mean scores for the AH3 test, as taken by three groups with different ethnic backgrounds

Group	Sample-size*	Mean test scores			
		Total	Verbal	Numerical	Perceptual
Native English (A)	316	72.05	22.86	26.19	23.00
European not English (B)	41	57.59	17.78	18.78	21.03
Non-European (C)	71	46.20	12.89	18.20	15.11

* 'Bridge' programmes 16 to 27 at the Polytechnic of Central London

Table 4.5(b)
Differences between mean scores obtained by the three ethnic groups

Groups compared	Differences between mean scores			
	Total	Verbal	Numerical	Perceptual
A–B	14.70	5.08	7.41	1.97*
B–C	11.39	4.89	0.58*	5.92
A–C	26.09	9.97	7.99	7.89

* Not significant at p> .001 (two-tailed)

Table 4.5(c)
Standard deviations for scores obtained by each of the three ethnic groups

Group	Standard deviations of test scores			
	Total	Verbal	Numerical	Perceptual
A	17.50	6.73	7.78	5.82
B	16.23	5.94	6.64	5.47
C	17.73	5.85	7.94	5.88

There are significant differences between the total test scores of all three groups, and also between the scores on verbal reasoning. There were differences in the numerical sub-test scores between native English speakers and the other groups, which are not themselves significantly different in their performance on this dimension. The non-Europeans did less well than the other two groups on the perceptual sub-test, who were themselves not significantly different in this respect.

At this point, test-users are faced with the possiblity that English speakers are superior in cognitive skills when compared with people from other ethnic

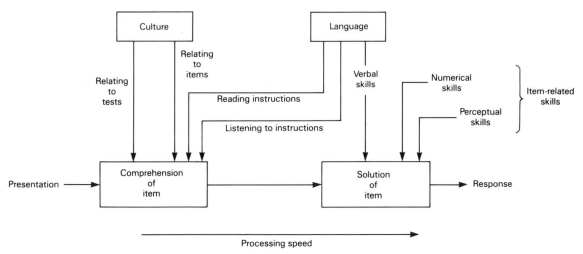

Figure 4.10   Factors affecting processing speed when taking an intelligence test

backgrounds, a hypothesis which seems unlikely if only because of the high level of qualifications found among the non-English speaking sample. The alternatives are: the test itself is culturally biased, or that the language problems shown in Figure 4.10 are the cause of differential test performance.

Table 4.6 reports the questions that produced significant bias in one or more of the paired group comparisons. It will be observed that these add up to a small fraction of all questions (120 in the whole test). Most of the biased questions were from the verbal sub-test, and in most cases a perusal of the test question revealed a likely cause. The clearest example was a question that depended on a knowledge of the pronunciation of various words ending in '-ough'. In several other cases, differences of general knowledge, or knowledge of word meanings seem likely causes. One verbal question that actually favoured the non-European group used letters rather than words and had relatively simple instructions. Some questions identified as possibly biased were attempted by only small numbers of the 'disadvantaged' groups.

The bias programme also provided details of the number of test-takers reaching each question, and confirmed the differences presented in Table

Table 4.6 **Number of AH3** **questions producing** **significant bias** *Sub-test*	SIGNIF. LEVEL P<	*Comparison 1* *questions favouring:*		*Comparison 2* *questions favouring:*		*Comparison 3* *questions favouring:*	
		Nateng	*Euro*	*Nateng*	*Non-Euro*	*Euro*	*Non-Euro*
Verbal	.05	2	—	5	—	1	—
	.01	1	—	3	1	—	—
Numerical	.05	1	—	—	1	—	—
	.01	—	—	1	—	—	—
Perceptual	.05	—	—	3	—	1	—
	.01	—	—	—	—	—	—

4.3(a). This pattern suggests language and cultural differences influenced speed on the verbal sub-test, with language only influencing speed on the numerical sub-test and cultural differences only affecting the perceptual sub-test.

Conclusions

Two categories of conclusion may be drawn from this case study: one set concern the research itself, and the other the wider implications for human resource strategists.

The research findings suggest that both language and culture influence performance on at least one popular test of general reasoning. The verbal questions presuppose a level of competence with the English language and a general knowledge base that is not necessarily possessed by non-English test-takers. It is also likely that the speed differences reflected the additional time that the non-English groups needed to read and comprehend the written questions. The argument could be advanced that 'ethnic minority' test-takers work more slowly solely because of cultural norms related to tests and examinations in general. This could be countered by pointing to the different races and cultures represented within the non-European group, and to their high level of qualifications. Such people are used to examinations and tests.

The wider implications may be itemized as follows:

1 Tests such as the AH3 cannot be used to assess fairly the reasoning ability of people who do not speak English as a first language or who have a non-Western cultural background. This caveat also applies to English candidates with poor reading competence. At the very least, tests with verbal instructions should allow generous time limits.

2 It may be perfectly legitimate for employers to assess reading comprehension, but that should be done with dedicated tests of reading skills.

3 Indicated reasoning abilities may have little to do with getting a job. A follow-up study of all 'Bridge' programme participants revealed that non-Europeans were no less successful than others in gaining employment (Table 4.7). Two possible reasons suggest themselves. Advice to improve skills in English may have been heeded, having a beneficial effect on acceptability. Alternatively, the professional training of minority members may have provided a knowledge of the specialist terms needed at interview, regardless of general English-speaking competence.

4 This case study illustrates the way in which administration can be broadened into research, to their mutual benefit. The 'Bridge' programme staff collected the test data as part of their everyday work. The important next step was to analyse this to discover whether it might have significance

Table 4.7
Comparison of employment outcomes for non-European (ethnic minority) group with all participants

	Non-Europeans	All participants
% known outcomes	70	75
Re-employment as % of known outcomes	88	92
Occupation-changing as % of known outcomes	43	60

for the way in which re-employment programmes should be run. Personnel departments, in the same way, collect and file data daily about candidates and potential candidates for jobs. Human resource strategists will not wish to leave it there. Valuable information may be obtained if administrative records are exploited for social research. If relevant skills are not available within the organization, academic or other research institutes can help. The assistance granted by NFER for the analysis of test data demonstrates that reputable test suppliers will be prepared to help users with statistical analysis and professional advice.

References

Angoff, W. (1986) 'A philosophical discussion: the issues of test and item bias', *ETS Developments*, **24**, 10.

Arvey, R. and Campion, J. (1982) 'The employment interview: a summary and review of recent research', *Personnel Psychology*, **35**, 281.

Atkinson, J. (1984) 'Manpower strategies for flexible organizations', *Personnel Management*, August, 28.

Bennison, M. and Casson, J. (1984) *The Manpower Planning Handbook*, McGraw-Hill (UK) Ltd, Maidenhead.

Dulewicz, V. and Fletcher, C. (1982) 'The relationship between previous experience, intelligence and background characteristics of participants and their performance at an assessment centre', *Journal of Occupational Psychology*, **55**, 197.

Heim, A., Watts, K. and Simmonds, V. (1974) 'AH2 and AH3: parallel tests of reasoning', *British Journal of Psychology*, **65**, 493.

Heim, A. (1975) *Intelligence and Personality*, Penguin Books, Harmondsworth, London.

Herriot, P. (1984) *Down from the Ivory Tower: graduates and their jobs*, John Wiley & Sons Ltd, Chichester.

Herriot, P., Glendinning, R. and Wingrove, J. (1984) 'Graduate pre-selection: a research note', *Journal of Occupational Psychology*, **57**, 169.

Herriot, P. (1988) 'Graduate recruitment: psychological contracts and the balance of power', *British Journal of Guidance and Counselling*, **16**, 228.

Herriot, P. (1989) 'Selection as a social process' in Smith, M. and Robertson, I. *Advances in Selection and Assessment*, John Wiley and Sons, Chichester.

Holland, P. and Thayer, T. (1986) *Differential Item Functioning and the Mantel-Haenszel Procedure*, ETS—RR 31 Educational Testing Service, Princeton, NJ, USA.

Kelly, G. (1955) *The Psychology of Personal Constructs*, W. W. Norton, New York.

McClelland, D. (1961) *The Achieving Society*, Van Nostrand, Princeton, NJ, USA.

McCormick, E. and Tiffin J. (1975) *Industrial Psychology*, Prentice-Hall International, New Jersey.

Monahan, C. and Muchinsky, J. (1983) 'Three decades of personnel selection research: A state-of-the-art analysis and evaluation', *Journal of Occupational Psychology*, **56**, 241.

Munro-Fraser, J. (1971) *Psychology: General, Industrial, Social*. Pitman, London.

Pearson, R. and Heyno, A. (1988) *Helping the Unemployed Professional*, John Wiley and Sons, Chichester.

Pearson, R. and Smith, P. (1990) *Language, Intelligence and Getting a Job: the test performance of ethnic minorities* (to be published).

Robertson, I. and Kandola, K. (1982) 'Work sampling tests: validity, adverse impact and applicant reaction', *Journal of Occupational Psychology*, **55**, 171.

Roethlisberger, F. and Dickson, W. (1939) *Management and the Worker*, Harvard University Press, Cambridge, Massachusetts.

Rodger, A. (1952) *The Seven Point Plan*, National Institute of Industrial Psychology, London

Smith, M. and Robertson, I. (1989) *Advances in Selection and Assessment*, John Wiley & Sons, Chichester.

Spurgeon, P., Patrick, J. and Michael, I. (1984) *Training and Selection of Computer Personnel*, Manpower Services Commission Research and Development No. 18, MSC, Sheffield. Permission granted by author and Training Agency.

CHAPTER 5 People and productivity

Productivity and change

In the previous chapter we took a hard look at selection theory and practice. The focus was the avoidance of stereotyping, either of jobs or people. Stereotyping is undesirable for strategic, economic, legal and social reasons. Outdated perceptions cause inefficiencies in the labour market and restrict the opportunities for both employers and workers. Underestimating skill requirements leads to poor job performance; drawing the selection criteria too tightly restricts the number of potential candidates.

The purpose behind effective selection is a productive workforce, whether within an organization or nationally. Later in this chapter, we will be looking more closely at the concept of productivity. For the moment, the traditional definition will do—output divided by input. This concept is operationalized in official statistics as 'output per person employed'. Since input usually includes more than labour content, however, it is preferable to reduce both factors in the productivity ratio to monetary terms. In a labour market that favours high rates of wastage, both factors require careful attention. This is because prolonged training of new recruits increases input and reduces output. Productivity is determined not only by job design and incentives, but also by effectiveness in personnel selection.

What are the other strategic issues affecting productivity, and how should the human resource planner assess them? Much early writing on manpower planning was concerned with 'getting the numbers right', an obsession with the size of the payroll rather than the quality of purpose of work being done. The historical reasons are clear. In the UK, lack of industrial productivity was a continuing concern both of politicians and industrial managers. Trade unions were perceived, often by their own members, as frustrating attempts to improve productivity; the leaders' view was that they were 'protecting jobs'. Mrs Thatcher's victory in 1979 owed not a little to a perception by skilled manual workers that this situation had to change.

The emphasis on quantity rather than quality was compounded by the manpower planners themselves, as implied in Chapter 1. They were more at home calculating input–output ratios, and extrapolating trend lines for numbers of established jobs, rather than looking at work itself, and how it might change. Kemp (see Chapter 2) has described a similar bias in the eighteenth-century British economy. He claims that the failure of merchants to look beyond buying and selling, and to take a critical interest in the process of production, actually held back the onset on industrialization. Failure to look critically at the processes in the British motor industry some 200 years later led to its near collapse.

Strategic thinking requires, among other things, an appreciation of the ways in which work is changing, nationally and within each organization. Chapter 2 demonstrated that this appreciation comes from an awareness of historical trends and of the technological, market and social factors that will affect consumer demands in the future. Traditional ideas of productivity tended to be tactical rather than strategic, concentrating on the individual worker. Job design was a matter of ergonomics, and motivation a matter of union-negotiated incentive schemes. Strategic human resource planners need a broader view of the working environment.

Productivity: the concentric model

Figure 5.1 presents the factors affecting the productivity of individual workers as a series of the concentric circles. This does not give full expression to the importance of changes in technology and job design, which are the subject of later discussion.

At the centre of the model are the workers themselves, the traditional heroes or villains of the productivity drama. Personal performance is the subject of cajolery, threats or incentive schemes. The output of the individual is determined at this level by personal motivation and skills. Workers are often unaware of the full range of their skills, and the work for which they are best fitted. Vocational guidance is the luxury of the few, and job choice is as likely to be made on grounds of economic necessity as for any other reason. The allocation of workers to particular types of work, however, is the responsibility of management. As the first case study in Chapter 4 made clear, selection methods sometimes have little to do with this essential process. Strategic management of the human resource assumes that employers fully understand the work done in their organizations, and are professional in their selection and work allocation procedures.

Chapter 4 also had something to say about the way in which effectiveness of selection might be improved. Job analysis that takes account of the job content, the job context, and the skills required is more likely to result in the recruitment of satisfactory workers. Dissatisfaction, as Chapter 6 will demonstrate, may result in wastage from the workforce; it is also a cause of underperformance. The employer is the first to be blamed for feelings of dissatisfaction, and lowering productivity is the most obvious means of expressing resentment. Yet the factors that cause dissatisfaction vary with the individual—work in a busy social atmosphere is profoundly unpleasant for some people yet a delight for others. Work that demands commercial assertiveness has the same varied effect. The important point is that both skills and contextual factors should be taken into account during the selection or allocation of recruits. Lack of basic skills means lack of confidence and lack of motivation. Motivated workers, however, will strive to acquire additional skills in their work, whether formal training is provided or not (evidence for this is presented in Chapter 7).

Figure 5.1
Factors affecting
individual productivity

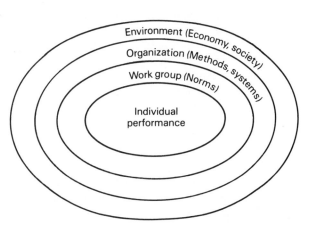

Given a professional selection procedure, which has taken account of skills and motivation, what else determines the output that each worker achieves? Figure 5.1 suggests that the work group has the next most immediate effect. The group is a source of social attitudes that the individual ignores at some peril. Groups can foster positive attitudes to work, rewarding team achievement, and exhibiting what is known in military terms as high morale. Examples of favourable group effects on productivity can be found in the *relay test room* experiments of the classic Hawthorne research (Roethlisberger and Dickson, 1939), and in many subsequent studies. The value of teamwork in car manufacture has been demonstrated at the Volvo plant in Sweden. To obtain a high level of commitment and performance, teams should be given a say in selecting their own members, and allowed to organize work within the group.

Groups may also police the behaviour of their own members in ways that limit rather than enhance productivity. Many cases are reported in the literature, sometimes based on participant observation by researchers. The *bank wiring room* observations in the Hawthorne research is a well-known example. A cash incentive scheme was undermined by tacit group agreement. Output was restricted in order that earnings would not fluctuate too widely, weaker workers would not be shown up, and so that management would not be aware of lax piece-rates. The restriction of output was enforced by a series of group sanctions. Physical closeness is not necessary for these powerful psychological forces to operate, though it usually intensifies them. Even a sales force, scattered geographically around the country, may fail to act in the competitive way desired by the sales manager because of hidden agreements among its members.

Social norms of acceptable behaviour effect absenteeism, as well as performance when the workers are present. Night work would appear both socially and physically undesirable, and greater absenteeism would be expected in consequence. Yet the opposite frequently occurs; absence is less than on day shifts. Workers are conscious at night of the need for psychological support, and absentees are felt to be letting the group down. This feeling is passed on to those who, in the groups' view, take too much time off. But they may also be made aware, as in all work groups, that a certain amount of voluntary absence is sanctioned by the group and will be 'covered' by colleagues.

The next circle in the productivity model is the organization and its systems. We have already considered one important aspect of this—the recruitment and selection system. As we have seen, this can be undervalued, unsystematic and unwelcoming. Enough has been said on that score already. The organization is the source of payment systems that are intended to reward productivity, but which may be subverted by the work group.

At its broadest conception, the organization is the support system for the worker, without which complex manufacturing, service or distribution functions cannot be performed. The ethos and efficiency of the support system has a powerful effect on productivity. The organization also chooses the technology, which may aid or retard the efforts of individuals, and the production control systems that determine the targets to be met. The organization also selects the raw materials or bought-in parts that are needed before work can begin. Efficiency in these support systems is at least as important as the efforts of individual workers. It is easy to think of situations outside the manufacturing industries where this is also true: teachers or doctors trying to work without adequate support will recognize the general point.

But organizations have styles as well as functions. Handy (1985), among others, has related style to function; the management styles of functional bureaucracies or task-oriented organizations appear to be related to their working methods and structure. These categorizations exist to be disproved, and in search of greater productivity they deserve to be. Following meticulous procedures is not the sole measure of success in most organizations; there are moves afoot to make branches of the British Civil Service more task-oriented and less bureaucratic. The ultimate purpose of the organization is not control of workers or managers, but to support their individual efforts.

The outermost circle of the model is the most powerful in its effect on both the organization and the individual worker, but appears to be outside the control of both. It represents the economic, social and political environment within which business is conducted, and services provided. Businesses and public services may complain that they are helpless in the face of these changes. Yet attitudes at this level of management distinguish the strategic thinkers from the rest.

Strategic decision-making is at once reactive and pro-active. Pro-activity is expressed by a purposive search for alternative strategies, and in making strategic choices. This includes scanning the environment for economic, social and political trends, and devising ways of profiting from them. But there is a limit beyond which even the most strategic organization will find it difficult to succeed. In modern managed economies, what the government decides to do, or not to do, will affect the productivity of the worker at the sales counter, the office desk or the factory bench. In the ultimate, productivity is managed nationally just like education or health are. Like an organization, the state can choose whether to control individual effort, or to support it.

An economy that discourages personal or corporate consumption, however sound the reasons, necessarily diminishes the market for the goods or services which workers produce. Exports may make up some of the slack, but these usually also depend upon a strong home market to carry some of the current costs and finance development. Individual productivity may be high but unsold goods provide no income. The productivity equation reduces to zero.

A government that permits high unemployment may claim that this is a necessary, if undesirable, outcome of encouraging high productivity. But what is the productivity of the unemployed? Even in an organizational context the ill-considered sacking of workers, in response to adverse markets or government policy, may have little strategic justification. During the middle 1980s, media attention in the UK turned rapidly from job losses to skill-shortages. In the first half of the decade, skilled people of all types were being ushered to the door of many large organizations. Better strategies are required at both organizational and national level to deal with the effects of an economic down-turn in employment.

Trade unions and productivity

Developing the human resource is about more than the effective use of high-calibre people who are starting or changing their careers; an equally important task is improving the skills and motivation of the longer-serving members of a workforce. Ability to do this depends on two constraints—trade unions and training.

In Chapter 1, the trade unions were perceived as a major preoccupation of personnel managers during the late 1860s and 1970s. Undoubtedly some improvements in productivity were achieved during this period, but nationally, performance languished.

Trade union membership, from the middle of the nineteenth century, was a barometer of industrial growth, reaching 12 million in 1979—well over 50 per cent of the workforce. Since then, structural change in the economy, unemployment and a change in public attitudes have wrought havoc on trade union membership, political influence and financial viability. For managers who want to change working practices, the situation has never been so favourable (Bassett, 1988). Workers in the new industries are not interested in joining unions, and managements have successfully resisted recognition claims where there has been union activity. Membership of TUC-affiliated unions has fallen to 9 million while the employed workforce has increased. A Gallup poll in 1976 showed that 85 per cent of the population thought that trade unions had influence; 10 years later, 65 per cent thought they had no influence.

In the UK, the sad fact is that trade unions give little attention to the business strategies of the companies and other organizations where their members work. The appointment of worker-directors has been rarely attempted and has not been a success. Looking after members' interests is seen only in terms of immediate rewards, and not as longer-term development for themselves or the health of the employer's business. Since job protection is the second item on the agenda, flexibility and mobility are not encouraged either. This state of affairs may owe its origins as much to the attitudes of employers as to those of trade union members and officers, but it has to be faced. The 1980s saw some rather brutal confrontations with established trade union power, and a reduction in membership and influence in government. One of the few trade unions in the UK to see its members' interests strategically, as training and adaptability, was expelled from the Trade Union Congress for its support for no-strike deals.

The values of trade unions were developed during an earlier phase of industrialization, and have not always altered with the changing realities of production. In days when loss of a job meant starvation, Luddism was understandable. Nowadays, union membership and institutions are sometimes based on skills, and skill differentials, that have no clear relevance to the tasks and objectives of modern organizations. A division still exists, for example, between sheet metal and woodworkers, working side by side in the same factory. The tools used are often identical, and the skills are transferable. This division was maintained during the 1980s in the face of commercial realities at one custom vehicle factory, resulting in closure. Perceptions are changing, of course, and multi-skilling is becoming accepted. Trade unions, perhaps of all large, slow-moving organizations, are the slowest to perceive themselves as part of a continuing process of change; the industralization that brought them into existence has moved from spinning-frames to microchips and lasers. Human skills cannot be institutionalized.

Recognition of valued skills as the basis of work organization and rewards is inhibited when all other sections of a unionized workforce demand parity with their most skilled members. This restricts management's ability to provide a better service by training and paying extra to those from whom special skills and commitment to work are required. Examples may be found in public sector employment.

Given the current orientation of trade union thought, human resource specialists must regard unions more as a constraint on strategic management than as contributors to it. This should not inhibit the consultation of individual members, or their local representatives, as part of the strategic process. Unions themselves will find a new role; employers should encourage helpful tendencies.

As work moves from the routine to the conceptual, and from mass production to customized output, unions representing unskilled and semi-skilled employees should consider two possible accommodations to the flexible labour market. One would be for unions themselves to become labour agencies, hiring work teams to employers who need their temporary services. More important, and more courageously, they should press for better education, not only at school, but remedially in later life, thus helping their members to take advantage of industrial change. Providing educational facilities for members has been an important aspect of EEPTU (the British electricians' and plumbers' union) policy in recent years. As the patterns of work continue to change in the direction of individual responsibility for aspects of the business, and with a concommitant growth in self-employment, the outlook for trade unions is bleak. What was appropriate for an earlier stage in industralization looks out of place at the end of the twentieth century.

Trade unions, of course, are not the only conservative force in a fast-changing world of work. Coulson-Thomas (see Chapter 7) has noted the need for the professional institutions to accommodate to transient membership as different specialisms engage the interest and attention of knowledge-workers. Restricting access to expertise is doomed to failure; expert systems already exist to give legal opinions on cases, and to diagnose illness from symptoms. This is not to deny the personal skills or status of the professions, but merely to point out that functions and attitudes will inevitably change. Both professions and trade unions should protect members' interests, not by holding back change, but by responding positively to it. Human resource specialists, working from an organizational base, should do their best to encourage the process.

Training and productivity

If trade unions ossify the categorization of workers in ways that restrict development, the enlightened provision of opportunities for education and training should have the opposite effect. Productivity, especially in the sense used later in this chapter, depends crucially on a well-educated workforce. This book does not discuss training theory or practice as there is copious literature on these subjects. An essential element, however, in the outermost circle of productivity (Figure 5.1), is the will to provide education and training for the sophisticated technology and markets of 1990s and the new century. The strategic outlook is far from encouraging.

Management education would be universally regarded as a necessary condition for a healthy economy, yet, as reports by Handy, and by Constable and McCormick (1987) pointed out, perceiving the need has not encouraged action. So what of the rest of the workforce?

Both major political parties in the UK believe that education and training of the workers both need to be vastly improved; the arguments are about how to achieve this desirable objective. Britain has one of the worst records in the industrialized world for retaining pupils in education after the minimum school leaving age. In Europe only Greece has a lower percentage of stayers. Few of the leavers go directly into work where there is organized, high-quality, vocational training. At the other end of the scale, only a small proportion of managers are graduates and few managers, whatever their educational background, receive regular training.

When these problems were first recognized in the UK, some 30 years ago, the 1944 Education Act had already been in force for 20 years. Its purpose had been to give appropriate education to pupils according to what were thought to be their natural abilities. Pupils were allocated to different schools following a test of scholastic aptitude at the age of 11. In the 1960s, this allocation was thought to be holding back many who could benefit from higher education, or whose aspirations were restricted by allocation to a secondary modern school. As one author put it (Newsom, 1963), we were ignoring 'half our future'. Three brave experiments were initiated to improve the level of education and skill of Britain's working population; the blending of separate schools to produce 'comprehensives', the expansion of university and polytechnic education, and the setting up of industrial training boards to encourage the level and frequency of training at work. Though all three measures had beneficial effects, they did not produce a highly educated and skilled workforce. It appears that mixing together pupils of widely different abilities, whatever the social advantages, does not engender a desire for education in those who would not otherwise have grasped it. The widening opportunities to acquire degrees were eagerly taken up by the children of an expanding middle class, but not by those of unskilled workers. In 1990, only 17 per cent of school-leavers proceeded to any form of full-time higher education.

The training board grants and levies intended to encourage training at work were a failure; the good employers continued their sound practices, while the others farmed the system to minimize their levy. Training boards were seen as yet another fiscal device. The strategic purpose of training, the radical improvement of workforce skills to prepare for change and new industries, was lost sight of in indifference, bureaucracy and training for the past instead of the future.

Ten years after the Industrial Training Act, a Manpower Services Commission was established, in an attempt to broaden the narrow, industry-based approach to training. As unemployment rose during the 1970s and 1980s, this organization was deflected from its original purpose, and became enmeshed in a series of schemes intended to provide help for those out of work. The best of these included training in computer skills or provided places on vocational postgraduate degree courses, but most of the time, and for most clients, the purpose was merely to provide alternatives to regular employment. At the end of the 1980s, the government policy was to return the responsibility for training to regional boards, under the direction of local employers. Some would say, 'This is where we came in'.

A major legacy of the Manpower Services Commission was the Youth Training Scheme, intended to provide employment and some level of training for the sizeable fraction of school-leavers who could not find work. A valuable social aim has been served by this means, but the scheme has been criticized for its low level of pay (it seemed that the government was using the scheme to reduce the levels of pay to which young workers had become accustomed) and the basic training provided. Many employers, understandably, saw the scheme as an adjunct to the concept of the flexible firm, the opportunity to hire unskilled people when needed. As such, the human resource specialist has a model for the hiring of general labour suggested above. Attempts are now being made, through the medium of a national curriculum, to provide all pupils with some basic levels of knowledge and competence. Human resource specialists should not look solely, or mainly, to politicians for solutions to their supply problems.

Liaison with local schools, often encouraged but seldom carried out, offers an opportunity to make pupils aware of the ways in which the labour markets are changing, and of the value of acquiring the best possible education. The immediate problem is with an existing workforce, often dedicated to stability in a changing world. Chapters 7 and 8 return to this topic.

A fair day's pay?

Productivity is a function both of skill and motivation. Many managers now take a sophisticated view of pay as a motivator. Following the Maslovian theory that is still the common currency of management courses, they believe that the intrinsic qualities of work matter more. They may well be right. A long career in industry, however, does not convince the author that all managers, particularly production managers, share this attitude. They see their own working lives to be dominated by a need to achieve, yet assume that the people who work for them do so only for cash. So well-established is this belief that 'payment by results' systems are still very popular.

The relationship between the common types of payment system are shown in Figure 5.2. To the strategic eye, it should be apparent that these are at best mere tactical devices. Incentive schemes are expensive to set up and maintain, and the expected benefits are seldom fully achieved in practice. Incentive payments are usually negotiated with the workforce, and the relation between effort and pay is understandably contentious. Work-study can be used to rationalize the argument, but work-study expertise and managerial time are themselves costly commodities. As discussed above, workers may voluntarily restrict output in case the payment rates are tightened, and so as not to penalize slow colleagues. Social and security needs are stronger than the need for immediate cash.

While 'payment by results' schemes do not necessarily increase output, they can discourage attention to quality. This is a poor form of motivation when quality and service are the keys to continuing markets. While 'pure' piece-work, in which pay is related solely to output, is still used for outworkers,

Figure 5.2
Common types of payment systems

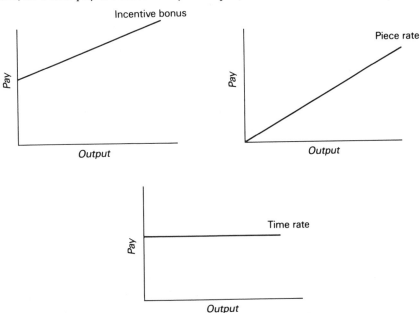

payment is now more likely to be based on 'incentive bonus' systems in which hourly pay is supplemented with premium payments based on output, and perhaps on quality. The influence of the group on productivity has been recognized in 'measured day work' which rewards group output above an agreed minimum with a shared bonus, The British motor industry, in the 1970s, swung unhappily between group and individual incentives. That systems and management were the key to higher productivity emerged ironically during the harsh decision-making of the 1980s.

'Time rate' is most often used to reward people in white-collar jobs, and it is an interesting reflection on our industrial heritage that middle-class workers are assumed to be motivated by professional standards of work commitment and quality, and to work diligently without financial incentives. As Martin Weiner (1981) has pointed out, the 'professionalism' of middle-class employees, recompensed by a just 'fee', is as much a product of industrialization as Marx's 'proletariat'. A changed perception seemed to be behind the late-1980s' interest in 'performance pay', especially for professionals in the public sector of the UK economy.

A fair day's work

Incentive payment systems are unlikely to be successful if the standards of performance are arbitrarily arrived at. Work-study is a set of techniques for making these judgements more objective, and is used to measure the detailed actions of the worker. The concept of work-study, as 'scientific management', is often ascribed to the American F. W. Taylor, and assumed to date from the turn of the century. It has its roots, however, at a much earlier stage in the history of industrialization, and is in fact integral to it. Andrew Ure (1835) perceived that taking the control of work away from the 'crafty workman' was one of the benefits of the factory system. In using this phrase, he was not complementing workers on their skilfulness. In the first Industrial Revolution (see Chapter 2), the fundamental process was organization, not mechanization. An important element in the organization of production was the control of manufacture that had hitherto been conducted as outwork. The first step in the continuing process of control is to get production into a factory building, under the eye of owners or managers. Once this has been achieved, they can turn their attention to the flow of work between workers, and the tasks each has to carry out. The economic advantages of specialization were apparent to Adam Smith as early as 1780. Specialization and control were necessary at the time, but are no longer the first priorities of an advanced industrial economy.

The next step was to study ways in which working methods could be speeded up. Technology was applied as owners and managers sought ways of replacing or augmenting people in the productive process. Managers planned and controlled; workers worked at their allotted tasks. The era of the professional manager had begun.

Work-study was Taylor's significant, but not iconoclastic, contribution to the continuing process of industrialization. The organization and mechanization of work had started long before his time, but he was one of the first to look closely at what workers actually did as they carried out their tasks. He favoured the 'one best way' of carrying out a manual task, fruits of the application of managerial intelligence to the details of labour. To his credit, he also saw that effort would only be applied in this way if workers were motivated to do so. The earlier stages of industrialization had taken place in countries where labour was relatively plentiful and motivated by hunger;

workers either worked or starved. As Kemp (1978) makes clear, American industrialization took place against a background of labour shortage, so that motivation by the threat of dismissal was not so easy. Effective use of both workers and technology was encouraged.

Taylor's deal with the workforce was to offer financial incentives in terms of higher pay for higher output, provided that the carefully developed methods were applied. Waves of newly arrived immigrants, with minds firmly set on making good in a new country, were susceptible to this method of motivation. They needed money to set up home and improve the lot of their families, and this objective could be achieved by doing the manager's bidding.

Taylor's original system would now be better described as method-study. He was concerned with the application of effort in the most economical way, thus increasing the output to effort ratio. A related, but distinct, issue is the time taken to carry out each operation in a repetitive task. Method-study should precede time-study because it is of little value to know the time taken to perform unnecessary or badly-sequenced tasks. Despite this fact, 'time and motion study' became the bane of twentieth-century working life, and the butt of many jokes. Chaplin's *Modern Times* was only one of the films to have guyed organized production and the work-study expert.

Workers do not remain passive in the face of scientific management. If economic and social conditions allow, they join trade unions in order to protect themselves against what they see as unreasonable demands. Perhaps more signficantly, they protect themselves within the work group against pressure to work beyond a certain speed. This protection consists of discouraging overzealous work in others, and by limiting their own immediate earnings in the interest of long-term wage stability. When they are timed by work-study specialists they ensure, whatever 'slack' is officially allowed in the timing, that they build in some of their own. The following quotation from Pagnamenta and Overy (1984) gives the flavour of the work-study culture as it is experienced on the shop-floor. The following extracts are quotations from workers in the British aircraft industry in the late 1940s:

> Once a new aircraft was started, then each particular item had to be priced, and after doing the first five or ten, including the prototype, then the rate-fixer used to come down on the shop-floor and he had to argue, or discuss, what the price should be for that particular item, or what number of hours would be allowed for the manufacture of a particular article . . .
>
> . . . If people, for example, worked in a blind hole, you used to tap and bang and the rate-fixer was outside listening to all this banging and tapping. They'd finish fitting this component an hour before, but they'd carry on running the rivet guns and tapping and banging, come out sweating and say, 'It's finished, stop the clock now'. They'd been stopped an hour. Earnings were very high on the assembly bays because they were very good talkers.

It should be mentioned that there was a strategic reason why timings were slack in the aircraft industry at that time: the customer was the government, and contracts were negotiated on a cost-plus basis. But the practice of 'fiddling the rates' is widespread.

Not all jobs to be rewarded by incentive payment schemes are subject to stop-watch timing. Predetermined motion timing allows the physical movements in a repetitive job to be divided into standard segments, for which standard times exist. The separate times can be aggregated for the whole job.

Office work is not immune from time and motion study. As the number of clerical workers increased, and manual workers decreased, attention was turned to the information factories that handle the requirements of a welfare state and the new service industries. Since office work more obviously (or more plausibly) requires thought as well as physical action, attention is paid to output rather than to the detail of how work is done. Clerical work measurement is concerned, say, with the number of forms processed per hour, rather than with the actions required to process each form. Both individual workers and departments can be assessed by this means.

Another method of measuring clerical work is activity sampling. The observer enters the department at random times and takes note of the activities that each worker is engaged on. This allows average times spent on each activity to be calculated. Potentially more valuable than their quasi-work-study role is the use of activity sampling and other forms of job analysis in wider areas of human resource planning. Job descriptions and personnel specifications could be greatly improved by careful observation of the way in which work is done.

Efficiency and effectiveness

From the human resource planner's point of view, the purpose behind studying motivation, payment systems and job evaluation, must be primarily to improve productivity. Planners are concerned not only with numbers of workers but also with the output obtained from each. But how should we measure productivity of individual workers? How much relevance does it have for a dualistic economy in a developing country, or in an advanced industrialized nation with a large proportion of workers in the service sector? And to what extent is the individual worker able to control his or her output in a complex organization?

The fault in much thinking about productivity is that it is often myopic, at best tactical, and never strategic. The reasons for this are the measures used, and narrowness of their application. Even at national level, a simplistic equation is created between national productivity and national well-being. Productivity is measured by an equally simplistic ratio that we have already used: output divided by input, each expressed in money terms.

Jones (1982) has pointed out the fallacy of this type of thinking by comparing the industrialized and less-developed countries. Bolivia, for example, emerged in the 1970s as the country with the highest productivity, because the value of its major product, tin, was then fetching a high price: output in money terms was high. Wages, on the contrary, were low. This combination of factors yielded, on paper, a very high figure for national productivity.

The *quality of life index*, however, told a different story—Bolivia was at the bottom of the world league. Britain, whose level of productivity in 1970s was something of a joke, nevertheless managed a reasonable rating in the quality of life table. So the relationship between productivity and quality of life is by no means direct or clear.

Jones explained the paradox by noting that the activities in an economy that contribute most to quality of life—education, health and social services—are also those where productivity is most difficult to measure. These benefits appear as costs, with no easy method of stating their value in cash terms. As the 1980s drew to a close, the British government appeared to be willing to let market forces establish the value of public services. To doubt the validity of using the market as the sole arbiter of aesthetic and social values is not, however, to support the alternative of state control. Services and social goods need some measures of efficient provision.

What is needed is a strategic approach that sees the factory, the office, the local authority, the national economy, as the complex systems they truly are. Glib oversimplications by politicians or managers place workers in a false position; their supposed lack of effort is the excuse for managerial failure. This is the analogy of ascribing failures to achieve 'Five Year Plans' under Communist regimes to 'sabotage', regardless of the massive system faults that exist in an overplanned economy.

The emphasis in what is left of manufacturing industry, in Britain and in many former 'industrialized' countries, is increasingly on automated and robotized production. Individual incentives based on units of output are clearly out of place. Given their dubious value even when the worker could increase output by individual effort, traditional payment by results schemes should now be phased out. Even if these payment systems work as incentives to higher mass production, they also rigidify the existing production methods and make regular changes in methods and technology more difficult.

This may not be appropriate advice for all situations; at the time of writing, Russian managers, after many years of command planning, are attempting to introduce a market economy and payment by results on the shop-floor. Given the yearning of its citizens for a better life, which they interpret in the Gorbachev era are more consumer goods and better food, the old Tayloristic principles may work. But as the technology available to Russian industrial managers begins to improve, they too will need to revise their thinking about shop-floor incentives.

In an age that increasingly relegates production to machines, or to computers, the role of the worker is undergoing a change at least as dramatic as was brought about during Britain's Industrial Revolution. Emphasis in these new conditions is not upon units of output, but upon the achievement of objectives, the design of systems and their availability when needed. Such tasks require high intelligence, training in problem-solving techniques and multiple skills. Salary levels will be determined largely by the market, but completion of a task on time and to the required quality can be specifically and explicitly rewarded by achievement-related pay.

Some jobs still require the diligent and timely completion of routine tasks rather than the application of special skills. Motivation may be best achieved not by work study and output-based incentives, but establishing the worker as the manager of his or her own business. In effect they have control over both input and output. Personal responsibility for success is clear, and workers themselves determine priorities and make choices. This inverts the Tayloristic philosophy: workers become managers, subject to the disciplines of the market within which they work. Effectiveness within a broad strategy is substituted for the narrow goal of efficiency in a subsidiary system. We could be entering a new era of the 'responsible worker', with a pre-industrial, rather than post-industrial logic. Options include home-working, especially its high-tech teleworking variant, or self-employment. Another model would be the commission only agents used by financial services companies—the business within a business. Management buy-outs, and hiving off subsidiary services from both private and public organizations in the 1980s, also showed the way.

The strategic forces that are dictating the swing away from 'economic man' to the 'responsible worker' are partly technological, but the market is also playing its part. People who want responsibility in their work also wish to exercise responsibility in their choice of goods. Market forces not only include price, but also personal satisfaction and the perceived effect of the purchase on the environment. The role of the worker can no longer be isolated from the role of customer, as it was during the earlier phases of industrialization. Quality and service are the responsibility of everyone in an organization, not merely tasks assigned to sales and maintenance staff. Performance pay, total quality management and quality circles are evidence that managers are taking these market demands seriously. These issues are further discussed in Case Study 5 at the end of this chapter.

Pay and motivation

The Eastern bloc has discovered the virtue of incentives that motivate a sense of personal responsibility at work; whether payment by results, on the old Western model, is the best way of doing this is a matter for debate. The market traders in Moscow have long been able to sell their produce at higher prices than the state shops, simply because they can supply customers with what they needed, when they needed it. Traders are motivated to take account of their markets in a way that the manager of a factory is not, because he is separated from his customers by a state purchasing system. Incentive is linked to responsibility. Russia, in short, wishes to motivate its workers, whatever techniques are eventually used to achieve this. But what is this intangible but apparently vital concept of motivation? We must make some attempt to understand such a commonly discussed topic.

In the physical world, we see two events occurring together, or in succession, and we may assume that one caused the other. Reference to Chapter 3 will show that philosophers of science now believe that cause cannot be proved, only disproved. The assumption of cause is necessary in everyday life, even if proof is impossible—if I turn on the switch the kettle will boil and I can make some tea.

For the psychologist and the manager, things may get more complicated; did the negotiated incentive scheme cause greater output, or was it the fact that management really talked to the workforce for the first time for 20 years? The additional assumption that we have to make is that human beings possess the conscious intentionality, something which makes them superior to animals and to computers. When someone is perceived to perform an action, it is assumed that he or she has willed to do it. The wish, the need to achieve some goal, has 'motivated' the action. If wishes determine actions, then it would seem possible to so arrange things that a person's wishes and actions are what another individual, or society at large, desires. One school of psychology, the behaviourists, believed that the unseen and unquantifiable 'wishes' could be ignored, and attention directed solely to the external arrangements, the management of contingencies. The classic experimental condition was the pigeon in a cage, performing simple tasks in response to a feeding regime. This may seem a poor model for our responsible worker, but one that some managers apply to the design of incentive schemes. Few psychologists, however, would now support a 'pure' behaviourist position, the assumption that mental events have no direct relevance to human action.

Most behaviourists would now accept that mental events have an information processing role to play in motivation, though the sensations of satisfaction or dissatisfaction that people report might still be regarded as irrelevant. More recent theories of motivation stress either the mental processes of motivation, or its emotional content.

Two well-known 'need' theories, which concentrate on the content rather than the process of motivation, are Maslow's (1954) *Hierarchy of needs*, and

Herzberg's (1959) 'two-factor' theory. These are interesting applications of humanistic thinking to the world of work, but neither theory could be accepted as scientific. They nevertheless have an intuitive appeal for managers attending business courses, and provide a useful storehouse of ideas for dealing with motivational problems at work. Schein (1970) has summed up the basically Maslovian categorization of motivations by stating that the manager is not dealing with 'economic man', 'social man', or 'self-actualizing man', but with 'complex man', whose needs are complicated, various and change with time. To assume that an incentive payment scheme will wholly and continuously motivate a particular worker to greater productive effort is to ask too much of a one-dimensional system. We will look more closely at motivational theory, and its relationship to job satisfaction, in the next chapter.

Is pay a motivator?

One problem with understanding motivation is that people do not like to talk about their deepest needs or fears. The automatic reaction to the question, 'Why do you go to work?', is to reply that you need the money. Britain's *Guardian* newspaper regularly publishes the results of a survey of its members' views on the world of work and the jobs they do. Figure 5.3 shows some results of a survey carried out in 1988. Pay does not figure strongly among the reasons given for working; nor does it appear, as such, in the theories mentioned in the last section, a reason for some managers' rejection of what they see as irrelevant psychologizing.

Redundancy and unemployment were discussed in Chapter 2. Being deprived of a source of income is the most immediate and worrying personal aspect of redundancy, but other feelings follow close behind. The redundant worker feels deprived of social relationships, self-esteem and, most important, the opportunity to make choices and to use valued skills.

The reader will observe that these aspects of work map neatly on to the 'content' theories described above, at least in so far as they relate to job satisfaction. Redundancy, in a sense, is an experimental justification for the theories of Maslow and Hertzberg. The deprivation that redundant workers feel is expressed in terms of social, self-esteem and self-actualization needs, despite their ignorance of motivational theory. One can only assume that what they now feel deprived of was once a benefit of being at work.

So losing a job does more harm than taking away a source of money. Work is an opportunity to use our skills, gain self-esteem and interact with a wide variety of people. Some forms of work, let alone unemployment, also leave the worker deprived of these psychological benefits (see Chapter 2). If so, pay assumes a greater importance, and it is possible to arrive at a situation in which pay is the only motivator. The 'instrumental' reward, pay, has superceded the 'intrinsic' satisfactions of work. This is not, of course, to say that the pattern of human needs has changed; simply that work is regarded solely as a source of cash, which will subsequently be used to buy satisfactions elsewhere. Pay also has a symbolic importance, giving feedback to the employee of his or her worth to the organization. Two quotations will make very different points about the instrumental and symbolic implications of pay:

> The Government's search for a new chairman for British Rail ended yesterday when Bob Reid of Shell UK was appointed to the job on a salary of £200,000—more than twice that of Sir Robert Reid the previous chairman . . . but he denied prolonging the Government's agony by holding out for a big salary: 'I could probably go elsewhere and earn £400,000.'
> (Harrison 1989)

Figure 5.3
Factors in job
satisfaction

	Important % Profile
The respect of people you work with	88
Personal freedom	87
Learning something new	86
A challenge	83
Seeing your suggestions acted upon	84
Helping other people	82
Being asked for advice	78
Respect of people in your field	76
Being well trained	74
Being liked by people you work with	74
Influencing events	72
Working conditions	71
Being offered increasing responsibility	69
Completing a project	68
Being part of a team	65
Meeting people through work	65
Influencing people	64
Working as an individual	63
Starting a project	61
Solving a human relations' problem	59
Security	55
Being praised by superiors	53
Status in your organisation	50
Being promoted	45
Solving a technical problem	45
Status of your organisation	42
Setting up new system	43
Making money	40
Exercising power	26
Social status	19

Source: Knight, G. P. 'Why work?' survey, January 1989, *The Guardian*

Lord Robens, Chairman of the Coal Board in 1960s, was understandably worried about the high rates of absenteeism in the pits. On one of his regular colliery visits, he asked a miner why he worked only four days a week. 'Because I can't earn enough in three', was the reply.

Herzberg listed pay as a 'hygiene factor'. Poor pay and inequitable payment systems generate dissatisfaction, causing demotivation. Even if pay is competitive and pay systems are perceived as equitable, however, there is no guarantee that workers will be motivated. Reduced to its essence, pay is a punishment, not a reward. Threatening its removal may be a crude way of influencing workers' immediate behaviour. As a way of encouraging steady improvements in productivity, it needs to be supplemented by psychologically valid rewards.

Mention of equitable payment systems raises another problem with pay as a motivator; what you earn is often not as important as what you earn in relation to others. In large organizations, with stable employment, this problem has been tackled by using a job evaluation, sometimes linking both staff and manual jobs. Much management effort, which could have been better applied to thinking strategically about the business, has been used in deciding the niceties of the job evaluation scheme, and in settling subsequent disputes. In any consideration of pay and productivity, however, it cannot be ignored.

Job evaluation

Apart from collective bargaining, and the operation of a market for scarce skills, is there any way in which the absolute worth of jobs can be established? The answer must be no, because the content of work varies widely and the value placed on various activities is determined by custom and culture. But it is possible, within a consistent value system, to determine the relative worth of jobs. The process is called *job evaluation.*

Job evaluation, self-evidently, depends on the evaluators having a thorough knowledge of the work to be evaluated, either through personal experience or from carefully prepared job descriptions. Once this knowledge is available, the methods used may be analytic or non-analytic.

Non-analytic methods include *job ranking* and *job grading*. In job ranking, jobs are placed in order of importance, but their relative value is not established. This technique provides a rough and ready, but cheap, method of ariving at a salary structure for a small unit.

For job grading, a scheme relating various types of work to grades must be available before evaluation is carried out. Jobs are then allocated to the most appropriate grade. This rationalizes the allocation process but, as with job ranking, relative worth is not established. An example of a job grading scheme is shown in Figure 5.4. Grading can be used effectively in organizations where all jobs contain a high administrative and clerical content, for instance an insurance company. Difficulties arise when the job content varies widely. In a multi-functional organization like a manufacturing plant, the jobs of technologists, accountants and production staff defy common grade descriptions. The same would be true of the pluralistic workforce within the health service. So problems of comparability are added to problems of relative value and sabotage the very objectives that job evaluation is intended to achieve.

To say how much more one job is worth than another, we need an analytic method that considers the job content in terms of skills, education and other qualities required, and which also compensates for stress or bad conditions. A popular example of an analytic method is points-rating. This technique has particular value for the human resource planner because, as suggested in Chapter 2, it opens the way to effective categories for workers. These would be based on the skills and other demands of the job rather than job titles.

The points-rating method, and indeed all analytic methods, depend on two important stages. The first is to identify factors that are common to much of the work performed in an organization. The second is to weight the relative importance of these factors to the organization's purposes. A simple, and oft-quoted example, suggests that jobs be evaluated on the following five factors; job knowledge, education required, mental effort, physical effort and working conditions. In a knowledge-based industry, more emphasis would be given to the first three than the others; in a heavy manufacturing plant the opposite might be the case.

The selection and the weighting of factors reflect both the activities of an organization and the culture within which it operates. They will also reflect, overtly or covertly, the market values of the skills required. Job evaluation is not scientific, in the sense that it avoids the application of value systems to

Figure 5.4
A job grading scheme

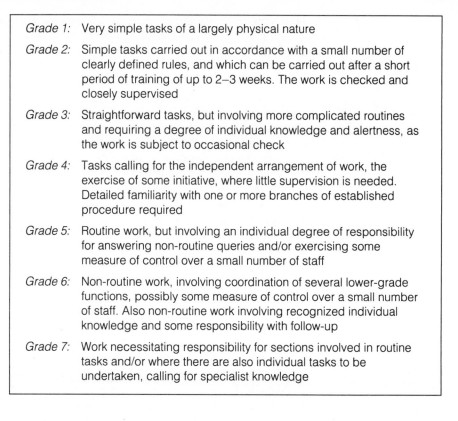

Grade 1:   Very simple tasks of a largely physical nature

Grade 2:   Simple tasks carried out in accordance with a small number of clearly defined rules, and which can be carried out after a short period of training of up to 2–3 weeks. The work is checked and closely supervised

Grade 3:   Straightforward tasks, but involving more complicated routines and requiring a degree of individual knowledge and alertness, as the work is subject to occasional check

Grade 4:   Tasks calling for the independent arrangement of work, the exercise of some initiative, where little supervision is needed. Detailed familiarity with one or more branches of established procedure required

Grade 5:   Routine work, but involving an individual degree of responsibility for answering non-routine queries and/or exercising some measure of control over a small number of staff

Grade 6:   Non-routine work, involving coordination of several lower-grade functions, possibly some measure of control over a small number of staff. Also non-routine work involving recognized individual knowledge and some responsibility with follow-up

Grade 7:   Work necessitating responsibility for sections involved in routine tasks and/or where there are also individual tasks to be undertaken, calling for specialist knowledge

work. Evaluating jobs is a branch of social research, and cannot evade the latter's value-laden aspects. It is also important to note that the factors are drawn from different aspects of a job analysis. Education and job knowledge should appear in the personnel specification rather than the job description; mental and physical effort, and working conditions contribute to the definition of job context. Job content, the activities and skills required, are not represented in this simple scheme.

Once a set of factors and weightings are established, however, the scheme can be used to evaluate jobs across all functions in an organization, and will provide relative numerical values upon which pay scales can be based. More elaborate job evaluation schemes include a wider range of factors (see the example in Table 5.1), and go some way towards overcoming the criticism that job evaluation concentrates on the context of jobs rather than their essential content. The scheme in Table 5.1 includes an evaluation of the analytic content of work, the requirement for logical thought and data processing skills. Another factor to be assessed is decision-making, the extent to which the job requires the job-holder to recognize and evaluate complex situations. A range of basic skills are subsumed within the factor. A job requiring high levels of accuracy, however, has implications for personality characteristics, rather than for skills. High rating on the numbers of staff supervised, and for liaison both inside and outside the organization, carry implications for both interpersonal skills and temperament.

Education is one of the most debatable factors in the scheme presented in Table 5.1, and it crops up in most others. Education, to be sure, is a rough and ready measure of intelligence, and of earlier motivation to succeed.

Depending on its vocational content, it may indicate the possession of job-related skills. But the assumption that a particular educational qualification is a necessity for carrying out many types of work flies in the face of experience. Professionalization introduces both justifiable and spurious requirements for qualifications, but the latter should not blind the strategic human resource planner to the true skill requirements of a job. Education provides some vocational skills, and the ability rapidly to acquire others; as a guide to the evaluation of work it is at best second-hand.

'Experience'?

If 'education' is a debatable factor, 'experience' is the most curious of all. It is at once the factor with the most potential for indicating skills, and in practice the most disappointing. It is measured solely in terms of time. Many readers will be familiar with the honoured member of a department who has performed, to management's satisfaction, the same routine job for many years. No doubt this merits some reward. But to suggest that long experience is a necessity for such work, or even that it is preferable, is plain nonsense. Given the rate at which such jobs are overtaken by technology, a replacement might not be needed at all.

Experience confers two things—job knowledge and skills. If it takes several years to acquire either there must be a problem with job design. Job knowledge should be codified and made available through an organization's information system. Allowing members of an organization to develop secret pockets of generally needed knowledge is to deny the usefulness of strategic thinking, as outlined in Chapter 1. To place too great a reliance on individual knowledge is also to overlook the potential for technology, as discussed in Chapter 2. The sharing of knowledge in an organization will be brought closer as effective artificial intelligence programs are developed. Databases allowing natural language interrogation, and expert systems, will show the way. Specialist knowledge will steadily cease to be the private property of professional employees. Even without this high technology, staff induction training should include the imparting of the essential, formalized knowledge required for effective job performance. 'Experience', as a necessary or even desirable, aspect of work is due for a strategic re-evaluation. Enshrining it in a job evaluation scheme now seems bizarre.

Sometimes, of course, an organization has need of highly specialized knowledge, legal, medical, technical or financial. In a flexible labour market, access to these should be obtained by hiring consultancy and not by recruitment. As Chapter 2 revealed, this is increasingly the pattern even for less specialized work. Significantly, when hiring experts, we are more interested in reported effectiveness than 'years of experience'. But there is another argument for not overstating the value of time spent in a job for its effective performance.

If job knowledge is truly acquired over a long period of time, then much work in that particular function must be carried out inefficiently or ineffectively. The same goes for job-related skills. Without doubt, workers vary in their effectiveness, but this is more likely to be caused by a skill deficit attributable to poor selection procedures or poor training, rather than to insufficient experience, interpreted as time in a previous job. So job analysis, purposive selection and effective and timely training, are the strategic answers to the need for appropriate skills, not qualification by long periods of sub-optimal work.

As human resource planners move towards performance criteria rather than the assessment of jobs on traditional lines, so 'experience required' will lose its importance, certainly in assessing human resources, and probably in job evaluation. The latter, as the reader may already have divined, is something of a digression from our stated topic—productivity defined either as efficiency or as effectiveness. Although the subjects of job evaluation are reassured that 'the job is evaluated, not the person', several of the factors in the system described in Table 5.1 appear to indicate personality traits of the successful incumbent. Other factors are there to deal with 'equalizing differences', as the economists describe them; extra points to compensate for working conditions.

Table 5.1
Range of factors in a
job evaluation scheme

Factors	Maximum points
1 Education	50
2 Experience	100
3 Relationships:	
(a) Internal	(50)
(b) External	(50)
4 Analysis	50
5 Work of others	25
6 Financial effect	50
7 Accuracy	50
8 Decision-making	50
9 Confidentiality	25
10 Property	25
11 Time schedules	25
12 Mental effort	25
13 Surroundings	10
14 Travel	20
	Total 605

Before writing off job evaluation as of little use to the strategic human resource planner, however, it is necessary to consider its potential contribution to the wider issue of job analysis. What could job evaluation, as presently constituted, tell us about the skills needed by a successful job-holder? If we know that, one requirement for greater productivity is within our grasp.

Rationalizing job analysis

In Chapter 4, the psychometric method of selection was described in terms of job analysis, leading from the unanalysed concept of the job to a job description and thence to a personnel specification, against which candidates would be measured. It was suggested that the job description, whatever the format used by particular organizations, should contain information about job context, job content and especially about the skills required of the job-holder. Job analysis for selection may differ from job analysis for reward. The former, as Fleishman (1984) has pointed out, requires the analyst to concentrate upon the tasks to be carried, the behaviour of the job-holder that contributes to task achievement, and the personal attributes (skills and attitudes) which make performance possible. While job context plays a significant part in success, possession of the appropriate skills is vital to it. This is the meaning of the central circle in Figure 5.1.

How far do the standard methods of job evaluation allow the analyst to explore jobs along Fleishman's dimension? The points-rating method tends to muddle the description of tasks and behaviour, and also to confuse job content and job context. Factors like 'experience required', which occur in most such evaluation schemes, emphasize behaviour by implying that the job-holder will be expected to repeat actions performed in previous work. To reward this aspect of work may seem ill-advised in today's fast-changing job market. Nevertheless, a high proportion of the available points are usually given over to this factor.

Other aspects of job analysis are, however, shared by both versions. Task characteristics are represented by such factors as 'numbers of staff supervised' and 'interpersonal contact'. Also to be found are factors that relate to attributes of the job-holder; 'analytical skill' is a good example. 'Number of staff supervised' merely implies skills of supervision, 'analytical skill' states the requirement directly. But the emphasis in analysis for job evaluation is on factors to be rewarded or compensated, it is not upon the essential skills required. Thus job analysis may achieve one organizational objective, a rational payment system, and fail to meet the requirements of another, effective selection.

Job evaluation, to borrow a concept from Chapter 4, lacks face validity. It does not reflect very accurately the way the job is seen by the job-holder; factors associated with job content, job context and skills used are weighted and evaluated in the same process, although their psychological impacts are quite different. Like most management techniques, job evaluation was suited to a particular period in post-war industrial history; that period when the search for 'economies of scales' had created large bureaucracies in both the public and private sectors, when white-collar work was beginning to overtake shop-floor manual labour in importance, and when there was a need to justify pay-scales to expanding white-collar unions. It is less well-adapted to a world in which products and customer demands are changing rapidly. It measures three aspects of jobs without considering the effort expended by job-holders, nor the results that they achieve. Organizations wishing to plan the use of their human resources strategically should use job evaluation with care; first as a research tool to discover whether existing pay scales have any rational basis. Revised pay scales should not be introduced, however, without considering whether the evaluation scheme itself is truly justifiable in the particular circumstances of the organization, and whether it is placing most value on those aspects of work and workers that are most needed in a changing market. This requires a shift from evaluating the job to evaluating the person who does it; from job content and job context to skills. As the redundancies of the 1980s have taught us, not without some pain, people are able to adapt to very different types of work when the situation demands. A strategic approach requires that this flexibility is made use of without the necessity for redundancy.

Skills: the elusive imperative

Job evaluation fails as a vehicle for job analysis: selection procedures often fail through being overconcerned with peripheral matters of 'personality' and 'social acceptability' at the expense of skills. The central issue in any selection decision should be the skills that a satisfactory candidate should possess.

One reason why skills play so small a part in the assessment of candidates is the difficulty of defining them. In Chapter 2, skills were described as belonging to one of two major categories, 'psychomotor' or 'symbolic'. Alternative names for these categories are 'action' and 'mental' skills. Beyond this, the identification of the fundamental skills becomes difficult. In practice, lists of 'skills' may remain at the level of tasks, or arbitrarily include personality characteristics such as 'initiative' (Rawling, 1982).

Analysis begins with listing the tasks required of the job-holder. It continues with the identification of the behaviours necessary to carry out those tasks. Finally, the tasks are inspected to reveal the job-holder attributes (traits) that are needed for the behaviour to be possible. The problem lies partly in the definition of skill itself, and partly in deciding when the skills listed are fundamental. Neisser (1983) is sanguine about the former difficulty, and points out that many psychological concepts are identified by attributes, rather than being capable of hard and fast definition. The attributes of skilled behaviour were discussed in Chapter 2.

The divisibility of skills may be illustrated by the following example. A task frequently found within a personnel manager's job description is 'negotiating with trade unions'. It might be necessary to identify an important contributory skill in this job as negotiation, partly because it could suggest that people with experience of negotiating in, say, sales, might be suitable despite the difference in job title. Can we, however, regard 'negotiation' as a fundamental skill? We are expressing a tautology by saying that 'negotiation with trade unions' requires the skill of 'negotiation'. If we return to the job itself, we may discover that the behaviours required for successful negotiation are meticulous preparation of a case, its forceful but diplomatic presentation, rapid revision while negotiations are in progress, and careful staff work once the negotiation is over. The emergent skills are data-gathering and analysis (research skills), interpersonal sensitivity, mental flexibility and orderly presentation on paper. These personal attributes could be classified in some cases as personality traits rather than skills, although the difference between the two is rather illusory. The important point is that all these attributes could be used independently of each other, and equally effectively in different human situations. Skills have the attribute of portability.

Table 5.2 shows a list of skills devised for use in research into the effect of job changes on the perceptions by the worker of his or her skills. Skills were classified as people-oriented, equipment-oriented and systems-oriented. Neither this classification, nor the lists of skills included are exhaustive nor ideal for all situations, yet it allowed respondents to record their perceived

Table 5.2
List of skills used in research into job changes

People	Systems
Interviewing	Accountancy
Languages	Analysing data
Leadership	Artistic
Negotiating	Clerical/secretarial
Selling/persuading	Computer programming
Public speaking	Creativity
Team-working	Design
	Problem-solving/diagnosis
Equipment	Report-writing
	Setting objectives
Electrical/electronic	Systems analysis
Keyboard	Using standard software
Mechanical	
Testing equipment	

skills before and after the change, with very little amendment. Townsend (1982) developed a practical categorization of transferable skills for use in the development of the Youth Training Scheme in the UK. Strategic human resource planning requires that we regard all such categorizations as provisional, but necessary in order to further the necessary process of research.

Examples of job analysis techniques that focus upon the skill requirements of jobs are the *position analysis questionnaire* (PAQ) and the *job components inventory* (JCI). According to Pearn and Kandola (1988), the JCI is used for jobs ranging from unskilled to technical and supervisory. It consists of eight sections, covering equipment used in the job, working conditions and skills needed. The skills are categorized as physical and perceptual, mathematical, communicative, decision-making and ability to accept responsibility.

The PAQ contains 194 job elements, 187 of which are related to job actitivies. The job itself is seen as an input–output system, rather as the human being was perceived in early behaviourist psychology. The analysis considers the information input needed in the job, the processing required of the job-holder, and the work output in terms of physical processing or the use of equipment. Attention is also given to the context in which the work is conducted. The PAQ is said to be particularly effective in identifying which other jobs relate closely to the job under consideration; that is in placing jobs within the appropriate 'family'. It also identifies the extreme and above average requirements of each job analysed, thus indicating the special needs of selection.

Managerial skills

During the late 1980s, educationalists became worried about two aspects of management training in the UK. The first was the nature of the training given, and the second was the small number of managers who appeared to receive any training at all. These fears were articulated in two reports, one by Handy (1987) and the other by Constable and McCormick (1987). The outcome was a decision by several public bodies to support an attempt to professionalize management, referred to as the *management charter initiative* (MCI). The pros and cons of professionalization will be discussed in Chapter 7. It is the aspect of managerial skills that concerns us here.

In order to achieve chartered status, managers were to be required to take three levels of education and training. The second and third of these already existed as courses on offer from colleges and business schools. These were the Diploma and Masters qualifications, which needed wider promotion rather than revision. A Diploma in Business Management was considered suitable for those who already carried some functional responsibility; the Masters' qualification was assumed to fit holders for the higher levels of management.

The criticism levelled at Masters' courses, and sometimes at the Diploma, was a perceived tendency to dwell on theory rather than practice. Economics and organization theory were seen to be given pride of place over the practical applications of financial decision-making and the management of people.

The innovation of the MCI was to be a certificate-level qualification aimed solely at competent performance of tasks rather than teaching the theory behind them. As we have seen in the preceding sections, identification of skills, or 'competencies' as the MCI authorities referred to them, is no easy matter. At what level is the junior manager required to be 'competent'? Can the 'competencies' be taught and assessed in isolation from other aspects of work?

The most intractable problem was the obverse of the theory-over-practice argument that had been used against the MBA courses. In performing skilled manual tasks, the major function of the brain is to coordinate the bodily actions that the skilled person is required to carry out. Knowledge of 'affordances' (see Chapter 4) is also necessary, though the skilled person might have difficulty explaining why. Symbolic skills are central to the performance of managerial work, however, and these imply some knowledge of context: social, technical, commercial, organizational and, sometimes, theoretical. It is not easy to see how 'competencies' can be attained in total isolation from the general knowledge surrounding managerial activity. Skills may be transferable, but they are not free-standing.

Whatever the force of this argument, it does not invalidate the use of job analysis to identify skills as an important precursor to selection and training. If many of these skills, or competencies, are transferable then we should be even less inclined to prescribe 'experience' in specifying the people needed for a particular role.

Productivity is a state of mind

This arresting phrase may be found in a quotation from an article by Hallett (1986). In its entirety it states 'Productivity is a state of mind; it is an ethic; it is a purpose'. Put like that, productivity begins to have the status at least of a strategic 'mission statement', as mentioned in Chapter 1. It may even rate as an example of the type of long-term objective, or corporate ethos, to be enshrined as policy.

Hallet writes of an America where the continuing worries about productivity match those of the UK, albeit from a higher base. Both countries have witnessed the run-down of manufacturing industry, brought about partly by changes in world markets and partly by an inability to provide what the customers want, at the price they want to pay, when they want it.

Hallet sees the definition of productivity as an economic ratio of output to input, which was used earlier in this chapter, as part of the problem. Those who would improve productivity on this measure tend to concentrate on inputs and outputs at the expense of the marketability of the product. Productivity, in its narrow definition, does not allow for good design or the assessment of customer satisfaction. The product has been efficiently but ineffectively made.

Hallet was discussing what has now become known as *total quality management* (TQM), defined in 'Personnel Management Factsheet no. 29' (1990) from the UK Institute of Personnel Management as:

> A cost-effective system for integrating the continuous quality improvement effort of people at all levels in an organization to deliver products and services which ensure customer satisfaction.

Efficiency has not been abandoned as an objective, but the emphasis on customer satisfaction, rather than on meeting quality control specifications, is clear. So is the necessary involvement of the whole workforce, together with their skills and creativity.

The move from a drive for efficiency towards a drive for effectiveness is essential if organizations, public or private, are to survive in an environment of rapidly changing consumer demand. Quality is no longer a matter of counting the rejects, which are representative of productive inefficiency rather than customer satisfaction. Quality is a function of market research, of design, of pride in work, of timely delivery, and of constant improvement; it is literally 'qualitative' rather than quantitative. A chief executive who stated, in the late

1980s, that his company was no longer interested in customer satisfaction, raised the eyebrows of his audience; he went on to say that the new target was 'customer delight'. That seems to sum up the position rather well.

The achievement of customer delight, of course, requires efficient and effective equipment, whether this is used to deliver a service or manufactured goods. The importance of flexible manufacturing facilities is illustrated in the case study at the end of this chapter. In human terms, 'customer delight' requires a great deal more. Not only must equipment be flexible, but so must the workforce. Studies of the 'flexible firm' (see Chapter 2) have so far tended to concentrate more on flexibility in contracts and working hours, not on the flexibility now required of people within the work they do. Many traditional aspects of organizational life, from 'custom and practice' to restrictive and union-based job demarcations, have patiently to be removed. In Britain, at any rate, those made redundant during the heavy unemployment of the 1980s could be helped to recognize their varied skills and to deflect them into occupations where employment prospects were brighter. Strategic human resource management now requires this level of professionalism at the place of work, without waiting for redundancy to make it necessary. The transfer of recognized skills is the key to both. 'Productivity as a state of mind' places a premium on the ability of management to conduct research into their markets, their products and, perhaps most important, the people who work for them.

CASE STUDY 5
Flexible manufacture— 'Britain's best factories'

The following case is taken from a survey of five factories that were judged by a consultant, on behalf of the British management magazine *Management Today*, to be world-class. It consists of extracts from an article (Ferguson, 1989), reproduced with permission.

Each factory had to prove that it could compete with global best practice in five areas: plant mission, organization, operations management, quality and technology. A clear understanding of mission indicates that a manufacturer knows where it is headed, while the other four categories show how it intends to get there. For a manufacturer to rate world-class, each area must reinforce and be reinforced by the others. It is here that Sony's colour television factory in Wales excels, demonstrating a superb mesh both within itself and with its parent, Sony Corp. of Japan.

Smart companies wield their manufacturing operations as business weapons, carving out a market share by meeting customers' demands for innovative, high-quality products delivered on time. Toshiba, for example, claims a doubling in market share from the improved quality of its products. ICL has gone one stage further and uses its Ashton factory as a show-piece. A marketing tool to show customers what ICL products can do, as well as how its computers are made, the factory helped to make an extra 200 international sales a year.

Today the best factories are maintaining or even reducing their controllable costs, they are delivering to schedule 99–100% of the time and their quality conforms to the highest requirements of consumer demand and company standards. By streamlining their manufacturing operations they are in a position to address today's demands from the market. Customers have come to expect competitive pricing, quality and delivery, and product life cycles shrink as they want new products even faster. Manufacturers must increase their flexibility by learning to produce both large and small volumes economically.

The order here is crucial: get the process right and then automate if necessary. The acronym-ed techniques with which any manufacturer must be familier today don't require masses of automated machines and computers to make them happen. Just-in-time production (JIT), materials requirements planning (MRPI), total quality control (TQC), or statistical process control (SPC) can, and must, be carried out as well by men as by machines. As Rank-Xerox found, it's hard to control a highly automated set-up if it isn't appropriate. Rank-Xerox ultimately went back to a relatively low-tech operation.

It is vitally important to recognize that the techniques above, and others such as manufacturing resources planning (MRPI)s, flexible manufacturing systems (FMS) and computer integrated manufacturing (CIM) are just that, tools, and not manufacturing strategies. The idea is to know where the business is now and where it is going, then use the relevant tools to get there.

To do this requires two basic abilities. The first is the ability to treat manufacturing in a scientific and pragmatic way. This is something at which the Japanese excel, which may explain the fact that two out of five factories are Japanese subsidiaries. Taking the view that if something works, it's worth doing, is often far more effective than conforming to a beautifully crafted strategy based rigidly on the latest techniques.

The other vital ability is to value the people who work in the factory as assets. After all, factories are no less people businesses than service companies. OAC (Oxford Automotive Components) asked its workforce what they thought could be done to streamline production. Toshiba discusses every aspect of its business with its employees via a company advisory board. Each of these factories undertakes a high level of communication and training and development for all of the staff and has placed responsibility for product and process quality directly in employees' hands. Team working is common to them all, and so is multiskilling of workers. The people who work at these factories don't leave their brains outside the gates because they're needed inside.

Of course, having a multiskilled workforce gives a factory much greater flexibility. If workers can build any product, then they can be deployed where they are most needed, as at ICL, for instance; or if the factory no longer needs an expensive and inflexible moving product line, it can build products from scratch in cells, as at Rank-Xerox. Capacity and volume are easily changed at short notice, as cells can be added or substracted, as distinct from the relative inflexibility of a line which must be rebalanced.

British detractors will point out that it is expensive to train all workers to do every job, yet that is half the point. For workers who now tend to be salaried and paid monthly, multiskilling provides an equable system of salary grading and promotion. 'It takes longer to train them but they stay', says Steve Young of A. T. Kearney, pointing out that, 'it's been shown to reduce staff turnover and absenteeism'. And a reputation for training is an added attraction when it comes to recruitment.

References   Bassett, P. (1988) 'Non-unionism's growing ranks', *Personnel Management*, March, **45**.
Constable, J. and McCormick, R. (1987) *The Making of British Managers*: a Report for the BIM and CBI into Management Training, Education and Development, British Institute of Management, Corby.
Ferguson, A. (1989) 'Britain's best factories', *Management Today*, November, **68**.
Fleishman, E. (1984) 'Systems for linking job tasks to personnel requirements', *Public Personnel Management*, **13**, 395.

Hallett, J. (1986) 'Productivity and quality: the never ending quest', *Personnel Administrator*, October. Reprinted in Ferris, G. and Rowland, K. (eds.) *Human Resources Management: perspectives and issues*, Allyn and Bacon, Boston.

Handy, C. (1985) *Understanding Organizations*, Penguin, Harmondsworth, London

Handy, C. (1987) *The Making of Managers*, Manpower Services Commission, National Economic Development Office, British Institute of Manager, Corby.

Harrison, M. (1989) 'Shell chief gets BR job', 7 December, *The Independent*.

Herzberg, F., Mausner, B. and Snyderman, B. (1959) *The Motivation to Work* (2nd ed.), John Wiley & Sons, Chichester.

Jones, B. (1982) *Sleepers, Wake!*, Wheatsheaf Books, Brighton.

Kemp, T. (1978) *Historical Patterns of Industrialization* Longman, London.

Maslow, A. (1954) *Motivation and Personality*, Harper & Row, New York.

Neisser, U. in Sloboda, J. and Rogers, D. (eds.) (1983) *The Acquisition of Symbolic Skills*, Plenum Press, New York.

Newsom, J. (1963) *Half our Future*, A report of the Central Advisory Council for Education (England), HMSO, London.

Pagnamenta, P. and Overy, R. (1984) *All our Working Lives*, BBC Books, London.

Pearn, M. and Kandola, R. (1988) *Job Analysis: a practical guide for managers*, IPM, London.

Rawling, K. (1982) *The Seven Point Plan Alec Rodger: new perspectives fifty years on*, NFER–Nelson, Windsor.

Roethlisberger, F. and Dickson, W. (1939) *Management and the Worker*, Harvard University Press, Cambridge, Massachusetts.

Schein, E. (1970) *Organizational Psychology*, Prentice-Hall International Inc., New York

Townsend, C. (1982) 'Skills needed for young people's jobs: Volume 1', Institute of Manpower Studies Report No. 40.

Ure, A. (1835) *The Philosophy of Manufactures*, from Beach, E. (1973) *Victorian Culture and Society*, Harper and Row.

Wiener, M. (1981) *English Culture and the Decline of the Industrial Spirit 1850–1980*, Pelican Books, London.

The unsatisfied worker

Worker satisfaction is a strategic issue

At the end of the previous chapter, it was suggested that 'customer delight' should replace 'customer satisfaction' as an organizational goal. If so, there are profound implications for the strategic use of human resources. While job satisfaction has been the subject of much research interest, little enough attention has been given to it at a practical level. Is it possible that 'customer delight' could be achieved without 'employee delight' as a subsidiary goal?

In the past, customer and job satisfaction have been seen as two very different issues. Customer satisfaction was less important when there was lack of choice and competition in the market. World wars and cartels both had powerful effects in restricting the availability of manufactured goods and services. Customers had to be satisfied with what they could get.

Quality control, where practised, was a matter of policing. Inspectors decided whether the output was within specification. Quality bonuses, or dismissal for poor performance, could ensure at least a grudging level of compliance. Payment by results systems were, however, often blamed for placing a premium on output rather than quality. They would also encourage disposal of half-finished goods when the operator realized that the item was substandard and completion would cost him wages. Worst of all, workers conditioned to accept Marx's 'cash nexus' as the basis of their relationship with their employer began to behave in ways that confirmed management's expectation: their sole reason for working was to earn money. Commitment to organizational objectives was irrelevant, and this included commitment to customer satisfaction, let alone delight. This system, which McGregor (1960) dubbed 'theory X', depends for any success it may have on the manipulation of rewards. Standards were defined and monitored, and rewards and penalties applied on the basis of their achievement. The complex of work-study and reward systems underlying 'scientific management' have already been discussed in Chapter 5. Figure 6.1(a) illustrates the relationship between worker, organization and customer under this regime.

Customers for manufactured products, of course, need never meet the people who make them; indeed they may have only the vaguest idea how and where manufacture takes place. If they have a complaint, this isolation can be maintained by a barrier layer of sales and customer service staff. Factory conditions are not brought to the notice of those who buy the goods. It is one of the ironies of modern life that environmental groups take more interest in the fate of animals used in research than in the conditions of humans in factories.

In service organizations, including the public sector, the customer and the employee have a much closer relationship, and customer satisfaction crucially depends upon it. Unsatisfied staff in a hotel or hospital can quickly bring either into disrepute. This may matter less if the hospital's patients have no choice but to use its service, but an unfriendly or unresponsive hotel is likely to go out of business. In the UK, local government was until recently the

Figure 6.1(a)
The relationship
between worker,
organization and
customer under
traditional management

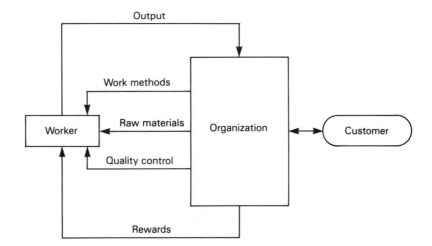

monopoly supplier of many services, especially those needed by the least well-off in the community. 'Privatization' of supply has at least allowed an assessment of costs, and a clearer understanding of productivity.

Encouraging competing suppliers to offer erstwhile local government services direct to the consumer is the next logical stage. Local authorities themselves are taking 'customer delight' seriously. Performance-related pay is determined on the basis of reports sent in by the authority's clients. This approach, coming as it does after years of fostering minimal, non-risk-taking performance in a bureacratic system, has taken some longer-serving employees by surprise. Yet it has much to teach employers not only in the service sector but also in manufacturing industry.

Employees are now made increasingly aware of the importance of the customer in maintaining employment. Customer feedback, related to performance pay, indicates a conscious decision to achieve this relationship; but the introduction of computer technology can have the same, perhaps unintended, effect. Computerized systems have removed layers of middle managers whose principal role was to process information. The information was collected from the periphery of the organization, including customers, and was analysed and passed to senior management. Their other role was to take decisions for members of staff who were in direct contact with the customer. Both of these activities can now be accomplished more effectively by database technology. Staff in direct contact with the customer are able to take decisions based on information directly available to them: senior management are immediately aware of the cumulative effect of those decisions, and the way in which customers are reacting. The British retail company, Marks and Spencer, long before computers were installed, realized the necessity of keeping information systems direct and simple. Now this advantage is within reach of many top-heavy bureaucracies, in both the public and private sectors of the economy. Figure 6.1(b) illustrates these revised relationships.

But Marks and Spencer also realized that simplicity was only one pillar of organizational success. Good relations with their employees was another. The people in direct contact with the customer could make or break the business; unsatisfied workers would swiftly lead to unsatisfied customers and to lower turnover. The John Lewis Partnership (Flanders, Pomeranz and Woodward, 1968), significantly also in the retail sector, recognized before the First World War that the attitude of employees was paramount in their successful dealings

Figure 6.1(b)
The relationship
between worker,
organization and
customer as they are
now emerging

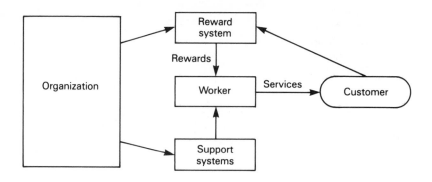

with customers; they gave partnership status to all who worked for them. Both Marks and Spencer and John Lewis have survived through many trade cycles in contrast with a number of apparently 'entrepreneurial' retail enterprises that have flourished briefly and then foundered in a matter of five years. The former's concern for the welfare needs of employees, including those of their suppliers, is praiseworthy. What lies behind this implicit theory of motivating employees is paternalism, a philsophy that can be traced back to industrial entrepreneurs like Titus Salt and Robert Owen in the nineteenth century. The concept that the employer is responsible for employees, as parents would feel responsible for their children, assumes that motivation to work productively stems from gratitude for this concern. It is also assumed that employees will wish to remain members of a supportive organization that offers fringe benefits, good working conditions, job security and predictable promotion. Recruitment and retention of employees should thus be easier for organizations that adopt this approach. The human relations school, influenced by the Hawthorne studies, built on the paternalistic idea that satisfaction with the job will lead to increased output. Paternalism, however, may only be a start. Scientific management regarded employees as irresponsible beings motivated only by carrot and stick. Is the kindlier, but still patronizing view of workers, any more effective? Well-treated employees are more likely than ill-treated ones to give a good standard of service to customers. But passive receipt of benefits does not encourage self-development or intiative. Both qualities are increasingly necessary in many forms of employment.

If employee satisfaction, even delight, is a necessary condition of a successful business, how can it be achieved? What should the human resource strategist's contribution be? What body of theory exists to stimulate and support research by strategic human resource planners?

Social and psychological contracts

The psychometric method of selection was described in Chapter 4, and Chapter 5 emphasized the importance of identifying the skills needed in a job. Chapter 4 also gave attention to the social processes in selection. Herriot (1984) has championed this neglected aspect, especially in relation to graduates. He believes that employee dissatisfaction, rather than lack of ability, is the more likely reason for terminating employment. This would be especially true of candidates of high general ability, but the principle can be applied to selection at all levels.

The importance of social exchange in selection and recruitment practice is that the candidate should be a willing and fully informed partner at each stage of the process, and should be capable of participating fully in the decision to join the organization. Later the two-way relationship should continue, so that the social contract established at recruitment can be regularly reviewed and adapted to changing needs. This assumes, incidentally, not a reduced emphasis on job analysis, but an increased one. In order to communicate the demands of the job to the candidate, the selectors themselves must fully understand them.

But is giving attention to the negotiation, and re-negotiation, of a social contract with employees any more than a higher paternalism? 'Niceness' starts a little earlier in the recruitment process, perhaps, and extends to meeting the employee's needs once the first contract has been established, but will this, of itself, lead to high performance? If freedom of information about a job, and freedom to renegotiate its context and content, are two ways of promoting job satisfaction, what else is necessary? For further ideas we have to move from the social to the psychological. The social exchange aspects of selection are the means by which an applicant becomes aware of the likely psychological demands and rewards of a particular job; it is the satisfaction of psychological needs that determine the acceptance of an offer, and subsequent decisions to remain in employment.

The importance to the human resource strategist of a basic psychological understanding of workers' motives and satisfactions has been demonstrated in earlier chapters of this book. An appreciation of the vagaries of categorization is necessary in order to comprehend labour markets, and an understanding of psychological contructs is necessary to distinguish between aptitudes, abilities and attitudes. Selection is necessarily a matter of measuring people by the use of these constructs. In Chapter 3 we made a brief detour into the psychology of unemployment. The psychology of motivation was introduced in Chapter 5, and it is now necessary to take this further.

One problem with the overt use of psychological ideas at work is that people are embarrassed to talk about them. Discussing satisfaction with work, especially psychological needs, sounds soft, and is avoided by both managers and employees. Another problem is that people often lack the language either to express their own feelings, or to categorize and understand the feelings of others as expressed in everyday language. Yet if contracts are to be negotiated, the language in which they are written and agreed should be understood by both parties.

Psychological theory is also a requirement of the general model of social research shown in Figure 3.1. Theory is needed to explain the implications of the accumulated data, thus providing a springboard for the development of strategy and policy.

Workers as individuals

Traditional manpower planning considered workers very much in the mass. Mathematical models are easiest to apply when organizations are large, and when each category of staff contains statistically stable aggregates of people. Any attempt to seek theories of motivation with the same premises leads us into sociology rather than psychology. We find ourselves ascribing 'class attitudes' to different groups, and examining the social forces leading to union membership. Managing individuals within that perspective is, however, inordinately difficult. So is accounting for the apparent quirkiness of individual behaviour. People resist categorization, because their perceptions of the world are different and change with time. Attitudes are determined at least partially by social forces, but individuals are members of diverse social groups, each of which has its own norms and values. Diversity of membership enriches individuality.

'Job satisfaction' is often associated in the public mind with the environmental conditions of work, social relationships and the physical nature of the equipment and workplace. Yet the psychology and the personal situation of the individual are as likely to affect this attitude. A preferred term would, perhaps be 'worker satisfaction', of which 'job satisfaction' would be a significant but partial element.

Motivation and satisfaction

Inherent in the two 'content' theories of motivation discussed in the previous chapter is the supposition that the human being is a satisfaction-seeking organism. The problem for managers who like all issues to be simple is that the same satisfactions can be achieved by pursuing different goals, and that goals can be achieved by many different behaviours; the most observable aspects of workers are the least informative. As managers and human resource planners, we would like to know what motivates workers, so that behaviour could be directed towards organizational goals. Behaviour is simply described, whereas motivation can only be inferred. In the terminology of Chapter 3, motivation is an explanatory construct.

Unfortunately, research into the behaviour of human resources cannot be restricted to mere description, the presentation of tables and diagrams summarizing the outcome of surveys. Explanation is needed if research is to make a contribution to strategic thinking, and to influence policy. Theorists provide human resource planners with insights rather than universal explanations. Theory is developed from a particular viewpoint and, in particular, experimental settings. The task for human resource strategists is to use what seems to be relevant in the body of theory to provide a coherent explanation of their own findings. As the case study at the end of this chapter illustrates, there is room for minority, if not individual, explanations within the broader generalizations of aggregated data. Human resource strategists need to keep an eye out for exceptions. A simple example will illustrate why human actions are difficult to explain.

The behaviour of a person making a foolhardy dash across a busy road is dramatically observable, and easily described; the explanation is more complex. We may be observing someone anxious to catch a train, or a criminal trying to evade capture. Is the person dashing for the train a workaholic concerned about late arrival at the office, or worried that a love affair will end if a partner is kept waiting? To what extent do people in these situations 'act on impulse' or make careful calculations of the benefits and risks of the action they are taking?

One method of understanding these questions is to separate the 'content' of motivation from the 'process' leading to action. The criminal escaping across a busy road may be doing so because he fears the loss of his liberty more than the chance of injury; we might infer that he has a 'need' for freedom of action, which capture will severely restrict. But is his action calculated or automatic? Is it the result solely of the 'content', the need to be free, or are the risks of capture or physical injury balanced against each other before action is taken? The latter explanation emphasizes the importance of cognitive processes; calculating his chance of reaching the other side unscathed requires not only a recognized need but also an assessment of skills and the problems faced in avoiding traffic. So motivation involves not only 'content', the satisfaction of a need, but also a 'process' of decision.

Figure 6.2
Maslow's hierarchy of
needs

Two well-known content theories of motivation are those of Maslow and Herzberg. Both were mentioned in Chapter 5 in relation to pay; both, through the medium of management courses over the last 40 years, have found their way into managers' vocabulary. With what degree of understanding, however, is questionable. Maslow's theory is really a typology of human needs, that has a powerful appeal to human experience, but which is not susceptible to experiment. It assumes that human needs are of five main types, and that these occupy a hierarchy. This concept is illustrated in Figure 6.2. The theory further assumes that higher needs will not become effective until lower ones are satisfied, and that individuals differ in the intensity with which they experience the various needs even when activated.

Maslow's theory was published in the 1950s and its appeal to managers facing the problems of the post-war period is not difficult to understand. Full employment policies were being pursued by governments fearful of the disruption caused by unemployment in the 1930s, and wartime losses had created many skill-shortages. The fear of dismissal could no longer be used to motivate workers, even if that were desirable. Managers had to look to higher needs than survival and shelter, which were increasingly assured by full employment, subsidized housing and welfare. Pay, of course, provided workers with the means to meet higher needs outside work, and piece-work incentives were popular. But piece-work rates, at least in the UK (Donovan, 1971) were a cause of shop-floor strife and, as described in Chapter 5, could be subverted. Maslow offered a way to motivate workers through satisfactions gained from the work itself. So managers were urged to give attention to workers' social, self-esteem and self-actualization needs. The job enrichment movement was under way.

But Maslow's hierarchy of needs also offers a managerial 'rule of thumb' for explaining the motivation of individual workers. Consider the following example.

A hitherto cooperative employee approaches a manager to explain that a proposed change to a technical process will not work. The manager has to judge whether the employee is right in his assumption and, if not, why he or she is being obstructive. Let us consider three possibilities, each with different psychological and managerial implications.

The first comes to light when the manager discovers that the employee has no technical data to support his or her contention, and there is general belief among the workgroup that the change will lead to redundancy. The employee recognizes the weakness of the technical argument, but is reluctant to go against the feelings of the group.

The second explanation hinges upon self-esteem, rather than safety and social needs. Again, there is a lack of technical data to back the assertion that the new process will not work. The employee refers frequently to his or her involvement some years ago in the development of the original process. This time the development has been conducted by a team of technologists from the research division, without reference to the employee.

The third explanation assumes that both self-esteem and self-actualization are the mainsprings of the employee's action. The manager recognizes that the employee has considerable technical skill, and has cooperated with the research team. This time there is copious and convincing proof that the assertion is correct, much of it reflecting the employee's expertise.

To have strategic importance, psychological theories must have practical application, either as suggestive frameworks, like Maslow's hierarchy, or as testable explanations. While some psychological research is unashamedly and correctly directed towards the development of theory, much research and psychological practice are aimed at solving problems. The occupational psychologist, no less than the manager, is interested in results; satisfied clients mean more business. So theory is used to achieve practical ends, and several different theoretical viewpoints may be required.

Maslow's theory has enjoyed a prolonged vogue in management courses, perhaps because it has the power of suggesting insights that aid managerial action. In the examples above, the action to be taken varies from discussion with the workgroup to finding a suitable reward for individual effort.

Maslow's hierarchy of needs was not intended solely to account for motivation at work; it covers the whole of human life, of which work is an important part. But human resource strategists would be wise not to concentrate on work to the exclusion of other human activities. When using psychometric methods of selection we gain insight into candidates' interests and skills by discussing what they do in their spare time, in addition to their previous work experience. In regarding recruitment and employment as social exchange, we accept that we are acquiring the services of a whole person, with needs outside the job in addition to those satisfied by the work itself. Where needs cannot be satisfied within work, a strategic solution could include providing opportunities outside the working environment for social contact, development of new skills or for gaining self-esteem.

Herzberg popularized Maslow's theory by applying it directly to the workplace. He also provided an experimental basis for what became known as the 'two-factor' theory of work satisfaction and motivation. His experiment consisted of asking people in professional work (engineers and accountants) to describe incidents that either made them 'feel good' or that made them 'feel bad' at work. The descriptions were analysed, and were found to fall into two distinguishable but overlapping categories. The first, which contained the 'felt good' incidents, concerned various aspects of the work itself; how much autonomy the job-holder was allowed, achievement and feedback about success. The second category concerned the conditions under which the work was carried out, including pay, and contained the 'felt bad' incidents. Herzberg realized that some factors in a job provided motivation to achieve, because of their positive effect on the mental well-being of the employee. Others needed attention by management because they could demotivate employees by inducing dissatisfaction. The latter, however, had no motivating power. The first group, appropriately, were called 'motivators', and the second, presumably because they were aspects of organizational housekeeping, were called 'hygiene factors'.

This approach to the management of people is a long way from that proposed by Taylor; the 'one best way of working' by means of which management would achieve its objectives of high productivity, and the workers, who were assumed to be motivated only by money, would also achieve theirs. Paternalism relates to Herzberg's hygiene factors, rather than to his motivators. From Herzberg's point of view, pay systems must not lead to dissatisfaction, but are unlikely to motivate workers to achieve their own or company goals. Giving workers control over their own work was the key to that. These ideas were controversial, but formed the theoretical basis for the experiments in job design that took place in the 1960s.

Herzberg's original research was based on a sample of professionally-trained specialists. Generalization of his findings to workers with other values has its dangers; experiments to establish its validity for shop-floor workers were not convincing. Taylor selected his sample for their individualistic interest in high pay. In developing and applying motivational theories it is advisable always to consider the context.

The idea that achievement is its own motivator was taken one step further by McLelland and his co-workers (1953), His theory of achievement motivation goes some way towards explaining why people might react in different ways to attempts to provide them with challenging and responsible work. McLelland saw 'the need to achieve' as a personal trait, developed by early influences of parents, teachers and reading matter. The experimental basis was the use of projective tests (ambivalent pictures) to discover whether childrens' descriptions contained imagery associated with need to achieve. Levels of 'need to achieve' were related to the importance given by parents to the achievements of their children and the extent to which they encouraged it. McLelland generalized his research to investigating the relation between the economic performance of countries at particular times and the literature generally available when the citizens were growing up. Achievement imagery in formative literature correlated with later economic success.

McLelland's ideas lead us from 'content' towards 'process' theories of motivation. The essential question is whether people follow urges, exhibiting behaviour as they do so, or whether they calculate the desirability of goals, and also the probability of success. In the second case, the observed behaviour is the product of a cognitive process.

The best-known 'cognitive' theory of motivation is Porter and Lawler's (1969) *expectancy theory*. This is illustrated in Figure 6.3. The assumption is that people consciously assess the attractiveness of available rewards. They also assess the probabilities that effort will lead to achievement and that achievement will lead to reward. They consider whether they have the required skills, and how those skills should be deployed (the role that they should adopt). If the assessment appears sufficiently favourable, they will behave positively towards the objective. Of course, the outcome of the calculation depends on the accuracy with which people perceive the goals, rewards, skills and role to be adopted. In the strategic use of human resources, it may be an important function of management to clarify employees' perceptions of these factors.

An important contribution of 'cognitive' theories is to separate the concepts

Figure 6.3
Expectancy theory of
motivation
Source: Open
University Course
P670, The Effective
Manager (adapted from
Porter & Lawler's
original theory)

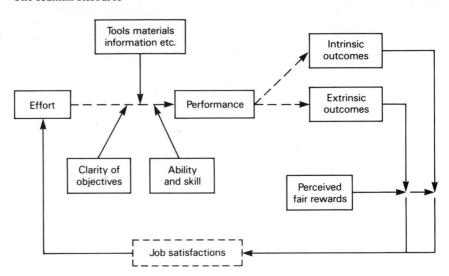

of goal and reward. Obviously, 'content' theories cannot be thrown overboard, because the idea of a reward requires a need to be fulfilled. But to what extent is goal achievement its own reward? For those with high 'need to achieve' this would appear to be so. More recent writers on the subject of motivation claim that the effective use of skills is the primary satisfaction to be gained from work; removal of the opportunity to use valued skills is one of the least desirable effects of redundancy.

Motivational theory has been reviewed comprehensively by Locke and Henne (1986). They accept the arguments concerning 'need' as the source of motivation, and also the classification of needs as contributing either to survival or to well-being, as in Maslow's hierarchy. Locke's analysis of motivation focuses on the setting of goals, and the strategy needed to achieve satisfaction through their attainment. People differ not only in the intensity with which they experience needs, but also in their perceptions of strategies and ways of implementing them. Readers may detect echoes here of the discussion of organizational strategy in Chapter 1.

Locke asserts that personal values ultimately determine people's choice of strategy; their ideas of right and wrong, and what may be classified as 'good'. Hedonists and Greenpeace enthusiasts, for example, might go about the task of selecting clothing very differently. Both would have the goal of keeping warm, but the Greenpeace people might reject out of hand the purchase of animal fur. If values are the strongest guiding principle in personal motivation, we should not be surprised that 'policies', whether these are explicit or not, similarly affect the choice of corporate strategy. Successful groups share values, which will also determine whether particular people will choose to join. Communicating the value system to candidates is an important aspect of social exchange in recruitment, as discussed in Chapter 4.

Deeply held personal values, like organizational policies, change slowly if at all. Not all personal values are shared, even within a group, and they may vary widely among the members of an organization. This presents a problem for the personnel administrator and those who design personnel policies. Incentive schemes, or disciplinary rules, are designed for the mass: individual responses may surprise those who devise them.

The process of satisfying needs within strongly held values is fraught with emotion. Goal achievement, by definition, brings satisfaction. Failure brings not only dissatisfaction, but also the possibility of anxiety and depression. In the process of choosing goals, situations may be assessed as threatening, or damaging to self-esteem. Susceptibility to each of these emotions is itself a response to the social learning of the individual.

Superficial discussion of 'job satisfaction', and the use of standardized questionnaires to measure it, tend to obscure the complexity of the issue at an individual level, and can mislead both managers and human resource specialists in their attempts to get the best from a workforce. Willingness to undertake tasks, especially the public observable assignments that characterize work, depends on the confidence of the individual worker. Bandura (1982) refers to this perception of individual ability as 'self-efficacy'. This is a broader concept than the assessment of personal skills which moderates the effort–performance link in *expectancy theory*, being more task-specific. 'Self-efficacy' is a term derived from Bandura's *social learning theory*, and this has implications for the training and development of employees; if 'efficacy' is determined by experience, managers should seek to develop 'efficacy' in their staff by providing tasks of graded difficulty. These would be intended to develop confidence and widen the repertoire of skills that employees can confidently apply. Once again, this requires personal attention to individuals, rather than attendance at group training programmes.

Locke and Henne (1986) dismiss all motivational theory, with the exception of Bandura's and what they describe as goal setting theory, as lacking sound experimental support. They believe that progress can be made in managing work performance by diverting attention from needs towards the goals intended to satisfy them. The former can be inferred only at second hand, while the latter can be specified in terms of measurable performance. Locke prefers values to needs as ways of accounting for goal selection. But it is the concentration on the goals to be achieved that characterizes his approach to motivating employees to high performance.

Locke points to the weight of research evidence for goal setting as a powerful motivator. He summarizes the latter as follows:

- Difficult goals lead to higher task performance. This contrasts with McLelland's (1953) theory of achievement motivation which suggests that those valuing achievement will seek goals of moderate difficulty.
- Specific and difficult goals lead to higher performance than vague or non-existent goals.
- Goals help by:
  – directing attention
  – mobilizing effort
  – increasing persistence
  – motivating the search for strategies.
- Feedback is needed to help people monitor their own progress towards the goal, but is not necessary for task completion.
- The function of money is to encourage goal setting, and within that the setting of higher goals.
- Goal setting effectiveness is not related to personal variables, personality, age or background.

Locke had some interesting things to say about the effects of feedback on motivation and satisfaction, which are seen as separate outcomes. Negative feedback is said to motivate people to better performance, but presumably only if clear goals have been set in the first place. Negative feedback also raises dissatisfaction with the task. How the worker responds to this feeling is moderated by his of her general confidence ('self-efficacy') and personal goals, which may not also be those of the organization.

Motivation by the work itself?

Maslow's hierarchy of needs applies as much to life in general as it does to work. Herzberg's two-factor theory is work-oriented, but refers to work only in terms of attributes, not its intrinsic nature. Locke's theory suggests that work will be most motivating when clear goals are set for the worker; it does not examine the nature of the actions carried out in achieving these goals. Bandura emphasizes the state of mind of the worker in preparing to achieve work-oriented goals, and McLelland the values that a worker holds about the worthwhileness of goal achievement itself. All leave an uncertain gap between motivation and satisfaction: why should satisfactions, once achieved, promote further action?

Hackman and Oldham (1980), whose ideas derive from those of Herzberg, go some way towards explaining why work itself might be both motivating and satisfying. Their research dates from the 1960s and 1970s, when job design had become a talking point among occupational psychologists and managers. The introduction of new technology was also forcing a reappraisal of working patterns. Jobs that were both motivating and satisfying were said to be those which provided skill variety, task identity, task significance, autonomy and feedback. While there are echoes here of other motivational theories, the nature of the task itself features in the first three factors of Hackman's scheme. Skill variety is plainly a function of the job. Task identity refers to the wholeness of the task—that element lost when scientific management is applied to work simplification and work-study. Task significance refers to the perception that work relates directly to the effectiveness of the organization. Autonomy and feedback, though also important aspects of job design, refer not to the work itself but to the environment in which it is carried out.

O'Brien (1986) shed additional light on the relationship between motivation and satisfaction, and between each and the job itself. He produced experimental evidence to show that work values and skill variety influence satisfaction, but that what matters most of all is skill use. O'Brien apparently includes in this category both the development of new skills and the full use of existing ones.

O'Brien's ideas have at least one major advantage. Concentrating on activity within the job itself resolves the ambiguity between motivation and satisfaction. Work is attractive to workers in the same way as games are attractive to those who wish to develop and display their sporting skills. Continuing challenge provides continuing satisfaction and motivation. Work that develops and fully uses skills is addictive, and the adjective 'workaholic' takes on a new meaning. O'Brien's corrollary is that workers will not derive satisfaction from work for which they have been overeducated. This makes the assumption that the quality of work is immutable; a contentious point. In common with other writers, however, O'Brien sees deprival of the opportunity to use and maintain skills as one of the less desirable aspects of redundancy and unemployment.

A unitary model of job motivation and satisfaction

The reader should be aware that the motivational theories we have discussed all interlock in various ways, and put emphasis on different aspects of motivation. These relationships are represented in Figure 6.4(a) and (b). The interaction of personal values with motivation and satisfaction has already been mentioned. While theorists may vary in the importance they ascribe to values as a moderator of behaviour, this factor does help to explain the differing responses of cultural groups to financial and other incentives. Values affect the relative salience of needs. They also affect the selection of goals and strategies. Shackleton and Fletcher (1984) believe that values are more important than personal interests in determining choice of occupation. Even the tendency to be motivated by work itself is the expression of a value.

Figure 6.4(b) demonstrates why human resource management is the most 'strategic' of managerial activities. Managers' output depends on some badly specified and fickle machinery. Personal needs vary from one employee to another. Some may seek to achieve goals outside the organization, through the medium of cash rewards. Some gain satisfactions within the organization, but independent of the job itself. Separately from these motivations and satisfactions, a job that uses and develops skills combines motivation, goal achievement and satisfaction in a virtuous spiral. Human resource strategists

Figure 6.4
(a) The relationship of motivation theory to the process of goal achievement

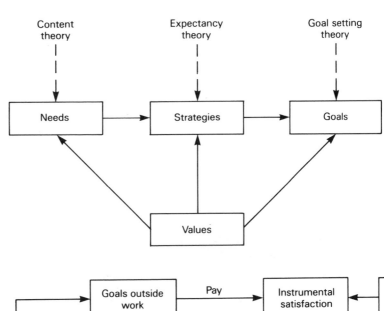

(b) Motivational routes to goal achievement and job satisfaction

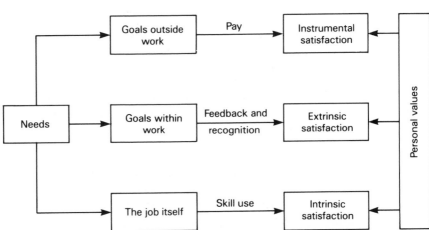

should regularly appraise the satisfactions that the organization can provide for employees. Payment systems are not enough.

The experimental evidence for the motivational effects of goal setting, and the motivating and satisfying effect of skill use, are quite strong, but strategic human resource planners should regard any or all of the theories discussed here as potential explanatory models. They should recognize that all theories have their limitations, but that explanations are required to support administrative action and, of course, to prompt a search for new data.

The psychologist, rightly, places emphasis on experimental verifiability. Human resource planners, however, need not reject earlier theories as a source of ideas. Verifiability is as verifiability does: if an idea suggested by Herzberg's or McLelland's theories results in improved performance, then it has helped to achieve strategic objectives. It is the essence of strategic thinking that 'theories' are regarded as both useful and discardable. Whatever the weight of general evidence for goal setting as the basis of human motivation, its practicality and effectiveness in a particular work setting needs to be established. 'Performance pay', 'total quality management' and the consequent revival of interest in management by objectives, are likely to dominate the management climate of the 1990s. Goal setting theory, which explicitly or implicitly underlies these practical attempts to improve the delivery and quality of goods and services, deserves both scrutiny and appropriate use.

The title of this chapter is 'The unsatisfied worker'. So far we have been concerned with motivation rather than satisfaction, but with the aim of making sense of both. At the level of skill use, where the job itself has its greatest psychological impact, the two are closely linked, and may be indistinguishable. This is not to deny the importance to the well-being of the worker of the other factors related to work environment, including organizational values, supervisory style and physical conditions. Satisfaction with goal achievement and skill use are not the only emotions experienced by workers in carrying out their daily tasks.

'Job satisfaction' as experienced

Strategists should be interested not only in the quantity of the human resource, but also in its quality. There is a British proverb which claims that 'one volunteer is worth 10 pressed men'. This refers to the days of the Napoleonic Wars, when warships were manned both by professional sailors, and by a motley crew of landsmen picked up on the streets of sea ports by the press gangs. The latter were forced to serve against their wills under a harsh disciplinary regime. Those interested in the history of industrialization will be aware that this took place at a time when people might also have felt themselves to be forced into factory work by economic circumstances. Motivational theory is older than we might suppose. Nowadays it is usually, but not always, recognized that workers respond in ways more creative and committed to rewards rather than punishment, and that the intrinsic value of work can be a powerful reward. Our previous discussion has helped to make this point.

Locke has commented on the feelings of dissatisfaction that accompany negative feedback. To what extent is dissatisfaction a necessary part of the motivational process, and to what extent is it dysfunctional, leading to poor performance, termination of employment or absence? What, in fact, are the sources of satisfaction in working life?

Job satisfaction, like motivation, has been a talking point in occupational psychology for several decades. As stated in Chapter 2, the discussion of work as a good in itself was a concomitant of the Industrial Revolution. Victorian thinkers took viewpoints ranging from the utilitarian ('work is a necessary evil') to the religious, as expressed in 'The Gospel of Work'. 'Happy is the man', said Carlyle, 'who has found his work'. These ideas live on in public consciousness, as well as in the papers of occupational psychologists. The British newspaper, *The Guardian*, regularly asks its readers to complete a questionnaire called the 'Why work?' survey. One of the questions in the 1988 survey, which was mentioned in Chapter 5 (Table 5.1), asked readers to say how important a range of factors were in providing them with job satisfaction. Those looking for support for both Maslow's and Herzberg's theories could take comfort from this survey.

Growth and self-esteem needs appear to be high on the agenda of professional workers (we are discussing the perceptions of *Guardian* readers) in the late twentieth century. The hygiene factor, 'working conditions', features as the twelfth item, but higher than several other factors that could be classified as 'motivators'. 'Making money' appears as twenty-eighth on the list, with 40 per cent of the sample seeing it as important in job satisfaction. The low need for security expressed by owners and partners in the sample (29 per cent thought it was important, compared with 55 per cent in the whole sample) emphasized the individual nature of needs and satisfaction. This sub-group valued personal freedom, however (91 per cent thought it was important). Managers placed a high value on gaining increased responsibility, on praise from superiors and on the respect of people they work with.

It seems that the concept of 'job satisfaction' is both understood and significant for a wide variety of workers, but is it also of value to those who seek to make the best use of human resources?

Job satisfaction: concept and measure

Like skill, job satisfaction is a commonly understood phrase that is difficult to define. Locke (1976) describes job satisfaction as 'a pleasurable or positive emotional state resulting from the appraisal of one's job or job experiences'.

Establishing that the pleasurable emotional state is a result of experience at work may not, however, be easy. The techniques have been discussed in Chapter 3. As in all attitudinal research, including market research, investigators use the interview and the questionnaire. Subjects are asked how happy they feel with various aspects of work, and each of these is rated on a standard scale. Referring back to Chapter 3, or perhaps to his or her personal experience, the reader will realize that this procedure is fraught with difficulty. In order that subjects should be systematically questioned, the investigator has to decide what aspects of work are likely to be sources of satisfaction and include relevant items. Individual reactions are sacrificed in order to obtain quantifiable and generalizable responses. The alternative is to use in-depth interviews or free response questionnaires to provide insight into the reactions of individuals at the expense of general concepts. The difficulties with the latter course are the time taken, and the problems of coding responses. The use of withdrawal behaviour, such as leaving and absence, as measures of job satisfaction results in a circular argument; job satisfaction cannot be used to explain its own measure.

In practice, the questionnaire method is generally used; standard measures are the *job description index* (JDI), the *Minnesota satisfaction questionnaire*, or the *Michigan measure of facet satisfaction*. Regular use does not make a questionnaire more reliable, however, and human resource specialists are recommended to check the suitability of a measure for the situation they wish to investigate. The *job description index* was devised by Smith, Kendall and Hulin (1969). Its simple wording allows it to be used to assess the feelings of people with comparatively low verbal skills.

The alternative to using structured questionnaires is to ask open questions about attitudes to work, and then to analyse the content of the respondent's statements for common themes. This was the method used by Herzberg in establishing his two-factor theory. One of the criticisms surrounding Herzberg's work is that the two factors, claimed as independent dimensions, nevertheless include some of the same elements, as revealed by the free response technique that he used. Working conditions, for example, occur in both dimensions, though more so in the 'hygienes' or 'dissatisfiers' than in the 'motivators' or 'satisfiers'.

As distinct from motivation, where there are a number of conflicting theories, job satisfaction is seen as an atheoretical concept (Griffin and Bateman, 1986). These authors argue that there are three ways of accounting for the popularly held concept. The first of these is to accept Herzberg's joint theory of motivation and satisfaction. The second is to view job satisfaction as a social product dependent on cues from fellow workers (Salancik and Pfeffer, 1978). The third is to see job satisfaction as an aspect of a worker's information processing (Landy, 1978). None of these offer the human resource planner a wholy acceptable or accessible explanation of job satisfaction.

In the common-sense world, indeed, job satisfaction is well understood. In research by Pearson and Heyno (1988), unemployed professional people who had subsequently returned to work were asked to rate the change in job satisfaction between their two employments—they had no difficulty in doing so. The *Guardian* 'Why work?' survey (see above) revealed that the readership of this newspaper, admittedly biased towards qualified professional workers, had no difficulty in understanding the idea and describing it from their own experience. The human resource planner, as we shall see later in this chapter, has to account for tendencies to stay away from particular jobs, or to leave them altogether. Explanations are likely to be situational and individual rather than general.

Job satisfaction and mental health

Another way of looking at job satisfaction is to consider what relationship it might have with general mental health, recognizing, of course, that factors outside work are also responsible.

Warr (1985 and 1987) has presented an interesting theory of job satisfaction within the general concept of mental health. He indentified two components of the latter, 'pleasure' and 'arousal'. He identified nine aspects of mental health that were available through work, and considered whether giving a person more of each would he helpful, neutral or harmful. He likened these factors to vitamins, some of which merely cease to be beneficial if taken in large doses, while others become positively harmful if taken in excess. The factors, and their effects, are listed in Table 6.1. Like O'Brien's emphasis on skill use, Warr's two-factor theory of mental health has the virtue of accounting for the way in which satisfaction can be a motivator. If activity itself is pleasurable, it remains only for management to provide profitable opportunities for pleasurable performance. His 'vitamin' theory helps to explain the complexity of human responses to particular jobs. Management should be careful to avoid, by accident or design, giving employees too much of a good thing.

Table 6.1
Occupational factors
contributing to mental
health, some only in
limited amounts

* Opportunity for control
* Opportunity for skill use
* Externally generated goals
* Variety
* Feedback
   Availability of money
   Physical security
* Opportunity for interpersonal contact
   Valued social position

* indicates that too much of factor has adverse effect on mental health

Source: Warr, P. (1987) *Work, Unemployment and Mental Health*, by permission of the Oxford University Press, Oxford

Warr's theory both affirms the value of work in maintaining mental health, and suggests that satisfaction is more than passive contentment. Both chime well with everyday experience. Stress, in the sense of moderate anxiety about the successful outcome of work-based tasks, is good for mental health. The strain resulting from overwork can be relieved by job design, whatever the value of psychological counselling. Removing the opportunity for attainment of realistic goals, and for the display of competence and autonomy, will positively harm mental health. Facilitation, rather than 'resting' should be management's reaction to stress caused by overwork.

Poor mental health expresses itself as anxiety, depression, low self-esteem and poor sleep. These are symptoms commonly found in people who are out of work and also, as described below, in people who are employed but dissatisfied with their employment. 'Hard work', as the old saying has it, 'never hurt anyone'. Unemployment, and badly designed jobs, may well do so.

Much of the research by Warr and his co-workers has contributed to an understanding of the dissatisfactions of being out of work; job satisfaction revealed by deprival. Pearson (1989) has reported research in which it was possible to compare the mental health of two groups of professionals and managers, one of which were out of work, and the other which were employed but seeking guidance about how to develop their careers. The measure used was the *general health questionnaire* (Goldberg, 1978) which reveals situational anxiety and depression. Results for the two groups are compared in Figure 6.5. Interestingly, both groups exhibited a wide range of scores, from normal to highly distressed, but there was no discernible difference between the distribution of scores within the two groups. It seems that having a job does not automatically confer the benefits of mental health that unemployment might be assumed to take away. Job satisfaction and sound mental health are available to some workers, but not to all; nor does satisfying work necessarily make up for distress suffered in other aspects of life.

Job satisfaction and skills

Warr is not the only authority to study job satisfaction from the point of view of those deprived of it, particularly the unemployed. O'Brien included the underemployed in this category. Jahoda (1982) proposed a theory of psychological stress in unemployment based on 'deprival' of the benefits of work: workers are seen as deprived not only of money, but also of the social, time-structuring, skill-use, and self-esteem boosting aspects of work. But she is also aware of 'unhappy, psychologically unhealthy people in

Figure 6.5
Comparison between
mental health of
seekers and
unemployed managers
(spread of scores on
Goldberg's general
health questionnaire)

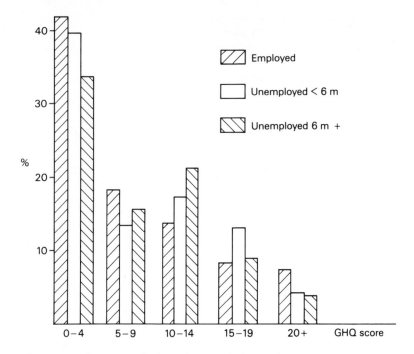

employment whose morale is as low as their productivity', as described in Chapter 2.

Work may be better than unemployment, but only just. It is hard to accept O'Brien's thesis of an overeducated workforce against this judgement. Much of the earlier justification for manpower planning was based on matching organizational needs with the labour market. Human resource strategy requires much more than this. Employers should re-design jobs to provide challenge and full use of skills; national strategy must be aimed at bringing the skills of the population as a whole to a high level.

For the moment, however, we need to consider how to interpret data which may indicate that workers are not satisfied, and that further study and remedial action are required.

Correlates of job satisfaction: aspects to consider

The outcome of social research at the workplace should be effective policies for human resource management. Explaining data that might suggest presence or absence of job satisfaction is not easy, but human resource planners may care to consider the following summary of research into this topic (Griffin and Bateman, 1986). As with motivation (see Figure 6.4), satisfaction is influenced not only by work content but also by the values that workers hold, including self-esteem and need for achievement.

Satisfaction is found to be positively related to educational achievement, age, income and occupational level. The last of these supports Jahoda's contention, quoted above: low job skill results in low job satisfaction. Satisfaction tends to decrease the longer a job is held, again supporting the contention that activity and skill development are both motivators and satisfiers. Once again, 'experience' is undermined as a measure of effectiveness.

Neither gender nor race have marked effects on perceived job satisfaction. As implied in Chapter 5, pay may have little relation to motivation. It does affect job satisfaction, but not in ways that are correlated with performance.

The openness of the payment system, perhaps because of its 'hygiene' status in Herzberg's terms, has been shown to be a factor in satisfaction. Clear connections between organization structure and job satisfaction have not been established, but participation in decision-making does have a beneficial effect, good news for those who believe in strategic management.

Locke has defined job satisfaction as 'pleasurable emotion'. He has also defined it as 'the achievement of one's job values in the work situation'. Satisfaction and dissatisfaction are the emotional reactions to work, which managers ignore at their peril, because they stem from the very heart of the employment relationship. Their direct relationship with intrinsic motivation and performance can be deduced from research described above. The relevance of extrinsic factors, the social and physical environment in which work is carried out, is perhaps more difficult to maintain. We now turn to two aspects of worker behaviour that are often explained by dissatisfaction with work.

The danger signals: absence and turnover

Negative emotions about work have one very clear-cut interest for the human resource planner—they are likely causes of 'wastage', which has been described by Bennison and Casson (1984) as 'the engine of manpower planning'. It is assumed that people leave organizations because they are dissatisfied with them, either in absolute terms, or by reference to a better organization elsewhere. Even if they don't leave they may indulge in taking time off. Sometimes this may be unexplained and sometimes it is sanctioned by reasons of ill-health, real or spurious. Wastage can, to some extent, be allowed for and this may be part of a conscious organizational strategy. Absenteeism, however, is disruptive for management and colleagues alike, and planning for it is difficult. The one-day absences that characterize voluntary absenteeism are particularly serious in this respect and cause additional costs through over-manning, or through lost output when resources are left idle.

For our present purpose, we will concentrate on the methodological problems involved in measuring turnover and absence. Once again the issues are those of concept and measure, validity and reliability, categorization and enumeration. Which wastage data will be worth collecting, and why? Presumably, the most interesting and worthwhile is the behaviour that lies within management control: voluntary severance, as distinct from death, sickness, or closure of a factory or office. Voluntary leaving is motivated by personal reasons, but how can we categorize these? If we conduct 'exit interviews' to try to discover causes, will we receive valid answers to our questions? Would discovering what sort of job the leaver is going to next be a better indicator? Finally, how will we categorize the replies when we receive them? Bowey (1978) provides a useful list of 'processes' leading to termination of employment (see Table 6.2).

Wolpin and Burke (1985) pointed out that absence and wastage should be correlated, since voluntary absence could be the first indication of an employee's dissatisfaction with an organization, and departure its final confirmation. Few research studies support this obvious prediction. Failure to use correct, compatible and consistent concepts and measures may be a reason for this. Certainly we need to try to distinguish between absence truly attributable to sickness, and that which arises from other reasons. Within 'other reasons' absence, we need to discover how much is entirely under the voluntary control of the employee. What status is to be given to absence caused by strikes, holidays and, as one overseas student put it, 'when we are

Table 6.2
Bowey's 'processes' in
learning behaviour

Reasons for leaving

—Moving for higher earnings
—Moving to advance career prospects
—Attraction to alternative job opportunties
—Leaving to avoid personal conflict
—Management run-down of staff
—Induction crisis
—Loss of unstable recruits
—Pressures from shortage of staff
—Pressures from change of working methods
—The availability of an alternative role

Source: Bowey, A. (1974) *A Guide to Manpower Planning*, Macmillan, London

told to go out on the streets and support the President'. A thorough review of research into absence and wastage some 20 years ago (Porter and Steers, 1973) revealed that researchers and administrators had frequently failed to differentiate sickness absence from that attributable to other causes. Sickness and voluntary absence follow very different patterns. These patterns are revealed by careful enumeration and appropriate description, once suitable categories have been recognized. There are two major descriptors for absence behaviour: severity and frequency.

- *Severity* measures the total time that an individual or group have been absent in a given period of time.
- *Frequency* measures the number of absences.

Severity is the better measure of true sickness absence, since this occurs infrequently but usually lasts for a week or more.

Frequency is the preferred measure for voluntary absences, most of which lasts only one day, but which happen much more often. Both should be calculated and recorded. The predicted patterns are, of course, general rules, and exceptions may be found in particular working environments. The study of absence behaviour is the subject of the case study at the end of this chapter.

Staff turnover, or wastage, was extensively studied in the early days of manpower planning. Sophisticated indices were computed, and elaborate computer models were programmed; the wonder is that so much labour resulted in so little impact on management or strategic thinking. One reason, undoubtedly, was that basic data were never collected; another that changes in the economy ('secular changes' in the terminology of social science) made projections on the basis of past wastage data a hazardous matter. Sources for the early work on this subject may be found in Chapter 1.

There are, however, simple indices that, when used with care, can provide the basis for human resource planning. One is known as the *BIM (or crude wastage) index*. The formula is shown in Table 6.3. Although the example is calculated for a period of one year, a shorter or longer time can be used, provided that consistency is maintained. In some industries, or cultures, a much shorter time would give more meaningful results. The index should not be regarded, in itself, as indicating that turnover is either good or bad; high turnover might be the norm for a particular industry. But indices can be used comparatively, perhaps showing up differences between one department and another, or between one company and another in the same business. Periods of time can be compared, to see whether turnover is increasing or decreasing. Comparative figures are the best guide to management action.

The 'crudity' of the 'crude wastage' index resides in a number of factors. First, the average number employed over a period of time will have little meaning if a large number of people leave. Secondly, the fast turnover of a small number of jobs will cause a spuriously high index. Thirdly, as will be evident when we consider cohort analysis, those with shorter service are the most likely to leave, so that the length of service profiles will affect the turnover index.

The *stability index* overcomes some of these disadvantages. This index focuses on stayers rather than leavers. The formula is shown in Table 6.3. Once again, the period of time for calculation of the index is arbitrary. It is advisable to calculate both BIM and stability indices when evaluating wastage. The problem of short-serving employees remains, and another index (Bowey, 1974) is available to remove the effect of the more mobile employees from the calculation. This is a matter of choice, because it may be important when designing strategy to include the effects of short-serving people on staffing levels.

Table 6.3
Measures of leaving
behaviour

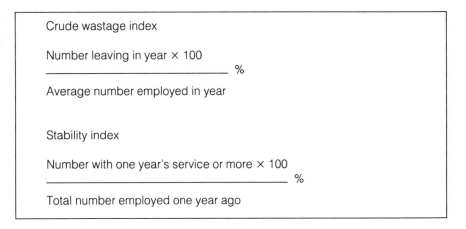

Crude wastage index

$$\frac{\text{Number leaving in year} \times 100}{\text{Average number employed in year}} \, \%$$

Stability index

$$\frac{\text{Number with one year's service or more} \times 100}{\text{Total number employed one year ago}} \, \%$$

Why short-service staff matter is demonstrated in Figure 6.6. This shows the typical leaving behaviour of a group of similar employees who join an organization at the same time, and whose work experience or training follow the same path. Such a group is called a cohort, and the recording and description of their subsequent leaving behaviour is called *cohort analysis*. It has obvious application to the planning for entry to, and losses from, training schemes, including those for graduates.

Early losses from a cohort might indicate poor induction procedures, or poor understanding by recruits of what was required of them. But some losses are to expected in the early stages of a training programme (the fallibility of selection was discussed in Chapter 4). Later losses might indicate that the cohort were disillusioned about career prospects once training was complete. The value of such analyses lies in the explanations that they suggest, and their implications for strategy and policy.

Gathering and interpreting cohort data is a lengthy business. In the case of graduates, for instance, accumulating significant cohort data takes several years, during which the economic outlook can have changed a number of times. So the final graph may be less regular than the idealized version in

Figure 6.6
Cohort analysis:
percentage of
employee group
remaining at various
times after recruitment

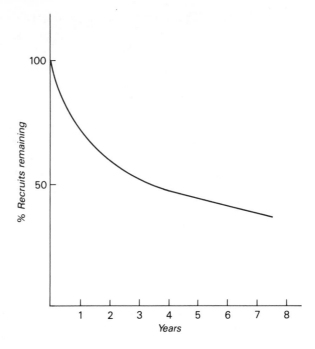

Figure 6.6. As a basis for forecasting future intake, they should be used with circumspection. They may, however, provide data for the scenario planning favoured by Bennison and Casson (1984) using the 'manpower map'. They could inform strategic planning by suggesting estimates of 'best' and 'worst' cases.

All research, whether large scale or confined to one organization, benefits from a unifying theoretical model. Steers and Rhodes (1978) provided such a model for absence behaviour. It owes its origins to an earlier literature review by Porter and Steers (1973). Steers and Rhodes draw attention to the need to consider 'ability' as well as 'motivation' to go to work. Their model for the causes of absence behaviour is shown in Figure 6.7.

This provides a suitable conclusion to this chapter, because it links the concepts of motivation and satisfaction, and shows them to be interdependent at the level of the work itself. These intrinsic satisfactions of the job are contrasted with the wider issues of economic need and values, and the limitations placed on attendance by physical location. Models like this lack the easy cause and effect relationships of earlier theory, but, combined with the intelligent and diligent gathering of data, offer more realistic support for strategic human resource planning.

Steers and Rhodes' model has recently been used to guide research into absence of care staff at a veterans hospital in the USA (Brooke and Price, 1989) and its basic assumptions shown to be tenable. Interestingly, for readers of Chapter 3, the research team had to modify the model because some of the theoretical constructs could not be operationalized.

Practical issues in the control of absence behaviour within an organization have been reviewed by Sargent (1989).

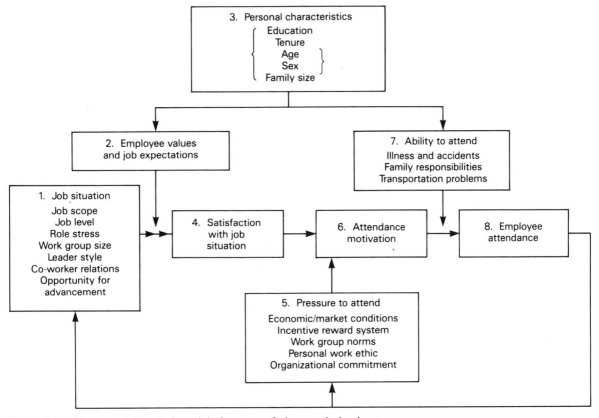

Figure 6.7 Steers and Rhodes' model of causes of absence behaviour
Source: Steers, R. and Rhodes, R. (1978) 'Major influences on employee attendance: a process model', *Journal of Applied Psychology*, 63, 391. © 1978 by the American Psychological Association. Reprinted by permission.

CASE STUDY 6
Measuring and accounting for absence behaviour

Oxford Road Products are a manufacturing company housed in an old cotton mill near the centre of Manchester, in England's North West. They produce a variety of rubber, or rubber-based, items. Manufacturing processes differ widely, as do the working conditions associated with each process.

Table 6.4 shows the major products and processes, and the workforce engaged in each. At the time of this study, absenteeism among shop-floor workers was between 10 and 20 per cent. The aim of the research was to compare patterns of absence behaviour between departments, and to discover how far working conditions might account for differences.

Entry and data source

The difficulties facing the manpower planner responsible for this study were those common to many other investigations of social systems. There were the problems of gaining entry to the organization, and of overcoming the suspicions of both line management and the personnel department towards an outsider. This could be crucial in gaining access to data. But, as readers of the foregoing chapters will realize, there were also problems of conceptualization, of understanding what absence behaviour might mean in this particular environment, and of interpreting that behaviour in such a way that management could understand it.

In the event, the personnel department and the general manager adopted a

Table 6.4
Factory at which the
study of absence
behaviour was carried
out: major products,
types of process, and
the workforce engaged
in each

Product	Department	Production methods	Group size
Rubber compounds	Mill	Rubber is masticated between hot rollers and blended with compounding ingredients, including carbon black	54 male
Rubber-covered rollers	Roller covering	Steel rollers to be used in textile machinery, are coated with rubber and vulcanized	35 male
Flooring for vehicles	Car mats	Rubber compounds are calendered into sheets, moulded into car mat shapes, vulcanized, trimmed and finished	48 male 45 female
Coated fabrics	Proofing	Compounds are dissolved in solvents, and spread in successive layers on fabrics, which are then dried and vulcanized	64 male
Solid rubber tyres	Solid tyres	Rubber compounds are extruded, formed onto metal bands, and vulcanized	27 male
Checked goods for despatch	Packing	Goods are generally packed in the manufacturing department. There is also a small team of loaders	20 male

neutral stance towards the research, allowing access at least to available numerical data. Their attitude to more direct contact with the workforce will be discussed later.

The personnel department revealed that there were two sources of information about absence behaviour, neither of them ideal. These were referred to as the Weekly Absence Reports, and the Timekeeping Records Cards. The Weekly Absence Reports (WAR) were produced by supervisors to record the numbers absent on each day of the previous working week. Absence was classified as 'sickness', 'long-term sickness' and 'other reasons'. The supervisor recorded which shift was affected.

The Timekeeping Record Cards (TCR) were maintained within the accounts department. Each card contained a space for each day of the working year. Should inspection of the employee's clock-card reveal that he was absent, the card was marked provisionally 'A' for absent, or 'P' if absence was sanctioned by the supervisor. When a doctor's note was received from the welfare department, the absence was re-classified as related to sickness, and marked with a 'D'. The affected shift was not recorded. More seriously, record cards for those leaving the company were destroyed.

The accounts department provided computerized personnel records that included age and length of service for each employee, and lists of recent leavers.

Assessment of data sources

As a record of total absence, the Weekly Absence Report was likely to be reasonably accurate, since the supervisor would be directly concerned with numbers absent each day. The allocation of absence to the major categories would, however, be rather arbitrary. Sickness absence usually lasts several days, and often several weeks. Doctors' notes were required after three days, and the supervisor would be unlikely to know their existence before submitting the report. Personal knowledge of individuals probably played its part in the allocation of absence to categories. Permitted absence was not separately recorded.

Timekeeping Record Cards were a good source of information about individual absence behaviour, distinguishing as they did between absence sanctioned by a doctor's note and other reasons. Permitted absence was rare and was eliminated as a separate category in this investigation. This source could provide data on both frequency and severity of absence. Systematic but random samples were obtained by selecting every fifth card in alphabetical order within departments.

The TCR, however, had one important weakness—leavers were not included. This was unfortunate because the absence behaviour of short-stay people might be particularly interesting, and also because removing it might bias the sampled data. This potential bias would, of course, vary with the turnover level in the department being considered. The turnover in some departments, however, was as high as 40 per cent, and some bias must have occurred.

All surveys of this type are subject to an important threat to validity—the period of time to which the data refers. No period can be said to be truly representative, because economic and social conditions vary continuously. At the beginning of this particular six-month period, there were slack trading conditions, and some lay-offs were taking place. Numbers employed decreased in some departments during the period, and one was closed shortly after.

Daily patterns of absence within departments

Figure 6.8 shows that there was a general pattern of absence behaviour in all departments. Mondays and Fridays tended to be the worst days; Thursday, being pay-day, showed the highest attendance. Closer inspection of the histograms reveals that most of the variation occurs in the 'other reasons' category, supporting the reliability of the supervisors' reports. Sickness absence remained steady at about five per cent from day to day, and from department to department. Absence attributable to long-term sickness (lasting more than 13 weeks) was usually the cause of higher than average percentages of sickness absence.

Night shifts, when long-term sickness was left out of account, revealed more favourable absence rates on four nights of the week than day shifts; Fridays were an understandable exception.

Only two female work groups were operating during the period covered by this investigation. Absence among females in the car mats department was significantly higher than for males only on Fridays. The high absence quality control department was later disbanded.

The daily variation in both sickness and 'other reasons' absence may be expressed in terms of the *worst day index*. This ratio compares in absence on the worst and best days (see Table 6.5).

The data gathered from the TCR and personnel records could be analysed either within departments or for the workforce as a whole. Figures 6.9(a) and (b) show some characteristics of the latter—the age and length of service profiles. The distribution of sickness absence, both as totals within the six-month period of research and as separate absences are shown in Figures 6.9(c)

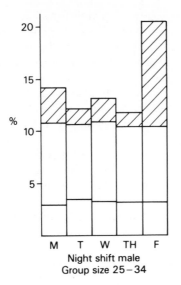

Figure 6.8
Daily patterns of
absence behaviour
within departments of a
multi-product factory

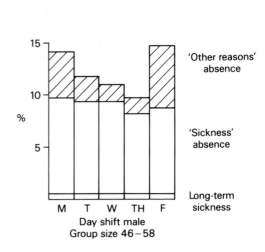

MILL

'Other reasons'
absence

'Sickness'
absence

Long-term
sickness

Day shift male
Group size 46−58

Night shift male
Group size 25−34

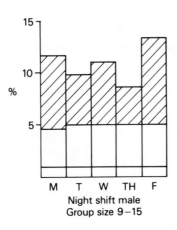

Night shift male
Group size 9−15

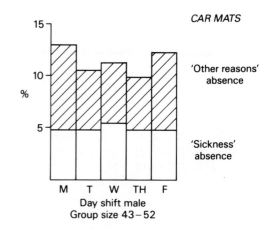

CAR MATS

'Other reasons'
absence

'Sickness'
absence

Day shift male
Group size 43−52

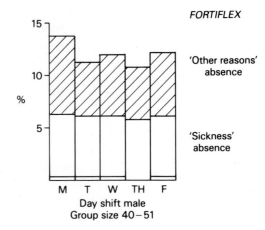

FORTIFLEX

'Other reasons'
absence

'Sickness'
absence

Day shift male
Group size 40−51

Figure 6.9
(a) Age distribution for
factory workforce

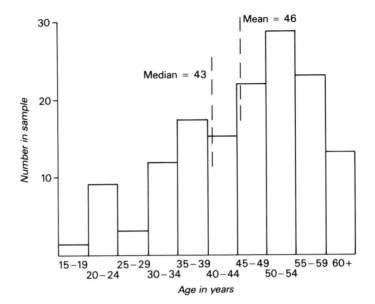

(b) Length of service
distribution for factory
workforce

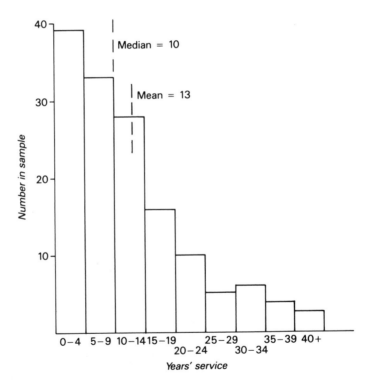

and (d). Table 6.6 shows the distribution of unsanctioned absence, for which a histogram is unsuitable.

The uneven ('skewed') distribution of particular behaviours within a group, familiar to many managers as the 80/20 rule, applies to absence, and has implications for both strategy and policy. This skewedness can be conveniently demonstrated by means of cumulative frequency graphs, also known as ogives. Figure 6.10 compares the distribution of voluntary and sickness absence for each department.

Figure 6.9
(c) Distribution of total sickness absences: six-month period

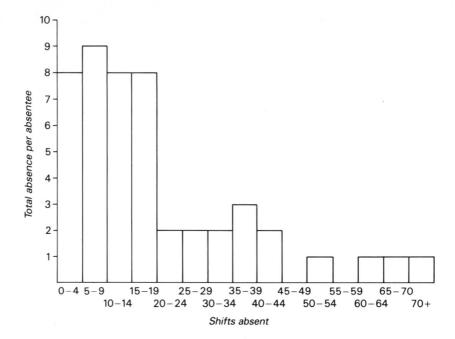

(d) Distribution of total voluntary absence: six-month period

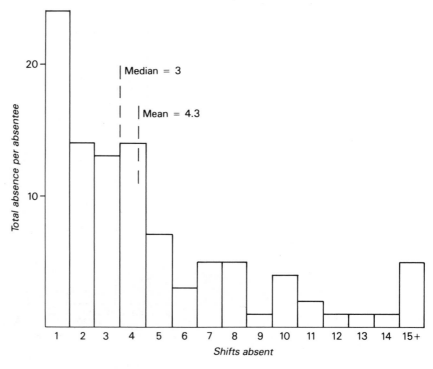

General characteristics of workforce and absence behaviour

The population of manual workers at the factory could be defined in the following ways:

- they had a median age of 43
- they had a median length of service of 10 years
- they work in departments manufacturing a range of products with different uses, and requiring a variety of skills

Table 6.5
'Worst day' indices by
department

Department	Sickness absence (WDI)		'Other reasons' absence (WDI)	
	Day shift	*Night shift*	*Day shift*	*Night shift*
Mill	1.2	1.1	4.1	7.1
Proofing	1.1	1.1	1.9	2.2
Roller covering	1.1	—	1.8	—
Fortiflex	1.1	—	1.5	—
Car mats (males)	1.2	1.1	1.8	3.8
(females)	1.1	—	1.6	—
Stores	1.1	—	3.7	—
CV extrusions	1.4	1.3	6.8	3.0
Calenders	1.6	—	3.0	—
Solid tyres	1.1	2.0	4.9	1.8
Packing	1.1	—	3.7	—
Engineers	1.2	1.1	1.4	4.0
Quality control (males)	1.1	—	1.6	—
(females)	1.2	—	1.8	—

* 'Worst day' index is the ratio of absences on the worst and the best days

Table 6.6
Distribution of
unsanctioned absence
within and between
departments

Absences	Instances	Duration (shifts)
All voluntary absences in sample	366	583
All voluntary absences lasting one shift only	305	305
% of one-shift voluntary absences	83	52

Their absence behaviour was characterized by a reluctance to attend for work on Monday and Friday, and a readiness to attend on Thursday, which was pay-day. Their patterns of sickness and unsanctioned absence were sufficiently variable to warrant separate consideration.

Sickness absence was absence covered by submission of a doctor's note, whether or not the absentee could be said to be truly ill. At this factory, and at this time, sickness absence often lasted at least 10 working days, and in some cases much longer.

Sickness absence affected seriously only about 20 per cent of the manual workers, and could be safely assumed to be representative of individuals rather than of the working environment. Sickness absence rates of five per cent appeared general in most departments, with long-term sickness absence affecting some.

Sickness absence occurred less frequently than unsanctioned absence, and when it did occur rearrangements of work lasting a week or more could be made. Unsanctioned absences, however, seldom lasted for more than one day, and amounted to a one-person lightning strike. As such, they could be highly disruptive of production. Unsanctioned absences were a more general feature of the workforce than sickness. Only about 20 per cent of them had not taken at least one day's absence during the six months covered by the research project. There were variations in both severity and frequency of absence between one department and another, as well as from day to day. As discussed

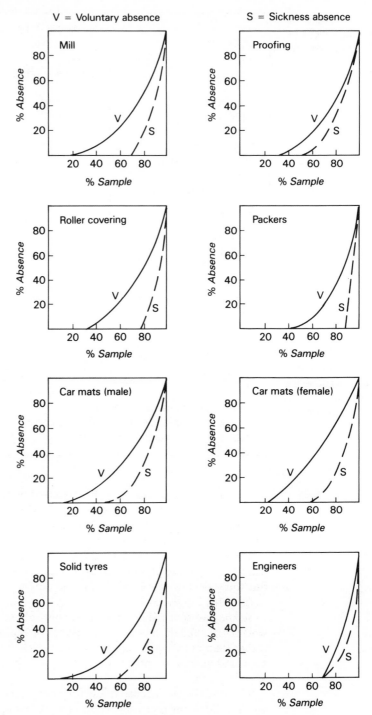

in Chapter 6, a complex interplay of personal, domestic and work-related variables could have been responsible. Nevertheless, absence did vary between departments, possibly because of the variation of working conditions. The latter would have included physical environment, the nature of the work done and the human relationships including style of supervision.

An interesting group, represented in each department, apparently took no time off at all. The manpower planner dubbed these 'the presentees'. The

Table 6.7
Characteristics of
workers who attended
regularly for work

Association between 'no sickness absence' and age		
Age	Number who were never absent	Number who were absent for any period
43 or over	70	28
42 or less	27	19
$\chi^2 = 2.3$, which is not significant for one degree of freedom		

Association between 'no voluntary absence' and age		
Age	Number who were never absent	Number who were absent for any period
43 or over	41	56
42 or less	8	39
$\chi^2 = 9.0$, which is significant at the % level for one degree of freedom		

Association between 'no sickness absence' and age		
Age	Number who were never absent	Number who were absent for any period
43 or over	70	28
42 or less	27	19
$\chi^2 = 2.3$, which is not significant for one degree of freedom		

Association between 'no voluntary absence' and length of service		
Service	Number who were never absent	Number who were absent for any period
10 years or over	24	43
9 years	18	50

association of this characteristic with age and length of service was tested as shown in Table 6.7. Unexpectedly, the no-absence group were older than other workers, but not necessarily longer-serving.

The frustrations of research

At this point it would have been both satisfying and revealing to change the research style from survey to fieldwork, and to have interviewed samples of both absentees and 'presentees' in depth. Of particular interest would have been the perceptions and motivations of the presentees. Another advantage would have been the opportunity to check whether worker's perceptions of their working conditions were the same as those of the researcher. Unfortunately, fearing a reaction from the trade union, management forbade any such investigation. Interviewing departmental managers, both as a group and singly, was permitted.

Creating synthetic variables

Despite the difficulties created by the ban on shop-floor interviews, the hypothesis that frequency of voluntary absence would correlate with the severity of working conditions was tested. A measure of the latter was compiled from separate assessments of major variables by the researcher: darkness, heat, humidity, repetition of work, pressure and group size. A maximum of five points was allocated to each of these factors. Since some factors did not apply to some departments, total scores varied from 4 to 25 points on each factor. At interviews with departmental managers, each was asked to comment on the closeness of supervision required, the physical conditions of the work and the cohesiveness of working groups. These comments were content analysed and departments were awarded up to a maximum of five points each according to perceived unpleasantness. When departments were ranked on each scale, the rank order was different only for the roller covering department, twelfth on the first scale and fourth on the second. This department was omitted from the subsequent analysis.

The final stage of the research was to test the hypothesis that there would be a significant correlation between the ranking of working conditions and the ranking of voluntary absence rates. Spearman's rank order coefficient was found to be 0.77, just significant at the 0.1 per cent level for a sample size of six.

This outcome does not, of course, necessarily imply that poor working conditions cause absence. For one reason, perceptions of working conditions by research workers or managers are not necessarily also those of the workers themselves. For another, the relationship could be caused by what is called 'an intervening variable'; for instance, the less satisfactory workers available to the labour department might have been allocated to work in the less pleasant departments. In the end, the outcomes and meaning of research projects of this type have to be decided on the balance of probabilities.

Research, strategy and policy

In a strategically managed organization, absence behaviour would be kept under continuous review. Over a period of time, this would be focused increasingly on probable causal factors. The results would be applied to studies of job and work design, and also related to validity of selection. They would, in Halsey's phrase, 'inform the political debate'. Decisions on disciplinary procedures, incentive schemes and health programmes would be taken in the light of continuous research. Attention would be given to the comparative rarity of sickness absence, and to the fact that some workers attend their place of work without fail. There would also be more openness in acquiring and discussing the implications of data with the workforce. That way, the strategic decision process would be assisted, and realistic general policies for handling personnel problems would be derived.

Readers may like to reflect on the different approaches that would be required in similar investigations in the factories described in the case study at the end of Chapter 5.

References

Bandura, A. (1982) 'Self-efficacy mechanism in human agency', *American Psychologist*, **37**, 122.

Bennison, M. and Casson, J. (1984) *The Manpower Planning Handbook*, McGraw-Hill (UK) Ltd, Maidenhead.

Bowey, A. (1974) *A Guide to Manpower Planning*, Macmillan, London.

Brooke, P. and Price, J. (1989) 'The determinants of employee absenteeism: An empirical test of a causal model', *Journal of Occupational Psychology*, **62**, 1.

Donovan, The Right Hon. Lord (1971) *Royal Commission on Trade Unions and Employers' Associations*, HMSO, London.

Flanders, A. Pomeranz, R. and Woodward, J. (1968) *An Experiment in Industrial Democracy*, Faber and Faber, London.

Goldberg, D. (1978) *General Health Questionnaire*, NFER–Nelson, Windsor.

Griffin, R. and Bateman, T. (1986) *Job Satisfaction and Organizational Commitment*, International Review of Industrial and Organizational Psychology, John Wiley & Sons, Chichester.

Hackman, J. and Oldham, G. (1980) *Work Redesign*, Addison-Wesley, Reading, Massachusetts.

Herriot, P. (1984) *Down from the Ivory Tower: graduates and their jobs*, John Wiley & Sons, Chichester.

Herzberg, F., Mausner, B. and Snyderman, B. (1959) *The Motivation to Work*, John Wiley & Sons, Chichester.

Jahoda, M. (1982) *Employment and Unemployment*, Cambridge University Press, Cambridge.

Landy, F. (1978) 'An opponent process theory of job satisfaction', *Journal of Applied Psychology*, **63**, 533.

Locke, E. (1976) 'The nature and causes of job satisfaction' in Dunette, M. (ed.) *Handbook of Industrial and Organizational Psychology*, Rand McNally, Chicago.

Locke, E. and Henne, D. (1986) 'Work motivation theories' in Cooper, C. and Robertson, I. (1986) *Work Motivation Theories*. Reprinted by permission of John Wiley & Sons, Chichester.

Maslow, A. (1954) *Motivation and Personality*, Harper & Row, New York.

McLelland, D., Atkinson, J., Clare, R. and Lowell, E. (1953) *The Achievement Motive*, Appleton Century, New York.

McGregor, D. (1960) *The Human Side of Enterprise*, McGraw-Hill (UK) Ltd, Maidenhead.

O'Brien, G. (1986) *Psychology of Work and Unemployment*, John Wiley & Sons, Chichester.

Pearson, R. and Heyno, A. (1988) *Helping the Unemployed Professional*, John Wiley & Sons, Chichester.

Pearson, R. (1989) 'Career change and redundancy: two sides of the same coin?' Paper presented to the British Psychological Society Occupational Psychology Conference, Windermere, January.

Pagnamenta, P. and Overy, R. (1984) *All Our Working Lives*, BBC Books, London.

Porter, L. and Lawler, E. (1969) *Managerial Attitudes and Performance*, Dorsey-Irwin, Holmwood, Illinois.

Porter, L. and Steers, R. (1973) 'Organizational, work and personal factors in employee turnover and absenteeism', *Psychological Bulletin*, **80**, 2, 151.

Salancik, G. and Pfeffer, J. (1978) 'A social information processing approach to job attitudes and task design', *Administrative Science Quarterly*, **23**, 224.

Sargent, A. (1989) *The Missing Workforce: managing absenteeism*, Institute of Personnel Management, London.

Shackleton, V. and Fletcher, C. (1984) *Individual Differences: theories and applications*, New Essential Psychology, Methuen, London.

Smith, P., Kendall, L. and Hulin, C. (1969) *The Measurement of Satisfaction in Work and Retirement: a strategy for the study of attitudes*, Rand-McNally, Chicago.

Steers, R. and Rhodes, R. (1978) 'Major influences on employee attendance: a process model', *Journal of Applied Psychology*, **63**, 391.

Warr, P. (1985) 'Jobs and mental health', The Third Alec Rodger Memorial Lecture, Birkbeck College, November.

Warr, P. (1987) *Work, Unemployment and Mental Health*, Clarendon Press, Oxford

Wolpin, J. and Burke, R. (1985) 'Relationships between absenteeism and turnover: a function of measures?' *Personnel Psychology*, **57**.

CHAPTER 7 Responding to new careers

The career concept and human resource strategy

The concept of motivation, whatever its psychological implications, can be reduced for our purposes to the assumption that work is done best by those who want to do it—ability is not enough. In the previous chapter we considered the value of clearly defined goals in motivating performance. Skill use emerged as joint motivator and satisfier. In considering motivation and job satisfaction, we were concerned with their immediate effects on job performance, rather than with the long-term relationship between employer and employee. A warning signal may be detected, however, in the observation (Chapter 6) that job satisfaction is diminished by staying too long in a job. Too much 'experience', it appears, will blunt the edge of both aspects of motivation: goals will no longer appear challenging, and skills will not be developed.

Pursuing a career could be seen as a way of ensuring that new goals are achieved and new skills acquired. Developing the careers of key employees would appear to be an important task in strategic human resource management. Provided, of course, that we know what careers are. With the demise of cradle-to-grave employment, the task of definition is now more difficult than it once seemed.

The traditional concept of a career is deeply ingrained in the working culture of industrialized nations. Career structures were the basis of early manpower planning theory. Redundancies, and the rise of a more individualistic work ethic, however, have made a mockery of both. Employees no longer act in ways that suggest that their 'careers' will be developed by a single employer or, indeed, by anything but their own efforts and choices.

To employers, careers have always been something of a fiction. The phrase 'make a career with us' in employment brochures often implied humdrum employment in clerical work, or even in manual occupations. The devaluation of the word has helped neither employers nor employees to understand the economic and psychological importance of continually upgrading their skills. The offer of a career, even to highly qualified people, was often little more than a promise to provide continuing employment; a promise withdrawn when the going got tough in the 1970s and 1980s.

The 1990s will see the further development of a new phenomenon—the individual career—in which regular opportunities will be taken to enhance both personal skills and knowledge, whether these coincide with the interests of particular employers or not. This presents employers with a strategic challenge. The 1960s and 1970s were decades of the management development department. Large organizations, particularly, found it difficult to fill senior positions when they fell vacant. They adopted policies of staff appraisal, backed by structured management training, to 'grow their own timber'. Well-meaning attempts to fill the ability gap were frustrated by the tendency of able, creative employees to leave, and of less able people to remain behind. Manpower planning, where adopted, was obsessed with measuring and predicting staff turnover. The rising numbers of graduates from expanded higher education were seen as a source of talent to be nurtured and developed in special schemes for 'high fliers'. Yearly losses of 10 to 20 per cent per year from these schemes were not unusual.

Strategic thinking, however, is not about beating one's head against a brick wall; it is about detecting and responding to realities. If the reasoning in Chapter 6 (see references to Herzberg, Locke and O'Brien) is valid, organizations should not be surprised if pensions, generous pay-scales and fringe benefits fail to hold unsatisfied workers within their career structures; these are, in Herzberg's terms, only 'hygiene' factors. If Locke and O'Brien are right, it is factors more closely connected with the work itself that both motivate and satisfy employees; goal setting focuses effort and motivates performance, the use of skills gives satisfaction. The larger the organization, the more opportunity there would seem to be for both. Keeping the more highly qualified person should be easier for the larger company and for the public service. Why is the reality so often different?

Large organizations do indeed have the potential to provide satisfying careers. But size also slows down organizational responses, both to the internal labour market and to employees' needs. Entrepreneurial talents are stifled by bureaucracy, and opportunities to use skills are limited by the ability of middle managers to recognize these in the people who work for them. Small wonder that employees use the external labour market as a measure of their worth.

Instead of fruitlessly trying to prevent turnover of skilled and creative people, human resource planners should turn to accepting and managing it. Designing a satisfying and profitable short-term assignment for a highly motivated but temporary member of staff presents human resource planners themselves with a motivating challenge. The earlier part of this chapter deals with the more traditional definition and management of careers; we will then turn to today's more individual approach.

Careers versus jobs

What are the characteristics of a career that distinguish it from a job? In the technical language of social science, what are the 'indicators' of the career concept? A list of features to be found in all careers would include at least some of the following:

- Entry based on educational attainment
- Vocational training with qualifying examinations
- Specific job experience required before promotion
- Recognized structure of promotional steps
- Membership of a 'professional' body, allowng careers to be independent of employers, or to be conducted on a self-employed basis
- Codes of professional ethics
- Progressive status and salary

One of the definitions of 'career' in Chambers Dictionary is 'advancement in profession or occupation'. So the idea of 'progress' or 'progression' appears to be fundamental: a career is a series of jobs in which the job-holder can demonstrate increasing competence and experience fulfilment. If this is so, careers require more than a 'nine to five' commitment; they also demand time devoted to study, unpaid overtime, and a social life that includes mixing with others following the same career. The final requirement is commitment to a professional code of ethics that may from time to time conflict with the objectives of a particular employer.

Traditional thinking about careers

In the UK, 'career' is an overused word; 'careers services' are forced to accept the realities of local labour markets in giving advice to young people, and 'careers handbooks' describe the range of employment in an organization, without any assumption that it will be progressive. While the traditional concept of a career might have most relevance for those entering one of the learned professions, the word is also used euphemistically in advertisements for junior clerical staff. For those with memories of mass unemployment in the 1930s, a 'career' was identified as a secure job with prospects of advancement. People who had experienced unemployment encouraged their children to seek out jobs that offered those benefits. The apparent security, and middle-class overtones, of the word 'career' may explain its use as an advertiser's hyperbole when 'employment' is intended.

The literature and techniques of manpower planning take career structures for granted. Students of human resource management might justifiably suspect that careers present yet another example of the familiar problem of categorization. It is, after all, of little value to carry out elaborate computer modelling and forecasting exercises on career structures if the grades fail to represent real differences in levels of competence and status, or if very few actually follow the paths that the manpower planners have assumed in their analysis.

Bennison and Casson (1984) emphasized the importance of establishing the true nature of the 'manpower system' before using it for forecasting purposes. They pointed out that the cherished beliefs of managers, even those of personnel specialists, need to be validated by reference to the personnel records. Is there evidence that grades are significantly different from each other, or are they merely devices for paying different salaries? If the levels of expertise are truly different, how often are staff recorded as actually making the transition between them? If policies of internal promotion are claimed, how often is recruitment to a grade made from external sources? The ratio of internal promotions to external recruitment is called, in Bennison's terms, the 'replacement policy'. Like so much in career management, 'policy' is too exalted a name for the series of casual decisions represented by this ratio.

Yet manpower planning, in the early 1980s, made much of the management of career structures, perhaps because 'slimming' had apparently become inevitable under the pressures of world recession. The Institute of Manpower Studies provided the statistical means, the concept of the career progression diagram, and computer programs that allowed it to be used as a forecasting technique.

Career progression diagrams: an exercise in methodology

Career progression diagrams (also known as *camera diagrams*) enabled manpower planners to assess the probability of staff reaching a particular grade in an organization, and at what age (Bennison and Casson, 1984). The use of this technique, valuable though it is in indicating the net effect of past manpower policies, betrays the origins of manpower planning in large, bureaucratic and hierarchical organizations. For smaller organizations, and for those of any size where turnover is large, camera diagrams can be highly misleading. Even when applying them to seemingly appropriate situations, the human resource planner should do so critically, looking carefully for evidence that the assumed career structure actually exists.

Figure 7.1(a), (b)
Staff within grades by
age group: as
(a) numbers and as
(b) percentages

(a)

Grade	Age group							
	20–24	25–29	30–34	35–39	40–44	45–49	50–54	55–60
Senior	0	0	50	75	100	70	70	80
Middle	0	300	450	425	250	200	100	200
Junior	2000	1500	1000	1000	650	330	250	120
Trainees	500	200	0	0	0	0	0	0
Total	2500	2000	1500	1500	1000	600	500	400

(b)

Grade	Age group							
	20–24	25–29	30–34	35–39	40–44	45–49	50–54	55–60
Senior	0	0	3	5	10	12	14	80
Middle	0	15	30	28	25	33	36	50
Junior	80	75	67	67	65	55	50	30
Trainees	20	10	0	0	0	0	0	0
Total	100	100	100	100	100	100	100	100

Camera diagrams represent career structures as smoothed, stacked histograms. They show the proportions of employees in each grade by age. The technique is best understood by means of an example:

- Figure 7.1(a) shows the numbers of staff within grades for five-year class intervals over a normal career span
- In Figure 7.1(b), these numbers have to be reduced to percentages, which are then plotted as a histogram in Figure 7.1(c)
- In Figure 7.1(d), the histograms have been smoothed to represent the current age–grade structure
- In Figure 7.1(e), the diagram has been further adapted to emphasize the proportion of staff reaching a particular grade, and the average age at which this grade is reached

Taken together, these statistics make up what is referred to as the 'career prospectus'. They do not imply that any particular person has actually followed a career that corresponds to the prospectus, or will do so in the future. This assumption needs to be separately validated from the personnel records. The name 'camera diagram' suggests correctly that it provides a snapshot of the career structure at the time the analysis is carried out. Use of this for forecasting career outcomes depends on both recruitment and wastage being at moderate and predictable levels.

Yet open and regular discussion of the career prospectus with employees should be an important element in the 'social exchange' that Herriot (Chapter 4) has suggested should characterize the employment relationship. Perhaps even more important is the use of the prospectus as a yardstick to measure the efforts of proposed policy changes. In a phrase used more than once in this book, camera diagrams and career prospectuses help human resource strategists to 'inform the political debate'.

These statistics can also be used to test the effectiveness of policy decisions.

Figure 7.1(c)–(e)
The development of a
career progression
diagram

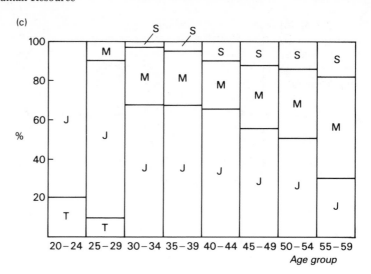

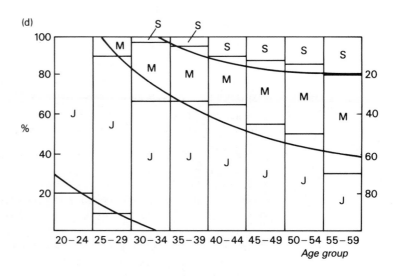

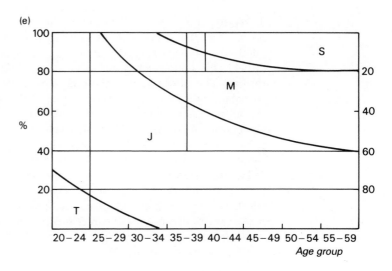

Separate career prospectuses could be plotted for different ethnic groups. Over a period of time, changes in these diagrams will show whether career prospects of the selected group are improving. The effects of decisions about external recruitment in relation to internal promotion can also be monitored.

Human resource strategists, while recognizing the value of career progression statistics, will wish to examine critically the methodology behind them. The model presented in Chapter 3, suggests that categorization is the aspect to consider. Grade structures often have curious histories; they are the fruits of compromises with trade unions, or directly with employees when labour market conditions gave them power. The work actually carried out by two or more grades may be similar, only the title indicating a difference. Alternatively, a single grade of employees may carry out work so various as to render the use of the grade as an occupational category almost meaningless. The motivational aspects of jobs are critically affected by their content, as is their value to the employer. While a human resource planner may be able realistically to re-classify current work into meaningful grades, the career progression diagram represents the outcome of many years of purposive or intuitive career management. If the true categories of work have changed over this period, and they probably will have done, the averaging effect of the career progression diagram may give spurious indications of career prospects. Projections by computer modelling are fraught with the same difficulty. Human resource stategists will be mindful of the continuing process of industrialization that both creates new categories of work and kills off older ones. There is no reason to suppose that this process will cease.

In organizations without official grade structures it will be necessary to devise 'notional grades' before the career prospectus can be calculated. Once again, the search should be for a structure that truly represents valid differences in job content, and a determination to keep these categories under review. In multi-functional and pluralistic organizations, unitary grade structures may be a near impossibility—a problem that also limits the use of grading as a method of job evaluation (Chapter 5). Camera diagrams may be used for each major career stream, but this will never truly represent the opportunities that exist. Job-evaluated grades are very unlikely to be appropriate for career analysis, based as they are on similarity of 'worth' rather than similarity of content.

But categorization is one problem, and enumeration is another. If the traditional grade categories have to be revised, or grade structures created for the purposes of career analysis, enumeration of personnel records could be a tedious and expensive business. Each job has to be considered for its new grading within the notional structure.

The camera diagram, and career prospectus, are a representation of policies developed over many years. These policies may have been explicit, tacit or unconscious. Enumeration of current percentages within the camera diagram will be a poor guide to the future unless the policies, past and future, are made explicit. Another threat to validity is the susceptibility of policies to changes in social and economic environments, and in technology. As emphasized above, the name 'camera diagram' is apt: snapshots reveal much, but they reveal change only when compared with snapshots taken at other times. The career prospectus and career progression diagrams are descriptive statistical devices, but what they describe requires careful evaluation and explanation.

When traditional career planning goes wrong

Important changes within the organization, and in the environment, are usually wide-ranging and sudden, and not the smooth transitions indicated by the forecaster's trend lines. Career management, if it is to have any meaning, must be judged by how it performs under real life conditions. In recent years, business cut-backs in the larger organizations have outnumbered expansions. How do organizations respond to a reduction in career opportunity, whether it has the benefit of career progression diagrams or not? Significantly some large companies disbanded their career development departments when redundancies increased in the early 1980s.

The first step is usually a call for early retirement. As Bennison has pointed out, this appears a painless step, but its effects are often lost sight of in the desire to reduce numbers. These are that both people and jobs are lost; those happy to accept the 'package' are often the more able, who see opportunities elsewhere. The jobs they vacate no longer appear in the career structure, thus reducing opportunities for those lower down. The same may be said for voluntary redundancy.

The ultimate weapon is forced redundancy. The rationality of this, least acceptable, stage in the process is clouded by agreements to protect longer-serving people, and by a preference for closing whole departments where possible. The transferable skills of redundant employees are seldom consciously considered. So haphazard and counter-productive are these situations that redundancy programmes are not a manifestation but a negation of human resource planning.

Smith (1989) has demonstrated that the most able people in an organization are also the most likely to be made redundant. His evidence is derived from an analysis of male job-seekers who sought the help of a major outplacement agency. Intelligence, particularly verbal intelligence, and variety of experience, predict the level of managerial responsibility, and redundant managers scored more highly on both measures than managers in general. Redundant managers were also more independent and venturesome. Smith explained these findings in two ways. The first is the tendency of able people to accept proffered redundancy 'packages' because they believe they can succeed elsewhere. Smith describes this as the 'mechanics of redundancy' explanation. The second is the tendency of organizations to go for safe options when under threat; the more able and independent are seen as a danger, and are nudged towards the door. This 'grit in the oyster' explanation casts an interesting light on the response of organizations to strategic challenge.

Business expansions, too, tend to be impetuous rather than calculated. Decisions are often taken without strategic attention being given to the availability of human resources, inside or outside the expanding organization. A good example is the now classic study of the Tyne labour market by Walshe and McGill (1982). The health authority were apparently planning for expansion with no knowledge or concern for local labour market realities. This required a careful examination, not only of numbers, but also of the quality of potential recruits. Human resource audits should include both.

Sudden expansions or contractions of organizations reveal the faults in traditional career thinking and manpower planning. The key to better management is thorough knowledge of the skills of the existing workforce. Contraction is then less likely because workers are fully used in the pursuit of profitability and good service to clients and customers. When expansions are contemplated, relevant data allows the human resource planner to make a valuable contribution to the strategic management of the change by injecting information about internal and external sources of talent.

The planned professional career and its demise

For the professional worker, however, careers tend to be identified not with bland phrases in career prospectuses, but with progressive levels of responsibility and salary, with portable qualifications and membership of professional bodies and with adherence to codes of practice and ethics. A prototype would be the hospital doctor, whose 'anticipatory socialization' may commence in the early teens, whose training may last until the age of 30, and who may hope for progressive appointments until the age of retirement.

In the UK, in other industrial countries, and even in the less developed economies, the concept of a 'career' is being called into question by continuing high levels of unemployment. Professionals and managers are less likely to be out of work than unskilled workers, but increasing numbers have faced the experience of redundancy in recent years. Long 'careers' with one employer are brought to a sudden halt, and the unemployed have to re-think their working lives from scratch. What have they to offer the job market in terms of skills and experience? Should they attempt to continue in the same sort of work, or change their 'career' paths? Are 'careers' necessarily publicly regulated and recognized, or can they also be expressions of an individual's personal development? For the purposes of this book, how should the human resource strategist respond to individual and corporate needs for flexibility in the ways people are used, and for different types of employment contract?

The traditional concepts of careers and professionalism overlap strongly. While we may, in our search for flexibility in employment, welcome the demise of careers devoted to a single occupation, do we also welcome the loss of commitment to professional standards that this flexibility might entail? Or do we suspect that 'professional standards' are also used as an excuse to resist change, and to maintain unnecessarily high manning levels that are sanctioned solely by 'professional' judgement? Human resource strategists should be aware of these issues as one element in their environmental scanning.

Professionalism

The reader may have noticed that Chambers Dictionary conflates 'profession' with 'occupation' in one of its definitions of 'career'. It is nevertheless possible to distinguish clearly between the two, and to assess the degree of professionalism in any occupation. Three categories of professionalism can be defined:

1 Those for whom the possession of legally recognized qualifications and adherence to a code of ethics are essential to the exercise of their duties (e.g. doctors, lawyers and chartered accountants).
2 Those who consider that their responsibility towards clients goes beyond carrying out certain specified actions for pay. Teachers and nurses, whether highly qualified or not, might see themselves as having a duty of care towards their students or patients that requires maturity, responsibility and a dedication not bought solely by salary. In return, they expect their professionalism to be recognized and respected.
3 Those in less well-defined career structures, where the emphasis may be less on care of clients than on commercial results, but who wish their occupations to be recognized as professions. The UK Institute of Marketing has chartered status. British personnel officers who qualify for membership

of the Institute of Personnel Management by examination may be said to be following careers, but their 'profession' is not yet recognized by statute.

In all of these categories, there is some 'fuzziness' in the interpretation of professionalism. Doctors in the UK have indulged in political lobbying against changes proposed by the government for the National Health Service. According to one's political viewpoint, this can be seen as a professional body doing its best for standards of client service, or as protection of outmoded vested interests that restrict the effective use of professional skills. The government has also claimed better service to clients as the rationale for proposed changes. The British Medical Association has been described by one ex-Minister of Health as 'the most powerful trade union in the country'. Attempts to reform the legal profession in the UK, especially in respect of the 'rights of audience' of solicitors (the members of the profession who deal directly with clients) in court, have had limited success. Professions, whatever else, are about power to restrict access to work. Nevertheless, the professional bodies responsible for the law and the medical profession are also there to protect the client by insisting on standards of conduct.

The professionalism of teachers has been called into question during a series of strikes and sanctions in support of pay claims. Some teachers refused to take part in this action because they believed that their duty to pupils was paramount. Others rejected the idea of professionalism, claiming that their work was 'just another job'. But the diminished esteem given to teachers by the general public is also a source of deep dissatisfaction. It is possible to desire professional status without accepting the means of attaining it.

Mary Warnock (1985), the Oxford philosopher and one-time headmistress, set out what she believed to be the requirements of professionalism in teaching. The first was a career structure, offering greater rewards at higher levels, that would be validated by a system of appraisal. The second was accreditation; by analogy with nursing, teachers would be accredited by a General Teaching Council. Her suggestions for professional conduct by teachers included giving both sides of the question in matters of public debate, being optimistic on behalf of their pupils, and while being willing to give guidance in matters of private morality, not taking upon themselves the role of other professionals, such as social workers. Encouragement and correction have no doubt always been the hallmarks of good teaching, though in the troubled and cynical mid-1980s they needed restating. In the ensuing battles over the national curriculum for schools, by which the government took upon itself the right to set standards of educational attainment (and by implication the standards of teaching), Warnocks' proposal for a professional body has been overlooked. Introducing this, together with the steeper career structure that Warnock also proposed, would have a marked effect on any strategic attempt to plan the use of teachers. Higher standards might entail greater rigidities.

We now turn to the third category of professional worker—those who would like to be so regarded. In commercial firms, at least, personnel managers would be unlikely to see themselves in the same relation to their employees as nurses to their patients, or teachers to their pupils. In spite of the existence of the British Institute of Management, and other bodies representing more specialist types of commercial activity, the reader might speculate how easy it would be to insist that no one be appointed a manager until he or she had passed a series of qualifying examinations, and had accepted a recognized code of ethics—and what, in the environment of everyday management, such a code might contain.

Ethics or no, is the model of a professional career, with its regulated structure and almost tribal overtones, the right way of looking at a 'career' in management, sales or even personnel? It would seem so. In the UK, the Institute of Marketing has recently acquired chartered status. The Institute of Personnel Management has made several attempts to gain chartered status for qualified personnel managers. The CBI, the Council for Management Education and Development and BIM are vigorously promoting the idea of the 'chartered manager', with qualifications to match.

But professional status does not necessarily imply a career based only on specialization. Doctors, the typical career professionals, are currently being urged to add management and budgetary skills to their clinical abilities, and to undertake administrative roles. While other occupations aspire to emulate medical specialization, medical professionals themselves are being asked to become generalists. Teachers are encouraged, not least by Warnock, to be professional in their relations with students, but they are also urged to improve their general management of resources. Technology, as discussed in Chapter 3, has many effects on the nature of work. It changes relationships with subordinates and it alters the type of decision to be taken in managerial and professional practice. Those who yearn for professional status, and those who already enjoy it, should consider carefully how their professional duties will be affected as database and expert system techniques begin to take over their processes of decision-making. Wherein will the essence of professional expertise reside?

In many countries, membership of a profession presupposes a high level of remuneration—Americans, for example, refer to a 'professional salary' as a desirable level of pay. Expectations of this sort are only one way in which professionalism can produce rigidities in the labour market. The status of the professions also plays a part in deflecting able people away from other economically useful work. The preference of academically able people in the UK for professional occupations rather than work in technology or industry has been seen as a cause of economic decline (Wiener, 1985). Yet high standards of training and professional conduct are also desirable in industrial activities, as German experience has shown. Need standards of excellence be bought only at the expense of professional rigidities and restrictive practices? The world of work is plainly at odds with itself about what it wants from professionals. One of the interesting and challenging problems for manpower and personnel specialists, in the next few years, will be how to resolve this ambivalence in a practical way. In Third World countries, the effective use of expensively trained professional resources could be the key factor in improving economic performance.

Professional associations themselves face a strategic challenge from this upheaval. Coulson-Thomas (1988) has surveyed the effects of changing career patterns on the associations, and on the professionals themselves. He identified two trends that support the analysis given earlier in this chapter: a widening gap between managerial and professional work, and the need for temporary membership of professional associations to match the occupational changes in personal career patterns. Coulson-Thomas sees managers as full-time employees, looking after the general direction of the business, assisted by professionals who are freelance operators, working for a number of employers simultaneously. This is the pattern also identified by Atkinson as the 'flexible firm'. Both managers and professionals will expand their expertise throughout their working lives, and they will require the support of differing professional bodies. Addressing the problem of categorization, Coulson-Thomas sees the boundaries between professional associations becoming less distinct, as each tries to cater for the fringe needs of its members. Another strategic challenge to the professional associations is the extent to which conformity to European standards of qualification will be both achievable and enforced.

The 'internal career' and self-development

So far in this chapter we have been concerned with what Schein (1978) has dubbed 'external careers'. These have a public face: entry is gained, qualifications are won and promotions are achieved; success is manifest. Many organizations have career structures, and are able to say how many of their employees occupy each grade. The degree of professionalism, as described above, varies across organizational and occupational barriers. In some cases, it has a strong regulatory effect on the work that particular employees may do, by limiting both access and content. This in turn places a limitation on the flexibility and productivity of professionals within an organization, which the human resource strategist cannot ignore.

From the employee's point of view, such limitation of function is more serious, since he or she has fewer degrees of freedom than the organization. This is particularly so as 'careers' rapidly become more varied, and less tied to occupations or employers.

Another definition of 'career' may also be found in Chambers Dictionary. It is described as 'progress through life'. This seems to suggest more than 'living'—what is implied is the development of a person, in terms of skills, values, needs and the changing goals that go along with this development. The reader may recall that these were the terms used in our discussion of job satisfaction. Schein (1978) differentiated between 'external' and 'internal' careers; the first being the publicly recognized progress through a given occupation, and the second a matter of personal development; a private concern of the individual. This humanistic sounding idea may nevertheless have considerable relevance for hard-headed managers and human resource planners as they recognize the need for a more flexible and better trained workforce. Professionalism, as defined above, has the value of setting standards and ensuring thorough knowledge of a particular line of work. But it can also 'type-cast' employees into roles that are inappropriate when organizational objectives change. The human resource strategist, with organizational needs as a first priority, should look closely at professional type-casting to see whether professional boundaries need be so rigid.

There is evidence that traditional career structures, where they can still be maintained, are positively unattractive to job-seekers. Yates (1987) has reported that central and local government, along with other organizations with traditionally rigid scales and remuneration packages, are having difficulty in recruiting professional specialists. At competitive rates of pay, job choices are decided first on job content, and secondly on organizational image.

The career professional, of course, is only one category of employee that suffers from type-casting. Members of skilled trades, reinforced by union demarcations, present the human resource planner with similar problems. A welcome change has been signalled by the acceptance during the 1980s of multi-skilling in response to new technology (Hendry and Pettigrew 1988). This should be emulated by the better qualified members of the workforce.

The organizational problems in encouraging and developing flexible careers are partly endemic and partly self-inflicted. All organizations have rigidities, by virtue of their existence; some organizations, exalting Weber's bureaucratic rule systems to an art form, find it impossible to recruit or promote more than mediocre talent.

The individual is under no such constraints and, given the confidence and vision, can play the field. For such a person, employment is a source of career development opportunities to be seized and acted on. To people without these qualities, employment often presents blocks to career progress that they feel powerless to remove. Indeed, the same situation, like many strategic issues, can be seen in both lights. Evidence for the opportunist nature of career development was presented in Chapter 2, and we return to this topic later in this chapter.

Careers can be seen only in retrospect. In middle life, the measured progress predicted by the brochures in the University Careers Library, for example, will seem a myth. Hall (1986) described mature managers' 'careers' as rationalizations of random events. Asking older people about their careers will provoke wry admissions to similar feelings. Redundancy has brought many steady organizational 'careers' to a sudden halt. It has also opened up opportunities for career development. People attending a programme for unemployed managers and professionals during the 1980s frequently obtained better paid employment, and showed surprising flexibility in switching between occupations (Pearson and Heyno, 1988). The 'opportunity' was forced upon them, but help was at hand, and hidden talents were revealed.

A career, then, can be seen as justification for the existence of professional institutions and manpower planners, or as the productive use of random events in working life. Schein (1978) offers us a way of conceptualizing these two approaches. The 'external' career is the traditional progress through what are now fast-changing professional or organizational career structures. The 'internal' career is an individual's perception of his or her personal development in terms of skills, experience and satisfaction derived from work. Internal careers are independent of formal professional training and organizational structures, and are an expression of life-long development. Which definition of 'career' seems the more likely to survive the 1990s?

Researching career mobility and occupational flexibility

Careers, internal or external, face human resource researchers with two major problems: sources of representative data, and methods of recording the important changes that occur. In fact, data is readily available in every personnel department, not only in the existing staff records, which may be biased in various ways, but also in applications for jobs. These are usually destroyed when the vacancy is filled, and much useful data is lost.

Keeping a simple career database on a computer need not contravene the Data Protection Act, since all reference to particular persons can be omitted. What is of interest is the number of career transitions and occupations that applicants have had—real data about the real job market of interest to particular organizations. Finding a satisfactory way of recording career paths accurately probably awaits the ministrations of experts in artificial intelligence; the dimensions are complex, as is the recording of skill development. But categorizing career experience by occupation requires only database technology (see Chapter 3, Case Study 2).

One of the research programmes described below tackled this problem, at least in part, by asking respondents to indicate their personal views of transitions in a simple coding system. The dimensions were organizational change, occupational change and increase in responsibility.

We will give further consideration to the meaning of two research projects, which were both described in outline in Chapter 2. One was concerned primarily with people attending training courses to help them change jobs, and the other with career and occupational changes made by members of the British Institute of Management. Both illustrate the fluidity of careers; a phenomenon that strategic human resource planners now have to face.

Three types of job-changer

The review of the changing labour market in Chapter 2 referred to three categories of job-changer—the *opportunists*, the *seekers*, and the *unemployed*. To recapitulate, their characteristics are as follows:

- The *opportunists* are the employed managers and professionals whose careers include unexpected opportunities to change occupation, raise the level of their responsibility and change employer. They travel hopefully and confidently, but seldom arrive in work that totally satisfies them. We owe knowledge of this group to Nicholson and West (1988).
- The *seekers* were described as people dissatisfied with their current job, but who lack the confidence of the opportunists. They are unsure of their skills and the outlets for them.
- The *unemployed* are managers and professionals currently without work, most often through redundancy. Their confidence is likely to have suffered from the enforced departure from their jobs, whatever their normal level of morale, but they have an additional financial incentive to find new work.

To maintain that these were totally distinct categories would be naive. They overlap in ways illustrated in Figure 2.6. The subsequent discussion of the issues of confidence and skills will, however, justify the categorization. The importance of this analysis to human resource strategists should be apparent. We have already discussed the tendency of redundancy to rid organizations of their more able people: 'opportunism' has the same effect. Revealing the presence of seekers within organizations, and discovering the sources of their lack of confidence and dissatisfaction, could provide human resource specialists with a second line of defence in their battle to deliver the skills needed for strategic development.

Confidence and flexibility

These have emerged, not unexpectedly, as central issues in the career patterns of today. Nor should readers be surprised that the two are closely related. Evidence for this assertion was obtained from the programmes run under the auspices of the Manpower Services Commission, for people who lost their jobs during the recession of 1980–1985 in the UK. Details of one such programme, designed to help unemployed managers and professionals in London, may be found in Chapter 2. That account also reports the very considerable job-getting success of participants. A full description of the programme and its outcomes has been provided by Pearson and Heyno (1988).

Those who attended the programme were free to join one of two tutor-led groups when entering the four-month programme. One of these covered self-assessment and confidence building; the other, strategies and good practice in job-seeking and in making applications. The latter group was chosen, usually correctly, by people who felt they had assessed their skills and the job market, but who saw job-seeking advice as a top priority. The others who chose the self-assessment group as the first stage moved on later to job-seeking. Choice of group took place at an introductory session, under the guidance of a tutor.

Applicants were invited to discuss their situation as they saw it, and to make the decision in collaboration with others.

The needs of people who opted for the self-assessment are illustrated in Figure 7.2, a diagram that was generated by one such group at their opening session. This included, without prompting, the twin concepts of flexibility and confidence. Another model, illustrated in Figure 7.3, formed the basis of tutorial guidance. It assumed that those who had lost confidence would also have lost the ability to perceive profitable options, initiating a downward spiral towards aimlessness and alienation. This model has theoretical support from the ideas of Seligman (1975) on 'learned helplessness', and from McLelland's theory of 'achievement motivation' described in Chapter 6. Research into the application of 'learned helplessness' theory to the long-term unemployed has been reported by Kearns (1987). The concepts from Chapter 6 on job satisfaction also apply in understanding unemployment. Locke's 'goal setting' theory is particularly relevant, since the opportunities to set goals in unemployment decrease with lack of job-getting success. O'Brien's assertion that 'skill use' is the prime source of job satisfaction provides yet another explanation for dissatisfaction and alienation in unemployment, as he himself has pointed out. Bandura's emphasis on 'self-efficacy' would provide another way of explaining situational loss of confidence. The programme was in no way an attempt to validate any of these theories. The theoretical concepts, however, provided ideas for the day-to-day development of the programme. Human resource strategists, in the daily work within an organization, should use theory in the same way.

Figure 7.2
Self-expressed needs
of a group of
unemployed
professionals seeking
career guidance

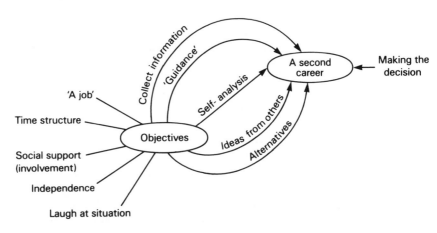

Figure 7.3
Model linking flexibility
and confidence in
finding new
employment

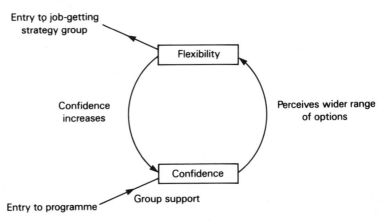

One theory that did not accord with experience was Rotter's (1966) categorization of people by the way they naturally perceive their lives to be controlled. 'Internals' perceive the locus of control within themselves, and 'externals' perceive themselves to be at the mercy of forces within society. These are assumed to be relatively enduring traits, and the ability of many people on these programmes to change their viewpoint, within a matter of weeks, does not suggest permanence. For a small minority of 'hard-core' unemployed, the theory may be valid.

How flexible are job-related skills?

Confidence cannot be built on false assumptions. People who already suffer from anxiety and depression bred by redundancy and unemployment, are doubly hurt by unsubstantiated claims that life is better than they think. If there really are no jobs, no opportunities to change career or occupation, then it would be preferable not to pretend otherwise. As evidence accumulated in the early programmes, however, it was possible to say with some assurance to subsequent participants that there were more opportunities than they had so far considered, and that they were likely to be successful in their job search. Thus, gathering data as the programme took place had the status of strategic research. Human resource planners with comparable data can give both management and employees a clear picture of career prospects.

The success of the programmes in getting professionals back to work is reported in Chapter 2. In brief, 92 per cent of known outcomes was a return to employment, 94 per cent for women and 88 per cent for ethnic minorities. The effects of these changes on financial status and job satisfaction are revealed in Figure 7.4. Those experiencing serious loss of both job satisfaction and financial reward amounted to only 10 per cent.

Of prime interest to the tutors, and to human resource specialists with other responsibilities, is the way this success was achieved at a time of job scarcity.

The organizers categorized the occupation of each participant when he or she joined the programme, and again when new employment was obtained. They began to be aware that, as often as not, the category had changed. An effective response to a narrow occupational job market was to widen it by including new job categories. What can be learned from flexibility under the stress of redundancy that might help human resource specialists make better use of their resources?

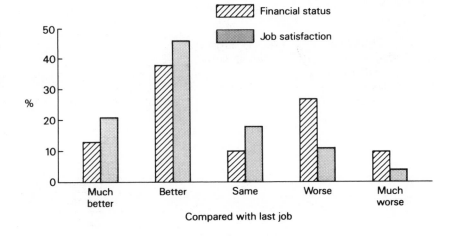

Figure 7.4
Effects of job change on financial status and job satisfaction

Are some occupations more conducive to career changes

Table 7.1 compares the distribution of occupational categories in the programme as a whole with that in the sample who changed occupation to get back to work. It demonstrates that those working originally in engineering and clerical jobs are less likely to change; those in administration and management have the highest probability of doing so. This could be because of self-stereotyping as a member of the engineering profession with defined but limited skills. But, by and large, current or recent occupation has little effect on the ability to find work within a different category.

Table 7.1
Effect of previous occupation on probability of changing occupational category when returning to work

Previous occupation	% of all participants (A)	% of occupation changers during re-employment (B)	B/A
Admin/management	17.2	24.8	1.4
Engineering	12.3	8.9	0.7
Buying/selling	10.9	11.5	1.1
Teaching	7.8	8.4	1.1
Finance	7.0	6.9	1.0
Clerical	6.7	4.0	0.6
Media/arts	6.5	6.1	0.9
Social work	3.4	4.3	1.3
Research	3.4	4.0	1.2
Technical	3.2	3.2	1.0
Marketing	2.5	2.3	0.9
Computers	2.3	2.0	0.9
Manual	1.6	0.9	0.5
Consultancy	0.6	0.0	0.0
Others (16 categories)	14.5	12.7	0.9
Total	100.0	100.0	
N	1,262	347	

Source: Pearson, 1988

Which occupational changes are possible?

Figures 7.5 and 7.6 (figures expressed as percentages) show the range of observed occupational changes from very different initial categories. These, of course, are by no means the only possible transformations. Figure 7.6 suggests a possible grouping of related categories.

How reliable are the categories?

In the terminology introduced in Chapter 3, occupations are polythetic categories. Prototypes of occupations are not always clearly understood by those who use them. Are the apparent changes merely artifacts of the category system, the result of calling the same occupation by two different names? In practical terms, the answer does not matter. If transfer takes place between valid categories, something has been learnt about transferable skills: if the categories are invalid in research they are also invalid in common usage. The apparent but illusory transfer nevertheless shows once again that a person's labour market is wider than he or she thought.

Aitkins (1988) checked the agreement between the original categorizations of representative job titles with those of a panel of categorizers consisting of

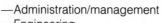

—Administration/management
—Engineering
—Teaching
—Finance
—Clerical
—Media/arts
—Social work
—Marketing
—Computers
—Consultancy
—Insurance
—Self-employment

Figure 7.6
Occupational changes
among professionals
gaining new
employment after
redundancy

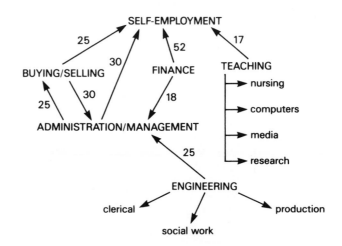

managers and professionals. Agreement by the panel with the original category was never less than 50 per cent, and in most cases is higher. Table 7.2 shows the percentage agreement and number of alternatives used by the panel for three of the most frequent categories. The less frequent categories are, by definition, the most specialized and therefore create the least disagreement. Those jobs for which the categorization is less certain plainly indicate options between which job-holders are able to move with ease, whether they realize it or not. Engineering (Table 7.2) is an unexpectedly permeable category.

Table 7.2
Agreement on the
occupational categories
of job titles (panel of
managers)

Category	% Agreement	No. of other categories
Administration/management	78	8
Buying/selling	78	4
Engineering	52	5

Another way of looking at permeable categories is to consider the percentage of moves taking place between them. Figure 7.6 indicates, by the percentage of people moving between related categories, the ease of transfer from one to another.

Free choice or desperation?

Readers will recall that the changes of occupation analysed here took place when professionals and managers returned to work after a period of unemployment. It is legitimate to wonder whether the change was a forced or a free choice.

There is evidence that confident people are more likely to change occupation than those whose self-esteem has been affected by their experience of unemployment. Table 7.3 demonstrates that the short-term unemployed are more likely to make changes of occupation than those out of work for long periods.

Table 7.3
Relation between occupation changing and time out of work

Duration of unemployment (months)	All participants %	Occupation changers %
Under 6	60	65
6 to 12	16	18
over 12	24	17

Although all participants in the programme were offered the option of working within career assessment seminars, nearly 50 per cent chose to go straight to the seminars on job-getting skills. The latter, generally speaking, were those who were already clear about their career options and objectives (and, perhaps, the closest in mental attitude to the opportunists described by Nicholson and West). Yet this group showed nearly as great a tendency to change occupations when getting a new job as those undergoing self-analysis and confidence building. It seems that occupational transfer is more likely to be a by-product of confidence than of desperation. A significant minority of occupational changes are from employed to self-employed status; this, too, suggests that confidence rather than desperation is the governing factor.

Age and occupational change

This is really another way of asking the previous question. Figure 7.7 shows that the distribution of occupation changers by age is the same as that for all participants in the programme. Increasing experience in one occupation need not result in increasingly narrow stereotyping, by either the job-seeker or by employers, but carefully designed career development programmes may be needed to change individual perceptions.

What is transferred when occupations change?

This is the most difficult question to answer. Skills are more likely to be transferred than knowledge, since both employer and job are new. The definition and categorizing of skills is difficult, however (see Chapters 2 and 5), and their transfer is more easily inferred than demonstrated.

Some unpublished research by Pearson (1989) suggests that job-changers feel their skill repertoire to be increased in taking up new employment, but this increase seldom exceeds three new skills.

The research was conducted by sending a questionnaire to 140 ex-members of the 'Bridge' programme, two years after attendance. The usable response was 46 per cent. Only five per cent of the usable sample reported continuing unemployment, but job mobility was rapid. The average number of jobs per person in two years was 1.8. Well over half the respondents had changed the category of their occupation, and three quarters perceived differences in job content since redundancy. Despite the perceived differences in work done and

Figure 7.7
Age distribution of
occupation changers,
compared with age
distribution of all
participants

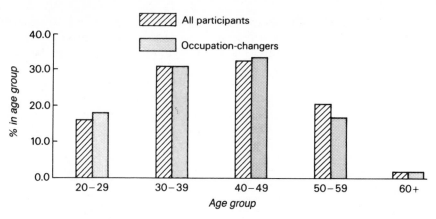

an average acquisition of three new skills, only 35 per cent reported receiving any formal training. 'Sink or swim' appears to sum up human resource policy in many organizations.

The research does not, as yet, positively support the transfer of skills. But, to borrow a phrase from the Management Charter Initiative, there do seem to be basic 'competencies' that people are applying to the development of flexible careers. Some of these must be related to job content, others may be general skills that facilitate getting to grips with a new job.

Career moves in a wider setting

Not all the people included in the research just described would see themselves as successful in their careers, or expect others to do so. For most, however, redundancy was an unfortunate episode in an otherwise progressive career, whether judged on 'external' or 'internal' criteria. They would have liked to have handled the transfer to another employer more pro-actively, but redundancy got there first. An open programme like 'Bridge' was bound to attract some exceptions, but the great majority of participants were no less talented than the general run of managers and professionals. The research by Smith, quoted above, indicated that they would often be more so.

What Nicholson and West (1988) have to say about job changes applies both to opportunists and to the unemployed, and is generally corroborative of research into career patterns of the latter. The following are quotations from their concluding discussion of career mobility:

> We have seen that there is a high and rising rate of management mobility— there are still some managers whose careers are stable and orderly but their numbers are dwindling. Most can expect to change jobs at least once every three years, and for the great majority job change will also mean a change of function. More often than not job change involves either a change of status, a change of employer, or both, for over half of all management job change is 'spiralling' in character, involving simultaneous functional and upward status changes.

> Perhaps the most surprising finding here is that employer changes are bridges typically crossed by successful travellers on the upward path to managerial success. Simply experiencing a series of promotions within an organization is less likely to lead to the top . . . The lesson for the ambitious manager would seem to be, boldness be thy friend.

This second quotation chimes well with Smith's research into the previous career patterns of successful managers: variety of experience was the key. It is where this variety of experience is to be obtained, and by whom, that provide the greatest surprise:

> It is also striking that proportionately more women than men, more young than old, and more specialists than generalists are following this route, a route that also passes through more of the new occupations and growing industrial sectors than the old and declining ones. It is in areas such as management services rather than industrial sectors and line management that fast and radical upward moves occur. (Nicholson and West, 1988)

This observation gives an added importance to Coulson-Thomas's comments about professional associations, in terms both of temporary membership and of encouraging acquisition of relevant skills. Since specialists, it appears, are more likely to become senior managers than those entering junior management, basic managerial skills ('competencies') must be acquired by both. But one is left with the suspicion that the essential ingredient of a senior manager's repertoire, a strategic approach to problem-solving, is currently more easily acquired in specialist roles than in junior supervisory work. If this is to change, more than 'competencies' should be considered when training junior managers. The steady drift of specialists to self-employed consultant status will, of course, affect their availability for senior managerial work. All these issues claim the urgent attention of the human resource strategist. One response might be to make better use of older employees. Hall (1986) has described, from an American viewpoint, how older managers become 'Protean', once family responsibilities are shed, and they feel free to take risks again. Nicholson and West did not detect older 'spiralists' in their sample, but pioneering human resource specialists could begin the process of exploiting this 'Protean', pro-active spirit among older people.

Boldness, be thy friend?

Clearly flexibility in careers is a product of confidence. The opportunists stressed their needs for challenge and the opportunity for growth, rather than for high quality of supervision or job security. Fifty per cent of their job moves involved a change of function and increased responsibility, often also a change of employer. They responded positively, and with high expectations, to the opportunities that suddenly came their way. As implied above, this group could include some of those temporarily unemployed. Since the response rate to Nicholson and West's survey of BIM members was less than 50 per cent, it is possible that their results are biased towards those who had made self-motivated career moves, and made them successfully.

The seekers, described in research by Pearson (1989), and referred to in Chapters 2 and 6, are more inclined to contemplation of opportunities than to action. They would be expected to be less confident than Nicholson's opportunists. Running a privately-funded programme alongside another sponsored by the Manpower Services Commission, allowed tutors to gather psychometric data for both seekers and the unemployed. The use of Goldberg's *general health questionnaire* to compare the mental health of seekers and unemployed was described in Chapter 6. The questionnaire is widely used in research into the psychological effects of unemployment (Warr and Jackson, 1985 and Stokes and Cochrane, 1984). Comparing mental states of those entering these programmes would have no validity if the samples were of very different people. Table 7.4 shows the demographic similarities between the employed seekers and unemployed. The latter are categorized as short-term (less than six months) and long-term (six months or more). The comparison of the mental health scores for the three groups was discussed in Chapter 6, and is summarized in Table 7.5.

Table 7.4
Demographic
comparison between
the seekers and
unemployed

	Employed (seekers)	Unemployed <6m	6m+
n	51	57	37
Average age	38.7	43.1	42.0
% female	17.7	14.0	5.4
% ethnic	9.8	15.8	21.8
% graduate	82.4	56.1	67.8
% management	15.7	28.1	16.2

Table 7.4
Demographic
comparison between
the seekers and
unemployed

Table 7.5
General health
questionnaire scores*

	Employed (seekers)	Unemployed <6m	6m+
Subjects	44	51	35
Mean	7.5	7.9	8.8
Median	6	7	8
% below cutting score	45.5	43.1	37.1

* simple scoring method

These data seem to suggest that the psychological dividing line should not nowadays be between employed and unemployed, but between those we have termed opportunists, whether employed or not, and those who need both to become more confident and to become more aware of their wide range of skills. Work with unemployed professionals on the 'Bridge' programme has often confirmed the close relationship between confidence and career flexibility. This could also apply to those in employment who need to change their jobs but who also need help in setting objectives. The expertise gained from working with unemployed professionals has a wider use, not the least by human resource specialists within organizations.

The collapse of traditional career structures will evoke varied reactions from members of an organization. Some, probably the most confident, will grasp the opportunity to make constructive moves as they become visible. Others will nurse dissatisfaction with their career progress, at some cost to mental well-being, until an opportunity is presented to them. Those made redundant have little choice but to re-examine their careers and, having done so, may make changes as productive and radical as the opportunists. The final chapter of this book contains a discussion of the ways in which public policy and private organizations should respond to these three categories of job-seeker.

The shock of the new: the transition process

Another of the strategically important points made by Nicholson and West (1988) is that a substantial number of the jobs to which the opportunists move are not only new to the transferee, but are also new to the organization. This would be expected in Western economies, which are going through rapid changes under the influence of consumer demand and technology (Chapter 2). But inferences from economic history and technological change are one thing, and direct evidence of the need to innovate when entering new employment is

Figure 7.8
Psychological states
during job change, as
reported by the
opportunists

another. Innovation is not confined to creating the content of a new job; older ones also have to be brought up to date.

Figure 7.8 has been adapted from Nicholson's model of role transitions to show the psychological states at each stage of the transfer from one job into another. Reporting their feelings some time after the transition had occurred, the opportunists sample did not generally recall the preparation period as one of anxiety. This contrasts with unemployed and seekers tested by Pearson, many of whom were highly anxious. But the two situations are not identical: for opportunists the die is cast; for both seekers and unemployed, there is as yet no new job. The opportunist can settle down to preparing, in a spirit of hope, for new and interesting challenges. The need to be pro-active, rather than reacting to a job offer, may well be more stressful.

In discussing selection (Chapter 4) and job satisfaction (Chapter 6), we have considered the importance of explaining clearly to candidates the nature of the job they will be asked to do (or innovations they will be required to make). This is an important element in what Herriot refers to as social exchange. Yet many of the opportunists questioned by Nicholson and West remembered the first days in their new jobs as a shock. Broadly, this took the form of surprise at both the responsibility they were given and their own ability to cope. It was accompanied, less happily, with surprise at the apathy of people they were to work with, and the lack of preparation and training they are given. Nevertheless they managed to cope with the difference between expectation and reality. Adjustment took longer, and was achieved through a variety of strategies. The strategy depended on both the new occupant and the job. The greater the novelty, and the greater the discretion afforded, the more the new job-holder was likely to innovate, influencing both the way the job was to be performed and his or her skills in the process. Personality variables also influenced the extent of innovation; a strong desire for control increased the likelihood of role innovation. Once again there was little evidence of undue levels of stress in adjusting to the new role. Nevertheless, as Nicholson and West pointed out, each transition left the opportunist manager with a residue of disappointment, sufficient to initiate another transition cycle if an opening should appear.

Nicholson and West's conclusions are supported by another study of job transition (Newton and Keenan, 1990)—on this occasion the effects of changing employer on graduate engineers. This group appeared to follow a pro-active strategy in adapting to their new work and, in so doing, experienced development of their skills. Growth was at least as important as any increase in salary.

It is difficult, in considering all three categories of job-changer, not to believe that the basic managerial 'competence' is that of managing transitions. To know when and how to innovate, and to enjoy doing so, seem quite basic to a satisfactory career, whether this is judged in external or internal terms. But these skills and attitudes can be taught; the programmes for the unemployed manager have shown that. Like 'learned helplessness', however, it seems that certain patterns of employment may stifle the natural innovatory skills that some managers and other staff possess. Frese (1982) described how personality could be influenced by employment. Even measured intelligence could be lowered by dull work; the more fragile psychological structures like need to achieve would be even more vulnerable.

Hall (1971), in days when life-long careers in one profession, or one organization, were a good deal more common, proposed a model of personal career development that he called 'sub-identity growth'. The 'sub-identity' is the fraction of one's identity, or self-concept, invested in a particular career. The diagram in Figure 7.9 shows how, after entry to the career or organization, investment might increase through steady achievement and growth of self-esteem. Failure to provide early challenge forces recruits either to leave in search of greater challenge, or to settle for second best, losing the opportunity and the motivation to innovate. We are back again, as in Chapter 6, with lack of skill use as a dissatisfier. Nicholson and West's sample of managers were not merely opportunist; they placed a high value on challenge, recognition of achievement, personal creativity and learning. They were more likely to find these in private sector companies. The rewards of working for bureaucracies—security, role clarity and prestige—did not appeal. Echoing evidence in Chapters 5 and 6, cash rewards were not a major factor in motivation. The opportunists, as predicted by Hall in a more stable environment, noticed, and were pleased by, the development of their self-concepts as new job challenges were faced.

In a more recent book, Hall (1986) draws a distinction between career planning for the individual and career management by the organization. Career planning sounds not unlike Schein's internal career; Hall refers to a

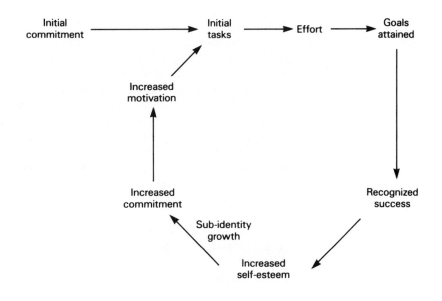

Figure 7.9
Hall's model of 'sub-identity' development during the early stages of a career
Source: Hall, D. (1971) Organisational Behaviour and Human Decision Processes, 6, 50

deliberate process of becoming aware of one's self, one's opportunities and one's constraints. Nicholson and West's sample, at least, have learnt to live with this process.

Career management is less in evidence in the UK. The pretence that long-term careers can be offered has been dropped. It will be suggested in the final chapter that career management is now a matter of intensity rather than longevity. High performance from highly skilled employees over comparatively short periods of employment should now be the major concern of human resource strategists. The 'flexible firm' (Atkinson, 1984) is now affecting all levels of work.

This chapter ends with another case study. The subject is, once again, graduates entering an organization. The problem is how to get them to perform effectively, through feedback and growing self-esteem. How, in fact, to achieve Hall's concept of sub-identity growth to the mutual profit of individual and organization.

CASE STUDY 7
Providing new recruits with a strategic challenge

British education has many faults, but one thing it is good at is serving the top end of the market—the PhD research student. In recent years, graduates have shown reluctance to invest three extra years in study to acquire a doctorate, on the grounds that the traditional market for their services, research fellowships and academic posts in higher education, were thin on the ground.

This was not the case during the 1960s, when the Swann Report (1968) was published. This attempted a constructive response to criticisms that postgraduate research deflected able students from industry, and that the narrowness of doctorate studies rendered those who pursued them unfit for the commercial world. The following quotation will make the point:

> . . . a new system might also make it possible to develop an environment for study which is more in line with that attaching to industrial and commercial operations (and come to that in local and national government). For example, one might realize the need to work to a tight timetable, to take a decision on open-ended problems with only limited data available, to work with and control the work of others, to give status to material things rather than those that appeal mainly as an intellectual challenge.

If this sounds like inviting intelligent people to think strategically, and to realize that the strategic process in business (of all types) is as challenging as research, then the author would not quibble with that interpretation.

The University of Aston responded to this demand by establishing an Interdisciplinary Higher Degree (IHD) Scheme; other institutions followed suit. IHD allowed suitably motivated students to conduct research into problems suggested by an outside body—often, but not always, a commercial firm. The problem had to be of the type that would be classified in Chapter 1 as strategic. A simple technical or operational difficulty taking a few months to solve was not sufficient. The problem also had to be investigated within two academic disciplines, justifying the interdisciplinary title, and meeting Swann's requirement for a broad approach. For instance, a long-standing problem with product quality would invite investigation both as a technical and as an occupational psychological project.

Supervision of projects was a joint responsibility of academic staff, and of the host organization, which provided what became known as an 'industrial supervisor'. The potential benefits of this procedure were many. The student could be trained to make rigorous yet practical analysis of real-life problems;

academic staff were themselves broadened by contact with commerical and public service organizations; the sponsor would gain inexpensive consultancy help, and encouragement to think broadly and strategically. That a scheme with such exacting requirements actually got underway, however, was entirely to the credit of the dedicated team that Aston University assembled to organize it. Several hundred research students enhanced their careers by taking IHD degrees over the 18 years of the scheme's existence. Financial stringency caused its closure in 1988.

The relevance of the IHD scheme to human resource strategy in the 1990s, and the career patterns that are emerging, should by now be apparent. The reasons for its success are rooted in the career advantages for both organization and student. It assists both career planning and career management.

Graduate recruitment has always been a chancy thing. Many employers who work hard to acquire able graduates lose more than half of them over the first five years of service. There are two major reasons. The first is a natural footlooseness that causes graduates to conclude that their first choice could have been better made, whether this is true or not. The second is a failure to use graduates' skills early in their careers, putting stress instead on aspects of work with which they are least familiar. The IHD scheme reversed this state of affairs, encouraging the graduate to get to know the organization thoroughly and to stay with it for at least three years. Providing an immediate intellectual challenge of a breadth that he or she would be unlikely to meet in traditional graduate employment has obvious benefits for organizations in sore need of management talent. The theoretical justification for these outcomes has already been discussed in this and the previous chapters. Locke (Chapter 6) would recognize the motivating value of clear objectives that were regularly reviewed, and O'Brien (Chapter 3) would note the satisfaction of using and extending one's range of skills. Hall's (Chapter 7) ideas of expanding self-concept are also relevant to the challenge of the research task and the self-esteem that achievement of an advance for their employers, and the research degree, would inspire.

To the financial advantage of sponsors, the projects were usually supported with grants from the Research Councils, and the consultancy work was provided at very small cost. While good R & D staff might attract some employers to the scheme, most also saw its potential as management training. In a company that the author knows well, participation in the scheme was seen as an effective method of attracting better graduates into industry, and of retaining their services long enough to get value from them. The projects provided recruits with early experience of productive teamwork with managers, other employees and the academic supervisors. In the event, IHD graduates tended to stay longer than those recruited in other ways, even when the stabilizing effect of the three-year PhD was taken into account. Those who left did so with a good impression of their first employment, and often to responsible posts with employers who recognized the value of their training. The following examples will illustrate this particular method of providing career opportunities that are even more relevant to the employment patterns of the 1990s.

David graduated in chemical engineering. He made an obvious, but ill-advised, career move into a large textile group to gain experience as an engineer. After 12 months he regretted this decision. Neither his otherwise successful degree studies nor his early experience with the textile firm really satisfied him. He applied for the IHD scheme because it seemed to offer an opportunity to reassess his career, and to make a productive change. He was given a project by a central personnel department that wanted a full analysis of absenteeism throughout the parent group. David was able to provide practical analysis and guidelines for management on a serious problem, while taking the opportunity to gain academic knowledge of mathematical modelling techniques and occupational psychology. He also took the opportunity to observe the workings of a variety of personnel departments. His PhD safely completed, he was offered a post as a personnel officer with one of the divisions that had provided the data for his analysis. He was able to contribute successfully to solving the problems that the division faced, including a major redundancy. Two years later, he was attracted by an advertisement offering an opportunity to set up a personnel department from scratch, and took it. Within five years, he was personnel director of a major commercial group. A reluctant engineer had become a successful personnel executive.

Technical projects did not type-cast students as a technologists, to the benefit of their career options. An engineer was given the task of improving the performance of hosepipes for transferring oil from terminals to tankers, taking account of both technical and commercial aspects. This required frequent visits to Nigeria, working in collaboration with experienced managers from other companies. His initiative and managerial skills developed quickly to meet the demands placed upon him.

Of course, these benefits are not achieved without effort or acts of faith, nor without risk; some projects failed spectacularly. But the failures were not failures of principle. Once projects had been brought to a successful conclusion, no one doubted the value of three years' hard labour.

The value and suitability of this type of early training for graduates will be further discussed in the final chapter.

References

Aitkins, M. (1988) 'Employment implications of transferable skills: analysis of data from the PCL "Bridge" programme', Unpublished MA thesis.

Atkinson, J. (1984) 'Manpower strategies for flexible organizations', *Personnel Management*, August, 28.

Bennison, M. And Casson, J. (1984) *The Manpower Planning Handbook*, McGraw-Hill Book Company (UK) Ltd, Maidenhead.

Coulson-Thomas, C. (1988) *The 'New Professionals'* BIM/Aston University, Birmingham.

Frese, M. (1982) 'Occupational socialization and psychological development: an underemphasized research perspective in industrial psychology', *Journal of Occupational Psychology*, **55**, 209.

Goldberg, D. (1978) *General Health Questionnaire*, NFER-Nelson, Windsor.

Hall, D. (1971) 'A theoretical model of career subidentity development in organizational settings', *Organization Behaviour and Human Decision Processes*, **6**, 50.

Hall, D. and Associates (1986) *Career Development in Organizations*, Jossey-Bass Inc, San Francisco.

Hendry, C. and Pettigrew, A. (1988) 'Multi-skilling in the round', *Personnel Management*, April, 36.

Kearns, A. (1987) 'London's longer-term unemployed', Paper presented to the British Psychological Society Occupational Psychology Conference, University of Hull, 5–8 January.

Newton, T. and Keenan, A. (1990) 'Consequences of changing employers amongst young engineers', *Journal of Occupational Psychology*, **63**, 113.

Nicholson, N. and West, M. (1988) *Managerial Job Change: men and women in transition*, Cambridge University Press, Cambridge.

Pearson, R. (1988) 'Creating flexible careers: some observations on a "Bridge" programme for unemployed professionals', *British Journal of Guidance and Counselling*, **16**, No. 3, 250–267.

Pearson, R. and Heyno, A. (1988) *Helping the Unemployed Professional*, John Wiley & Sons, Chichester.

Pearson, R. (1989) 'Career change and redundancy: two sides of the same coin?', Paper presented to the British Psychological Society's Occupational Psychology Conference Windermere, January.

Rotter, J. (1966) 'General expectancies for internal versus external control of reinforcement', *Psychological Monographs*, **80**, 1.

Schein, E. (1978) *Career Dynamics*, Addison-Wesley, Reading, Massachusetts.

Seligman, M. (1975) *Helplessness: on depression, development and death*, W. H. Freeman, San Francisco.

Smith, J. M. (1989) *Job Loss—the paradoxes of talent*, Coutts Career Consultants Ltd Occasional Papers.

Stokes, G. and Cochrane, R. (1984), 'A study of psychological effects of redundancy and unemployment', *Journal of Occupational Psychology*, **57**, 309-322.

Swann, The Lord (1968) 'The flow into employment of scientists, engineers and technologists', Cmnd 3760, HMSO, London.

Walshe, K. and McGill, D. (1982) *The Tyne Labour Market*, DHSS Information Division, Brighton, Sussex.

Warnock, M. (1985) 'Teacher teach thyself: the 1985 Dimbleby Lecture', *The Listener*, March, 10.

Warr, P. and Jackson, P. (1985) 'Factors influencing the psychological impact of prolonged unemployment and re-employment', *Psychological Medicine*, **15**, 795.

Wiener, M. (1985) *English Culture and the Decline of the Industrial Spirit*, Pelican Books, London.

Yates, J. (1987) 'Retaining specialists', Institute of Manpower Studies Report No. 145., IMS, Brighton.

Policies for people and jobs: research and action

Policies, strategies and action

The purpose of this final chapter is to bring together issues that have been raised elsewhere in the book, and to relate them to practical action by human resource planners. Practical action includes the development of explicit policies.

This book is dedicated to two propositions: that people are the crucial component in any organizational strategy, and that the first duty of human resource specialists is to contribute to strategic management through effective research. This is not to suggest a return to the 'manpower planning' of the past, with its emphasis on statistical forecasting techniques. The statistical approach to manpower planning encouraged managers to think about the supply and demand of human resources, and it prompted questions about the categories that should be used in evaluating them. Demand planning will now depend more upon scenarios than trend line forecasting. Human resource planners, from whatever part of the world, will be able to sense the likelihood of changes in work and labour markets by reference to the process of industrialization discussed in Chapter 2. The time-scale of the expected changes is another matter; overprecision in numerical forecasts can bring the planning enterprise into disrepute. The focus in human resource strategy will move from groups to individuals; their abilities, perceptions and aspirations will matter every bit as much as the statistical analysis of large career structures. These human attributes are the subject of human resource auditing, which is itself the basis of a strategic response to the continuing but unpredictable changes in an organization's social, political and commercial environment.

The relationship between policy, strategy and research was discussed in Chapter 1. Policy, expressed as the embodiment of a principle, sounds remote from managers' daily concerns. It is often seen merely as an irksome constraint on managerial actions, rather than as contributing constructively to them. Policy however, is the framework within which strategy is selected, and action is taken; clear policy statements are important for both. Decisions to treat the human resource as people, and to apply certain principles to guide this treatment, are derived from values that transcend the strategic process. The net result of both policy-making and strategic analysis, however, should be a healthy and successful organization. If not, there is no purpose in policy or strategy, and no future for employees.

This chapter returns to the topic of policy, in order to consider its meaning, structure and practical derivation. Policy is shown to be part of the framework within which strategic management takes place. The importance of research in developing both policy and strategy is affirmed. Practical action to improve an organization's human resource strategies and policies is then reviewed.

Policies and people

Pigors and Myers (1973) described policy as 'a special kind of decision and directive', which could 'affirm a general principle or long-term corporate aim'. So, in dealing with policy we are not setting out rules and procedures, nor are we, as some writers seem to hold, pursuing strategic management. The formal distinctions between and policy and strategy are those of time-scale and the concepts involved.

The policies of an organization, however expressed and understood, are slow to change. Strategy, or more strictly strategic management, is a continual review of the organization and its environment. The product of policy-making is the principle or long-term corportate aim. Policy could be written either to guide the actions of employees, or as a long-term business objective. Strategic thinking, on the other hand, results in plans that have to be implemented and monitored, but which have a finite outcome. Once strategic thinking has reached the implementation stage, further reviews of the organization's strategic position begin. A strategist's work is never done; a policy maker's may be a joy for ever. Both policy and strategy, however, should be based on well-researched data.

Neither policy nor strategy are necessarily the products of careful research and consultation, of course. Both are subject to different interpretations in the management literature (see Chapter 1), let alone in management practice. One such is to see strategy as the 'vision' of the chief executive. From this, he or she develops a scenario for the future development of the organization, which others are required to implement. In the same way, policy might be presented as a *fait accompli* to managers and staff. Such practices are not unknown. Here we will assume that Pigors and Myers' advice has been taken, and that policy is developed in a participative way, gaining commitment in the process.

The source of ideas for policy formulation could be anywhere within the organization, and not solely within the minds of senior management or the chief executive. As an example, we might cite a departmental manager who feels unsure about his or her responsibilities in relation to equal opportunities, and the quality of staff whom he or she appoints. Pigors and Myers suggested that once a need for policy has been raised, the task of developing it should be allocated to a representative committee. The committee should thoroughly investigate the problem that has been drawn to their intention, seek data, establish the basic principles involved, and formulate a draft document. This looks very like the process of strategic management.

More obviously than strategy, policy is a political matter; it should be presented with enough supporting data to counter objections of fact. Data alone will not convince chief executives or other managers to adopt a particular policy, however. Objections based on personal bias or interest are much more difficult to deal with than factual argument. Nevertheless, a steady water-drip of objective data will erode the grip of badly-founded policy. Defensible data is as important to policy development as to strategic management.

Like the strategic process, once again, policy development should be nurtured by discussion. Equal opportunity policies, to return to our example, imply more jobs for one group at the expense of another that has been over-favoured in the past. If the policy is to have more than casual support, its implications must be fully understood. Modification should be accepted on the basis of factual arguments. Once agreed, the policy should be carefully drafted as an official policy aim; the shorter and the more easily understood this document is, the better.

Policy, as interpreted here, is the expression of organizational philosophy. The principle could be either 'promotion on merit', or 'equality of opportunity'. The agreed policy aim, say Pigors and Myers, should commit management to take account of the stated principle, thus promoting consistency of behaviour, but should invite discretion within stated limits; policies are not procedures or rules.

Finally, a new policy should be congruent with existing policies, never quite so easy as it sounds. Employees need general guidance if they are to use their discretion appropriately. Pigors and Myers suggested that the policy aim should be supported by additional statements to assist its application in practice. The list of statements within a published policy document would be as follows:

- statement of policy aim
- applicability (whom should be included within its scope)
- responsibility (how application of policy is to be monitored and by whom)
- limitations (under what circumstances policy will not apply)

The statement of applicability would advise managers whether the equal opportunity policy should apply, for instance, to both full- and part-time staff. Responsibility should rest, wherever possible, with line managers. Specialist advisers, who might well include the human resources strategist, should have the joint tasks of monitoring progress towards policy objectives and of modifying the policy in the light of valid complaints. Each of these responsibilities should be clearly set out in the policy document.

The statement of limitations is important in enabling everyday management to continue without confusion, thus gaining greater acceptance for both policies and policy makers. Policies, being very general principles, tend to overlap and conflict in ways familiar to a moral philosopher but irritating to a practical manager with a profit to make or a service to provide. For an example, we return to a topic that arose in Chapter 4.

To what extent is a single organization, acting on its own, responsible for equality of opportunities in employment for local minority populations? Are undereducated and underskilled recruits to be hired in order to redress social inequalities that are none of the employer's making? It may well be that the employer will decide that the principle of fitness for the job should override the principle of equality. A policy of giving financial and other assistance to schools might be seen to be a better way of meeting social obligations than hamstringing the organization with unsatisfactory workers. The statement on limitations could make this clear, thus enabling the individual manager to apply the policy wholeheartedly but realistically.

Even without these useful refinements, however, a statement of policy that is communicated explicitly to managers is clearly preferable to an implicit policy, picked up by listening to 'how we do things round here', or by 'knowing the boss's mind'. Successful organizations are likely to have formal policies, if only to guide their strategic thinking. Explicitness in one area encourages explicitness in another.

Policy-making and research

The similarity between the strategic process and the development of policy has been illustrated by Pollitt and others (1979). Their book is concerned particularly with public policy, but the basic principles are universal. In their view:

> Policies are a *process* of decision-making activity. They customarily involve a *series* of decisions taken over an extended period of time, an exercise in *power* and *rationality*. [italics in the original]

Public policy, however, is developed within a more rigid framework than Pigors and Myers envisaged for personnel policy within organizations:

> This process of decision-making takes place *mainly*, though not exclusively, within a framework of prescribed organizational roles. In the case of public policy, these roles are those constituting a series of formal institutions with special legal characteristics. They are the institutions of state.

The institutions of state, of course, impinge also upon the development of organization policy; indeed they may be the trigger for the policy-making process. An important example, for the employer, is the legal framework within which employment decisions are taken, and organizational policies operate. Health and safety policies are required by law for all but the smallest organizations in the UK. Equal opportunity is enshrined in statutes dating back to the mid-1970s.

An internal policy statement has rather more force for the average manager, however, than laws that seem remote from his or her own experience. Sometimes managers may believe even that there is tacit organizational encouragement to flout the law as it stands. Good organizational policies, and good policy-making, give managers security and a reason to do the right thing.

One objective for manpower and social research is to provide a sound basis for policy-making. At national level, for example the development of policies for the labour market will require appropriate categorization, enumeration and description of the current workforce. Effective action to deal with unemployment and with skill-shortages depends on the objectivity with which this is done. An explanation of likely trends will also be required, in terms of theory or of comparison with other labour markets.

Policy-making, like the strategic process, requires reflection; the 'fermentation' noted by Pfiffner (1960). Administrative action, however, often takes place in an atmosphere of crisis. An AIDS epidemic, a shortage of National Health Service nurses, and the 'greenhouse effect' are examples from 1980s Britain. The media attention that these newsworthy matters attract fades long before rational analysis has taken place. In these situations, politicians and administrators wish to be seen to be taking action, albeit on shaky and hastily assembled data. Once action has been taken, often with the expenditure of public money, neither politicians nor administrators like to admit that they were wrong.

Yet anyone with scientific or technical training knows that out-of-line data can occur by chance; two or three points occurring away from an expected trend line do not necessarily mean that a significant change has taken place. Is the sharply changing trend that triggers the sense of crisis, and the call for administrative action, mathematically significant? If not, the action taken to correct the trend may be wholly inappropriate. Political power and careers have been invested in unsuitable action, and no one wants to admit mistakes.

Those caught in this situation have been described by Campbell (1969) as 'trapped administrators'. Such people see their political futures to be related to a particular course of action, rather than to the solution of a social problem. This fixation, in turn, limits the objectivity of evaluative research. Research workers will be under heavy pressure to come up with findings that demonstrate that the action was correct. Policy, in Campbell's view, should be aimed at the solution of social or organizational problems, not at affirming particular courses of administrative action. The latter should be based on the best evidence available from social research and should itself be seen as experimental. Changes in administrative action in the light of new data should not be regarded as admission of failure.

Campbell contrasts the 'trapped' administrator, limited to one course of action to be defended at all costs, with the 'experimental' administrator who is free to take different courses of action as new data becomes available. He lists the reasons for invalidity in social research, and how these are related to policy-making and administrative action. The subject of validity was discussed in Chapter 3.

Sharp-eyed readers will have spotted that Campbell's analysis, though highly relevant to the ill-informed decisions that are made from time to time in public life and in private organizations, fails to distinguish between strategy and policy. The types of decisions Campbell uses to illustrate his argument, such as the raising or lowering of speed-limits in American states, are not themselves matters of fundamental ethical or long-term importance. They are a strategic response to data obtained by public servants and, perhaps to the clamour of pressure groups. To be sure, administrators are taking into account, however dimly, such principles as the sanctity of human life and the freedom of movement. What is less certain is the extent to which a legal restriction of freedom will actually result in greater saving of life. This is a matter of survey and observation, which may indicate that further changes of regulations should take place. The relation of research to strategy will be explored in the next section. To describe changes of regulations as changes in policy is to confuse policy, yet again, with strategy, the legitimate tool of the 'experimental administrator'.

Another reading that makes some interesting links between policy and social research is Halsey's(1972) account of the relation of official education policy in the UK to the research carried out on behalf of the Plowden Committee. This was set up in the late 1960s to inquire into the effectiveness of education in primary schools. Halsey drew a distinction between value assumptions, which express what is desirable, and the findings of social science, which indicates what is possible. Thus, 'equality of educational opportunity' may be desirable, but ability to achieve it may be limited by the attitudes of parents to the educational process, and by social conditions that lie outside the jurisdiction of the educational service. It was in this connection that Halsey made the comment, quoted already in this book, that 'the purpose of social research is to inform the political debate'. This implies that social researchers, whatever their own political convictions, should try to let the facts speak for themselves. Readers who work in Civil Service departments, or other highly political environments, will know how difficult this requirement can be. In some cases, however, even a meagre amount of well-presented data can do a great deal to 'inform a political debate', since previous discussion has taken place in total ignorance of the facts! This is the human resource specialist's greatest opportunity. It will be exploited best in an environment that clearly perceives strategic management, and strategic thinking, to be processes rather than products. Data affects interpretations, policies and strategies for two reasons: the quality of the information improves, or the situation that the data represents is itself changing. Either may require the revision of business plans or administrative action.

One cannot, of course, escape from the need to balance value assumptions against strategic requirements. How are we to meet the needs of 'organizational efficiency' within a policy affirming 'equality of opportunity'? How is 'the sanctity of human life' to be recognized within a strategic requirement for 'cost effectiveness in public health care'? At organizational level, it is these dilemmas that Pigors and Myers attempt to resolve with their suggestion for a statement of limitations in support of a policy aim. Policy makers should think through, for the guidance of those who operate within policy decisions, where one principle will override another. These issues are universal, not confined to the UK nor to one sector of the economy: never have the analytical powers of the social and manpower researcher been more necessary.

Granted the distinction between enduring principles encapsulated in written policy, and the continuous, data-driven, review that is implied by the strategic process, are there nevertheless any aspects of business life, in its broadest interpretation, that require fully articulated policies? The answer must be 'yes', because of the large number of organizations that already have them. Policies setting out organizational values in relation to customers, to safety and the environment, and to employment are either legally enforced, or rendered advisable by an increasingly aware and articulate public opinion.

Enduring policy may also be needed in the successful pursuit of commerical objectives. Tom Peters (1989), the management writer and consultant who had much influence during the 1980s, had remarked on the need to bring the customer fully into the design of new products. This is the direct opposite of the mass production strategy that Galbraith (1987) observed in the post-war period, the force-feeding of consumers with mass-produced, standardized, output sold through heavy advertising. In 1950s Britain, customers were expected to sign away their common law rights in accepting the guarantee for a new car. Now the trend is to bring the customer into the factory, if not in body at least in mind. Manufacturing methods and relations with employees are mentioned in sales literature, and customized options allow personal preferences to be expressed in otherwise mass-produced items. The need to excercise legal rights of redress is excluded not by asking customers to forego them, but by making such action unnecessary. In the expanding service sector as in manufacturing, there is a need to bring employees' interests closer to those of customers. The principles governing personal behaviour need to be stated as clearly as those guiding corporate decisions.

Another need for policy is posed by the 'green' issues that began to influence politics in the 1980s and which are unlikely to go away; never was there an issue so bedevilled by conflicting principles and lack of hard data to guide strategy or policy. To select just one ethical confusion: is Third World development to be held back because the process of industrialization might cause further harm to the environment? Are the claims for environmental harm irrefutable? How do we balance obvious starvation against possible inferences from a meteorologist's chart? The answers to these questions affect employment world-wide. Policies, explicit and implicit, are strategic issues, and require a sound research base if they are not to compound the problems they set out to solve. We now return briefly to the relationship between research and strategy.

Strategic management and research

The conflation of 'strategy' with 'business policy' was discussed in Chapter 1. Sometimes this is overt, as in Johnson and Scholes (1988) opening chapter, or implicit. According to Thomas (1983), policy formulation is the:

Nature and process of choice about the future of independent enterprises by those responsible for decisions and their implementation.

Like the formation of public policy, this process is political, because different stakeholders are involved. Policies may, for instance, bring the interests of employees and shareholders into conflict. Like Pigors and Myers, Thomas sees policy as distinct from procedure—policy-making is more than the preparation of business plans and monitoring them. Business policy is concerned with scenarios about the future environment of the business, with the life-cycle of its current technology, and with the gap between commercial targets and their attainment. From such considerations, the relationship between the strategy of the organization and its structure have to be resolved.

Interestingly, human resource policy is seen by Thomas as subsidiary to business policy, echoing the corporate approach to manpower planning described in Chapter 1. 'Paternalism' as Thomas describes concern for employees' welfare, is perceived as being beyond the scope of business policy formation, and only to be indulged in if the philosophy of management demands it. Human resource policies are part of what Johnson and Scholes describe as 'recipes'. Policy, on this reckoning, is mostly about profit in the short run.

Strategy and strategic thinking are much more than the limited vision implied by Thomas's description of business policy. The interpretation favoured in Chapter 1, and implicit throughout the rest of this book, is Mintzberg's concept of organizational learning. No business plan is ever ideally suited to the organizational purposes it is intended to serve. Its execution in practice is never certain, especially in relation to time limits. Management control data exists to inform those responsible that corrective action is needed, sometimes amounting to reappraisal of the original objectives. This is the everyday currency of managerial work.

Yet the idea that research data, especially where this concerns workers as people, might be used in the original selection of objectives is nothing like so obvious. The subordination of manpower planning to corporate objectives was not only passively accepted, but lauded as correct procedure in the early days of the subject. Such an attitude holds one aspect of the strategic process, the chosen objectives, as sacrosanct, and the provision of human skills as a subsidiary facet of strategic implementation. When the objectives are not achieved, the human resource specialist can be blamed for not carrying out his or her alloted task. The defensiveness evoked by this approach to planning inhibits organizational learning, the essence of strategic management.

Change is continuous, and demands constant review of the internal state and the external situation of the organization. Review requires open discussion, and a corporate culture in which cherished assumptions can be challenged without risk to reputation or job. It requires research to provide the best available data at every stage of the strategic process, and an acceptance that the message conveyed by the data will change with time. Better decision-making, awareness and commitment to the organization are the benefits. No one, in Campbell's phrase, should feel themselves to be 'trapped administrators'. Open and honest appraisal of success and failure is the source of the strategic learning process.

Research, in its many and varied forms, is the lifeblood of strategic human resource management. This may take the form of an on-going analysis of employee records, so that management, and the workforce itself, may be made aware of changing demographic patterns and career prospects. Human

Figure 8.1
The relation between
strategy, policy and
research

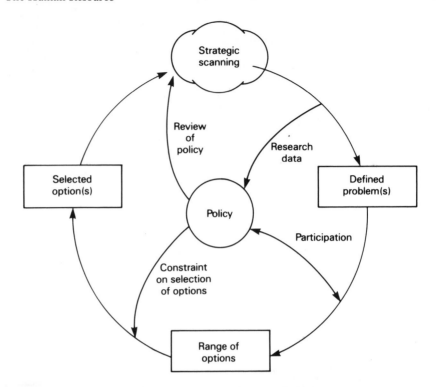

Figure 8.1 The relation between strategy, policy and research

resource audits are a powerful trigger for strategic thinking. The discussion of business opportunities identified by market research may signal the need for an investigation by the human resource specialist into the availability of technical skills. Human resource managers who can think in this way, and can rise to the challenge, need not fear redundancy; they can leave much of their administrative tasks to the computer without feeling that they have no other work to do.

But there is a cultural gap to be bridged, as mentioned in Chapter 3: Churchill's dictum that 'scientists should be on tap but not on top', expressed more recently by those who believe, in preparing succession plans, that research is an activity that renders its practitioners unfit for management. As Churchill himself might now put it; 'some research, some management'. Wartime technology required rapid implementation of ideas, and the scientists usually delivered the goods. When post-war stringencies dictated output at all costs, the scientists' ideas for new processes and products were less welcome. At the time of Prime Minister Wilson's 'White-hot technological revolution' in the mid-1960s, commentators were remarking on the inability of British manufacturers to keep up with developments elsewhere. If the demanding customers' needs are to be met at the price they are prepared to pay, or if Third World poverty is to be moderated let alone ended, the marriage of management with effective research is essential. This is not confined to technology but extends also to the understanding of markets and human resources.

By way of summary. Figure 8.1 illustrates the relation between strategy, policy and research. Policy is both a constraint on strategic management and a benificiary of the concommitant research findings.

In Chapter 1, it was suggested that the narrow concept of manpower planning, with its aura of unsuccessful forecasting and dependence on

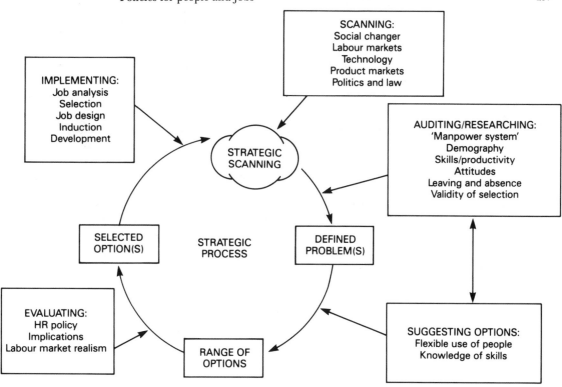

Figure 8.2 The contributions of the human resource planner to the strategic process

decisions made elsewhere, be abandoned in favour of a wider interpretation, that of human resource strategy. This was defined as: 'A process of social research whose primary objective is improving the quality of work'.

The rest of this chapter will be taken up with spelling out the implications of this definition for those who aspire to be human resource strategists. This will take the form of suggestions for action.

The human resource strategist in action

Strategic analysis: the human resource audit

Figure 8.2 illustrates, yet again, the process of strategic management. This time the diagram also includes the specific contributions to be made by the human resource planner, and which have been discussed in previous chapters.

The first and most important concern of the human resource specialist is the existing workforce. There are two reasons for this: first, the internal labour market affects most immediately the performance of the organization, and the human resource specialist will rightly be expected to be knowledgeable about it; second, it is the basis for categorizing the external labour market. Case Study 2 illustrates the problems encountered in auditing the staff of a medium-sized company.

The first methodological problem in conducting a human resource audit is shared with all survey research, the problem of categorization. To a first approximation, workers can be categorized under the headings used for current work, the familiar departmental names and job titles. A histogram like Figure 3.4 will show the accumulated expertise of existing staff and will suggest new areas of business development that that expertise would support. Defining 'significant experience' needs careful thought and measures will become more perceptive as the human resource planner accumulates data about the manpower system. The rough and ready categorization used in Case Study 2 will get strategic analysis underway.

While the use of work experience as a category system might be appropriate for a fairly static organization, there are advantages in finding more rigorous ways of discovering the skills that are available. Skills are notoriously difficult to define; Neisser (Chapter 2) suggested that they could be recognized, like other psychological concepts, by their attributes. The analysis of job descriptions for their task and skill content is described in Chapter 5. This type of investigation will generate copious data, but the computer comes to the rescue. Some large organizations write skills-based job descriptions for employees and record the results on computer databases. Others allow employees to list their own skills on free-report forms, and analyse these for computerized records (Windsor 1988). The use of systematic testing programmes and assessment centres can open management's eyes to the unrealized potential of those who work for them. Opinions vary about the ethics and legality of keeping detailed psychological data about individuals; openness about intended use is probably the deciding factor.

Another method of internal auditing is to use a points-factor job evaluation scheme. This reveals the skill-related factors that are highly rated in each job. This in turn provides a database that can be used to suggest transfers between nominally unrelated forms of work, thus widening the available labour market.

Categorizing significant experience, and identifying and listing skills, both make a substantial contribution to the effective use of an established workforce. It should, of course, be accompanied in the database by more traditional demographic information. Useful items include age, length of service, gender, ethnic origin, current department, level of managerial responsibility, educational level and date of last career move. Case Study 2 shows how these can be presented, perhaps by means of a graphics facility on a personal computer. Regular updating is needed, since the information must be timely if it is to contribute to strategic management. As part of this process, management colleagues should be consulted about new ways of categorizing workers that could be helpful to them. The greater the involvement of the strategic team in the human resource analysis, the greater the acceptability and utility of the results.

The foregoing has emphasized the need to record skills-based information; apart from that, the recommendations for recording data may not seem remarkable. Nevertheless, human resources specialists may be surprised how little information is readily available in the files kept for personnel administration. Research will be needed to establish reliable databases. In managing the 'flexible firm' (Chapter 2), it is necessary also to pay special attention to the part-time and temporary labour forces, because strategic use depends on an assessment of their numbers and availability. Yet, because of their limited administrative responsibility for these categories of worker, personnel departments often lack records.

Employment legislation has forced personnel departments to record, if not to analyse, data concerning employee absence and departure from the organization. Tribunal cases can be won only if management can justify its actions. The human resource planner will wish to go much further than this negative use of information; analysis of both patterns of behaviour (Chapter 6) is an important aspect of auditing the human resource performance of an organization.

Using people more effectively is assisted by good record-keeping, and by appropriate and regularly revised categorization, but knowledge of people as people, rather than as contributors to databases and histograms, is also a strategic requirement. The dividing line between 'manpower planning' and 'manpower development' was always rather artificial. An effective human resource strategist will get out and about among the workforce, interviewing at least representative samples of grades and occupations, watching for signals that indicate greater utility, willingness to train and indications of dissatisfaction. People rated particularly high, and particularly low, in staff appraisal should claim special attention; critical incidents reveal much about the organization apart from individual performance.

The skills required here are rather more than may be mentioned in books on manpower planning: good interview technique requires the interviewer to be clear what his or her objectives are; line management are unlikely to be happy if key employees are taken away from their work for long periods. Within the time available, the interviewer should offer every opportunity for interviewees to answer questions in their own way. The use of non-directive 'open' questions is the key to this.

Existing factual data should also be checked. Employees, for example, may not have reported the recent acquisition of education or professional qualifications. The main purpose of such interviews is to gather information not normally available within the personnel records. If skills have not been assessed elsewhere, the interview is the time to do it. Mobility can be appraised indirectly from remarks made about home life and past job moves, and questions can be asked about the motivating and satisfying aspects of current work. Employees should be reassured that, while the more sensitive information may be reported to management as anonymous data, it will be used for decisions about individuals only with their express permission. To meet the requirements of the Data Protection Act, all computer records should be open to checking.

The human resource audit, then, will contain demographic data, supported by specific information about skills and test results, and demonstrating attendance and leaving patterns of significant groups of workers. The more sophisticated human resource strategist will also wish to include in the audit the 'soft' data about employee attitudes and 'internal' career aspirations (see Chapers 6 and 7) that has been gathered during interviews.

Strategic analysis: career structures

Traditional manpower planning made much of career structures—those convenient categorizations of staff that were susceptible to the techniques of mathematical analysis at which the early practitioners excelled. Career structures may be attractive to analyse, but they can also restrict the effective use of the workforce, particularly its most talented members.

That being said, human resource strategists should explore, conceptualize and validate the existing career structure of the organization. In Bennison's terms (Chapter 1), strategists need a picture of the 'manpower system', particularly its main entry points. Camera diagrams (Chapter 7) will assist a strategic team in visualizing the effects of past promotion and recruitment procedures, and their suitability for the future. The Institute of Manpower Studies (1987, 1988) has developed software that allows career progression diagrams to be used interactively, testing the effect of assumptions about growth, contraction and career prospects. Human resource audit data, of course, should nowadays be represented on a computer graphics suite, allowing strategists to demonstrate the effects of different assumptions. The emphasis, especially at the stage of strategic analysis, should be on options and mutability, rather than on the apparently rigid constraints of past practice.

Using data to support policy

Policy development and monitoring, no less than strategic management, are supported by human resource auditing. For example, the data discussed above can be used to check the career progress of women. This aspect of monitoring is more than a social duty, it is a strategic necessity in the 1990s when, more than ever before, employers will depend on the skills of the female workforce. Employment opportunities for women are there in plenty; what is by no means so obvious is that career opportunities are there to match. Chapman's research, reported in Chapter 2, suggests strongly that they are not. The prejudice and discrimination surrounding womens' career development is but one aspect of the stereotyping and lack of imagination that also blights the opportunities of satisfying work for many men. Sex discrimination is, of course, none the less reprehensible for that. A survey by Metcalfe (1990) suggested, however, that women's employment was limited by the practicalities of combining home-life and work, rather than by prejudice and stereotyping. The human resource strategist's role will be to encourage the provision of enhanced maternity benefits, child-care facilities and career breaks. Data supporting the valuable contribution made by female workers will strengthen the case.

According to Meager and Metcalfe (1988), 'The key to becoming an equal opportunity employer lies in policies to revise and monitor personnel practices and procedures'. A crucial aspect of the research needed to support effective policies is the use of benign discrimination—categorizing minority groups in order to follow the progress of each within the manpower system. Common parlance, often racially prejudiced to begin with, tends to lump the minorities together as 'blacks', a singularly unhelpful category system. The Commission for Racial Equality suggests the following categories:

- White
- Black (Caribbean)
- Black (African)
- Black (Other: please specify)
- Indian
- Pakistani
- Bangladeshi
- Chinese
- Other(please describe)

and for some purposes that will be too crude. As a matter of courtesy, members of a minority should be allowed not to state what their origins are, but only after the reason for collecting the data has been explained to them. It is also important to discover whether minority members are new to the country, and to what extent they have absorbed the local culture and acquired the language (see Case Study 4).

The correct use of the psychometric model of selection is highly relevant to equal opportunity policies, whether intended to counteract sectarianism in Northern Ireland, racial bias in Malaysia, tribal discrimination in African countries, or sexism in the selection of computer programmers in the UK. Valid selection is fair selection.

Bennison's 'manpower systems' and 'career progression diagrams' record the accumulated effects of previous policies, whether or not these were ever made explicit. They can be used to assist the development of improved human resource policies, along the lines suggested in Chapter 7.

Validating selection

Whatever the methods used, one of the chief duties of human resource specialists in the 1990s will be to validate selection procedures. For years, tests have been used in personnel selection but, once recruits were appointed, validation was overlooked. The attitude seems to be that the die is then cast, and that it is no good wondering what might have been. Validation is even less likely if the sole method of selection is the interview; in that case the predictive measure, let alone the criterion of future success, is often far from clear. Since large sums of money, in revenue and in managerial time, have been expended in selection procedures, it is a pity not to validate their use.

Validation need not be a complicated process; it is easiest when a range of candidates is appointed at approximately the same time. Selectors are required to rate candidates in order of suitability, for later reference. They should be asked to give reasons for their ranking. If they can be persuaded also to accept some candidates who would otherwise be rejected, so much the better. All recruits are given a chance to settle into the organization and become familiar with the work. Ratings of performance, preferably based on appraisal, are then obtained. These can be converted to a ranking of criterion performance, which in turn is correlated with the ranking at selection, to see how the two compare. This rough and ready coefficient of predictive validity (Chapter 4) is the guide to future adjustments to the selection procedure.

Another approach is appropriate when a test is used as predictor. Again, there has to be agreement to accept, for the purposes of validation, a wide range of apparent ability. Table 8.1 shows how a two by two matrix can be used to assess the accuracy of judgements made on the basis of an intelligence test.

Table 8.1
Validation of an intelligence test by comparison with supervisors' ratings of subsequent performance

	Performance satisfactory	Performance unsatisfactory
Above minimum test score	24	10
Below minimum test score	20	26

Chi^2 test for significance shows that test scores above the accepted minimum are positively associated with subsequent job performance

In the process of collecting criterion data for validation, any 'failures' should be investigated to discover whether job-related factors were to blame. One possibility could be poor induction, which will be discussed later in the chapter.

Strategic options: flexible use of people

The audit of existing resources, some aspects of which are illustrated in the case studies, has two main purposes. It suggests further research, perhaps to discover why people joining a certain grade often leave the organization rather than achieving promotion. The audit also provides relevant language and concepts for the discussion of human resource problems and opportunities with colleagues. Audits and labour market reports are the equivalent of the data contributed to strategic analysis by the accountant and the market analyst.

If the human resource specialist's contribution were to stop here, however, it would be as if the accountant had no ideas about sources of finance, or how the funds available to the organization could be restructured.

The first responsibility in the 1990s is to bring home to colleagues the scarcity of human resources, and the problems of developing and conserving them. Nicholson and West's (1988) contribution to our knowledge of rapid career movement for managers (Chapter 7) is particularly important. We should also take note of the hidden dissatisfaction expressed in questionnaires by those who had spent too long in one job. What applied to an identifiable white-collar group in the 1980s will apply with equal force to a wider group of employees in the 1990s. Multi-skilling will blur an already indistinct line between manual and non-manual occupations, as the maintenance of complex systems demands higher levels of technical competence. In the service sector, giving the employee more responsibility for relations with the customer will enhance skills and expectations. So career mobility will increase as aspirations are raised, together with frustration for those who don't achieve it.

A promising response would be to introduce more active career development policies (in the full meaning of the phrase), and this means more than merely offering 'incentives' to stay. Cheap mortgages, for example, are initially attractive, but in the long run do not make up for lack of challenge and personal development through work. When job satisfaction falls away, people feel trapped, and approach their job with the sullen dissatisfaction uncovered by Nicholson and West's survey. Well-motivated performance is more important than long service. Employers embraced the idea of the flexible firm in the 1980s; now they must come to terms with the flexible employee.

Good performance is promoted by steadily increasing challenge and a good appraisal system. The theoretical backing for this assumption was presented in Chapters 6 and 7. Hall, in 1971, was writing of the need for challenge and recognition of achievement early in a career if new entrants were to develop personal commitment. In 1986, Hall had recognized that we were dealing not with a single career, but with several during the course of a lifetime. Nevertheless, the same general principle applies: expect high performance and you are more likely to get it. O'Brien's contribution (Chapter 6) on the primacy of skill use in job satisfaction leads to the same conclusion.

Ironically, it is the people that an organization is most likely to lose who will give the best service for the duration of their stay. This is a problem only if the human resource specialist has not prepared other managers for this eventuality. Organizations still mourn the loss of some valued employee ('I thought she was happy here!'), and request the personnel department to find a replacement, 'but someone who will stay this time'.

The content of work is changing fast, under the influence of technology, global politics and consumer awareness. Both new technology and the sophistication of consumer demands make it advantageous to give employees more freedom, virtually, to run their own businesses within the organization.

Division of work into defined projects, rather than ongoing routine, also favours less rigid organizational structures, and better use of transient employees. What seemed a rather odd way of selling life insurance in the early 1980s now has potential in many other businesses. Project management, hitherto the speciality of the construction industry, is now the way to organize many other industries' output, according to Cooke-Davis (1990). A sense of the industrial past helps managers to appreciate the dramatic changes in the content and structure of work over the last 200 years. The process will not stop now.

In addition to taking a positive line on the loss of valued employees, the human resource strategist will be required to suggest ways of dealing with 'skill-shortages'. One response to perceived shortages is to develop strategies for the effective use of existing workers. The starting point is the audit described above, and the major topics in this book—productivity, human skills, worker satisfaction and careers—would all be relevant to a review of skill requirements. Whether to provide equitable rewards by means of a job evaluation scheme, and whether to provide career development opportunities, are matters of organizational policy.

This discussion of human resource options is intended to promote creativity in the use of people; not to restrict the possibilities that might be suggested during the development of organizational strategy. Particular employers will perceive their own interpretations of the general principles discussed in this book. Some of these will be evident during the human resource research phase, and others when problems have been defined. Strategic analysis, to use Johnson and Scholes' phrase, is an iterative process; listing options generates a need for more data.

Strategic evaluation: human resource implications

This is the stage in the strategic process at which financial evaluation of options will become paramount. Nevertheless, the human resource strategist should be prepared to point to options that are more likely to have beneficial human resource outcomes. Knowledge of local and national labour markets will be an important contribution at this stage of the strategic process, together with a fresh look at the implications of business options for employee development.

As opinion begins to firm up on one or other of the business options, the human resource planner should gather data for the *manpower map*. This is the term used by Bennison and Casson (1984) for a forecasting technique that shows the recruits needed over a range of wastage rates and expansion or contraction rates for the organization. Table 8.2 shows an example from Walshe, McGill and Pearson (1982) for ambulance drivers required by a health authority in the UK. The informed guesses of all members of the strategic team will give the forecast more validity than predictions based on traditional staffing levels. As strategy is implemented, and circumstances change, human resource requirements can be adjusted in accordance with the manpower map.

Table 8.2
Manpower map for an annual local recruitment need for ambulancemen

	Annual growth in numbers		
	+1%	no change	−1%
Current (low) wastage	29–33	25–29	22–25
High wastage	64–65	57–59	54–56

The map shows that the recruitment need will lie between 22 and 65 on any likely range of assumptions, and indicates what combination of factors will put the need to the top or bottom of the range.

Source: Walshe *et al* (1982) *The Methodology of Labour Market Analysis*. Reproduced with the permission of the Controller of HMSO

Strategic implementation and the human resource

Once the preferred option has been selected by the strategic team, the human resource specialist will acquire reponsibilities for implementation. Each major change of direction for an enterprise presents opportunities for improving the management of human resources, but only if relevant ideas and information are available. If the human resource planner has contributed fully to the earlier stages of the strategic process, the data can be taken for granted. Ideas should have been generated by brainstorming at the stage of strategic analysis.

Recruitment

Specifically, the human resource specialist will be faced with the task of selecting, internally or externally, suitable people for the tasks detailed in the agreed strategic plan. Knowledge of the validity of selection procedures, and their relevance to local labour markets, as discussed in Chapter 4, will be important at this point, as will the manpower audit.

The human resource specialist should recognize that selection is only one phase of a continuing process, that starts with a vague recognition of the need to recruit, proceeds through the first definition of the personnel specification, and continues with re-definition of the job after the recruit has occupied the post long enough to stamp a personal style upon it. The crucial stage is the impact that the actuality of the job makes on the new incumbent immediately after starting work.

Selection procedures will rely increasingly on the use of tests to identify skills that are needed in current jobs, or later as the content of work changes. Valid general aptitude tests have their place in assessing both candidates and existing employees but more attention must be given to work-sampling (see Chapter 4). Apart from having greater face validity than intelligence tests, personality questionnaires and interviews, the candidate is able to experience the emotions associated with the work, and to make a personal assessment of his or her suitability. He or she can also make an estimate of the room for innovation and personal development. Interviews, never a very reliable method of selection, will be used more appropriately to conduct the informational and negotiating requirements of social exchange.

Selling real jobs

Human resource departments both buy talent, and sell job opportunity and satisfaction. As Chapter 6 revealed, the prime sources of job satisfaction are the opportunities for skill use and skill development that the job affords. To locate suitable employees is one thing; to attract them is another. What is it that the people we wish to hire will be looking for, in terms of personal development?

Market researchers use a concept called 'market segmentation', which can also be applied in the strategic management of human resources. An example in Chapter 4 illustrates this approach.

Job descriptions should state explicitly the skills needed, and the opportunities for skill development that the job affords. They should also make clear the tasks to be carried out and, particularly, the objectives to be achieved. Finally they should also describe the context in which all this will happen. Explicit job descriptions will help the human resource planner to construct personnel specifications that stress transferable skills rather than ill-defined 'experience', and that accept the ability of people to achieve success in different ways. Personality characteristics should be stipulated sparingly, the emphasis being on the recruit's rapid effectiveness within a particular team and under a particular management style. A frank statement of job demands in advertisements and at initial interviews are the first stages in effective social exchange with candidates, encouraging self-assessment.

Personnel selection has suffered in the past from failure to specify what is required, first within the job itself, and secondly in terms of personal attributes. In the 1990s, more than ever, changing job requirements must be recognized by regular revisions to job descriptions. Particular attention must be given to changing skills, and not only when recruitment is in prospect. Neither job descriptions nor personal specifications should contain unnecessary conditions that would further restrict the effective size of an already narrow market for talent. Discrimination against women and ethnic minorities is best tackled at this stage. This means avoiding any implication that only men, or members of the majority culture, would be suitable. It also requires consideration of what would help to widen the field of suitable applicants; child-care, and language and cultural training are examples.

As with existing staff, it is the human resource specialist's task to make new recruits aware of the climate of change, especially necessary if this is their first work experience. They should under no circumstances be led to believe that life-time employment can be provided. Instead it will be the organization's intention to provide opportunities for self-development and regular career counselling.

Induction and job design

Valid selection is only part of the implementation stage. Whether new jobs are to be filled from outside or inside the organization, the 'shock of the new' (Chapter 7) can affect performance or satisfaction. Attention must be paid to induction, in the fullest sense of the term, of the newcomers. In personnel management parlance, this all too often means little more than viewing a video about the company, followed by a lecture on safety. Here we are discussing the need of new employees, at all levels, for meaningful yet comprehensible work when they begin a new appointment. Jobs should be designed with these factors in mind.

Chapter 5 presents some general ideas on the relations between the organization, the employee and the client, which can be used to stimulate new ideas for job design, especially if technology is involved.

Setting up work as projects has particular relevance to new employees, especially the more able. Case Study 7 in Chapter 7 showed how the Interdisciplinary Higher Degree Scheme could help graduates by allowing them to change career and develop new skills. They acquired not only a new specialism but also confidence and the adaptability to make further radical career changes. The scheme helped organizations by solving problems that would otherwise require a consultancy team. But IHD is not the only way in which this type of project-based training could be set up. Organizations with strong research departments could allocate some of their projects to recently graduated scientists and technologists. These would be required also to work, for example, with commercial staff on the market demand for the proposed product. These cross-functional projects would provide some of the benefits of the interdisciplinary scheme, and develop a strategic approach in the new employee. Although the well-organized Aston scheme is no longer available, informal collaboration with universities and colleges should be welcomed as they are encouraged to respond to the needs of industry and the public services. Able graduates see the advantages of interdisciplinary projects as a promising start to their careers. They will not be trapped in a narrow specialism, and they will learn a strategic approach to management. They are unlikely to leave before completing the project, which provides a defined and motivating goal. If they move on later, the employer can count the tangible benefits of the successful project against recruitment and training costs. The need for flexible managers was emphasized in two surveys that addressed the human resource needs of the 1990s: Coulson-Thomas and Brown (1989) have pointed to the requirement for customer responsiveness; Atkinson (1989) has seen mobile and flexible staff, and transnational product management, as strategies for the Single Market.

Development   Developing the human resource is about more than the effective use of high-calibre people. An equally important task is improving the skills and motivation of the longer-serving members of a workforce. Chapter 5 had something to say about this aspect of improving the human resource. Coping with an uncertain labour market begins with regular analysis of the jobs to be filled. To what extent can they be redesigned, or eliminated? Job descriptions, as suggested in Chapter 4, should distinguish clearly between the routine and judgemental aspects of work. Routine, in this sense, means carrying out, repeatedly, administrative or technical tasks. Dealing with the general public should not be classified as routine, however menial the job may appear. Service work has often been denigrated in this way; interacting with customers effectively requires a high level of skill, and is crucial to the success of a business. Poor training and poor skills in many who do this work are not logical reasons to deny its value.

Truly routine aspects of work should be carefully scrutinized to see whether technology could replace people, in the short or longer term. Cash-point machines were greeted with some reserve when they first appeared, but are now welcomed as a round the clock service. This requires only standard database technology, but as artificial intelligence systems are developed, expanding opportunities will exist to replace the routine and programmable with machines, a late phase of the mechanization that began 200 years ago. The reasons, then as now, have as much to do with expanding business as with labour replacement. If obsolescence can be foreseen, it would be wise to include this in the job description. At the other end of the scale are the key tasks by which performance is measured and upon which the success of an organization will depend. These should be carefully described with, wherever possible, the control data. This will assist selection, training and later appraisal of performance.

Education, the least satisfactory aspect in the quality of the British workforce, should not be made an unnecessary barrier in the promotion or flexible use of employees. There is a limited supply of graduates, even of people educated beyond school age (17 per cent of school-leavers). Focusing upon skills and general intelligence, rather than looking for educational labels, expands the available market. Training can go some way to overcome the deficiencies in education; it should be aimed principally at improving current performance. Relevance and professionalism in training is rarer than might be supposed, given the many organizations offering their services. But training should not end with competent instruction in the requirements of the current job. Trainees who respond well to this should be encouraged to improve their general education, and to acquire the skills they will need as work changes. Encouragement and success in their first training experience after leaving school may begin to repair years of discouragement. Day-release education still has much to commend it. A really effective Youth Training Scheme would concentrate on this rather than upon being a source of cheap labour.

As the routine is removed from a wide range of jobs, the value of appraising performance in those aspects where the job-holder has discretion becomes more obvious. This applies to both managerial and specialist work. Training should be linked, primarily, to improving performance in key tasks. But training, like strategic management, depends on a climate in which improvement is the norm: 'Productivity is a state of mind' (see Chapter 5). An organization that takes its human resources seriously will be one that also provides opportunities for self-development, even if these are not directly related to job performance or might lead to employees seeking other work. It is the climate of excellence that counts. Subsidizing courses at local colleges, or with the Open University, help create that climate.

Allowing and encouraging staff to take change in their stride is as much organizational development as the set-piece group exercises run by consultants. The traditional process of 'unfreezing—change—refreezing' is not only lengthy and traumatic, it also implies that employees are set in new ways as much as they were in the old. 'Unfreezing' by personal development implies that people then become ready to accept change whenever needed. They are aware of development in their own lives, are prepared to accept and encourage it in others, and are not surprised when the whole organization has to make adjustments in its relations with customers. Bureaucracy gives way to 'adhocracy', the department to the project team.

Rajan's model of simultaneous change in products and technology was mentioned in Chapter 2 and has been referred to elsewhere in this book. Although it was derived originally from a study of changing manpower requirements in the City of London's deregulated finance industry, it has wider implications. Rajan entitled an article on the subject in *Personnel Management* magazine 'Today the City, tomorrow . . .?' The model (Chapter 5) of the new relationship between worker, customer and employer is plainly applicable to the service sector, but Case Study 5 shows that it is also vital to the success of the best manufacturing firms. It illustrates the concept of the responsible employee who is given discretion and technological support, which should characterize strategic human resource management as the twentieth century draws to its close.

Relocation Human resource specialists should take every opportunity to promote personal and organizational flexibility. One particular opportunity is the decision to move location, whether this is the result of strategic discussion or imposed. Matrices (see Table 8.3) can be a good way of analysing and presenting the data. This should not, of course, be gathered at the time the move is announced, but should already be available in the human resource database. Needless to say, people will not always appear in the most desirable quadrants of the diagram, but the opportunities for staff development, and the necessity for recruitment at the new location, together with the need for management to provide incentives, should all be clear. As an aid to strategic decision-making, a preliminary analysis may make the move itself seem less desirable.

Table 8.3
Matrix for the predicted outcome of a proposed relocation of a head office

Mobility	Essential workers	Non-essential workers
Prepared to move to new office	26	28
Not prepared to move to new office	10	85

Strategic scanning The human resource strategist, as implied in the previous paragraphs, cannot concentrate full time on the organization and its immediate concerns. We have already discussed the external labour market as an important source of data for strategic analysis and strategic implementation; it is also a source of 'triggers' for strategic change, alongside technology and changing consumer demands. The interaction between technology and labour markets was discussed at some length in Chapter 2. The difficulty is one of maintaining a satisfactory line between the irrelevance of large amounts of data, and the danger of overlooking the less obvious aspects of change. This, of course, is a problem for all strategic management; generally speaking it is better to have too many sources of information than too few. Some useful ones are mentioned in Chapter 2.

The need to recruit new employees is no longer predicted by the age distribution. Nicholson and West have revealed that only one in ten of their professional and managerial sample had experienced no change of employer. Since these people might be expected to be among the more stable members of a workforce, few indeed must see their future with only one employer. The redundancies of the last 15 years have added considerably to mobility initiated by employees themselves. Many employees will leave an organization long before retirement, and will need to be replaced. The position of older workers in the labour force is more like that of the ethnic minorities than that of women; the problem is not so much one of facilitation (see above), but of prejudice and stereotyping. Metcalfe and Thompson (1990) have surveyed employers to discover that older people are still thought not to be retrainable, especially in information technology. Human resource shortages may change attitudes.

The human resource manager has ceased to be the gate-keeper to a stable workforce, and is becoming more like the casting director of a film company. Projects are set up, technicians and actors are hired, and all are dispersed again once the filming is complete. Pay while working, of course, has to be sufficient to cover resting periods, a concept not yet fully accepted by employers.

As work ceases to be routine, and becomes more project-oriented, the human research strategist must become adept in assembling teams and dispersing them once again into the labour market. The construction industry, like the entertainment business, operates in this way. The short-term contract, and the contract for service rather than of service will become the common way of acquring skilled assistance. Certainly we are seeing the end of the career for life. This has profound implications for the way in which recruitment should be handled.

The first requirement is to know the labour markets in which temporary or short-service workers are to be found. Human resource specialists must be prepared either to do their own research or to rely increasingly on the expensive help of outside consultants. Since the latter tend to deal in people whom they deem to be readily saleable, the market is unnecessarily restricted and competitive. A human resource specialist working within an organization can bring to it a strategic view of transferable skills, and the use of less immediately visible sources of talent than the salesmanship of the consultant will provide. Advertisements based on restrictive job titles will no longer serve the purpose. Most jobs now require some degree of innovation from the new incumbent (see Chapter 7), and many have not been done by anyone before the job-holder is appointed.

National and regional information about human resources can only be a back-drop to effective recruitment; the figures are often over-aggregated, and do not reveal the detail necessary to identify opportunities for transferable skills. Yet personnel departments for years have collected data about their labour markets. Recruitment advertisements bring in many more applications than personnel staff could cope with. After short-listing, which is the most hazardous stage of selection for prejudice and discrimination, much of this valuable market research data is destroyed. Now, at least, it is both possible and advisable to code and record basic information about candidates on a computer spreadsheet or database. This need not risk problems with the Data Protection Act, since identifying individuals is not necessary—it is the pattern of the data that is strategically useful. Application forms could, however, contain a box to be ticked by those who would not object to personal data being retained for future reference. But the patterns of data on age, qualifications, gender, coded employment history (see Chapter 3) and location, would help the organization to know where suitably qualified recruits might be found. Research-minded human resource specialists, who understand the stages in social research described in Chapter 3, will do a better job than recruitment consultants as the quality of their databases become an accurate source of information about sources of candidates.

Human resource strategy in a national context

It would take another book to discuss the implications of a strategic approach to human resources at national level fully. Some remarks have, however, been made about labour market information, training schemes and education. Perhaps the greatest single contribution that politicians and civil servants could make to the effective use of human resources would be continuity of policy. A similar plea is often expressed by businessmen in relation to economic policy, and by universities in relation to the government's plans for education. The 1980s saw a constant chopping and changing in policies (or procedures) in measures to help the unemployed, and for workforce training.

Government should also recognize that, if careers are no longer 'for life', then sensible arrangements must be made for periods when talented people will find themselves temporarily out of work. This is their opportunity to acquire new or updated skills, and to reorient their careers. To allow this to happen in a haphazard way is not to allow it to happen at all. Educational institutions should be encouraged to provide a range of courses, flexibly designed, to meet these needs. Perhaps it is also time to reconsider the undignified, ill-targeted, concept of unemployment benefit. This would be better presented as a social wage to which those without current full-time employment would be entitled as a right. The original motive behind redundancy payments, when these were introduced in the 1960s, was to encourage flexibility in the workforce. In the UK we seem to have returned to the premise that people given benefits will not work, and that pressure should be applied to make them do so. That way of looking at unemployment makes assumptions about workers, work, and the potential for human development that do not accord with the ideas presented in this book.

Qualities needed in human resources management

The management of human resources will demand special qualities in those who are charged with devising strategies and putting them into effect. It is doubtful whether the traditional role of the personnel department, and its traditional specialisms, are relevant to the new patterns of work and work behaviour. The old distinction between the manpower planner, as previously defined, and the personnel manager has disappeared. The administrative function that has typified personnel departments over the years should now be relegated to technology, which is ideally suited to the maintenance of personnel records and routine information. Administration that requires no more than record-keeping should be combined with other central administrative functions in the organization. The contribution of the human resource expert is to strategy; the focus is the future.

That a suitable person would be numerate goes without saying; that they should be research-minded should be apparent from this book. This requires productive scepticism about current practices, and especially about current categorizations and expectations of employees' abilities.

What they should not be sceptical about is people themselves, and the potential for development that extends well beyond their existing work. Steady improvement in the performance of a workforce, and in the clarity that other managers have of the people who work for them, are the essential measures of success. The ability to inform the 'political debate' in the organization with well-chosen and researched information about external and internal labour markets, is the measure of their strategic contribution.

References

Atkinson, J. (1989) *Corporate Employment Policies for the Single European Market*, IMS, Brighton.

Bennison, M. and Casson, J. (1984) *The Manpower Planning Handbook*, McGraw-Hill (UK) Ltd, Maidenhead.

Campbell, D. (1969) 'Reforms as experiments', *American Psychologist*, **24**, 409, in Brynner, J. and Stribley, K. (1979) *Social Research: principles and procedures*, Open University, Milton Keynes.

Cooke-Davis, T. (1990 'Return of the project manager', *Management Today*, May, 119.

Coulson-Thomas, C. and Brown, R. (1989) *The Responsive Organization: people and management: the challenge of the 1990s*, BIM/Aston University, Birmingham.

Galbraith, J. (1987) *The Affluent Society* (4th ed.), Penguin Books, Harmondsworth, London.

Halsey, A. (ed) (1972) *Educational Priority Areas: Vol 1 EPA problems and policies*, HMSO, London.

Institute of Manpower Studies (1987) *A Practitioner's Guide Microprospect*, IMS, Brighton.

Institute of Manpower Studies (1988) *Computer Applications for Manpower Planning*, IMS, Brighton.

Johnson, G. and Scholes, K. (1988) *Exploring Corporate Strategy*, Prentice-Hall International (UK) Ltd, Hemel Hempstead.

Meager, N. and Metcalfe, H. (1988) 'Equal opportunity policies', Institute of Manpower Studies Report No. 156, IMS, Brighton.

Metcalfe, H. (1990) 'Retaining women employees: measures to counteract labour shortage', Institute of Manpower Studies Report No. 190, IMS, Brighton.

Metcalfe, H. and Thompson, M. (1990) *Older Workers: employers' attitudes and practices*, IMS, Brighton.

Nicholson, N. and West, M. (1988) *Managerial Job-Change: men and women in transition*, Cambridge University Press, Cambridge.

Peters, T. (1989) 'New products, new markets, competition, thinking', *The Economist*, **310**, 7592, 27.

Pfiffner, J. (1960) 'Administrative rationality', *Public Administration Review*, Summer, 125–132.

Pigors, P. and Myers, C. (1973) *Personal Administration* (7th ed.) McGraw-Hill, Tokyo.

Pollit, C., Lewis, L., Negro, J. and Patten, J. (1979) *Public Policy in Theory and Practice*, Hodder and Stoughton/Open University Press, Sevenoaks, Kent.

Thomas, R. (1983) *Business Policy*, Philip Allan, Oxford.

Walshe, K., McGill, D. and Pearson, R. (1982) *The Methodology of Labour Market Analysis*, DHSS, Brighton, Sussex.

Windsor, G. (1988) 'How high tec helped uncover hidden talents', *Personnel Management*, March, 37.

Index